Confederate Cemeteries

Volume 1

Mark Hughes

HERITAGE BOOKS
2006

HERITAGE BOOKS
AN IMPRINT OF HERITAGE BOOKS, INC.

Books, CDs, and more—Worldwide

For our listing of thousands of titles see our website
at
www.HeritageBooks.com

Published 2006 by
HERITAGE BOOKS, INC.
Publishing Division
65 East Main Street
Westminster, Maryland 21157-5026

Copyright © 2002 Mark Hughes

Other books by the author:
Bivouac of the Dead
Confederate Cemeteries, Volume 2
The Unpublished Roll of Honor

All rights reserved. No part of this book may be reproduced or transmitted in any form or by any means, electronic or mechanical, including photocopying, recording or by any information storage and retrieval system without written permission from the author, except for the inclusion of brief quotations in a review.

International Standard Book Number: 978-0-7884-2050-X

In memory of my father, S.J. (Jack) Hughes, who taught me the value of hard work.

In honor of my mother, Clara Humphries Hughes, who showed me the joy of reading.

Contents

Acknowledgements vii
How to Use This Book ix
Abbreviations x
List of Reference Numbers (VA1, VA2, ...) xii
List of Original Burial Sites xiii

Section I
Burying the Confederate Dead (An Overview) 1

Section II
Cemetery Descriptions 25

Section III
List of Burials 55

Appendix
Photographs 387
Bibliography 413
About the Author 421

Acknowledgements

No one writes a book in a vacuum. Since I began researching this book fifteen years ago, many people have helped me. I must thank:

My wife of thirty years, Patty Hughes, deserves most of the credit for this book. Without her understanding and moral support this book could have never been written. My daughter, Anna Grace Hughes, went on research trips disguised as vacations. She recorded inscriptions on monuments, swatted bugs, ate picnic lunches in cemeteries, helped me locate books in libraries, and made copies. Thank you both.

Electronic technologists are not trained in the nuances of the English language. Without a good editor, they are lost. Mrs. Pat Anderson proved to be an excellent editor. However the mistakes are mine, not hers.

Many people furnished information about cemeteries. Mr. Greg McMillen, Assistant to the President of Emory and Henry College, supplied information about the cemetery at Emory. Ms. Julie Bushong, Library Associate for the Culpeper County Library, located a list of burials at Culpeper in the library's vertical file.

Mrs. Barbara Blakey, Assistant to the Director of the Virginia Military Institute Museum, and Mrs. Jesse Sellers, President of the Woman's Memorial Society, supplied information about Confederate burials in and near New Market. Mrs. Blakey also supplied information on the VMI Cadets killed at New Market as did Mr. Troy Marshall, Visitor Services Supervisor at New Market Battlefield State Historical Park, and Ms. Diane B. Jacob, Archivist at Virginia Military Institute's Preston Library.

Mr. Hatcher P. Story supplied a list of Confederate Soldiers buried at Courtland Baptist Church. M. Wright supplied a list of Confederate Soldiers buried in the Bruton Parish Churchyard.

Employees of the National Park Service are always helpful to authors. Mr. Mac Wycoff, Historian of Fredericksburg & Spotsylvania National Military Park, supplied a copy of the burial roster of Spotsylvania Confederate Cemetery. Mr. Robert E.L. Kirk, Historian of Richmond National Battlefield Park, provided information on the location of burial records for several cemeteries. Ms. Diane K. Depew, Supervisory Park Ranger at Colonial National Historical Park, provided information about the two Confederate cemeteries at Yorktown. Mr. Jim Anderson, retired Chief Ranger at Kings Mountain National Military Park, provided names of National Park Service rangers to contact, as did Mr. Chris Revels, the Chief Ranger at Kings Mountain National Military Park. Mr. Revels is a walking directory of Park Service employees.

Don Cunningham, WB4QAQ, and Phil Baker, WD4CGC, gave me tips in purchasing a camera and photographing tombstones. Don also retouched several photographs using PhotoShop™.

The administration, staff, and faculty of Cleveland Community College also supported and encouraged me. Special thanks to Dr. Steve Thornburg, President, Dr. Ron Wright, Vice President of Academic Programs, and Mr. Mike McSwain, Dean of Vocational / Engineering Technologies for their support.

The library staff at Cleveland Community College, Ms. Barbara McKibbin, Ms. Nettle Durant, Mrs. Elizabeth Stone, Mrs. Ellen Williams, and Ms. Shirley Anthony (now retired) ordered books via interlibrary loan and encouraged me. Mr. Phil Reid, Mr. Danny Scruggs, and Mike Sisk of the Information Technology Department offered advice on some of the finer points of Microsoft Word™ and Microsoft Access™.

My Cousin, Hugh Hughes, encouraged me to begin this project, unfortunately he died before it was completed. I will miss his encouragement and expert advice.

How to Use This Book

This book contains the names of 9,528 soldiers and civilians buried in 30 cemeteries. The vast majority of the soldiers listed died during the Civil War, though the names of a few veterans are included. All of the civilians listed died as a direct result of the war. Most were killed while manufacturing gunpowder. The names of the soldiers are listed alphabetically in section III. A reference number (VA01, VA14, ...) is assigned to each name. These reference numbers are listed on page xi. A short description of each cemetery is included in section II. Sometimes soldiers were moved to a centrally located cemetery from battlefields. A list of battlefields and alternate names for locations is on page xii. A list of abbreviations is on the next page.

Of course this list contains errors. There are errors in the records kept by cemetery sextons and hospital orderlies. One of the major problems faced by the keepers of burial lists was the inability of the average Civil War soldier to spell his name. During World War I, my wife's grandfather, John William Boyce McDaniel, was stationed at Camp Jackson, South Carolina. McDaniel was assigned to the 156th Depot Brigade. He explained how he came to be detailed as a hospital orderly: "One morning at roll call the sergeant told us: 'If you can read, step out'. Only McHaffey and I stepped out. The sergeant told us: 'Report to the hospital, you're going to be an orderly.' The last time I saw the rest of them (the remaining 98 men in his company) they were digging a ditch."

If a soldier could not spell his name, the orderly attempted to spell it phonically. I have seen my last name, Hughes, spelled in a variety of ways: Huges, Huse, Hewes, Huzz, Huze, ... Many times, of course, the "keeper of the book of the dead" followed the unwritten rule that most students follow when confronted with a question they can not answer. If in doubt, scribble.

The compiler of the list of names of the soldiers buried in Richmond's Hollywood Cemetery said it best: " Amid the confusion incident to the time when the Confederate dead were buried, and their names recorded, errors in spelling and in assignment to their respective Companies, Regiments or States, may have arisen; the Register is presented, therefore, as simply a careful and laborious compilation from all the sources of information available, with such accuracy in detail as circumstances rendered it possible to secure."

List of Abbreviations

Bat. - see the note below
Batt. - see the note below
Capt. - Captain
Co. - Company
Corp. - Corporal
DOD - Died of Disease
DOW - Died of Wounds
KIA - Killed in Action
Lt. - Lieutenant
MW - Mortally Wounded
Sgt. - Sergeant
VMI - Virginia Military Institute

VA01 to VA30 are reference numbers for cemeteries. These cemeteries are listed alphabetically in section II. Please refer to the list of reference numbers on the next page.

Bat. and Batt. are abbreviations used in the original documents. These may stand for either battery or battalion.

Key to Reference Numbers

These cemeteries are listed alphabetically in section II of this book.

VA01 Ball's Bluff National Cemetery
VA02 Williamsburg - Bruton Parish Church
VA03 Courtland Baptist Church
VA04 Alexandria National Cemetery
VA05 Covington - Cedar Hill Cemetery
VA06 Clarke County - Old Chapel
VA07 Upperville
VA08 Woodstock
VA09 Yorktown National Cemetery
VA10 Fairfax
VA11 Mount Jackson
VA12 New Market - Saint Matthews Cemetery
VA13 New Market - Zirkle Cemetery
VA14 New Market - Cedar Grove Cemetery
VA15 New Market - Emmanuel Cemetery
VA16 Centreville - Saint John's Episcopal Church
VA17 Richmond - Hebrew Confederate Cemetery
VA18 Culpeper
VA19 Richmond - Shockoe Cemetery
VA20 Emory and Henry College
VA21 VMI Cadets Killed at New Market
VA22 City Point National Cemetery (Hopewell)
VA23 Front Royal - Prospect Hill Cemetery
VA24 see City Point National Cemetery
VA25 Richmond - Hollywood Cemetery
VA26 Newport News
VA27 see Newport News
VA28 Spotsylvania Confederate Cemetery
VA29 Culpeper National Cemetery
VA30 New Market - Mount Zion Cemetery

List of Original Burial Sites

This book lists soldiers that died in the following locations. If a cemetery is listed as "moved to" another cemetery, that means the remains of at least some of the soldiers buried there where moved to the cemetery listed. This does not imply that all the remains of Confederate soldiers were moved from one location to another. There are at least 3,300 Confederates buried in the Fredericksburg Confederate cemetery while only a few soldiers that died at Fredericksburg were moved to the Spotsylvania Confederate cemetery.

Alexandria
Ball's Bluff
Centreville
Chancellorsville - moved to Spotsylvania Confederate
    Cemetery
City Point
Clarke County
Cold Harbor - moved to Hollywood Cemetery - Richmond
Courtland
Covington
Craney Island - see Newport News
Culpeper
Drewry's Bluff - moved to Hollywood Cemetery - Richmond
Emory and Henry College
Fairfax
Fort Harrison - moved to Hollywood Cemetery - Richmond
Frazier's Farm - moved to Hollywood Cemetery - Richmond
Fredericksburg - moved to Spotsylvania Confederate
    Cemetery
Front Royal
Gaines Mill Station - moved to Spotsylvania Confederate
    Cemetery
Gaines' Mill - moved to Hollywood Cemetery - Richmond
Gettysburg - moved to Hollywood Cemetery - Richmond

Guinea Station - moved to Spotsylvania Confederate
    Cemetery
Hamilton's Crossing - moved to Spotsylvania Confederate
    Cemetery
Hopewell - see City Point
Jerusalem - see Courtland
Malvern Hill - moved to Hollywood Cemetery - Richmond
Mechanicsville - moved to Hollywood Cemetery - Richmond
Mount Jackson
New Market
Newport News
Quincy Station - moved to Spotsylvania Confederate
    Cemetery
Richmond
Savage's Station - moved to Hollywood Cemetery - Richmond
Seven Pines - moved to Hollywood Cemetery - Richmond
Sharpsburg - moved to Hollywood Cemetery - Richmond
Spotsylvania Court House
Todd's Tavern - moved to Spotsylvania Confederate Cemetery
Upperville
Waite's Shop - moved to Spotsylvania Confederate Cemetery
West Farm - moved to Newport News
Wilderness - moved to Spotsylvania Confederate Cemetery
Williamsburg
Williamsburg - moved to Hollywood Cemetery - Richmond
Woodstock
Yellow Tavern - moved to Hollywood Cemetery - Richmond
Yorktown

Section I

Burying the Confederate Dead
An Overview

Burying the Confederate Dead
An Overview

After the Civil War ended in the Spring of 1865, most of the combatants started home. However, over half a million of the soldiers never returned home. They were buried on the battlefield where they fell, in cemeteries near the makeshift hospitals where they died, or near the prisoner of war camps were they died. United States Army Surgeon General Joseph K. Barnes reported a total of 304,369 Union soldiers died during the war. About 16 percent of these men were killed in battle. Some 18 percent died of wounds. Disease accounted for over two-thirds of the Union losses.[1]

Burial of Union soldiers was the responsibility of the Quartermaster Corps. The Quartermaster Corps established 72 national cemeteries to bury most of the Union dead.[2] Two other national cemeteries were established by state associations. Of these 74 cemeteries, 305,492 Union soldiers were supposed to have been buried there, but in reality only 296,296 Union soldiers were buried there. The Federal Government deliberately misstated the number of Federal soldiers buried at the Salisbury National Cemetery in North Carolina in an attempt to make it appear that more Union soldiers died in Southern POW camps than number of Confederate soldiers that died in Union POW camps.[3] By 1877, over four million dollars had been spent developing these cemeteries, recovering bodies from battlefields and local cemeteries, and reintering them in these cemeteries. Later, over one million dollars was spent on headstones to mark these graves.[4]

In sharp contrast to the major (and costly) effort to recover the bodies of Union soldiers, there was no national effort to preserve the graves of Confederates. The Confederacy had ceased to exist, most Southerners were concerned with surviving. There was no money for luxuries such as tombstones. The Federal Government had no interest in caring for the graves of rebels.

Because there was no central organization responsible for the burial of Confederates after the war, no one knows how many Confederates died during the war. Estimates range from 180,000 to 258,000. This last figure was reported by the Adjutant General's office in 1885. The same report listed 359,528 Union deaths.[5] In 1892, a former officer of the Confederate Medical Corps estimated 200,000 Confederate deaths.[6]

About 16 percent of the Union casualties were killed outright in battle. It is likely that over 30,000 Confederates were killed in action. One of the fruits of victory was the task of burying the dead. Normally the members of a regiment would bury the dead of that regiment. Graves that contained bodies that could be identified were often marked by a wooden headboard. Because dog tags had not been invented, often the only way to identify a dead soldier was by personal effects found on the body. Sometimes a letter with the soldier's name was found on the body.

Unfortunately, thieves would sometimes search the bodies before a burial detail could arrive. In his book, *Recollections of a Veteran or Four years in Dixie*, J. Polk Racine describes the robbing of the dead that occurred after the battle of Antietam:

> Every man's pocket was turned inside out. Sometimes a piece of money, a pocket knife, or something else, would fall from the hands of the midnight robbers.... The watches were taken, and everything else of value. One young man had a little Testament lying by his hand, and written on the flyleaf were the words: "Think of the Lord Jesus and your dear old mother." Of course they had no use for that. [7]

Many casualties were never identified.

The victorious army also had to dispose of the dead of the opposing army. Captain Wilburn Hill King of the Missouri State Guard (CSA) described this unpalatable duty after the Confederate victory at Wilson Creek (Oak Hills), Missouri:

> The Yankees left us to care for their dead and wounded, among the dead being their very able commander-in-chief Genl. N. Lyon. Caring for the dead proved to be a dreadful task, as the weather was fearfully hot, decay set in early, [firm ground] in which graves could be dug and the tools to work with were both exceedingly scarce; and the battlefield and the country round about it, by midnight became unbearable from the stench, and those engaged in the horrible but necessary duty of burial were to be pitied. [8]

After the Battle of Antietam, Union Private S.M. Whistler's unit was detailed to bury the Confederate dead. Whistler later wrote:

> In the burial of the dead on this particular part of the field, the 130th Regiment, by reason of having incurred the displeasure of its brigade commander, was honored in the appointment as undertaker-in-chief. The weather was phenomenally hot, and the stench from the hundreds of black bloated, decomposed maggoty bodies, exposed to a torrid heat for three days after the battle, was a sight truly horrid and beggaring all power of verbal expression. Over head floated large numbers of those harpies of the air, buzzards, awaiting an opportunity to descend to earth to partake of the cadaverous feast. Just over there in Muma's field in one ditch you placed 185

Confederate corpses, the one on top of the other, and indecorously covered them from sight with clay. [9]

At least these Confederates were buried. On the South Mountain (Maryland) battlefield a Union burial detail simply dumped 58 Confederate bodies into a well owned by a local farmer named Wise. [10]

Some Union soldiers took their duties more seriously. In 1896 a former Union soldier, Michael Deady, wrote the *Confederate Veteran*:

> After the Battle of South Mountain, Md. Sept. 1862, I was detailed to bury the dead. Among them I found a Confederate officer, on whose coat was pinned a paper with these words written in pencil: Capt. H.Y. Hyers, Mad River Lodge, North Carolina...' He must have placed the paper there himself so he might be known if he fell. He was buried as tenderly as could be under the circumstances. I cut on a board, letter for letter, what was on the paper and placed it at the head of the grave. [11]

Just because a soldier had a headboard did not mean his grave would be permanently marked after the war. The wooden headboards often rotted. The wooden headboards were also a cheap source of fuel for people too lazy to cut their own firewood. In many cases local farmers simply plowed over the graves.[12] Some farmers took care to protect the graves. After the battle of Piedmont, Virginia, in 1864, local farmers buried the dead Confederates where they rebuilt their wooden fences. That way they would not plow up the bodies and disease would not be spread. [13]

Soldiers from Maryland fought on both sides during the war. Early in 1864, the State of Maryland granted the charter of the Antietam National Cemetery. One provision of the grant was: "The remains of the soldiers of the Confederate Army [are] to be buried in a part of the grounds separate from those of the Union Army." [14] By 1867, the Confederate dead had not been moved to the cemetery, prompting R.E. Fenton, the Governor of New York, to write the cemetery's trustees reminding them of their duty to bury the Confederate dead. The trustees discussed "the question" on December 9, 1868.[15] They took no action, however. As Steven R. Stotelmyer wrote: "To many veterans of the North, burying Confederates at Antietam would have been the same as burying the Japanese at Arlington after World War II."[16] In 1870, $5,000 that the Maryland legislature had appropriated for burying the Confederate dead at Antietam was turned over to the board of trustees of Washington Cemetery in Hagerstown, Maryland to establish a Confederate Cemetery. The bodies of 1,721 Confederates were moved to the cemetery.[17] With the other southern states under carpetbagger rule, Maryland was the only Southern state to make a concerted effort to care for the Confederates buried within their borders.

At least the families of soldiers that were killed in battle knew of their loved one's fate. Most Confederate units were comprised of soldiers from one county. After the war the surviving comrades of a dead soldier would be able to tell a soldier's relatives where he was killed in action. Perhaps they could assure the family that their son or husband had received a Christian burial. Unfortunately, families often never knew the fate of soldiers who died in hospitals or prisoner of war camps.

Hospitals were established away from the front lines. Any hamlet near the railroad soon had at least one hospital. Churches, schools, and hotels were quickly converted to hospitals. At the hospitals established at the University of Virginia in Charlottesville, 1,370 soldiers died. Typhoid fever claimed 365 of these soldiers, while 353 succumbed to pneumonia. Only 97 died of gunshot wounds. Without modern sanitation practices and antibiotics, disease claimed over two-thirds of the victims of the Civil War. The dead at Charlottesville came from eleven Southern states.[18] Ten Federal soldiers died in the hospital, but the disposition of their bodies is not known. There is no record of their being removed to a National Cemetery.[19] Apparently many of the bodies of the soldiers were "removed by friends." The University's Confederate Cemetery contains only 1,097 graves. [20]

It is impossible to determine how many soldiers were brought home by family. For example, my great-great-grandfather, James Lewis Jones, was in his sixties when he was "enrolled" in Company B of the First South Carolina Artillery. He died near Wadesboro, North Carolina, during General Joseph Johnston's retreat. After hearing of his father's death, one of his sons hitched the family's mule to a wagon and proceeded to bring the body back home. Not every one managed to make it home with the remains of their loved ones. The death roster for the hospital at Charlottesville contains this cryptic note: "This soldier died in Richmond. The intention of carrying his remains to his home was frustrated by the season and the interment took place here." [21]

Prisoners of war were packed off to prison camps in the North. In February 1863, 387 of the 3,884 Confederates held at Camp Douglas, Illinois, died. This is a death rate of almost 10 percent (9.96 percent). [22]

One "guest" of Federal authorities was Capt. Robert E. Park. Capt. Park was held at Fort Delaware on Pea Patch Island. The prison doctor, a Doctor Miller, was a "youth of perhaps twenty years." A total of 2,509 Confederates were buried at nearby Finn's Point, New Jersey. As Capt. Park reported:

> The dead prisoner is carried to the "dead-house," stripped of his clothing, placed by strangers and enemies in a rough, unpainted pine coffin, hoisted in an old cart, and hurried to the burial ground, like the carcass of some

dumb brute, without the presence or ministrations of a single friend. They are carried across the bay, when not sunk within it, and buried on the Jersey shore. The graves are seldom marked, or it is done in a very careless manner, easily erased in a short time by the action of the elements. [23]

The Federal Government had little interest in preserving graves of Confederate POW's. By 1893 the Confederate Cemetery at North Alton, Illinois, was being used as a pasture.[24] In the late 1870's, the United States was offered the burial grounds at the Camp Chase Prison near Columbus, Ohio, for $500. Quartermaster General Montgomery C. Meigs stated in his report that the government had no reason to protect the "rebels and enemies of the county" buried at Camp Chase. The Republican dominated Senate Committee on Military Affairs thought otherwise. After tongue-lashing Secretary of War McCrary, who had endorsed Meigs' report, the committee voted to purchase the land. The Confederate graves were not marked, however. [25] [26]

Not only did the Federal Government decline to mark the graves of Confederates that were buried in National Cemeteries, it refused to grant permission for anyone else to mark them. Resourceful Southerners used several ploys to circumvent these rules. In 1879, the Southern Memorial Association of Alexandria, Virginia, received permission to disinter the bodies of 34 Confederate POW's from Alexandria National Cemetery. The soldiers were reburied in a mound in the Christ Church Yard in Alexandria. The association then erected a monument with the soldiers' names.[27]

Philadelphia's United Daughters of the Confederacy took a different approach. Rebuffed in their efforts to mark the graves of 224 Confederate prisoners at Philadelphia, they arranged to erect a boulder in Richmond's Hollywood

Cemetery. One bronze tablet on the granite boulder is inscribed:

> **Dying in Captivity and Denied a Monument in Philadelphia Where They Lie Buried**
> **This Stone is Erected in Their Everlasting Honor in the Heart of the Confederacy** [28]

Thirty-four years after the war ended, President McKinley made a speech in Atlanta, Georgia. In this speech the President said: "Sectional feeling no longer holds back the love we [north and south] bear each other." After referring to the precious legacy of the dead, President McKinley continued: "Every soldier's grave made during our unfortunate Civil War is a tribute to American valor... the time has come... [that] we should share with you in the care of the graves of Confederate soldiers." [29] McKinley, who had been breveted major for "gallant and meritorious service" during the war, realized that old passions had cooled, and caring for Confederate graves was one way to heal the nation's wounds.

President McKinley's concern might have been genuine, but perhaps he had a political motive. He had won election in 1896 with 61 percent of the electoral vote but only 52 percent of the popular vote. His opponent, William Jennings Bryan, had carried all the Southern states.[30] Could McKinley have seen marking Confederate graves as one way of wooing Southern voters? We do not know. McKinley was assassinated in 1901.

On June 6, 1900, Congress appropriated $2,500 to reinter the Confederate prisoners buried in Arlington National Cemetery. A total of 264 prisoners were reinterred and their graves were marked with permanent headstones.[31]

Various Confederate veterans groups began petitioning Congress to provide care for the graves of other Confederate prisoners. In March 1906, Congress allocated $200,000 to locate these burial sites, purchase them, and mark the graves with headstones. By 1912, a total of 25,560 graves had been marked at a cost of $149,020.09. One reason for the delay was that the first two commissioners died while in office. The commission was authorized to locate and mark the graves of Confederates who ". . . died in Federal prisons and military hospitals in the North . . . ." The commission did not mark the graves of the several thousand Confederates who died while prisoners in the South. [32]

Not all the graves marked by the commission were soldiers or sailors. Of the 1,140 Confederates buried at Jefferson Barracks near Saint Louis, 161 were male civilians. Mrs. Jane N. Foster was a "Confederate civilian" from Randolph County, Arkansas.[33] Most of the civilians were political prisoners. President Lincoln had suspended the right of writ of habeas corpus. Many people were arrested and held without evidence. Rev. Isaac W.K. Handy, D.D., spent fifteen months at Fort Delaware as a political prisoner. In his book *United States Bonds* (subtitled *Duress by Federal Authority*), he detailed his confinement. Apparently he had made a few comments in private that were deemed treason.[34] Not all the civilians that are buried with Confederate POW's were political prisoners, however. Sister Consolata Conlon of the Sisters of Charity succumbed to typhoid fever at Point Lookout, Maryland, while she was nursing sick prisoners. [35]

Ultimately, the women of the former Confederacy cared for most of the graves of Confederate soldiers. Some years ago my father, S.J. "Jack" Hughes and I were discussing how eight Union occupation troops came to be buried in Rosehill Cemetery in York, South Carolina. "Mark," my father told me, " the good women of York took care of them. They [the Union soldiers] were someone's sons, and these women had sons that died during the war. They treated the

Union soldiers' graves just like they hoped someone had treated their sons' graves." He was right; the ladies of the South banded together to care for the graves of both Confederate and Union soldiers buried in their area.

Shortly after the war, most towns in the South had a Confederate Memorial Association or a group by a similar name. One of the first obstacles facing these groups was raising money to purchase land for cemeteries, moving the dead to these cemeteries, and purchasing monuments or headrocks. The ladies used a variety of methods to raise money in the cash-poor South. Ladies in Georgetown, Kentucky, raised $1,000 to bury 18 Confederate soldiers and erect a 20-foot monument. To raise the money, the ladies solicited $1.00 contributions.[36] In Fayetteville, North Carolina, a group of ladies and schools girls quilted 3,000 squares into a quilt. By selling $1.00 chances on the quilt, the ladies raised $300.[37] Former general Robert E. Lee donated a lock of his hair to the Confederate Cemetery Association of Springfield, Missouri, "to be sold at an entertainment gotten up to raise funds for the cemetery."[38]

As William Allan wrote about the ladies in Winchester, Virginia:

> After the war, the ladies of Winchester, from the midst of saddened and desolate homes, continued their self-denying care for the ashes of the brave men to whose comfort and encouragement they had contributed so freely in life, and by whose suffering cots they had often watched in sorrow, danger, and death. Under the leadership of Mrs. Philip Williams, they gathered the thousands of Confederate dead from the surrounding battle-fields and placed them in the 'Stonewall Cemetery'- - a monument not more to the patriotism of man than to the devotion of woman.[39]

Even if someone donated land for a cemetery, developing the land took work and money. The land that was donated for burial of Confederate soldiers at Raleigh, North Carolina, was "covered with native oaks and pines and was full of gulches. On the west side was a deep ravine and the cost of removing superfluous trees by the roots, grading, terracing, opening the walks and graves more than absorbed all the money raised, and a further call for funds had to be made." [40]

Most of the soldiers buried at Raleigh had died in the hospitals there and were buried alongside Federal soldiers who died in the same hospitals. According to an account of the development of the Confederate Cemetery:

> It is . . . proper to mention that we were forced to re-inter [sic] the remains of our noble soldiers before the Cemetery [sic] was in readiness, because of the heartlessness of the wretch sent by the authorities at Washington City to prepare a Cemetery for the Federal dead in which confiscated ground most of our dead were buried. This said Nero sent insulting messages to the Memorial Association insisting on the removal of the Confederate dead before the cemetery was in readiness for the graves to be opened and finally threatened that if our dead were not removed in twenty-four hours their remains would be thrown in the public road.
>
> It is needless to say this inhuman conduct and threat, coming from such a source, moved to activity every loyal citizen of the town and with commendable alacrity they responded to the call of the ladies and preparations were immediately begun for their removal to the Cemetery. This work was done almost entirely by the young men of the city

who had fought side by side with their comrades. It was a 'labor of love.' They came with picks and wheel barrows determined never to cease until the last Southern soldier was removed to a place of safety. They were assisted in this work by our faithful women walking by their sides, cheering and encouraging them as they trudged the weary distance between the two cemeteries under a scorching summer sun. One good woman, seeing them almost overcome by the task, begged a cask of beer and walking by their sides gave it out as she saw they needed it. Just here a touching little incident. One of the coffins had been a little strained at its joinings, by handling, allowing a long, half curled lock of fair hair to escape, which hung down as the coffin was lifted from the wagon.[41]

Occasionally money to develop a cemetery came from unexpected sources. Mr. John C. Latham, of New York, was walking in the Hopkinsville, Kentucky, Cemetery when his escort, a Mr. H.C. Gant, showed Mr. Latham the unmarked graves of soldiers who had died during the Civil War. Upon his return to New York, Mr. Latham mailed the Hopkinsville City Council a check for $1,500.00. The Hopkinsville city council supplemented this amount by $500.00 and erected a monument to the Confederate dead.[42] The monument of Confederate dead in Goldsboro, North Carolina's Willow Dale Cemetery bears this inscription:

A generous foe contributed to the erection of this memorial.

Sometimes the inscription on a monument caused problems. Caption A.J. Beale wrote about the difficulties encountered by the committee trying to erect a monument to the 47 Confederate dead buried in Cynthiana, Kentucky: "We were all too poor to do much in that line at that early date. The Wolf and the Yankee were both after us. We chose our inscription for the monument, as you see it, but it was not inscribed thereon for a number of years after. We were deterred by the persecutions of our friends in the farther South and the continued waving of the bloody shirt by our friends, the enemy. But as reason has resumed its sway, the monument has the inscriptions now." What were the inscriptions that caused such concern?

ERECTED MAY 27, 1869, BY THE CYNTHIANA CONFEDERATE MEMORIAL ASSOCIATION IN MEMORY OF THE CONFEDERATE DEAD WHO FELL IN DEFENSE OF CONSTITUTIONAL LIBERTY.

The reverse of the monument bears the inscription:

THEIR NAMES SHALL NEVER BE FORGOT, WHILE FAME HER RECORDS KEEPS AND GLORY GUARDS THE HALLOWED SPOT WHERE VALOR PROUDLY SLEEPS. [43]

At least the memorial association got to use the word "Confederate" in its title. The Ladies of New Orleans could not. The ladies' organization stated three goals: "(1) To provide artificial limbs for Confederate soldiers, no public provision having been made for such. (2) To mark and protect the graves of Confederate dead and when deemed necessary and found practical to remove their remains for more perfect and satisfactory protection. (3) To aid and assist the destitute widows and orphans of Confederate soldiers." [44]

Major General Phillip Sheridan was in command of the Union troops in Louisiana "and [upon] hearing of the purposes of the ladies stated that no association bearing the title "Confederate" could organize under existing laws." The ladies decided to rename their organization the "Ladies' Benevolent Association of Louisiana" and applied for a charter. Apparently General Sheridan's approval of the charter was required. In a letter to the District Attorney of the First Judicial District of Louisiana, General Sheridan wrote: "I have no objection to the purposes of the Association and trust that the high character of the ladies connected with it will confine it strictly to the objects set forth."[45] Apparently Federal officials were suspicious of any gathering of whites after the war. At least once the annual meeting of the Kings Mountain Baptist Association in North Carolina was interrupted by a visit from Federal occupation troops.

Approximately 150 men died at Weldon, North Carolina. They were buried in the "soldiers burying ground" which was never properly marked because the owner would not allow any improvements. After a number of years the property passed into the "hands of a highly respected Negro, David Smith." Mr. Smith deeded the land to the Junius Daniels Chapter of the United Daughters of the Confederacy. The County Commissioners then cleared the land of trees and brush. [46]

Sometimes government bodies changed their minds about Confederate cemeteries. In 1866, the Legislature of South Carolina gave the Ladies Memorial Association of South Carolina $1,000 to mark the Confederate graves in Charleston. The Legislature also donated the association marble and granite that was not needed to construct the new State House in Columbia. However, before the association could arrange to transport the material to Charleston, a carpetbagger government came to power. The unsympathetic government refused to release the materials, but the association's president, Mrs. Mary Snowden, refused to give up. According to Col. A. C. Haskell: " . . but for her persistent efforts the granite and marble would have not been procured." The marble was used to make over 800 headstones. The granite was used as a base for a monument. [47]

Mrs. Snowden had less luck with U.S. Quartermaster General Meigs when she tried to arrange to bring the bodies of 84 South Carolina soldiers buried at Gettysburg back "home" to Charleston. General Meigs refused to allow the removal of bodies that were buried in the Gettysburg National Cemetery. Finally Mr. Samuel Weaver, who had supervised removal of the Union dead to the Gettysburg National Cemetery, convinced Gen. Meigs to release the bodies. Unfortunately Mr. Weaver was killed in a railroad accident before the bodies could be removed. [48]

Mr. Weaver's son, Dr. R.B. Weaver, continued his father's work. However, some Gettysburg residents refused to allow Dr. Weaver to exhume Confederate bodies without payment. A Mr. Blocker refused Dr. Weaver permission to remove two Georgia soldiers from his farm until one soldier's brother telegraphed his consent for the removal. Blocker had removed the gold dental plate from one soldier and then refused to release the plate until Dr. Weaver paid him ten dollars.[49] From 1870 to 1873, Dr. Weaver exhumed the remains of 3,320 Confederates and sent them South.

It was expensive to develop and maintain cemeteries. Headstones for the soldiers in Charleston, South Carolina, cost $1,897.27, even though the state had donated the marble. From 1866 to 1880, the Memorial Association spent $1,006.63 on "care of the grounds" at Charleston. (X4)

Unfortunately the names of many soldiers buried in cemeteries have been lost. Mr. John K. Campbell recorded the names of the 150 or so soldiers buried at Weldon, North Carolina. When Mr. Campbell died in 1865, the "list was found among his papers, [but] it was not preserved." [50]

Some 150 Confederates of the 13th Mississippi and the 17th Mississippi that were stationed near Leesburg, Virginia, were buried in the Union Cemetery at Leesburg. Mrs. Lizzie Worsley wrote the *Confederate Veteran*: "At one time their names were all known, but the list [of names] was destroyed with other papers considered valueless after the death of the lady who had kept the list."[51] Approximately 30 unknown Confederates are buried near Red Sulfur Springs, West Virginia. The "gentleman in the neighborhood" that kept the burial register lost it.[52]

One way to preserve the names of soldiers buried in a cemetery would have been to erect headstones. But headstones cost money, and few organizations in the cash-strapped South had sufficient funds to properly mark the graves. Also, there were people who did not care for rows of headstones. The editor of the *Confederate Veteran* expressed this view in 1928:

> The Veteran makes the suggestion that we make a point to always preserve trees in such places [cemeteries]; just clear out the underbrush, and perhaps remove some trees if they are too thick; but trees and grass, and perhaps some shrubs here and there, will make any plot beautiful and restful to look upon, and the little grave markers are not really necessary. Just secure a list of those buried there and keep it in a safe place; or perhaps have a large bowlder with the names carved thereon. Let's make these places restful with shade; not lying out in the broad sun with rows and rows of markers glaring white. Think of the strength and beauty of trees, the restful color of the green grass, and the enjoyment we can have in blooming shrubs--and all this can be had at much less expense than stone markers.[53]

Sometimes entire cemeteries disappeared, not just the list of names. Sometime during the late 1940's, the graves of

36 Confederate soldiers and marines buried at Charleston, South Carolina, were paved over during construction of a football stadium. Mrs. Wendy Burbage, who spent eight years researching the cemetery, said: "It [paving over the graves] was more cost effective than moving them...." [54]

During the Great Depression, farmers who farmed the Champion Hill Battlefield in Mississippi were paid ten dollars for every skeleton of a Confederate soldier they plowed up. The bodies were then reburied in the Vicksburg Confederate Cemetery.

The names of some 5,000 Confederate dead buried at Vicksburg were recorded by a Union officer. This list was lost, but in the 1960's the local chapter of the United Daughters of the Confederacy was donated a trunk filled with Civil War documents. Included in the documents was a ledger containing the names of 1,600 Confederates buried at Vicksburg. The Veterans Administration supplied markers for these soldiers in 1980. [55]

Eleven years after a monument to 101 unknown Confederate dead at Hopkinsville, Kentucky, was erected, a book containing the names of 168 soldiers buried there was discovered in some rubbish in an old desk in the Bank of Hopkinsville. (41) While researching at the National Archives in 1994, I discovered the names of 16 Union soldiers, one civilian, and one Confederate prisoner of war who had been buried at Orangeburg, South Carolina. The local Boy Scout Troop assisted me in erecting headstones on their graves.

Between 1865 and 1871, the Quartermaster General's Office published 27 volumes of the *Roll of Honor.* These volumes list the names of approximately 180,000 identifiable Union soldiers who died during the Civil War. While a handful of books have been published listing burials in individual Confederate cemeteries, no one has written a series of books listing burials in all the cemeteries that can be found. The *Confederate Cemetery* series will rectify that omission.

Notes

[1] Joseph K. Barnes (Surgeon General of the United States Army), *The Medical and Surgical History of the War of the Rebellion*. (Washington, DC: 1870), p. xxxvi.

[2] Oscar Mack, *Report of the Inspector of National Cemeteries for the Years 1870 and 1871*. (Washington, DC: 1871), p. 98.

[3] Mark Hughes, *Bivouac of the Dead*. (Bowie, Maryland: Heritage Books, Inc., 1995), p. 217-220.

[4] Mack, p. 99.

[5] National Library of Medicine. *Medicine of the Civil War*. (n.d.), p. 9.

[6] Joseph Jones. *Southern Historical Society Papers*. (1892), p. 114.

[7] J. Polk Racine. *Recollections of a Veteran: or Four Years in Dixie*. (Elkton, Maryland: Appeal Printing Office, 1894), p. 47.

[8] L. David Norris. *The Autobiography of Wilburn Hill King*. (Hillsboro, Texas: Hill College Press, 1996), p. 21.

[8] *Boonsboro Oddfellow*. November 22, 1866.

[10] Oden Bowie. *A Descriptive List of the Burial Places of the Remains of Confederate Soldiers, who fell in the Battles of Antietam, South Mountain, Monocay, and other Points in Washington and Frederick Counties in the State of Maryland*. (Hagerstown, Maryland: Free Press, n.d.), p. 51

[11] *Confederate Veteran.* (January 1896.), p. 27.

[12] Bowie, p. 16.

[13] Donahue Bible. *Vaughn's Brigade at Piedmont.* (Mohawk, Tennessee: Dobson Creek Publishers, 1995.), p. 14.

[14] Bowie, p. 3.

[15] Bowie, p. 4 – 10.

[16] Steven R. Stotelmyer. *The Bivouacs of the Dead* (Baltimore, Maryland: Toomey Press, 1992.), p. 36.

[17] Calvin Mumma. *Washington Cemetery* (Pamphlet in the files of Antietam National Battlefield, n.d.).

[18] Richard Heath Dabney Papers (University of Virginia - Albert H. Small Special Collections Library- accession # 2533).

[19] Hughes, p.270.

[20] Roster of Buried Confederate Soldiers Collection (University of Virginia - Albert H. Small Special Collections Library - accession # 1235)

[21] Richard Heath Dabney Papers.

[22] Hughes, p. 17.

[23] Robert E. Park. *Southern Historical Society Papers.* (No. 3), 182-185.

[24] Clipping from unnamed newspaper – October 24, 1893. (Original in National Archives Record Group 92-576. "General Correspondence and Reports Relating to National and Post Cemeteries." 1865-1890).

[25] Ibid.

[26] *Washington Post.* August 6, 1879.

[27] Carrie White Avery. "Cemetery Records" (Library of Congress, 1923).

[28] Ladies' Hollywood Memorial Association. *Our Confederate Dead.* (Richmond, Virginia, 1916), p. 13-14

[29] Charles Broadway Rouss Camp - United Confederate Veterans. *Report on the Re-Burial of the Confederate Dead in Arlington Cemetery.* (Washington, DC: Judd and Detweiler, 1901), p. 10.

[30] Jams West Davidson, et al. *Nation of Nations.* (Vol. 2, New York: McGraw-Hill, 1990. 2 vols.), p. 785.

[31] Charles Broadway Rouss Camp of United Confederate Veterans, p. 37.

[32] James H. Berry. *Report of the Commissioner for Marking Confederate Graves.* (1912), p. 3.

[33] Veterans Administration. "Station Data Sheet - Jefferson Barracks National Cemetery." (n.d.).

[34] Isaac K. Handy. *United States Bonds.* (Baltimore, Maryland: Turnbull Brothers, 1874), p. 620.

[35] Mauriel Phillips Joslyn (ed). *Valor and Lace.* (Mufreesboro, Tennessee: Southern Heritage Press, n.d), p. 180.

[36] *Confederate Veteran.* (No. 6), p. 59.

[37] S.L. Smith (Mrs.). *North Carolina's Monuments and Memorials* (Raleigh, North Carolina: Edwards and Broughton, Co., 1941), p. 62.

[38] *Southern Historical Society Papers.* (Vol. 38), p. 365.

[39] William Allen. *Southern Historical Society Papers.* (No. 43), p. 163.

[40] Confederated Southern Memorial Association. *History of the Confederated Southern Memorial Associations of the South.* (n.d.), p. 229.

[41] Ibid., 230

[42] *Confederate Veteran.* (No. 7), p. 106-7.

[43] Bettie Alder Calhoun Emerson. *Historic Southern Monuments.* (New York and Washington: Neale Publishing Company, 1911), p. 135-7.

[44] Confederated Southern Memorial Association., p. 169.

[45] Ibid., p 170-1.

[46] *Confederate Veteran.* (No. 36), p. 93.

[47] Ladies Memorial Association [Charleston, South Carolina]. *A Brief History of the Ladies Memorial Association of Charleston, SC.* (Charleston, South Carolina: H.P. Cooke and Co., 1880), p. 1-3.

[48] Ibid., p. 7.

[49] R.B. Weaver. "Letter to K.L. Campbell." (Oct. 9, 1871, "Weaver File." Gettysburg National Military Park)

[50] *Confederate Veteran.* (No. 36), p. 93.

[51] *Confederate Veteran.* (No. 32), p. 355.

[52] *Confederate Veteran.* (No. 13), p. 564.

[53] *Confederate Veteran.* (No. 36), p. 93.

[54] "Senator wants to know why graves of Confederate soldiers were covered." *Times and Democrat* (Orangeburg, South Carolina. March 18, 1993.), p 3B.

[55] "Soldiers' Graves Ready For Ceremony Next Month." *Sunday Post.* Vicksburg, Mississippi. April 26,1981.), p 2.

[56] *Confederate Veteran.* (No. 36), p. 93.

Section II

Cemetery Descriptions

The cemeteries are listed in alphabetical order by the city (or town) where the cemetery is located. National Cemeteries are listed by the name of the cemetery.

Alexandria National Cemetery

Most of the 3,598 soldiers buried in the Alexandria National Cemetery died in hospitals in the area around Washington, DC. By 1866, one citizen and two "white females" were also interred in the cemetery.

Thirty-four Confederate soldiers who died while prisoners of war were also buried in unmarked graves. In 1879, these bodies were moved to the Christ Churchyard in Alexandria where a monument was erected, inscribed as follows:

**How sleep the brave who sink to rest
By all their Country's wishes blest."
Beneath this mound lie the remains of
34 Confederate soldiers, which were
disinterred
from the Alexandria Soldiers Cemetery
(Federal) and
reinterred in this ground on the 27th
day of December, 1879, under the auspices
of the
"Southern Memorial Association" of
Alexandria, Va.**

A list of 34 names follows, then concludes:

**a Lieut and one private unknown. These
men were prisoners of war who died in the
Federal Hospital in this city.**

RESURGEMUS

Ball's Bluff National Cemetery

What a Congressional committee called the "most atrocious military blunder in history" occurred on October 21, 1861, when troops under Colonel Edward D. Baker of the 71st Pennsylvania Infantry crossed the Potomac River to make a "slight demonstration." Colonel Nathan (Shanks) Evans's command waited until Baker's troops had crossed the river and then opened fire. Baker and 48 other Union troops were killed, 158 Union soldiers were wounded, and 714 were either captured or missing in action. Thirty-three Confederates were killed, 115 were wounded, and one was reported missing.

It is unclear how many Federal soldiers are buried at Ball's Bluff National Cemetery. The small plot contains one headstone with a name, and 24 graves marked simply: "Unknown." It appears that the plot may contain as many as 54 bodies. During the 1950's, the Quartermaster's Department proposed closing the cemetery, but Congress did not approve the plan. For more information about the history of Ball's Bluff National Cemetery, see the author's *Bivouac of the Dead*.

One Confederate soldier is buried near the cemetery. About 120 feet west of the cemetery's fence is a gray stone marker with the inscription:

CLINTON HATCHER
1840-1861
Co. F 8th VA REGT.
C.S.A.
FELL BRAVELY DEFENDING HIS NATIVE STATE

According to local legend, Clinton Hatcher's parents asked the War Department for permission to bury their son inside the cemetery's fence, but their request was refused. The National Archives' National and Post Cemetery file does not contain any correspondence that verifies this legend, but the as one archivist put it: "As you know, the material on National Cemeteries before 1920 is incomprehensible."

Ball's Bluff National Cemetery may be reached by way of a rutty, unpaved road that runs from U.S.15. The road, about two miles north of VA7, is marked with a green sign.

Centreville

Major Chatham Roberdeau Wheat commanded a "tough but unruly" battalion of Louisiana soldiers known as Wheat's Tigers. Two of his soldiers were shot by a firing squad on December 9, 1861. These are reputed to be the first soldiers executed by the Army of Northern Virginia. On December 9, 1979 the bodies of these two soldiers were exhumed and reburied at Saint John's Episcopal Church. The Church is located at 5649 Mount Gilead Road in Centreville.

City Point National Cemetery

Most of the soldiers buried in the City Point National Cemetery died in hospitals in the area. Construction of the cemetery was begun in late 1865 or early 1866. Reinterrments of soldiers from temporary cemeteries near hospitals commenced in July 1866. However, clear title for the land was not acquired until January 25, 1868, when the land was "purchased by appraisement from E. Comer." The Quartermaster Corps often began burying bodies on land designated as a National Cemetery without first buying the land.

By 1871 a total of 5,156 Union soldiers had been reinterrd in the cemetery:

	Known	Unknown
White Union Soldiers:	2,937	850
Colored Union Soldiers:	782	587

Major Oscar Mack, the Inspector of National Cemeteries, noted in his 1871 and 1874 reports a total of 151 rebel soldiers in the cemetery. Some years later, F.E. Kavanagh, the cemetery's superintendent, prepared a typewritten list of 98 Confederates known to be buried in the cemetery. Superintendent Kavanagh noted the cemetery contained fifteen unknown Confederates; however the "total number of Confederate graves" was 106. Soldiers on Kavanagh's list are labeled VA22 in section III. Twelve of these men are not listed on the cemetery's current (2001) burial roster.

Existing records in the National Archives do not state when the Confederate graves in the cemetery were marked. It appears the 12 soldiers that do not appear on Kavanagh's list are buried as unknowns.

In 1865, the United States Christian Commission published a list of 15 Confederate soldiers buried in and near

City Point. These soldiers are labeled VA24 in section III. Six of these soldiers are listed on City Point's current burial roster. It appears that these were the 15 unknown Confederates on Kavanagh's list.

City Point National Cemetery is located at the intersection of Davis Street and 10th Avenue in a residential neighborhood of Hopewell, Virginia.

Clarke County
Old Chapel

"Old Chapel" church was erected circa 1790. Monuments in the church cemetery honor 91 Confederate soldiers. Old chapel is located in Clarke County near Boyce and Millwood.

Courtland
Courtland Baptist Church

Courtland was known as Jerusalem during the War. The first Baptist church building in Jerusalem was erected in 1846. During the Civil War, between 40 to 45 members of Roberson's Brigade of Hood's Texas Division died while hospitalized at Jerusalem. They were buried in the church's cemetery. According to *Courtland Baptist Church's Ancestral History* these bodies were later moved the Suffolk Cemetery. However, because Federal troops were also buried there the bodies were moved back to Jerusalem in 1882. According the records of the U.S. Quartermaster Corps, there were 221 Federal soldiers buried "at Suffolk," but these bodies were moved to the Hampton National Cemetery before 1868.

In 1919, Mrs. Mattie Rochelle Tyler wrote the Texas United Daughters of the Confederacy requesting help in marking the graves of the soldiers buried in the church's cemetery. On September 17, 1924, a monument supplied by the U.D.C. of Texas was erected in the church cemetery. Unfortunately, a fire in 1893 destroyed many of the church's records. Mr. H.P. Story provided a list of 23 soldiers who died "at Jerusalem" and may have been buried in unmarked graves in the church's cemetery. Courtland Baptist Church is located on Main Street in Courtland.

Cedar Hill Cemetery
Covington

At least three Confederate soldiers are buried in Covington's Cedar Hill Cemetery. One of these soldiers drowned, while another died of measles.

Culpeper Fairview Cemetery

Most of the burials in Culpeper's Fairview cemetery apparently came from hospitals in the area. A list of 369 soldiers that are known to be buried in the cemetery was prepared by the ladies of Culpeper and published in the *Culpeper Observer* on May 27, 1866.

These soldiers are buried in a mound beneath the Confederate monument in Fairview Cemetery. Fairview Cemetery is located on US522 (Sperryville Road) five blocks west of Main Street in Culpeper, Virginia.

Culpeper National Cemetery

Culpeper National Cemetery was located some 200 yards east of the Orange and Alexandria Railroad. The Federal Government acquired the six acres of land for the cemetery by a "Degree of Condemnation" on April 27, 1867. The former owner, Mr. Edward B. Hill, was paid $1,400.00 for his land. The cemetery was in "plain sight of the rail-way station," which proved very convenient when some 350 bodies were moved to the cemetery from the Cedar Mountain Battlefield.

By the time Major Oscar Mack inspected the cemetery in 1871, a total of 448 known and 901 unknown Union soldiers had been buried in the cemetery. Major Mack did not report any burials of Confederates, but 1st Lt. D.J.V. Martin of company H of the Palmetto Sharpshooters is buried in the "officer's circle" along with some of the other 20 Union officers buried in the cemetery.

Culpeper National Cemetery is located at 305 U.S. Avenue in Culpeper.

Emory and Henry College

A stone obelisk in Emory's Holston Conference Cemetery honors the memory of 203 known and three unknown Confederate soldiers who died in the hospital at Emory and Henry College. Like many other Confederate cemeteries, the individual soldiers' graves are marked with numbered stone markers. Each number corresponds to a name on the bronze plaque located on the obelisk so each soldier's grave can be located.

On the south face of the obelisk, above the plaque of names, the following is etched into the stone:

206
Southern Soldiers
War 1861-65

At the top of the plaque of names is the following heading:
Our Confederate Dead

At the base of the obelisk is the following name:

J.W. Vermillion

It appears that he is the artist (stone mason) responsible for the obelisk.

The cemetery is not on the campus of Emory and Henry College, but just north of the heart of campus. The cemetery can be accessed from Elm or Linden Streets.

Fairfax Court House
Fairfax City Cemetery

From Fairfax to Appomattox 1861 - 1865

Erected to the memory of the Gallant Sons of Fairfax whose names are inscribed on this monument, but whose bodies lie Buried on Distant Battlefields; And to the memory of their 200 unknown comrades whose remains are at rest beneath this monument. These were men whom death could not Terrify whom defeat could not dishonor.

Thus reads the inscription on the 26-foot monument of Richmond granite in Fairfax City Cemetery (formerly called the Cemetery for the Burial of the Confederate Dead). The monument, dedicated on October 1, 1890, also lists the names of 100 men from Fairfax County who died during the war. These men's names are coded VA10 in section III of this book.

Sources disagree on the number of unknown Confederates buried in the cemetery, but it appears somewhere between 200 to 500 men are buried there. One private marker near the monument honors J. Douglas Martin, of Company A, 6th Regiment of South Carolina Volunteers.

Front Royal
Prospect Hill Cemetery

At least 186 Confederates are buried in Front Royal's Prospect Hill Cemetery. The names of 91 of them are known. Seven of these men were members of Col. Mosby's command who were executed while being held as prisoners of war. Col. Mosby would later explain the circumstances:

"At the time this affair occurred I was away from my command, wounded. Sheridan, with an overwhelming force, was pushing Early up the Shenandoah Valley. He had sent Torbert with two divisions of cavalry to cut off his retreat at New Market. Wickman, in command of Fitzhugh Lee's cavalry division, had repulsed them at Milford, and Torbert was retreating down the valley. Captain Sam Chapman, with a detachment of fifty or sixty men went to the valley to strike a blow that would impede Sheridan's march, by breaking his line of communication . . . . At Front Royal Chapman saw an ambulance train under an escort of cavalry coming down the pike. As he had not heard of Torbert's defeat and that he was retreating down the valley, and not dreaming that a corps of cavalry was in supporting distance immediately behind it, he attacked the escort and drove it back on the main body. Having leaped into the midst of overwhelming numbers, he had to call off his men and abandon what he had won. A body of cavalry was sent around to intercept his retreat, and formed across his path. Merritt's whole division was in pursuit. When Chapman's men came upon the cavalry in the road that barred their way they opened upon them with their six-shooters and cleared away the obstruction. There was no time to parley or to take prisoners. The momentum of Chapman's charge swept away all before it. The enemy had attempted to cut off Chapman, and had got cut off; but six of Chapman's men were captured."

The monument to these men is inscribed:

**ERECTED
1899
BY THE SURVIVORS OF
MOSBY'S COMMAND
IN MEMORY OF
SEVEN COMRADES
EXECUTED
WHILE PRISONERS OF WAR
NEAR THIS SPOT
SEPTEMBER 23rd, 1864
MOSBY'S MEN.
DULCE ET DECORUM EST
PRO PATRIA MORI
IN EVERLASTING HONOR OF
THOMAS E. ANDERSON,
DAVID L. JONES,
WILLIAM THOMAS OVERBY,
_____CARTER,
LUCIEN LOVE,
HENRY C. RHODES,
ALBERT C. WILLIS,
FORTY-THIRD BATTALION,
VIRGINIA CAVALRY,
MOSBY'S COMMAND,
C.S.A.**

The soldiers in the cemetery are buried in a circle around a monument that is inscribed:

> They died in the cause of honor
> And justice

> Erected by the Ladies
> Memorial Association
> August 24th 1882

> In memory of the one Hundred
> And eighty six honored men
> who lie buried here, from this
> And other Southern states. They
> gave their lives in Defence
> of truth and Right.

> Virginia Honor the Brave

Prospect Hill Cemetery is located on Prospect Street. From the Court House, go south three blocks on Royal Avenue (US340). Then turn right on Prospect Street. The monument to Mosby's men is located near the cemetery's entrance. The Confederate graves are located to the left near the crest of the hill.

Mount Jackson

The military hospital at Mount Jackson was established in September 1861 under the direction of Dr. Andrew Russell Meem. Dr. Meem, a native of the area, was a graduate of Princeton University and the University of Pennsylvania Medical College. The hospital had three two-story, 150-foot long buildings. Dr. Meem was assisted by the ladies of Mount Jackson, who according an appeal for funds to beautify the cemetery ". . . oft have . . . heard the sighs heaved by dying soldiers . . . ." The appeal listed the names of 238 soldiers buried in the cemetery, with the notation: "There are 112 graves unknown."

Today the names of the known dead are listed on two large bronze tablets. A statue of a bare-headed Confederate soldier is located in front of the tablets. The soldier's head is bowed as in prayer. Inscribed on the base of the statue is:

TO ALL CONFEDERATES

The cemetery is fenced. A metal arch above the stone gateposts reads:

OUR SOLDIERS CEMETERY
1861 - 1865

Mount Jackson's beautiful Soldiers' Cemetery is located on the west side of US11 near its junction with VA1314.

New Market

The Battle of New Market (May 15, 1864) pitted approximately 6,500 Union troops under General Franz Sigel against approximately 5,300 Confederates under General John C. Breckinridge. When General Breckinridge decided that Sigel had no intention of attacking him, he decided to be the aggressor: "I shall advance on him. We can attack and whip them here, and I'll do it." By 4:00 PM, Breckinridge had defeated Sigel and the Shenandoah Valley, a major source of the Confederacy's food, was safe (for awhile).

Some of the 50 or so Confederates who were killed at New Market are buried in five area cemeteries. Ninety-nine known Confederates are buried in Saint Matthews Cemetery, located behind the Reformation Lutheran Church. This cemetery also contains the graves of 33 unknown soldiers.

Emmanuel Cemetery contains the graves of 37 Confederates. Five Confederates rest in Zirkle Cemetery. Zirkle Cemetery is located on VA Route 617, three-tenths of a mile east of VA Route 728. Cedar Grove Cemetery, located on US11 north of New Market, contains the graves of four Confederates. One Confederate is buried in Mount Zion Cemetery. Mount Zion Cemetery is west of New Market on VA Route 728.

The Battle of New Market is most famous for the charge of a battalion of cadets from Virginia Military Institute. Five of the teenage cadets were killed in action and five were mortally wounded. The 14 charter members of the Woman's Memorial Society of the Lost Cause, founded in 1867, "desired that their fathers, husbands, sons, and betrothed be remembered." On May 12, 1898, a monument in "memory of the Southern Soldiers and the VMI Cadets" was erected in Saint Matthews Cemetery. However, none of the ten VMI Cadets who died as a result of the battle are buried in New Market. Six of the Cadets are buried under a monument on the campus of VMI. The rest were interred in private cemeteries.

Newport News

At least 167 Confederate prisoners of war died in a Federal prison camp in Newport News. These deaths occurred between April 27, 1865, and July 4, 1865. The bodies were buried on the "West farm." In 1890, these men's bodies were removed and buried in a large mound in Greenlawn Cemetery. Apparently, the bodies of three POW's who died on nearby Craney Island were moved there also. The burials on Craney Island are coded VA27 in section III of this book. According to one note found in the Virginia State Library and Archives: "The bones of a dozen or more men were dug up from various farms, several from Andrew Jones' place and buried under the monument. Unfortunately, the names were not known. At least, they were not recorded."

Richmond
Hebrew Confederate Cemetery

Some sources state that Hebrew Confederate Cemetery in Richmond is the only Jewish military cemetery in the world outside of Israel. Others dispute this claim, pointing to the Jewish sections of the military cemeteries operated by the Commonwealth War Graves Commission. This commission is responsible for maintaining cemeteries established after World War I and World War II for the burial of British and other troops from the British Commonwealth.

The cemetery, located on Shockoe Hill in Richmond, contains the graves of 30 Jewish Confederate soldiers. The names of all but one of the soldiers buried here are known. A bronze plaque at the cemetery lists the names of the 29 known soldiers along with the following inscription:

**TO THE GLORY OF GOD
AND
IN MEMORY OF
THE HEBREW CONFEDERATE SOLDIERS RESTING
IN THIS HALLOWED SPOT**

**ERECTED BY
HEBREW LADIES MEMORIAL ASSO.
RICHMOND, VA.
ORGANIZED 1866**

Richmond
Hollywood Cemetery

Almost as soon as the Civil War started, soldiers started flocking to Richmond. Richmond, the seat of the Confederate Government, was the major objective of the Union Army. Hospitals in Richmond treated tens of thousands of sick and wounded soldiers. Most of the soldiers who died in Richmond were buried in two cemeteries: Hollywood Cemetery and Oakwood Cemetery. Both have nearly the same number of Confederate burials. One of the first burials in Hollywood was that of Young Wyatt, of the 1st North Carolina Regiment. The burial roster published in 1869 lists him as the "First Martyr."

On May 3, 1866, the ladies of Richmond met at St. Paul's Church and organized The Ladies Hollywood Memorial Association. The Association's goal was "to collect funds to be applied in enclosing, arranging, returfing and otherwise placing in order the graves of the Confederate dead interred in Hollywood Cemetery . . . ."

The Association selected May 31, 1866, as the first Memorial Day in Richmond. Citizens of Richmond sent flowers to Grace Episcopal Church, ". . . where they were made into wreaths and taken to Hollywood." It is interesting to note that the citizens of Richmond were not allowed to go to the cemetery that day. According to an account written in 1916, "An address was *printed* and *published*, as at this time, the Federal authorities, who were in control, would not allow crowds to congregate or an address to be made openly by the people of this city." Apparently the First Amendment to the Constitution had been suspended by these Federal authorities.

In November 1866, the Association held its first bazaar to raise funds to construct a monument in the cemetery. This first effort raised $18,000, a fortune in the cash-strapped South. Fundraising continued until $26,000 was raised. In 1869, the Association constructed a pyramid 45 feet square and 90 feet high of "irregular blocks of James River granite." The pyramid's capstone was set in place by a "convict sailor who was given his liberty after accomplishing this daring deed." The inscriptions on the Memorial Pyramid are:

ERECTED BY THE HOLLYWOOD MEMORIAL ASSOCIATION A.D. 1869

TO THE CONFEDERATE DEAD

MEMORIA IN AETHRNA

NUMINI ET PATRIAE ASTO

Charles Henry Dimmock, who had served as a Captain in the Confederate Corps of Engineers, designed the Memorial Pyramid. A bronze tablet near the base of the pyramid honors Mr. Dimmock who was an architect, engineer, and lawyer during his brief life, 1831-1873.

While the monument was being designed and constructed, bodies from battlefields near Richmond were being moved to Hollywood. Many of these interments came from battlefields of the Seven Days Campaign and Grant's 1864 campaign. Unfortunately, many of these bodies were never identified.

Improvements were made in the cemetery. Normally when a grave was filled after a burial, dirt was mounded over the top of the grave. Then as the wooden casket rotted, the dirt would fill in the grave. By 1869, the graves had been leveled. Granite blocks were installed to mark the corners of each section.

Also in 1869, the Association published a register listing the names of 6,878 soldiers known to be buried in the cemetery. Around 5,000 unknown soldiers were buried in the cemetery by that time as well.

In 1872, the Association arranged to have the remaining bodies of Confederate soldiers removed from Gettysburg and reinterred in Hollywood. Bodies of soldiers known to be from South Carolina, North Carolina, and Georgia had already been returned to their home states. The names of the known dead removed from Gettysburg will be included in an upcoming edition of the *Confederate Cemeteries* series.

At least five and perhaps as many as seven Confederate Generals are now buried in Hollywood: J.E.B. Stuart, Edward Johnson, John R. Cooke, Fitzhugh Lee, and Eppa Hunton. General Richard Brooke Garnett was killed in action leading his troops at Gettysburg. His body was never identified after the battle; it is likely that his body was removed to Hollywood in 1872. A stone marker to his memory has been erected in Hollywood. The souvenir pamphlet *Our Confederate Dead*, published by the Association in 1916, lists John Pegram as a general; however, D.S. Freeman in *Lee's Lieutenants* states Pegram was a "Colonel of Artillery" when he was mortally wounded at Hatcher's Run on February 6, 1865. At one time General A. P. Hill was buried in Hollywood, but in 1892, his remains were moved to the site where he was handed his commission as Brigadier General.

After his death in 1889, Jefferson Davis, the only president of the Confederacy, was buried in Hollywood. A small marble headstone marks the grave of Davis's son, Joseph, who died after he fell from a window in the "Confederate White House." The headstone's inscription reads:

JOSEPH
Son of Our Beloved President
Erected by the Little Girls and Boys of the
Southern Capital

In 1914, the State of Virginia appropriated $8,000 to place the cemetery in perpetual care. On Monday, May 31, 1915, a bronze plaque commemorating this appropriation was unveiled:

**A MEMORIAL TO THE
CONFEDERATE WOMEN
OF VIRGINIA, 1861 - 1865
THE LEGISLATURE OF VIRGINIA
OF 1914, HAS AT THE
SOLICITATION OF LADIES
HOLLYWOOD
MEMORIAL ASSOCIATION
AND UNITED DAUGHTERS OF
CONFEDERACY OF VIRGINIA
PLACED IN PERPETUAL CARE
THIS SECTION WHERE LIE BURIED
EIGHTEEN THOUSAND
CONFEDERATE SOLDIERS.**

Hollywood Cemetery is located at 412 South Cherry Street in Richmond.

Richmond
Shockoe Cemetery

In 1820, Richmond's City Council purchased four acres of land on Shockoe Hill for a public cemetery. During the Civil War, the majority of Confederates who died in or near Richmond were buried in two larger city-owned cemeteries: Hollywood and Oakwood. The interment records of Shockoe Cemetery list a total of 316 burials directly related to the Civil War. The names of 208 Confederate soldiers are recorded, along with the names of 93 Federal soldiers who died while prisoners of war.

The interment records also list 13 civilians who were killed during the war. Two civilians died in an explosion at a "C.S. Laboratory" (gunpowder plant) on February 6, 1862. This explosion was a forerunner of the Friday the 13th disaster on Brown's Island. The explosion and fire there on March 13, 1863, claimed at least 55 lives. Most of the victims were young teenage girls. Nine girls, ages 12 to 16, were buried on Shockoe Hill.

Explosive shells remained dangerous long after the war. Mr. William B. Burch was "killed by [an] explosive shell" January 18, 1866. He was 29. Virginia S. Smith, age 24, was "killed in an engagement with the Federal Army" on March 15, 1865. A Mr. Webster, who was hung as a "Yankee spy," is also interred in Shockoe.

A plaque in the northeastern corner of the cemetery reads:

In this vicinity are buried 220 Confederate soldiers and 577 Union soldiers who are recorded, as well as hundreds of other soldiers of whose burial no record was made

This plaque was erected some years after the war. It is unclear what source was used for the numbers on the plaque.

Almost all of the Confederate soldiers whose names appear in the interment records were buried in plots purchased by their comrades. The records show the names of the purchaser(s) of a plot. However, the records do not show a soldier's military unit. The majority of these graves were never marked with any type of permanent marker.

It appears the Federal soldiers buried in Shockoe were never moved to a national cemetery. Their names do not appear in the 27 volume *Roll of Honor* series that lists Union burials, nor is there any record of removals from Shockoe in other existing records of the Quartermaster's Corps.

Shockoe Cemetery is located at 2nd and Hospital Streets in Richmond.

Spotsylvania Court House

On May 7, 1864, General U.S. Grant began to move his army from the bloody Wilderness battleground toward the tiny hamlet of Spotsylvania Court House. General Robert E. Lee's Army of Northern Virginia reached Spotsylvania Court House first. Grant's army attacked on May 10, but was repelled. Before dawn on May 12, Hancock's II Corps attacked the Confederate lines. The Federals broke through at the "mule shoe" salient, but the advance was stopped. The two armies remained in place until May 20, when Grant began disengaging his command.

In 1866, ladies in the area formed the Spotsylvania Memorial Association and established the Spotsylvania Confederate Cemetery on five acres of land donated by Joseph and Quincy Sanford. The bodies of 570 Confederates were removed from nearby battlefields and cemeteries and reinterred in the cemetery. Most of the Confederate dead buried in the cemetery are identified. Following a practice often used by the Federal Government when establishing national cemeteries, the soldiers were buried by state. Soldiers from ten Southern states-Alabama, Arkansas, Georgia, Louisiana, Mississippi, North Carolina, South Carolina, Tennessee, Texas, and Virginia are buried in the cemetery.

In 1918, local groups erected a granite monument, topped by a Confederate soldier in the cemetery. The inscriptions on the monument read:

Front:

**Erected and dedicated
May 12, 1918
By the Spotsylvania Chapter
United Daughters of
The Confederacy.
Confederated Southern
Memorial Association and
Citizens of Spotsylvania County.
To Commemorate and
Perpetuate the valor and
Patriotism of the sons
of Spotsylvania County,
Virginia, and other
Confederate soldiers who
repose in this cemetery.
1861   1865
Confederate Soldiers**

Right Side:
**Love makes Memory
Eternal.**

Left Side:
Lest We Forget

Rear:
**We have gathered the
sacred dust,
of warriors tried and true,
who bore the flag of
our nation's trust,
and fell in the cause**
'Tho lost, still just and died for me and you.

In 1931, the Federal Government supplied headstones to mark the graves in the cemetery. Spotsylvania Confederate Cemetery is located on Virginia Route VA208, about ½ mile northeast of the junction of VA208 and VA608.

Upperville

Sixteen Confederates, two unknown, are buried in Upperville. Two of these soldiers were killed in a skirmish at Upperville on June 21, 1863. The soldiers' graves are around a stone shaft inscribed with the words:

**Erected 1894 Restored 1984
United Daughters of the Confederacy
District of Columbia and Virginia Divisions**

The cemetery is located on US50 in Upperville.

Williamsburg
Bruton Parish Church

Thirty-three known and six unknown soldiers who were killed in the Battle of Williamsburg on May 5, 1862 are buried in Bruton Parish Churchyard. This battle was a delaying action during General J.B. "Prince John" Magruder's retreat up the peninsula of Virginia. Bruton Parish Church, an Anglican church, was constructed in 1715. Also buried in the churchyard are a soldier who died in 1861, two veterans, and two other unknown soldiers.

The names of 29 soldiers are listed on a monument that is inscribed:

**LORD KEEP THEIR
MEMORY GREEN**

**ERECTED IN MEMORY OF THE
CONFEDERATE SOLDIERS WHO FELL
IN THE
BATTLE OF WILLIAMSBURG MAY 5,
1862, AND LIE BURIED
UNDER AND AROUND THIS
MONUMENT**

Inside the church is a plaque that reads:

> **IN MEMORY OF**
> **THE**
> **CONFEDERATE**
> **SOLDIERS**
> who fell in the
> **BATTLE OF WILLIAMSBURG**
> May the 5th 1862
> And of those who died of
> the wounds received in
> the same.
> **THEY DIED FOR US.**

Bruton Parish Church is located inside Colonial Williamsburg and local directions to the church are suggested.

Woodstock

Sixty-three Confederates are buried in Woodstock's Massanutten Cemetery. Their graves are marked with individual headstones arranged in a circle around a monument. Several of these soldiers were killed in battles "in and around" the town. However, the majority of these soldiers died of wounds or disease in the hospital at Woodstock.

Massanutten Cemetery is located on Benchoff Street off US11 on the south end of Woodstock. The Confederates are buried in the section of the cemetery located behind the military academy.

Yorktown National Cemetery

After a month-long siege, Yorktown fell to General McClellan's army on May 3, 1862. McClellan proceeded to move "on to Richmond" and disaster in the Seven Days campaign. The Yorktown National Cemetery was established near the site of the siege lines during the 1781 campaign that ended the Revolutionary War. The land, around three acres, was purchased for $490.00. Bodies were moved to the cemetery from 27 different locations, some as far as 50 miles away. However, most of the bodies came from Yorktown and the Williamsburg Battlefield.

In 1874 Major Mack reported a total of 2,183 interments:

	Known	Unknown
White Union Soldiers and Sailors	713	1,410
Colored Union Soldiers and Sailors	11	17
Citizens	9	6
Rebel soldiers	16	1
	749	1,434

According to research conducted by Joseph C. Avent III, a volunteer at the Colonial National Historical Park, there are 14 marked graves of Confederates in the cemetery. All but one of the soldiers died in 1862, and all but one were from North Carolina units. Most of the Confederates buried at Yorktown were wounded and captured at the Battle of Hanover Court House on May 25, 1862.

Yorktown National Cemetery, located within the Colonial National Historical Park, is one of 14 national cemeteries maintained by the National Park Service. A second Confederate cemetery is located in the park's boundaries. There is a small monument at what was shown on an 1867 military map as a Confederate cemetery, but no records on burials in this cemetery have been located.

Section III

List of Burials

Cemeteries are coded (VA1, VA2, ...) See page xi for more information.

___ , Andrew J. - VA12
___ , Godfery - VA12
___ , ___ - Died at Hill's Mill   VA18
___ , ___ C. - "C" 57th Virginia   Oct. 9, 1861 VA25
___ , ___ - Died on the [train] cars at Gordonsville
    - March 30, 1862   VA25
A___, M. - Co. K 18th Georgia   Oct. 14, 1861 VA25
Aaron, M. - North Carolina   VA17
Aaron, W.J. - Co. E 17th North Carolina August 30, 1864
    VA25
Abanath, G.C. - Co. K 35th North Carolina   March 7, 1865
    VA25
Abaver, W.A. - Co. C 49th North Carolina   March 13, 1865
    VA25
Abbacombie, J. - Co. G 14th South Carolina   June 10, 1862
    VA25
Abbacombie, James - Co. C 14th South Carolina   June 9, 1862
    VA25
Abbanathe, D. - Co. D 1st Engineer Corps   July 6, 1864 VA25
Abbanathe, J.S. - Co. C 28th North Carolina   July 21, 1864
    VA25
Abbett, J. - Co. F 50th Georgia May 22, 1863   VA25
Abbey, ___ - July 5, 1862   VA25
Abbeynethe, A.J. - Co. K 25th North Carolina   April 17, 1865
    VA25
Abbliss, W.H. - Co. F 21st Mississippi   July 9, 1863 VA25
Abbliss, W.S. - 1st Georgia Oct. 16, 1861 VA25
Abbott, G. - Co. E 5th Alabama   June 8, 1862   VA25
Abbott, J. - 8th Louisiana   March 28, 1862 VA25
Abbott, J.J. - 59th Georgia   July 20, 1864   VA25
Abbott, V. - Co. F 17th Mississippi   Jan. 2, 1863 VA25
Abbott, Walter R. - KIA July 2, 1862   VA19
Abney, B. - Co. H 49th Georgia   June 5, 1864   VA25
Abney, J.R. - Co. B 7th South Carolina   August 4, 1864
    VA25

Abshin, A. - Co. F 52nd North Carolina Sept. 9, 1864 VA25

Acerman, D.S. - Co. C 5th South Carolina Cavalry   June 23, 1864   VA25

Ackler, W.R. - Co. I 4th Alabama June 27, 1862   VA25

Acklin, W. - Co. I 4th Alabama Aug. 1, 1862   VA25

Ackridge, R.M. - Co. F 18th Mississippi Infantry   VA08

Adams, A. - Co. I 10th Alabama July 22, 1862   VA25

Adams, A. - 2nd South Carolina July 21, 1862   VA25

Adams, A.R. - Co. B 22nd North Carolina Sept. 2, 1864 VA25

Adams, D. - Co. F 20th South Carolina August 10, 1864 VA25

Adams, E.D. - Co. C 5th Louisiana June 27, 1862   VA25

Adams, F. - Co. H 49th Georgia June 23, 1864   VA25

Adams, H. - Co. A 27th South Carolina Nov. 1, 1862 VA25

Adams, H.C.- Co. I 44th North Carolina Nov. 2, 1864 VA25

Adams, H.G. - Died Nov. 23, 1862 VA19

Adams, H.M. - 38th North Carolina August 31, 1862 VA25

Adams, J.C. - Co. A 13th Georgia Dec. 23, 1863   VA25

Adams, J.J. - Co. G 42nd Mississippi June 4, 1862 VA25

Adams, J.T.- Co. C 5th North Carolina June 3, 1862 VA25

Adams, J.W.- 2nd South Carolina VA11

Adams, James - POW - Federal Soldier Died April 17, 1862 VA19

Adams, John - 11th North Carolina Died 1861   VA23

Adams, John - Louisiana April 16, 1864 VA25

Adams, Joshua - 8th Virginia Infantry   VA10

Adams, N.T. - Co. D 54th North Carolina June 11, 1864 VA25

Adams, R. - Co. G 47th North Carolina Oct. 22, 1864 VA25

Adams, S.D.- Co. F 62nd Georgia Oct. 8, 1864   VA25

Adams, S.W. - Mississippi VA20

Adams, W. - Co. K 52nd Virginia June 22, 1864   VA25

Adams, W.H. - 11th North Carolina Sept. 30, 1861 VA25

Adams, W.J. - Co. A 44th Georgia June 5, 1864   VA25
Adams, Wm. H. - 8th Virginia Infantry VA10
Adcock, J.D. - Co. E 12th North Carolina July 5, 1862 VA25
Adcock, J.P. - Co. B 25th Virginia June 17, 1864   VA25
Addens, J.S. - Co. C 5th Alabama July 8, 1862 VA25
Adderhood, __ - Cobb's Legion (Georgia) June 22, 1862 VA25
Addington, J.P. - Co. H 5th Alabama July 10, 1862 VA25
Addington, Thos. - Co. B 38th Georgia Aug. 12, 1862 VA25
Addis, R. - Co. H 15th South Carolina Oct. 5, 1864 VA25
Addison, John - Lt. - Co. G - 17th Virginia - KIA - Battle of Williamsburg - May 5, 1862 VA02
Ade, S. - Co. E 25th Virginia Nov. 3, 1863   VA25
Adkins, Chas. - Virginia VA20
Adkins, J.C. - Co. I 44th Georgia March 24, 1865 VA25
Adkins, Jo. - POW - Federal Soldier Died June 19, 1862 VA19
Adler, Henry - 46th Virginia VA17
Aeres, E.W. - 42nd Virginia   VA18
Agecock, F.F. - Co. B 55th North Carolina May 11, 1862 VA25
Agecock, John - Co. G 9th Louisiana May 22, 1862 VA25
Agecock, R.C. - Co. B 14th North Carolina June 26, 1862 VA25
Agecock, R.J. - Co. A 14th North Carolina July 27, 1862 VA25
Ageton, W. - Co. B 26th North Carolina March 11, 1865 VA25
Ahisa, J.F. - Co. F 57th North Carolina Oct. 29, 1864 VA25
Aiken, William B. - Pvt. - Co. E 15th South Carolina Died May 18, 1864   VA28
Ainsley, L.B. - Co. B 18th Georgia Oct 23, 1864 VA25
Akin, W.C. - Co. G 2nd Louisiana May 16, 1862 VA25
Albert, T.J. - Co. D 45th North Carolina VA11

Albright, John - POW - Federal Soldier Died Dec. 9, 1861
    VA19
Albright, Samuel A. - Lt. - 53rd North Carolina Died May 13,
    1864   VA28
Aldred, James Aaron - Pvt. - Co. H 22nd Georgia Died May
    14, 1864   VA28
Alexander, __ - 5th Alabama   VA18
Alexander, H.H. - 10th Alabama Jan. 2, 1862 VA25
Alexander, J. - Orr's Rifles (South Carolina)   Aug. 3, 1864
    VA25
Alexander, J. F. - Co. K 49th North Carolina Aug. 27, 1864
    VA25
Alexander, J.H. - Co. F 15th Georgia Aug. 30, 1864 VA25
Alexander, J.W. - South Carolina Aug. 10, 1864 VA25
Alexander, J.W. - Co. D 27th South Carolina Feb. 17 1865
    VA25
Alexander, L. - Co. E 8th Virginia Aug. 21, 1862 VA25
Alexander, Margaret - Civilian -Killed in explosion of C.S.
    Laboratory - March 21, 1863 age 15   VA19
Alexander, W. - Co. Q _th Mississippi Battalion
    Jan. 10, 1862   VA25
Alexander, W.C. - - Pvt. - Co. B 13th North Carolina Died
    June 27, 1865   VA26
Alexander, W.M. - 5th Alabama   VA18
Alfred, J. - Co. K 38th North Carolina June 21, 1864 VA25
Aligood, J.B.W. - Co. C 26th Georgia   VA11
All, A. - Co. F 44th North Carolina Sept. 29, 1864 VA25
Allan, J.S. - Co. I 20th Virginia May 22, 1863   VA25
Allan, John - Lt. - Died April 15, 1865 VA19
Allen, A.A. - Co. D 8th Georgia Nov. 20, 1864   VA25
Allen, A.J. - 7th Virginia VA18
Allen, A.P. - Pvt. - Co. H 8th Georgia Bat.. Died May 23,
    1865   VA26
Allen, A.S. - Lt. VA06
Allen, Andrew Jackson - Pvt. - Co. D 52nd North Carolina
    Died May 12, 1864 VA28

Allen, D.H. - Lt. - Clark Cavalry VA06
Allen, E. - Co. A 23rd South Carolina Oct. 7, 1864 VA25
Allen, E. - Co. G 44th North Carolina Oct. 22, 1863 VA25
Allen, G. - Co. G 8th Louisiana Jan. 11, 1862 VA25
Allen, Garland - DOW July 26, 1862 VA19
Allen, H. - Co. B 4th North Carolina Sept. 22, 1862 VA25
Allen, H. - Co. B 53rd Virginia Aug. 8, 1862 VA25
Allen, J. - Co. I 21st North Carolina Dec. 30, 1863 VA25
Allen, J. - Co. D 54th North Carolina Sept. 24, 1862 VA25
Allen, J. W. - Co. D 2nd South Carolina Jan. 13, 1863 VA25
Allen, J.C. - Alabama April 21, 1862 VA25
Allen, J.G. - Sumpter Artillery May 27, 1862 VA25
Allen, J.H. - Co. I 3rd Virginia Sept. 2, 1862 VA25
Allen, J.J. - Co. B 25th North Carolina March 28, 1865 VA25
Allen, J.P. - Co. D 48th North Carolina Sept. 14, 1864 VA25
Allen, J.S. - Co. K 24th Georgia June 25, 1862 VA25
Allen, J.T. - 22nd North Carolina May 6, 1861 VA25
Allen, J.T. - Sept. 10, 1862 VA25
Allen, J.W. - Co. F 1st South Carolina July 19, 1862 VA25
Allen, John - Lt. KIA age 32 VA19
Allen, L.W. - South Carolina July 30, 1864 VA25
Allen, T. - Co. B 32nd Virginia June 8, 1862 VA25
Allen, T. - June 5, 1862 VA25
Allen, T.W. - Orr's Rifles (South Carolina) July 29, 1864 VA25
Allen, T.W. - Co. K 53rd Georgia Aug. 2, 1862 VA25
Allen, W. - Co. I 14th Alabama Sept. 1, 1862 VA25
Allen, W.H. - Co. K 33rd North Carolina March 23, 1863 VA25
Allen, W.J. - Co. C 24th Georgia July 20, 1862 VA25
Allen, W.T. - Co. C 24th Georgia June 20, 1862 VA25
Allen, W.T. - Nov. 1, 1861 VA25
Allen, __ - Co. I 14th Georgia Sept. 2, 1862 VA25
Allenton, __ - 49th Georgia July 1862 VA25
Allesvine, G.D. - 13th Alabama Sept. 1, 1861 VA25

Alley, J.H. - Co. B 24th Alabama   May 23, 1862 VA25
Alley, W.H. - Co. A 7th Virginia   June 4, 1862 VA25
Alley, W.H.- Co. H 22nd Alabama   May 18, 1862 VA25
Alley, Wm.- 4th Alabama   July 30, 1861 VA25
Allgood, A. - Co. G 66th North Carolina   July 11, 1864 VA25
Allgood, W.W. - Co. C 7th Georgia   July 18, 1862 VA25
Allington, T. - July 8, 1862 VA25
Allison, D.H. - Co. G 5th South Carolina   Oct. 10, 1861 VA25
Allison, D.M. - Co. B 8th Alabama   July 4, 1861 VA25
Allison, J. - 4th Virginia Cavalry,   April 21, 1865 VA25
Allison, J.H. - Co. I 3rd Virginia   Sept. 3, 1862 VA25
Allison, J.S. - Co. B 13th Mississippi   Feb. 8, 1863 VA25
Allison, M. - Co. A 5th Florida   Sept. 1, 1862 VA25
Allison, W.L. - Co. I 11th Mississippi   Oct. 1864 VA25
Allman, J.A. - Co. E 45th Georgia   July 23, 1862 VA25
Allman, W. - Co. A 5th Florida Sept. 1, 1862 VA25
Allmond, F. - 20th Georgia VA18
Almond, Ethelwin A. - Pvt. - Co. I 6th Virginia   Veteran Died Nov. 6, 1933 VA28
Alnad, M. - 22nd North Carolina March 23, 1865 VA25
Alphin, T. - 4th Texas Dec. 7, 1862 VA25
Alsop, A.B. - Co. A 9th Virginia Cavalry   Aug. __, 1864 VA25
Alsop, T.C. - Mississippi March 16, 1865 VA25
Alston, J.W. - DOW July 21, 1862 age 17 VA19
Alston, Samuel T. - Lt. - Co. K 12th North Carolina MW May 12, 1864   Died May 25, 1864 VA28
Alverson, John T. - Pvt. - Co. D 5th Texas Died May 10, 1864 VA28
Alvis, A.N. - Talley's Battery   March 28, 1863 VA25
Amber, A.K. - Lt. - Co. F 2nd North Carolina   July 11, 1863 VA25
Amerson, Andrew J.- Pvt. - Co. C 59th Georgia Died May 12, 1864 VA28

Ammerson, J.R. - Co. D 13th Alabama June 25, 1862 VA25
Amos, Harry - Co. L 21st North Carolina VA11
Anall, L.J.W. - 21st North Carolina April 1, 1865 VA25
Anders, E.R. - 49th Virginia VA18
Anderson, ____ - Capt. Crawford's Company May 23, 1862
    VA25
Anderson, __ - 1862 VA25
Anderson, A. - Co. F 52nd North Carolina Oct. 8, 1864
    VA25
Anderson, B.C. - Sept. 9, 1861 VA25
Anderson, D.C. - Co. H 20th Georgia March 19, 1863
    VA25
Anderson, E. - Co. E 10th South Carolina July 12, 1862
    VA25
Anderson, Elbert T. - Corp. - Co. D 50th Virginia KIA
    Spotsylvania C. H. VA28
Anderson, F.F. - Sgt.- Co. I 7th Tennessee Sept 3, 1863
    VA25
Anderson, G. - Co. C 5th Georgia Died Jan. 2, 1863 VA25
Anderson, G.A. - Pvt. - Madison Artillery Died June 19,
    1865 VA26
Anderson, H. - 37th North Carolina Oct. 6, 1862 VA25
Anderson, J. - Co. F 28th Georgia May 13, 1862 VA25
Anderson, J.B. - Co. G 27th North Carolina Sept. 28, 1864
    VA25
Anderson, J.B. - 13th South Carolina April 7, 1864 VA25
Anderson, J.C. - Sgt.- Co. C 8th Georgia Oct 21, 1864
    VA25
Anderson, J.C. - Co. C 8th Georgia Died Oct. 21, 1864
    VA25
Anderson, J.H. - Co. G 6th South Carolina Oct. 30, 1862
    VA25
Anderson, J.M. - Georgia Sept. 19, 1864 VA25
Anderson, J.N. - 4th Texas Nov. 9, 1861 VA25
Anderson, John - Co. G 23rd Georgia June 28, 1862 VA25

Anderson, John W. - Lt. - South Carolina Feb. 12, 1863 "disinterred and conveyed to South Carolina " VA19

Anderson, L. - Young's Virginia Artillery Died June 26, 1863 VA03

Anderson, L.A. - Hampton's Georgia Legion Oct. 14, 1864 VA25

Anderson, N. - Co. F 16th Mississippi Oct. 4, 1864 VA25

Anderson, S.M. - Co. B 2nd Louisiana May 27, 1862 VA25

Anderson, Thomas D. - Pvt. - Co. C 26th Georgia Died May 12, 1864 VA28

Anderson, Thomas E. - Mosby's Virginia Cavalry shot while POW - Sept 23, 1864 VA23

Anderson, W. - Sgt. - Co. F 14th South Carolina April 1, 1865 VA25

Anderson, W.A. - Co. A 3rd Virginia June 10, 1862 VA25

Anderson, W.A. - 9th Louisiana Nov. 30, 1862 VA25

Anderson, W.H. - Pvt. - Co. I 3rd South Carolina Died March 16, 1863 VA28

Anderson, W.J. - Co. G 38th Georgia July 28, 1862 VA25

Anderson, W.S. - Co. D 3rd Georgia July 8, 1864 VA25

Anderson, W.T. -Co. F 21st South Carolina June 20, 1864 VA25

Anderson, William - KIA July 9, 1862 VA19

Anderson, Wm. - 9th Louisiana Aug. 3, 1861 VA25

Andrews, G.W. - POW - Federal Soldier Died Oct. 16, 1861 VA19

Andrews, George W. - POW - Federal Soldier Died Oct. 15, 1861 VA19

Andrews, J Co. F 13th South Carolina June 22, 1864 VA25

Andrews, Thos. H. - Pvt. - Co. C 10th Virginia Artillery Died May 22, 1865 VA26

Andrews, W.G. - Lt. - Co. C 10th Virginia Died June 11, 1865 VA26

Andrews, W.N. - Pvt. - Georgia 1865 VA22

Angel, M. - Louisiana Sept 23, 1864 VA25

Angel, W. - 18th Georgia Oct. 2, 1861 VA25

Angling, G.W. - Co. F 14th Alabama July 28, 1862   VA25
Anthony, G - Co. D 4th Georgia July 12, 1863   VA25
Anthony, Mark C. - Pvt. - Co. G 59th Georgia Died May 10, 1864   VA28
Anthony, W.D. - Co. E 22nd Georgia July 17, 1864 VA25
Antony, S - Co. K 2nd Louisiana Jan. 19, 1864   VA25
Appberwhite, James - Co. G 17th Georgia June 2, 1862   VA25
Apperson, J - Co. G 27th Georgia Nov. 22, 1862   VA25
Apple, J.R. - Died Nov. 10, 1862 VA19
Apple, S.A. - Co. E 22nd North Carolina July 8, 1862 VA25
Apple, __ - 27th North Carolina July 9, 1862   VA25
Arbogast, Jefferson - Pvt. - Co. F 31st Virginia KIA Spotsylvania C. H. - May 12, 1864 Headstone reads: "Arborgast"   VA28
Arborgast, Jefferson - see Arbogast, Jefferson - VA28
Archball, J.F. - Co. G 3rd Louisiana June 26, 1862   VA25
Archer, E.S. - Co. I 21st Mississippi July 5, 1862   VA25
Archer, W.A.L. - Co. G 22nd Georgia Sept. - 18, 1864   VA25
Ard, J.A. - Co. E 8th Alabama Jan. 2, 1863   VA25
Arehart, W. Harvey - Grave not marked VA15
Arliff, J.N. - Co. G 28th Virginia June 6, 1862   VA25
Arman, __ - Co. H 15th Georgia July 3, 1862   VA25
Armer, J. - Co. E 15th Alabama Jan. 19, 1863   VA25
Armistead, R.W. - Louisiana Sept 23, 1862 VA25
Armstrong, A. - Sgt. - Co. F Orr's Rifles (South Carolina) July 17, 1862 VA25
Armstrong, A.C. - 1st South Carolina Sept. 19, 1862   VA25
Armstrong, J. - Louisiana Aug. 21, 1861 VA25
Armstrong, J.C. - Co. F 15th North Carolina June 14, 1864   VA25
Armstrong, M.A. - 6th Alabama May 3, 1862   VA25
Armstrong, Robert - 11th Mississippi   VA18
Armstrong, T.H. - Co. D 7th South Carolina Oct. 9, 1864   VA25

Armstrong, W.F. - 14th Alabama Infantry - KIA - Battle of Williamsburg - May 5, 1862 VA02

Armstrong, William Thomas - POW - Federal Soldier Died Jan. 17, 1862 VA19

Arnold, A - Co. H 53rd North Carolina June 25, 1864 VA25

Arnold, B.G. - Co. G 16th North Carolina June 25, 1864 VA25

Arnold, J. - 1st North Carolina VA18

Arnold, L.A. - Co. H 22nd Virginia June 7, 1864   VA25

Arnold, W.A. - Co. A 24th Georgia Dec. 28, 1862 VA25

Arrent, J.A. - Co. I 3rd South Carolina Nov 17, 1862 VA25

Arrington, Joshua P. - Pvt. - Co. G 38th Georgia Died May 10, 1864   VA28

Artop, B. - Co A 33rd Virginia June 9, 1863   VA25

Arundell, John T. - Mosby's Cavalry   VA10

Arvin, F. -   Co. F 24th Georgia May 17, 1863   VA25

Ash, H.N. - Cobb's Legion (Georgia)   June 29, 1862 VA25

Ashbern, A - Co. G 56th North Carolina Jan 2, 1865 VA25

Ashburn, Theodore - POW - Federal Soldier Died Dec. 6, 1861   VA19

Ashbury, Daniel - Kentucky   VA20

Ashby, B. -   Co A 17th Mississippi April 20, 1862   VA25

Ashby, J.L. - Clark Cavalry   VA06

Ashford, Chas. H. - Co. D 17th Virginia Infantry   VA10

Ashley, J.H. - 20th __   VA18

Ashlor, N - Co. G 7th South Carolina Cavalry April 24, 1865 VA25

Ashoy, J.M. - Clark Cavalry   VA06

Ashton, R.W. - Major - 2nd Louisiana July 1, 1862   VA25

Ashworth, J.W. -   Co. C 24th Virginia June 8, 1864   VA25

Atcherson, J. G. - Co. B 13th North Carolina May 20, 1862   VA25

Atcherson, J.M. - Co F 5th Texas Aug 1, 1862 VA25

Atchison, J.P. - 8th Georgia VA18

Atkins, A. - Lt. - Co. C 24th Virginia Cavalry   Oct. 5, 1864   VA25

Atkins, F. Sgt. - Co. F 14th North Carolina VA28
Atkins, J.F. - Co. A 12th Louisiana June 4, 1863 VA25
Atkins, James A. - Sgt. - Co. C 2nd Mississippi Died April 22, 1863 VA03
Atkins, L.M. - Co. H 5th Artillery VA11
Atkinson, C.M. - Sgt. - Co. E 7th South Carolina Aug. 21, 1864 VA22
Atkinson, G.W. - Co. H 16th Georgia May 27, 1862 VA25
Atkinson, P.P. - Co. B 41st Virginia June 28, 1862 VA25
Atkinson, W.H. - Co. I 57th Virginia May 28, 1862 VA25
Atterberry, John - 9th Alabama Oct 31, 1862 VA25
Attergia, O. - Sgt. - Co. K 27th North Carolina Oct. 18, 1864 VA25
Attrick, J. - Co. G 53rd Virginia July 22, 1862 VA25
Attwood, J.C. - Co. I 2nd North Carolina March 5, 1864 VA25
Atwill, Samuel Francis - Corp.. - VMI Cadet - MW - Battle of New Market - May 15, 1864 DOW - July 20, 1964 - Buried at VMI
Augustine, James - VA04
Austen, W. - Co. C 8th Virginia VA08
Austin, A.M. - Hampton's Legion (Georgia) April 25, 1862 VA25
Austin, H.E. - Co. E 3rd Texas July 1, 1862 VA25
Austin, Isaac G. - Pvt. - Co. B 3rd South Carolina Battalion Headstone reads "3rd South Carolina Infantry" VA28
Austin, J - Co. C 61st North Carolina Aug. 30, 1864 VA25
Austin, J.H. - Co. D 5th Virginia VA11
Austin, J.W. - Co. G 6th South Carolina Oct. 22, 1864 VA25
Auther, William - Louisiana July 24, 1861 VA25
Averent, L.A. - Co. I 21st South Carolina July 25, 1864 VA25
Avery, S.A.P. - Co. F 14th Alabama Feb. 13, 1863 VA25
Avery, T. Co I 66th North Carolina Oct. 24, 1864 VA25
Avery, W.R. - Co. G 47th Alabama May 30, 1864 VA25
Avett, J.H. - Co. H 14th North Carolina Headstone reads: "Avitt" VA28

Avitt, J.H. - see Avett, J.H. VA28
Ayers, J - Co. H 15th Georgia Dec. 12, 1862 VA25
Ayers, L.S. - 25th Virginia Battalion May 12, 1864 VA25
Ayers, Solomon K. - Sgt. - Co. F 7th North Carolina Died May 12, 1864 VA28
B __ , L.G. - 1st North Carolina Sept. 9, 1862 VA25
B __ , William G. - Co. A 3rd North Carolina VA11
Babb, J.T. - Co. E 14th South Carolina June 16, 1862 VA25
Babbitt, W. - Co. I 53rd Virginia July 17, 1862 VA25
Baber, A. - Sgt. - Co. I 17th North Carolina Sept. 7, 1864 VA25
Baber, W. - Co. G 34th Georgia June 21, 1862 VA25
Babler, N. - Co. A 2nd North Carolina March 28, 1862 VA25
Bachrach, M. - Lynchburg, Virginia VA17
Bachrach, S. - Lynchburg, Virginia VA17
Baerty, E. - Co. G 9th Virginia May 20, 1862 VA25
Bagat, A.S. - Co. E 1st Georgia Reserves March 2, 1865 VA25
Bagby, W.B. - Co. B 50th Georgia April 22, 1865 VA25
Baggers, W. - Co. E 4th North Carolina Feb. 26, 1865 VA25
Bagget, A. - Co. A 13th Alabama Oct. 6, 1861 VA25
Baggett, Robert - Pvt. - Co. H 20th North Carolina MW May 19, 1864 Headstone reads: " Baggott" VA28
Baggott, Robert - see Baggett, Robert VA28
Bagnall, T. - Co. G 13th South Carolina July 23, 1861 VA25
Bagne, D.D. - 14th Alabama July 4, 1861 VA25
Bagne, T.W. - Co. F 26th North Carolina July 9, 1864 VA25
Bagnell, W.H. - Co. H 26th Alabama May 12, 1863 VA25
Bagward, A.R. - Co. B 18th Alabama May 23, 1862 VA25
Bagwell, __ - 4th South Carolina VA18
Bagwell, __ - Aug. 3, 1863 VA25
Bagwell, W.H. - Co. C Holcombe's Legion Nov 18, 1864 VA25

Bahan, __ - Co. 3 Washington Artillery (Louisiana) Oct. 10, 1861 VA25

Bahan, G.W. - Washington Artillery (Louisiana.) Nov. 26, 1861 VA25

Bail, J. - Co. G 48th North Carolina Sept 3, 1863 VA25

Bailess, C.M. - Co. B 6th South Carolina May 21, 1862 VA25

Bailey, H. - Co. B 3rd Virginia May 18, 1862 VA25

Bailey, J. N.. - Co. H 3rd South Carolina Battalion Nov. 30, 1862 VA25

Bailey, J.H. - 4th Alabama VA18

Bailey, J.H. - Cobb's Legion (Georgia)   Feb. 17, 1864 VA25

Bailey, J.M. - Co. A 3rd Virginia Artillery May 20, 1862 VA25

Bailey, J.M. - Co. I 16th Georgia Died May 11, 1863 VA25

Bailey, J.P. - Co. E 47th North Carolina Sept. 30, 1864 VA25

Bailey, J.W. - Co. F 4th South Carolina June 27, 1864 VA25

Bailey, John - 2nd South Carolina Aug 26, 1861 VA25

Bailey, P. - Co. B 1st Louisiana July 24, 1862 VA25

Bailey, W. - Lt. - Co. H 15th Georgia Oct 5, 1864 VA25

Bailey, W.B. - Co. C 60 Georgia Aug. 13, 1862 VA25

Bailey, William - Co. A 6th Alabama June 20, 1862 VA25

Baine, G.W. - 14th Alabama June 7, 1862 VA25

Baird, A.N. - Co. B 56th North Carolina May 23, 1864 VA25

Baker, __ - Co. H 15th Louisiana Jan. 13, 1863   VA25

Baker, A.A. - North Carolina Battalion June 25, 1864 VA25

Baker, B.J. - Co. T 8th South Carolina Cavalry June 27, 1864 VA25

Baker, C - Co. C 13th Alabama August 23, 1862   VA25

Baker, Dickson L. - 2nd. Lt. - Co. B 24th Georgia Vol. Infantry April 24, 1830 - Aug. 16, 1864 This name does not appear on Julia D. Smith's list in the Virginia State Library and Archives. VA23

Baker, F.M. - 38th Virginia June 14th, 1862 VA25

Baker, F.W. - Lt. - 12th Georgia Battalion VA25

Baker, J. - Georgia Jan. 25, 1864   VA25
Baker, J. - Co. E 7th Virginia March 14, 1862   VA25
Baker, J. - Lt. - Co. E 8th North Carolina Oct. 4, 1864
    VA25
Baker, J.A. - Co. H 60th Georgia Jan. 30, 1863   VA25
Baker, J.C. - 2nd North Carolina Cavalry   VA18
Baker, J.H. - Kentucky   VA20
Baker, J.J. - Co. G 35th Georgia June 9, 1864   VA25
Baker, James - 5th North Carolina   VA18
Baker, Job Co. I 11th North Carolina   VA23
Baker, John Co. A 6th Alabama May 4, 1862 VA25
Baker, Joseph H. - Pvt. - Co. D 1st Virginia Cavalry KIA at
    Todd's Tavern - May 7, 1864   VA28
Baker, S.J. - Co. E 33rd North Carolina July 14, 1864 VA25
Baker, V - Co. A 27th South Carolina Oct. 26, 1864 VA25
Baker, William H. VA15
Balcrum, S. - Co. A 30th North Carolina Dec. 12, 1863
    VA25
Baldridge, William -18th Mississippi Infantry - KIA - Battle
    of Williamsburg - May 5, 1862   VA02
Baldwin, C.F. - Pvt. - Co. A 3rd Alabama Died May 12, 1864
    VA28
Baldwin, J. - Co. D 1st North Carolina July 21, 1862   VA25
Baldwin, J. - Co. D 36th Virginia   VA11
Baldwin, Nich. - Co. F 11th North Carolina Died Oct 8, 1861
    VA23
Balentine, J.B. - Co. H 13th South Carolina June 18, 1862
    VA25
Balian, G.B. - Co. 3 Washington Artillery Oct. 10, 1861
    VA25
Ball, __ - Virginia   VA07
Ball, G.C. - Co. E 49th Georgia July 20, 1862   VA25
Ball, G.H. - Capt. - May 13, 1864   VA25
Ball, J. - Co. H 26th North Carolina July 25, 1864 VA25
Ball, J.M. - 2nd Florida June 29, 1862   VA25
Ball, M.A. - Co. D 45th Georgia July 15, 1862   VA25

Ball, Summerfield - Co. I 11th Virginia   VA10
Ball, W.J. - Co. A 25th Virginia April 29, 1863   VA25
Ball, W.W. - Co. A 13th Mississippi May 25, 2864   VA25
Ballard, T.E. - Virginia July 13, 1865   VA25
Ballentine, William P. - Pvt. - Co. I 15th South Carolina Died at Cold Harbor - June 15, 1862   VA28
Ballinger, J. - Pvt. - South Carolina Aug. 15, 1864   VA22
Ballinger, James - 8th Virginia Infantry VA10
Balls, F. - Co. K 10th Georgia   VA11
Bamburg, William - Lt. - 42nd Mississippi   VA04
Bandy, George M. -Sgt. - Co. D 60th Georgia Died May 10, 1864   VA28
Baney, Thad. - Clark Cavalry VA06
Bangor, J.F. - Co. I 26th Alabama May 20, 1863   VA25
Banks, C.C. - 2nd South Carolina   VA18
Banon, __ - 1862 VA25
Banton, A - 27th Virginia Aug 14, 1861   VA25
Barber, A - Co. A 3rd North Carolina Feb 16, 1863 VA25
Barber, G.A. - Co. K 3rd Georgia June, 1862   VA25
Barber, J - Co. C 11th South Carolina June 19, 1864 VA25
Barber, J. - Clark Cavalry VA06
Barber, T - Co. H 51st Georgia 1862   VA25
Barber, Thomas D. - Co. B 4th North Carolina   VA28
Barber, W.A. - Co. F 51st Georgia Aug 7, 1862   VA25
Barber, W.B. - 5th North Carolina   VA18
Barber, W.G.- Co G 49th North Carolina Sept 9, 1864 VA25
Barber, Wm. C. - 56th North Carolina VA24
Barber. J.T. - Co. I 49th Virginia June 15, 1862   VA25
Barbour, J.F. - VA20
Barbour, James - 28th Virginia VA18
Barclay, W.J. - 13th Alabama June 25, 1862   VA25
Bard, Alex. - Virginia   VA20
Barefield, __ - Co. B 8th South Carolina Oct. 1862   VA25
Barefield, H - Co. E 1st South Carolina Aug. 7, 1862 VA25
Barefield, J. - Co. C 20th Georgia March 13, 1863   VA25

Barefield, J.B. - Co. B 37th North Carolina July 8, 1862 VA25
Barefield, John - Co. A 22nd Georgia Dec. 1861 VA25
Barefield, W.D. - Co. F 22nd Georgia Jan. 7, 1863 VA25
Barefoot, J. - Co. G 5th North Carolina April 20, 1862 VA25
Barehead, A. - 5th Texas Nov. 26, 1861 VA25
Barham, C. - Artillery Oct. 1863 VA25
Barham, N. - Co C 8th Louisiana April 29, 1862 VA25
Barhaw,___ - Co H 14th North Carolina June 30, 1862 VA25
Barker, ___ - 13th North Carolina July 3, 1862 VA25
Barker, P.G. - Co. E 6th Georgia July 30, 1864 VA25
Barklew, H.L. - Co. H 8th Alabama Aug. 2, 1862 VA25
Barklin, T. - 1862 VA25
Barlett, J. - 12th Virginia Battalion Aug. 17, 1862 VA25
Barlett, W. - Cooper's Rifles Nov. 15, 1861 VA25
Barlind, W. - Artillery June 23, 1862 VA25
Barlow, J.B. - Co. F 37th North Carolina Dec. 23, 1862 VA25
Barnes, A - Co. C 17th North Carolina Aug. 26, 1864 VA25
Barnes, A.S. - Co. C 24th North Carolina June 15, 1864 VA25
Barnes, C - Co. B 66th North Carolina Aug. 9, 1864 VA25
Barnes, C.A. - 13th Alabama Oct. 30, 1861 VA25
Barnes, H.R. - Corp. - Co. A 53rd North Carolina July 14, 1864 VA25
Barnes, Henry S. - Pvt. - Co. - A 35th Georgia DOW (Fredericksburg) Dec. 14, 1862 VA28
Barnes, J - Co. D 8th Louisiana Feb. 16, 1862 VA25
Barnes, J - Co. G 4th Texas Dec. 30, 1862 VA25
Barnes, J - Co. H 7th North Carolina Nov. 15, 1864 VA25
Barnes, R. Pvt. - Co. C 16th Georgia Died June 23, 1865 VA26
Barnes, Saml. L. - Co. D 17th Virginia Infantry VA10
Barnes, T. - 5th North Carolina - VA18
Barnes, T.F. - 22nd North Carolina June 26, 1862 VA25
Barnes, W - Co. B 5th Florida Nov. 7, 1862 VA25

Barnet, N.G. - VA06
Barnett, __ - Co. I 25th North Carolina July 8, 1862 VA25
Barnett, A.A. - 16th North Carolina Aug. 2, 1862 VA25
Barnett, J Co. G 22nd South Carolina July 31, 1864 VA25
Barnett, J.F. - Co. C 37th North Carolina July 28, 1864 VA25
Barnett, James - 19th Virginia Infantry - KIA - Battle of Williamsburg - May 5, 1862 VA02
Barnett, Jos. J. - Co. B 5th South Carolina Died April 6, 1863 VA03
Barnett, W.R. - Co. E 56th North Carolina Sept. 9, 1864 VA25
Barns, H. - POW - Federal Soldier Died June 19, 1862 VA19
Baron, S - Co. D 14th Alabama May 26, 1862 VA25
Barr, G.A. - Cobb's Legion (Georgia) June 10, 1862 VA25
Barr, T. - VA06
Barrad, William - POW - Federal Soldier Died June 12, 1862 VA19
Barred, O.W. - Co. B 58th North Carolina Aug. 27, 1864 VA25
Barrentine, S.L. - Co. D 12th __ Artillery July 30, 1862 VA25
Barrett, __ - Co. D 16th Georgia Nov. 7, 1862 VA25
Barrett, A.G. - Co. A 1st Mississippi July 3, 1863 VA25
Barrett, H. - Co. K 19th Mississippi May 23, 1863 VA25
Barrett, J.G. - Co. D 6th Georgia Nov. 8, 1862 VA25
Barrow, H.T. - Co. G 38th Georgia May 5, 1864 VA25
Barry, G. - Pvt. - Virginia April 19, 1865 Cemetery roster lists this soldier as "C. Barry" VA22
Barta, B - Co. G 5th South Carolina Sept. 14, 1864 VA25
Bartholomew, F - Co. F 9th Louisiana April 29, 1862 VA25
Bartlett, J. - Co. D 4th North Carolina Aug. 1, 1862 VA25
Bartlett, W.J. - 12th Alabama June 31, 1861 VA25
Barton, J.J. - Co. C 48th North Carolina June 21, 1864 VA25
Barton, J.M. - 5th Georgia VA18
Barton, S - Co. I 1st South Carolina July 5, 1864 VA25

Barton, William - Braxton's Artillery (Virginia) VA11
Barwick, N. - 11th ___ VA18
Base, R - Co. K 9th La May 27, 1862 VA25
Baskin, George P. - - Pvt. - Co. F 8th Louisiana Died May 10, 1864 VA28
Baskin, Hugh P. - Pvt. - Co. A 4th Georgia Died May 10, 1864 VA28
Baskin, Samuel C. - see Baskins, Samuel C. VA28
Baskins, Samuel C. - Pvt. - Co. C 16th Mississippi Died May 12, 1864 Service record lists this soldier as: "Samuel C. Baskin" VA28
Baskins, Thomas Pros. - Pvt. - Co. L 5th Virginia Died May 10, 1864 VA28
Bass, A. Alabama Nov. 22, 1862 VA25
Bass, A. - Co. K 19th Mississippi Sept. 22, 1862 VA25
Bass, A.C. - Co. H 64th Georgia July 21, 1864 VA25
Bass, A.P. - Co. G 18th Mississippi June 20, 1862 VA25
Bass, D.J. - Sgt. - Co. K 28th South Carolina Sept. 5, 1864 VA25
Bass, E.C. - Co. C 6th South Carolina May 22, 1862 VA25
Bass, E.T. - Co. E 47th North Carolina March 2, 1865 VA25
Bass, J.M. - Co. K 17th Georgia Jan. 7, 1862 VA25
Bass, M. - Sumpter Artillery May 22, 1862 VA25
Bass, W.W. - 16th Georgia Nov. 12, 1862 VA25
Bassen, H.B. - 2nd North Carolina April 1, 1862 VA25
Bassett, R.W. - Co. G 1st North Carolina Jan. 9, 1863 VA25
Basterskin, W.W. - Co. A 1st South Carolina Sept. 4, 1862 VA25
Batchelor, __ - 30th North Carolina Sept. 22, 1862 VA25
Batchelor, D. - Co. F 50th Georgia May 23, 1863 VA25
Batchelor, J - Co. E 7th North Carolina Aug. 24, 1862 VA25
Batchelor, M.L. - Co. K 3rd Alabama Jan. 16, 1862 VA25
Batchelor, R. - Co. B 66th North Carolina Oct. 8, 1864 VA25
Bates, F. - Corp. - Co. E 11th Virginia Died May 3, 1865 VA26
Bates, J.F. - Arkansas May 3, 1862 VA25

Bates, R.E. - 3rd Virginia Cavalry VA18
Bates, William - Bedford Rifles (Virginia) VA18
Bates, __ July 16, 1862 VA25
Batte, Wm. - POW - Federal Soldier Died Nov. 18, 1861 VA19
Battle, H. Nicholas - Pvt. - Co. I 13th Georgia Died May 12, 1864 VA28
Battle, W.H. - Co. I 6th Virginia Cavalry VA11
Battle, W.T. - Sumpter Artillery May 28, 1862 VA25
Baugh, B.F. - Co. I 46th Georgia Jan. 8, 1864 VA25
Baulderson, B. - Co. I 9th Virginia June 9, 1862 VA25
Baum, A. - 11th North Carolina April 25, 1865 VA25
Baum, H.J. - Co. C 38th Georgia May 4, 1864 VA25
Bavar, A - Co. C 57th North Carolina April 10, 1863 VA25
Bavins, W - Co. I 2nd North Carolina July 25, 1864 VA25
Baxter, George - May 28, 1862 age 55 VA19
Baxton, J.C. - Critcher's Artillery March 4, 1865 VA25
Bayheart, A - Co. H 57th North Carolina Nov. 24, 1862 VA25
Bayken, B.B. - Corp. - Co. A 15th North Carolina Died June 4, 1865 VA26
Bayley, C.W. - Co. K 60th Virginia Sept. 26, 1862 VA25
Bayley, J.G. - April 10, 1862 VA25
Bayley, R. - April 26, 1862 VA25
Bayley, T.W. - Co. F 30th Virginia July 14, 1864 VA25
Bayley, W.A. - Co. G 14th Alabama Feb. 17, 1862 VA25
Bayliss, Boyd - 3rd Tennessee VA18
Baylop, J.G. - Cobb's Legion (Georgia) Sept. 9, 1861 VA25
Bayne, D.C. - 14th Alabama July 3, 1862 VA25
Bayne, J. - North Carolina Oct. 30, 1862 VA25
Bayner, W.F. - 40th Georgia Nov. 26, 1862 VA25
Baynor, R.H. - Co. E 4th North Carolina July 26, 2862 VA25
Baysinger, __ - Co. F 22nd South Carolina July 9, 1862 VA25

Beach, Garrison - 4th Virginia VA10
Beach, J. - Co. D 17th Virginia Infantry VA10
Beach, J.T. - Lt. - 5th Louisiana May 28, 1863 VA25
Beach, William - 4th Virginia VA10
Beadfield, T.W. - Co. G 11th North Carolina Sept. 22, 1864 VA25
Bealder, A. - Pvt. - Alabama March 28, 1865. VA22
Beam, D.A. - Pvt. - Co. A 4th North Carolina DOW (Spotsylvania Court House) on June 15, 1864 VA28
Beam, Mr. - Died Dec. 13, 1862 VA19
Bean, W.J. Pvt. - Co. F 23rd Virginia Died June 24, 1865 VA26
Bear, Sam - Georgia VA17
Beard, J.W. - Co. K 17th Georgia May 18, 1864 VA25
Beardon, C. - Co. D 22nd North Carolina Aug. 2, 1864 VA25
Bearly, J.F. - Louisiana July 15, 1861 VA25
Bearly, T.G. - Co. H 21st Virginia May 20, 1863 VA25
Beasley, William R. - Pvt. - Co. F 15th Alabama Died May 12, 1864 last name is also spelled "Beasly" VA28
Beasly, William R. - see Beasley, William R. VA28
Beatty, C. - Co. C 15th North Carolina Aug. 5, 1864 VA25
Beaty, George R. - Co. C 22nd Georgia VA28
Beauford, A.B. - Co. H 47th Mississippi Died June 28, 1863 VA06
Beaver, L.W. - Co. B 4th North Carolina July 1862 VA25
Beaver, W. - Co. E 34th North Carolina June 21, 1862 VA25
Beavers, Fenton - Mosby's Cavalry VA10
Beck, A.A. - Co. A 42nd Mississippi Aug. 11, 1862 VA25
Beck, E.W. - Co. B 42nd Mississippi Aug. 11, 1862 VA25
Beck, Jacob H.R. - Co. B 14th North Carolina VA28
Beck, William - KIA July 5, 1862 age 22 VA19
Beckham, B. - Pvt. - Co. F 1st South Carolina Artillery Died May 6, 1865 VA26

Beckham, J.R. - Co. H 4th South Carolina   July 20, 1864   VA25
Beckham, L. J. - Co. E 32nd North Carolina   Oct. 22, 1864   VA25
Beddingfield, J.G. - Co. E 46th North Carolina   Aug 13, 1864   VA25
Beddingfield, John W. - see Bedingfield, John W.   VA28
Bedingfield, John W. - Pvt. - Co. H 14th Georgia   Died May 12, 1864   name on headstone - "Bediedingfield"   VA28
Bedsaul, Wm. - Virginia   VA20
Beele, M.A. - Co. D 45th Georgia   July 15, 1862   VA25
Beetlee, E.G. - Died Dec. 21, 1862   VA19
Beggs, Wm. - Co. E 5th Alabama   July 20, 1862   VA25
Beham, C. - Washington Artillery (Louisiana)   VA18
Beins, H. - POW - Federal Soldier   Died June 19, 1862   VA19
Belcher, A. - Co. A 13th South Carolina   July 10, 1862   VA25
Belcher, Wm. - Co. F 4th Georgia   Sept. 3, 1862   VA25
Bell, __ - 3rd North Carolina   July, 1862   VA25
Bell, __ - Georgia   April 2, 1862   VA25
Bell, A. - Co. H 9th La   June 13, 1863   VA25
Bell, A.G. - Co. D 11th North Carolina   Feb. 20, 1865   VA25
Bell, H. - 18th Georgia   Sept. 6, 1862   VA25
Bell, H.F. - Co. F 59th North Carolina   Oct. 14, 1864   VA25
Bell, J. - 13th Virginia   July 10, 1862   VA25
Bell, J.P. - Co. A 15th Alabama   Nov. 18, 1864   VA25
Bell, J.T. - 28th Virginia   VA18
Bell, Jas. - Clark Cavalry   VA06
Bell, John - 9th South Carolina   Nov. 27, 1862   VA25
Bell, Jonah - Clark Cavalry   VA06
Bell, M.P. - Co. E 33rd Virginia   MW May 12, 1864   Died June 10, 1864   VA28
Bell, O - Co. G 51st North Carolina   July 13, 1864   VA25
Bell, R.M. - Co. I 5th North Carolina   Sept. 1, 1864   VA25

Bell, S.N. - Co. I 12th South Carolina June 1, 1863   VA25
Bell, T. - Co. D 14th North Carolina May 29, 1862   VA25
Bell, T.J. - Co. H 11th Alabama June 9, 1862   VA25
Bellah, J.B. - 7th Georgia   VA18
Bellert, __ - June 25, 1862   VA25
Bellette, Charles H. - Pvt. - Co. I 31st Georgia Died May 13, 1864 name on headstone - "Billett"   VA28
Beloat, J.W. - 4th Virginia Heavy Artillery June 21, 1862   VA25
Belton, F. - Co. F 23rd Virginia   VA11
Belton, J.H. - 14th North Carolina June 25, 1862   VA25
Belvin, J.W. - 9th South Carolina Oct. 27, 1861   VA25
Benaman, A. - Co. C 4th North Carolina March 15, 1865   VA25
Benberring, K. - Co. G 8th Georgia June 17, 1863   VA25
Benga, J.B. - Co. B 2nd Mississippi July 3, 1863   VA25
Benjamin, J. - Co. I 8th Virginia May 13, 1862   VA25
Bennet, J. - VA12
Bennett, C.S. - Lt. - July. 19, 1862   VA25
Bennett, D.H. - Co. B 2nd Florida June 17, 1862   VA25
Bennett, G.L. - Lt. - Co. K 8th Alabama Aug. 14, 1862   VA25
Bennett, George W. - Pvt. - Co. E 35th Virginia Cavalry Died May 15, 1864 also listed as: "Burnett"   VA28
Bennett, J.W. - Co. H 66th North Carolina July 25, 1864   VA25
Bennett, R.W. - Co. G 20th North Carolina July 30, 1862   VA25
Bennett, W.G. - 5th Alabama   VA18
Bennick, John S. - VA15
Bensley, __ - 7th Louisiana VA18
Benson, B.N. - Co. B 26th Mississippi June 25, 1862 VA25
Benson, J.T.   15th Alabama VA18
Bentley, H. - Co. F 1st North Carolina Aug 26, 1862 VA25
Bentley, H. - Co. A 28th North Carolina Aug 1862   VA25
Bentley, James - 48th Georgia March 9, 1863   VA25
Bentley, P.H. - Co. F 1st North Carolina Aug 27, 1862 VA25

Bently, J.S. - Jeff. Davis' Artillery   Nov. 6, 1861 VA25
Benton, F. - Co. B 46th Georgia April 2, 1865   VA25
Benton, J.W. - Co. B 15th North Carolina July 16, 1864 VA25
Benton, S.G. - 57th North Carolina June 18, 1864   VA25
Benton, W.A. - Co. A 4th North Carolina Cavalry   VA18
Beny, Mulina - Georgia   VA20
Berdgooman, F.H. - 4th Virginia May 9, 1863   VA25
Bernage, G.W. - Co. C 42nd North Carolina Nov. 5, 1864 VA25
Bernhardt, Martin A. - Corp. - Co. B 2nd North Carolina MW May 12, 1864 Headstone reads: "Baneheart"   VA28
Bernheart, Martin A. - see Bernhardt, Martin A.   VA28
Berry, A. - Co. E 15th North Carolina Aug 26, 1863   VA25
Berry, A.T. - Virginia   VA20
Berry, F. - Co. F 52nd North Carolina Sept 9, 1864   VA25
Berry, G.S. - Sgt. - Co. A 56th North Carolina   Sept. 13, 1864 VA25
Berry, J. - Co. G 43rd Mississippi Sept 29, 1862 VA25
Berry, J.W. - Virginia   VA20
Berry, James - Co. E 17th Mississippi May 7, 1862   VA25
Berry, L. - Co. K 9th Georgia June 18, 1862   VA25
Berry, N.C. - Hampton's Legion (South Carolina)   Oct. 7, 1864   VA25
Berry, T.S. - Co. G 42nd Mississippi Sept 29, 1862 VA25
Bervis, J. - Co. C 10th Georgia May 10, 1863   VA25
Best, Robert - Lt. - KIA May 17, 1863   VA19
Best, W.H. - Co. H 18th North Carolina Infantry   VA08
Betts, J.H. - Co. C 9th Georgia May 22, 1862   VA25
Betts, J.M. - Co. E 7th Georgia Sept. 2, 1864   VA25
Beverage, Harry - see Beverage, Harvey   VA28
Beverage, Harvey - Lt. - Co. E 31st Virginia MW May 12, 1864   Died June 10 (15), 1864 also listed as "Harry Beverage"   VA28
Beverage, Joseph (MD) - medical doctor   VA12

Bevins, D.H. - Lt. - Dec 1, 1864 "Killed by Scott - removed to Oakwood Nov. 9, 1892"   VA19
Bibb, S.P. - Page's Sharp Shooters (South Carolina) VA25
Bickerstaff, R.I. - DOW July 8, 1862   VA19
Bicks, George - May 20, 1862 VA25
Bidingfield, N.C. - Co. A 4th Alabama July 23, 1862   VA25
Biedler, Daniel - VA15
Bigger, A.B. - Co. A 1st South Carolina   VA11
Bigger, Q. - Co. I 48th North Carolina April 12, 1865   VA25
Bigger, R.N. - Corp. - Co. B 26th Georgia   July 16, 1864   VA25
Biggs, J.H. - North Carolina Oct. 1862   VA25
Bigley, W.J. - 48th Virginia VA18
Bilbro, W.T. - Sgt. Major - Co. E 32nd North Carolina   VA28
Biles, __ - June 29, 1962   VA25
Billett, Charles H. - see Bellette, Charles H.   VA28
Billon, J.W. - Co. E 2nd Georgia July 22, 1862   VA25
Binder, W. - Co. I 19th Georgia   May 23, 1862   VA25
Bingham, J. - Co. A 6th South Carolina   May 28, 1862 VA25
Bingham, J.H. - Co. A 5th South Carolina Sept. 27, 1864   VA25
Binn, J. - Co. A 45th North Carolina June 25, 1864   VA25
Binston, R. - Co. A 27th Georgia July 15, 1862   VA25
Binzinger, A. - Medical Doctor - Co. D 10th Virginia Cavalry   1862   VA25
Bird, J. - Co. H 15th Alabama   Nov. 18, 1862   VA25
Bird, P.C. - 9th South Carolina Oct. 7, 1861   VA25
Bird, R. C. - Co. G 57th Virginia July 2, 1862   VA25
Bird, S.F. - Co. R 36th Virginia   VA08
Bishop, G. - Co. I 13th Alabama   Jan. 10, 1863   VA25
Bishop, J.W. - POW - Federal Soldier Died Dec. 8, 1861   VA19
Bishop, Wm. G. - POW - Federal Soldier Died Dec. 18, 1861   VA19
Black, __ - Nov. 21, 1862   VA25

Black, C. - Co. C 48th North Carolina April 25, 1865   VA25
Black, J. - Co. B 18th South Carolina   July 17, 1864   VA25
Black, J. H. - Co. D 8th Georgia   Oct. 5, 1864   VA25
Black, J. T. - Co. H 35th Georgia   July 17, 1862   VA25
Black, P.M. - Tennessee   VA20
Black, S.A. - Co. I 9th Alabama   Nov. 24, 1862   VA25
Black, S.C. - Corp. - Co. G 15th North Carolina   June 26, 1864   VA25
Black, W. - Co. H 38th North Carolina   Nov. 19, 1862   VA25
Black, W.M. - 4th Virginia VA18
Blackard, J. - Wise Artillery   Feb. 6, 1862   VA25
Blackburn, G.M. - 10th Alabama Infantry - KIA - Battle of Williamsburg - May 5, 1862   VA02
Blackburn, J.C. - Co. H 48th Mississippi   Oct. 29, 1864   VA25
Blackburn, L. - Co. I 27th North Carolina   Oct. 3, 1864   VA25
Blackburn, R. - Co. I 1st Texas   July 2, 1862   VA25
Blackburn, T.C. - Co. C 2nd North Carolina   May 16, 1863   VA25
Blackey, __ - Co. E 52nd Virginia   May 5, 1865   VA25
Blackman, __ - 2nd South Carolina   Aug. 15, 1861   VA25
Blackman, J.W. - Co. E 12th South Carolina   Oct. 4, 1864   VA25
Blackmore, G.R. - Co. H 8th North Carolina   Dec. 24, 1864   VA25
Blacknall, B. - Co. G 30th North Carolina   Aug. 12, 1864   VA25
Blacknel, __ - Aug. 1, 1862   VA25
Blacknell, __ - Co. K 1st South Carolina   June 29, 1862   VA25
Blackriller, J.R. - Co. E 60th Georgia   May 29, 1863   VA25
Blackwell, __ - Aug. 24, 1862   VA25
Blackwell, B.H. - Co. C 2nd North Carolina April 28, 1864   VA25

Blackwell, G.W. - Co. H 66th North Carolina Aug. 1, 1864 VA25

Blackwell, James W. - Sgt. - Co. C 60th Georgia Died May 12, 1864 VA28

Blackwell, R. - North Carolina Aug. 16, 1861 VA25

Blackwell, R.B. - Co. D 49th Virginia May 29, 1863 VA25

Blackwell, S.W. - Feb. 26, 1862 VA25

Blackwell, T. - Co. E 11th Georgia March 3, 1865 VA25

Blackwilder, A. - Co. G 42nd North Carolina July 11, 1864 VA25

Blackwilder, J.L. - Co. I 7th North Carolina May 20, 1863 VA25

Blackwilder, W.A. - Co. I 1st North Carolina July 11, 1864 VA25

Blackwood, W.R. - Co. H 9th La Feb. 19, 1862 VA25

Blader, G. - C.S. Navy March 20, 1863 VA25

Blair, G. - Co. I 19th Georgia May 24, 1862 VA25

Blair, Wm. M. - Pvt. - North Carolina April 21, 1865 VA22

Blakeley, L.L. - Co. F 14th South Carolina Oct. 3, 1864 VA25

Blakeley, William J. - Pvt. - Co. B Jeff Davis Legion (Mississippi) - KIA near Culpeper on Sept. 13, 1863 Headstone reads: "Blakely" VA28

Blakely, William J. - see Blakeley, William J. VA28

Blakeney, Hugh - see Blakney, Hugh VA28

Blakey, J.B. - Co. C 37th North Carolina June 30, 1862 VA25

Blakney, Hugh - Lt. - Co. D 8th South Carolina Died May 9, 1864 Headstone Reads: "Blakeney" VA28

Blalock, J.J. - Co. B 13th North Carolina Sept. 1862 VA25

Blalock, Rube W. - Co. D 1st Texas VA28

Blaman, B. - Co. B 17th Georgia July 30, 1864 VA25

Blanchard, P. - 8th Louisiana VA18

Blanchel, W.J. - Co. F 10th Georgia Aug. 10, 1864 VA25

Bland, J.J. - Co. R 50th Georgia May 2, 1863 VA25

Bland, W.T. - Co. C 49th Georgia Aug. 28, 1862 VA25

Bland, __ - Co. C 49th Georgia Sept 4, 1862   VA25
Blandheart, M.P. - Co. H 26th South Carolina Dec. 24, 1862 VA25
Blankenship, S. - Pvt. - Co. C 56th Virginia   Died June 26, 1865   VA26
Blankinship, A. - Co. C 34th North Carolina Aug. 27, 1864 VA25
Blanton, A. - Co. D 16th North Carolina June 24, 1862 VA25
Blanton, D.J. - Co. K 26th South Carolina Feb. 26, 1865 VA25
Blanton, J.J. - Co. H 2nd Georgia Aug. 12, 1865   VA25
Blanton, J.W. - Co. G 51st North Carolina July 13, 1864 VA25
Blanton, W.G. - Co. E 23rd Georgia June 13, 1862   VA25
Blanton, W.H. - Page's Sharp Shooters Oct. 11, 1864 VA25
Blanton, William - April 29, 1862   VA25
Blasingham, C. - 8th Louisiana Jan. 14, 1861   VA25
Blask, M. - Co. D 48th North Carolina Infantry   VA08
Blaylock, David - Corp. (Sgt.?) - Co. E 20th North Carolina DOW (Spotsylvania Court House)   May 16, 1864   VA28
Blaywake, D.O. - Page's Artillery (Virginia) July 5, 1864   VA25
Bledsoe, H.H. - Co. H 11th North Carolina Died Oct 3, 1861 VA23
Blindly, A.B. - Co. E 12th Alabama   VA11
Blinkey, R - Co. B 26th North Carolina June 20, 1864   VA25
Blinton, J.D. - 2nd Georgia April 19, 1865   VA25
Blivens, E.A. - Co. K 37th North Carolina June 6, 1864 VA25
Blizzard, H.P. - Co. K 38th North Carolina July 8, 1862 VA25
Blockwell, __ - 5th Alabama June 12, 1861   VA25
Blount, John W. - Died March 2, 1864 age 40   VA19
Bloxom, G. - Pvt. - Co. E 32nd Virginia Died May 5, 1865 VA26

Blue, Daniel M. - Sgt. - Co. G 8th Georgia Died May 12, 1864   VA28
Blue, H. - 8th South Carolina July 15, 1861   VA25
Bluett, R. - Capt. - 2nd Mississippi Battalion   July 10, 1862   VA25
Blunder, H. - Co B 15th Virginia June 19, 1864   VA25
Blunt, A.G. - 9th Louisiana May 4, 1862   VA25
Blunt, J. - Co. G 55th North Carolina June 17, 1863 VA25
Blyen, J. - Co. K 27th Georgia May 24, 1862   VA25
Blyth, H. - Co. I 2nd Louisiana Infantry   VA08
Blyth, M.S. - Co. I 2nd Louisiana Infantry   VA08
Boatman, R. - Co. H 28th South Carolina Feb. 26, 1865   VA25
Boatner, C. - Phillip's Legion   VA11
Bob, J.C. - Co. E 44th Georgia Sept. 2, 1862   VA25
Bodeford, D. - 28th Georgia VA18
Bodell, William - VA12
Boden, J.H. - South Carolina   VA20
Boden, James - Nurse - W Virginia   VA08
Bodenheimer, E.P. - Co. B 51st Georgia July 21, 1864   VA25
Bogat, F.M. - Co. K 50th Georgia June 13, 1863   VA25
Boggs, James K. - Pvt. - Co. A 8th Georgia Died May 13, 1864   VA28
Boggs, W.W. - Co. H 35th Georgia Sept. 17, 1863   VA25
Bohanan, A.H. - Co. D 60th Georgia July 20, 1863   VA25
Bohanan, A.H. - July 9, 1863 VA25
Boland, J.A. - Co. H 29th Virginia June 21, 1863 Headstone reads: Jordan Efferson Boland 1818 - 1863" VA25
Boland, Jordan Efferson - see Boland, J.A.   VA25
Boles, Wm. - Co. D 21st North Carolina Died Jan 10, 1862   VA23
Boley, I. - 33rd Virginia VA08
Bolin, John C. - "see Bowlin, John C."   VA19
Boling, W.J.   2nd Georgia VA18
Bolinger, D.B. - Co. B 24th Georgia July 15, 1863   VA25
Bolling, Jo. - Died June 28, 1862 age 40   VA19

Bolton, O.E. - Co. D 13th Mississippi Jan. 15, 1863   VA25
Bolton, S. - Co. I 56th North Carolina Sept. 24, 1864   VA25
Bomar, Richard Meredith - Capt. - Co. A 15th Texas Cavalry Died May 10, 1864   Headstone reads: " Co. A 4th Texas Infantry"   VA28
Bon, B - 3rd Alabama Aug. 5, 1862   VA25
Bonan, G.N. - Co. F 19th Georgia May 27, 1862   VA25
Bond, A.B. - Co. I 38th Georgia June 12, 1864   VA25
Bond, A.D. - Co. E 16th Virginia June 1, 1863   VA25
Bond, F.H. - Co. A 14th Tenn. March 2, 1865   VA25
Bond, J.D. - Co. G 28th Virginia Aug. - 30, 1862   VA25
Bond, W. - Co. B 47th North Carolina Dec. 16, 1863   VA25
Bonden, Richard - Co. E 1st North Carolina Cavalry Died Jan 25, 1862   VA23
Bone, H. - Co. I 30th North Carolina Nov. 19, 1862   VA25
Bonham, S.E. - VA06
Bonish, J.T. - 2nd Mississippi June 27, 1862   VA25
Bonnell, J. - Co. H 4th Florida July 10, 1864   VA25
Bonner, M. - Co. B 4th Texas Nov. 9, 1862   VA25
Bonner, Wyatt - Alabama   VA20
Bonon, L.B. - Co. F 26th Virginia May 12, 1865   VA25
Bonon, M.N. - Page's Legion (Georgia) Nov. 25, 1865   VA25
Booker, James C. - Pvt. - Co. A 11th Georgia   VA28
Booker, W.E. - Co. A 11th Georgia May 15, 1862   VA25
Bookheart, S. - "Doctor" - South Carolina - Sept. 4, 1861   VA25
Boomite, Thos. - 8th Georgia   VA18
Boone, J.W. - 8th South Carolina   VA18
Booth, J. - Co. G 28th Georgia Dec. __,1864   VA25
Booth, J.W. - Co. B 8th Florida Oct. 8, 1862   VA25
Boreman, J.C. - 51st Georgia March 11, 1863   VA25
Borhan, C. - Co. F 3rd Alabama Aug. 6, 1862   VA25
Boring, J.M. - Co. A 22nd Georgia Oct. 1, 1862   VA25
Borman, B.C. - Co. F 8th South Carolina May 20, 1862 VA25
Borough, W.E. - 2nd Reserves March 10, 1865   VA25

Bosman, J. - Co. B 14th Alabama March 5, 1862   VA25
Bosman, J.F. - Co. E 3rd Georgia Oct. 26, 1864   VA25
Bosnart, H. - Co. H 2nd Georgia Sept. 29, 1862   VA25
Bosner, A - Co. F 11th Florida Sept. 17, 1864   VA25
Boss, W.N. - Co. B 35th Georgia June 24, 1862   VA25
Bostick, F. - Hampton's. Legion (Georgia)   July 8, 1862   VA25
Bostick, F. - Capt. - Co. E 47th Virginia Aug. 14, 1862   VA25
Bostick, F.M. - Co. G 14th Georgia Aug. 14, 1862   VA25
Bostick, W.R. - Co. K 49th Georgia Dec. 27, 1862   VA25
Boswell, J. - 7th South Carolina   VA18
Boswell, J.L. - 7th South Carolina Aug. 17, 1861   VA25
Boswell, R.W. - Lt. - Co. H 2nd Louisiana Sept. 30, 1862   VA25
Bothers, J.R. - Co. A 51st North Carolina Sept. 24, 1864   VA25
Bott, H.T. - Co. I 14th Louisiana July 3, 1862   VA25
Botterford, W.A. - 11th Georgia VA18
Bottleford, A. - Co. A 20th Georgia April 20, 1862   VA25
Bottoms, J.E. - Died Oct. 31, 1862   VA19
Bottoms, J.M. - Co. I 10th Georgia May 23, 1863   VA25
Botts, Francis M. -   POW - Federal Soldier Died June 19, 1862 VA19
Bourgle, V.A. - Louisiana June 2, 1862   VA25
Bouzman, D. - Co. B 1st South Carolina June 4, 1862 VA25
Bowden, H. - Co. C 23rd North Carolina June 2, 1864 VA25
Bowe, T. - 15th Georgia Oct. 22, 1861   VA25
Boweing, __ - Co. A 24th Virginia Sept. 1862   VA25
Bowen, __ - Lt. - Co. F 6th Alabama Infantry   VA08
Bowen, A. - Co. A 35th Georgia July 12, 1864   VA25
Bowen, F.S. - Co. C 46th Virginia June 24, 1864   VA25
Bowen, W.T. - Cobb's Legion (Georgia)   June 21, 1862   VA25
Bowers, __ - Aug. 5, 1862 VA25
Bowers, J.F. - Co. A 23rd Virginia Feb. 23, 1865   VA25

Bowers, John - Co. F 5th North Carolina VA11
Bowers, R. - Co. E 17th North Carolina Sept. 19, 1864 VA25
Bowers, S.D. 16th Georgia Sept. 8, 1861 VA25
Bowers, Z. - Cobb's Legion (Georgia) Aug. 16, 1862 VA25
Bowes, M.A. - 4th North Carolina June 5, 1862 VA25
Bowett, W.N. - Co. K 50th Georgia March 24, 1863 VA25
Bowing, A.F. - Co. K 61st North Carolina Oct. 11, 1864 A25
Bowing, J.A. - Cobb's Legion (Georgia) Aug. 15, 1863 VA25
Bowing, W.H. - Co. C 45th Georgia Aug. 14, 1864 VA25
Bowland, A. - Co. C 31st Georgia July 25, 1864 VA25
Bowlar, B.F. - Co. I 7th Virginia Jan. 10, 1863 VA25
Bowlar, W.A. - Co. C 4th Virginia Cavalry May 11, 1862 VA25
Bowles, J.W. - VA12
Bowlett, G. - Louisiana. Rifles June 1, 1862 VA25
Bowlicks, T. - Co. H 28th North Carolina Oct. 26, 1864 VA25
Bowlin, J.W. - Co. I 24th Georgia Dec. 28, 1862 VA25
Bowlin, John C. - Nov. 24, 1862 VA19
Bowling, __ - Virginia Artillery June 18, 1864 VA25
Bowls, R.S. - Co. H 17th North Carolina June 14, 1864 VA25
Bowman, B. - Co. D 40th Virginia July 10, 1862 VA25
Bowman, David - Pvt. - Co. E 32nd North Carolina MW May 10, 1864 VA28
Bowman, J.R. - VA12
Box, D. - Co. D 15th Alabama July 5, 1862 VA25
Boyce, A.B. - DOW July 11, 1862 VA19
Boyd, A. - Co. B 31st North Carolina March 13, 1865 VA25
Boyd, A. - 57th Virginia Jan. 25, 1862 VA25
Boyd, A.E. - Co. B 37th North Carolina July 8, 1862 VA25
Boyd, A.J. - Co. K 8th Alabama July 25, 1862 VA25
Boyd, B. - Co. B 22nd Georgia Jan. 1, 1862 VA25
Boyd, E.V. - Co. E 49th Virginia July 6, 1862 VA25

Boyd, J. - 3rd Virginia June 8, 1862   VA25
Boyd, J.L. - Co. B 2nd Mississippi June 14, 1862   VA25
Boyd, N.F. - Co. A 14th South Carolina May 17, 1863 VA25
Boyd, T. - Co. K 8th North Carolina July 25, 1862 VA25
Boyd, T.M. - Co. D 12th Virginia July 16, 1862   VA25
Boyd, W.T. - July 1862   VA25
Boyd, Wm. - Virginia   VA20
Boydston, W.S. - 13th __   VA18
Boyer, Robt. B. - Virginia   VA20
Boyle, Charles - Pvt. - Co. F 11th Virginia Died May 1, 1865   VA26
Bozeman, David L. - Capt. - Co. A 44th Alabama Died May 8, 1864   VA28
Brackett, J. - Co. F 55th North Carolina July 16, ____   VA25
Bradberry, J. - Co. I 16th Georgia Oct. 16, 1861   VA25
Bradberry, J.J. - Co. K 27th North Carolina April 27, 1865   VA25
Bradberry, W. - Co. B 16th Georgia Sept. 16, 1861   VA25
Braddock, William C. - Co. I 8th Artillery   VA11
Braden, B. - Co. F 10th Alabama July 18, 1862   VA25
Bradfield, A.J. - 8th Virginia Infantry   VA10
Bradford, T.B. - Co. H 17th Mississippi May 12, 1862   VA25
Bradles, W.M. - 9th Louisiana Aug. 6, 1861   VA25
Bradley, __ Alabama Nov. 18, 1862   VA25
Bradley, G. - Co. G 3rd Alabama Jan. 13, 1863   VA25
Bradley, G.W. - Co. A 24th Georgia June 14, 1862   VA25
Bradley, J. - Co. E 55th North Carolina Oct. 3, 1864 VA25
Bradley, J.L. - Co. A 13th Mississippi July 1862   VA25
Bradley, J.M. - Co. A 64th Georgia Feb. 28, 1865   VA25
Bradley, J.W. - Cobb's Legion (Georgia)   Sept. 4, 1861   VA25
Bradley, Jno. - 9th La, Aug. 4, 1861   VA25
Bradley, John - Died May 18, 1864 age 28   VA19
Bradley, John - KIA May 18, 1864 disinterred July 8, 1874   VA19
Bradley, L.M. - Morris's Artillery July 25, 1862   VA25

Bradley, Thomas M. - Jeff Davis Artillery (Alabama)   Died May 12, 1864   VA28
Bradley, W. - Co. G 14th South Carolina May 20, 1863 VA25
Bradley, W.H. - Co. B 1st South Carolina Nov. 8, 1862 VA25
Bradley, Z. - Co. A Morris's Artillery July 25, 1862   VA25
Bradshaw, C.H. - Feb. 25, 1865 VA25
Bradshaw, T. - Co. G 10th Georgia Aug. 14, 1864   VA25
Bradshaw, W.T. - 4th Georgia March 4, 1865   VA25
Bradway, W.C. - Co. B 5th Alabama June 30, 1862   VA25
Brady, J.M. - Corp. - Co. K 64th Georgia   Feb. 27, 1865   VA25
Brady, Patrick - Mississippi Feb. 1, 1862   VA19
Brady, R.M. - Pvt. - South Carolina May 16, 1865   VA22
Brady, W. - Co. C 4th North Carolina Sept. 18, 1862   VA25
Braford, A. - Co. E 44th North Carolina Oct. 4, 1863 VA25
Braghill, J.W. - Co. A 7th North Carolina July 28, 1864 VA25
Braisanman, R.K. - Co. C 18th Mississippi May 24, 1862   VA25
Brake, G.W. - Co. A 12th North Carolina Aug. 24, 1864   VA25
Bramlett, Charles - Co. G 3rd South Carolina   VA11
Branch, E.W. - Capt. DOW Aug. 5, 1863   VA19
Brand, James - Died May 18, 1863 age 22   VA19
Brand, James A.   DOW May 18, 1863   VA19
Brand, M.D. - 44th North Carolina Sept. 1863   VA25
Branden, P.W. - Peyton's Artillery Aug. 1864   VA25
Brandon, B. - Co. A 19th Mississippi July 10, 1862   VA25
Brandon, C.C. - Co. K 13th Mississippi July 16, 1862   VA25
Brandon, J. - Co. B 10th Louisiana May 26, 1863   VA25
Brandon, J.N. - Co. G 44th North Carolina April 12, 1864   VA25
Brandon, P. - Co. C 5th Louisiana Aug. 16, 1864   VA25
Brandon, W.G. - Co. B 38th Virginia Nov. 18, 1862   VA25
Brandy, V. - Co. E 7th Georgia Cavalry   June 26, 1864   VA25
Brant, Andrew J. - Co. D 13th North Carolina   VA11

Brantley, H. - Co. E 2nd North Carolina March 31, 1865 VA25
Brantley, J. - Louisiana Nov. 13, 1862   VA25
Brantley, T.C. - Co. D 59th Georgia June 2, 1864   VA25
Brantly, Green - Co. A 28th Georgia   VA11
Braswell, S.S. - Co. I 48th North Carolina Nov. 25, 1862 VA25
Brausen, F. - Co. A 27th Virginia May 17, 1864   VA25
Brausen, J. - Co. B 13th Alabama Aug. 15, 1862   VA25
Bravaux, S. - 3rd Louisiana. Artillery Aug. 24, 1862   VA25
Braver, H. - Co. B 4th North Carolina June 17, 1862 VA25
Braver, J.H. - Co. F 18th Georgia June 24, 1864   VA25
Braver, J.W. - Lt. - Co. C Washington Artillery (Louisiana) Aug. 23, 1862   VA25
Brawer, __ - 27th North Carolina June 1862   VA25
Bray, A. - Co. H 34th North Carolina Oct. 3, 1864 VA25
Bray, D.C. - Co. D 1st North Carolina March 7, 1865 VA25
Bray, M.D. - Co. E 44th North Carolina Sept. 1863   VA25
Brazell, A.T. - 7th South Carolina Artillery   July 24, 1861 VA25
Brazewell, W.J. - Co. G 60th Alabama June 2, 1864   VA25
Brazil, G.W. -11th Alabama VA18
Breakein, J.W. - Co. F 9th Alabama July 14, 1862   VA25
Breakenridge, J. - Co. D 45th Georgia July 16, 1862   VA25
Breckenridge, John - DOD   VA19
Breckens, J. - 8th Alabama Aug. 8, 1862   VA25
Breeden, J.O. - Co. B 5th South Carolina Nov. 12, 1864 VA25
Breimer, J.W. - Lt. - Louisiana Artillery Sept. 4, 1862   VA25
Brener, W. - Lt. - Co. G 15th North Carolina   Oct. 22, 1864 VA25
Brensfield, W.P. - Co. H 45th North Carolina Oct. 28, 1862 VA25
Brent, __ - July 1862   VA25
Brett, Everett J. - Pvt. - 18th North Carolina Infantry DOW June 14, 1862   VA09
Brewer, A. - Co. D 52nd North Carolina July 1, 1864 VA25

Brewer, Eli H. - Pvt. - North Carolina Oct. 13, 1864 VA22
Brewer, J. - Co. H 9th Mississippi April 20, 1865 VA25
Brewer, Matthew - Sgt. - Co. G 44th Alabama Died May 8, 1864 VA28
Brewer, W.A. - Co. K 12th South Carolina July 5, 1862 VA25
Brewrton, H.W. - Pvt. - Co. K __th North Carolina Died May 17, 1865 VA26
Brewten, O.D. - Alabama Aug. 20, 1861   VA25
Briant, R.A. - Co. D 5th Alabama Aug. 23, 1862   VA25
Brick, H. - North Carolina Oct. 20, 1862   VA25
Bridges, D.P. - 10th Virginia July 28, 1861 VA25
Bridges, F.G. - Sgt. - 4th Virginia Battalion   June 2, 1862 VA25
Bridges, George - Pvt. - Co. E 61st Georgia Died at Hamilton's Crossing (1863) VA28
Bridges, J.J. - Co. C 66th North Carolina July 30, 1864 VA25
Bridges, J.W. - 13th Alabama VA11
Bridges, Joseph J. - Lt. Colonel - Co. F 20th North Carolina Headstone reads: " Sgt. Major - Co. G 32nd North Cavalry" VA28
Bridges, W.D. - 15th North Carolina May 21, 1862   VA25
Bridlen, J.M. - Co. E 15th Georgia July 17, 1864   VA25
Brien, B.C. - Alabama June 4, 1862 VA25
Brien, P.O. - 10th Virginia July 29, 1861   VA25
Briene, J.C. - Co. C 17th Alabama Aug. 12, 1862   VA25
Briggs, D.J. - Co. F 21st Virginia May 14, 1862   VA25
Briggs, Jno. - Co. B 6th South Carolina Cavalry Aug. 28, 1864 VA25
Bright, E. - Co. B 32nd North Carolina Feb. 10, 1865   VA25
Bright, J.W. - Pvt. - North Carolina   May 17, 1865 VA22
Bright, John W. - Pvt. - Co. E 44th Georgia Died May 10, 1864 VA28
Bright, M.B. - Co. D 21st North Carolina May 23, 1863 VA25
Brightaupt, C. - Lt. - Co. C 2nd Md.   Oct. 4, 1864   VA25

Brigman, James - Pvt. - Co. C 14th North Carolina MW May 12, 1864 DOW May 17, 1864 VA28

Brill, A.S. - Virginia - Note in the burial roster reads "Winchester" Nov 21, 1863 VA25

Brindle, G.S. - Co. H 54th North Carolina May 24, 1863 VA25 1865 VA25

Brinkley, J.H. - Co. A 28th North Carolina Aug. 5, 1862 VA25

Brinkley, R.B. - Co. D 42nd North Carolina Sept. 3, 1864 VA25

Brison, H. - Co. H 49th North Carolina Sept. 1, 1864 VA25

Brist, H. - Co. A 7th Georgia Nov. 26, 1862 VA25

Bristoe, N.P. - Pvt. - Co. A 34th Virginia Died July 2, 1865 VA26

Britt, Alexander - Pvt. - Co. K 3rd North Carolina Died June 27, 1865 VA26

Britt, Enos - Co. I 23rd North Carolina VA11

Britt, H.A. - Co. I 16th Georgia June 14, 1862 VA25

Britt, H.P. - Co. B 10th Georgia Aug. 26, 1864 VA25

Britton, L. - 9th Louisiana VA18

Britton, M. - 16th North Carolina VA18

Broadway, J. - Co. A 26th North Carolina Nov. 26, 1863 VA25

Broadwell, Harrison Mitchell - Lt. - Co. A 32nd Georgia (headstone reads 22nd Georgia) Died May 14, 1864 VA28

Brock, Granville - Co. G 3rd Ten Died Jan 11, 1862 VA23

Brockley, M. - 5th North Carolina VA18

Brockman, B.T. - Colonel VA25

Brockman, J. - Co. I 21st Arkansas Feb. 4, 1865 VA25

Brockman, Jesse Kilgore Capt. - Co. B 13th South Carolina Died May 28, 1864 VA28

Brockwood, Geo. - Pvt. - Co. C 18th North Carolina Died May 29, 1865 VA26

Brogdon, W. - Co. E 51st North Carolina June 19, 1864 VA25

Bronough, G.D. - Aug. 5, 1862 VA25
Bronought, W.N. - Major - 2nd Ark July 5, 1862 VA25
Brooks, A. - Oct. 21, 1862 VA25
Brooks, David S. - POW - Federal Soldier Died Oct. 21, 1861 VA19
Brooks, H. - July 16, 1862 VA25
Brooks, Hesekiah - KIA June 3, 1862 VA19
Brooks, J. - Sept. - 17, 1863 VA25
Brooks, J.D. - Co. E 9th Virginia VA11
Brooks, J.F. May 2, 1862 VA25
Brooks, J.G. - Co. E 11th Georgia Sept. 26, 1864 VA25
Brooks, J.J. - Co. F 18th Georgia Sept. 14, 1861 VA25
Brooks, J.J. - Co. G 11th Virginia May 14, 1862 VA25
Brooks, J.M. - Co. G 17th Georgia Aug. 17, 1862 VA25
Brooks, James H. - Resident of Confederate Soldiers Home Died Dec. 29, 1898 age 60 VA19
Brooks, John S. - Lt. Colonel - Co. E 20th North Carolina May 12, 1864 VA28
Brooks, Mary Louisa - Resident of Confederate Soldiers Home Died June 20, 1902 VA19
Brooks, S.M. - Capt. Patterson's Company May 16, 1861 VA25
Brooks, W.T. - Co. E 49th Georgia July 6,1862 VA25
Brooks, Whitefield - KIA June 12, 1862 age 19 VA19
Brookshire, G. - Co. K 7th North Carolina July 19, 1862 VA25
Broom, James - Co. E 1st South Carolina Rifles VA28
Brooway, S.W. - Co. D 48th North Carolina Oct. 8, 1864 VA25
Broterton, J.W. - Co. C 26th North Carolina June 27, 1864 VA25
Brothers, G. - Co. A 10th Alabama May 24, 1862 VA25
Browers, John J.H. - Resident of Confederate Soldiers Home died March 13, 1918 VA19
Browing, S.W. - Co. D 10th Alabama April 28, 1862 VA25
Brown, __ - 1st South Carolina July 5, 1862 VA25
Brown, Alfred - Co. G 30th North Carolina VA11

Brown, Anderson - 20th Georgia VA18
Brown, Anderton - 3rd North Carolina VA04
Brown, B. - Co. E 28th North Carolina VA11
Brown, B.A. - Aug. 2, 1864 VA25
Brown, C. - Co. H 14th Virginia March 12, 1862 VA25
Brown, C.C. - 16th Virginia Cavalry VA11
Brown, E. - Rockbridge Artillery (Virginia) June 6, 1863 VA25
Brown, F.S. - Co. C 46th Virginia Feb. 23, 1865 VA25
Brown, G.P. - Battery Number 8 July 8, 1862 VA25
Brown, G.W. - Co. G 16th Virginia July 20, 1863 VA25
Brown, G.W. - Co. A 5th Texas Sept. 20, 1862 VA25
Brown, Green - Alabama VA20
Brown, H. - Co. I 48th Alabama May 12, 1865 VA25
Brown, H.H. - Co. H 34th North Carolina June 23, 1863 VA25
Brown, Hamilton Rutledge - Pvt. - Co. B 3rd South Carolina Battalion Died May 8, 1864 Headstone reads "3rd South Carolina Infantry" VA28
Brown, J. - Pvt. - Stribling's Virginia Bat. Died June 19, 1865 VA26
Brown, J. - 10th Alabama Nov. 30, 1862 VA25
Brown, J. - Co. E 30th North Carolina May 21, 1864 VA25
Brown, J. - Phillip's Legion (Georgia) May 13, 1863 VA25
Brown, J. - Co. A 25th South Carolina Sept. 7, 1864 VA25
Brown, J. B. - Co. D 33rd South Carolina Nov. 24, 1862 VA25
Brown, J.C. - Co. F 38th Georgia July 5, 1864 VA25
Brown, J.D. - South Carolina VA20
Brown, J.E. - 5th Alabama VA18
Brown, J.F. - Co. I 26th Alabama May 21, 1863 VA25
Brown, J.H. - Lt. - Co. A 3rd Alabama Aug. 12, 1862 VA25
Brown, J.M. - Co. C 6th North Carolina May 11, 1862 VA25
Brown, J.M. - Co. B 13th South Carolina July 5, 1864 VA25
Brown, J.N. - Co. B 17th Virginia June 26, 1863 VA25

Brown, J.S. - Co. E 48th North Carolina Oct. 11, 1864 VA25
Brown, J.W. - Co. D 48th North Carolina Oct. 8, 1864 VA25
Brown, J.W. - Capt. - Co. C 47th North Carolina Oct. 5, 1864 VA25
Brown, James W. - POW - Federal Soldier Died May 14, 1862 VA19
Brown, Jas. A. - Co D 2nd Md Infantry KIA Gettysburg July 2, 1863 ("in memory of") VA23
Brown, John - POW - Federal Soldier Died Dec. 11, 1861 VA19
Brown, John Levi - Lt. - Co. C 48th North Carolina MW at Chancellorsville - May 3, 1863 Died May 17, 1863 VA28
Brown, Joseph - POW - Federal Soldier VA19
Brown, L. - Co. A 17th South Carolina Nov. 18,1862 VA25
Brown, L. - Capt. - Co. C 66th North Carolina July, 6, 1864 VA25
Brown, L. - Co. A 4th Mississippi Oct. 20, 1864 VA25
Brown, M. P. - Co. G 33rd North Carolina Dec. 26, 1862 VA25
Brown, Morton L. - POW - Federal Soldier Died June 10, 1862 VA19
Brown, R. - Co. C 13th Georgia Aug. 9, 1862 VA25
Brown, R. - Co. F 5th South Carolina July 14, 1864 VA25
Brown, R.H. - Co. G 15th Louisiana May 1863 VA25
Brown, R.W. - Co. C 58th Georgia Oct. 7, 1863 VA25
Brown, Sheldrick - Pvt. - Co. K 35th Georgia KIA - Fredericksburg - May 13, 1862 VA28
Brown, T. - Co. B 5th Georgia Oct. 1, 1862 VA25
Brown, T. - Co. D 5th North Carolina Dec. 2, 1862 VA25
Brown, T. - Co. G 37th North Carolina Sept. 2, 1864 VA25
Brown, T.C. - 7th South Carolina Aug. 1864 VA25
Brown, T.M. - Co. B 1st North Carolina Aug. 9, 1863 VA25
Brown, Thos. - North Carolina Nov. 9, 1862 VA25
Brown, Virginius - Sgt. - Co. G 49th Virginia VA28

Brown, W. - Co. A 14th North Carolina Oct. 28, 1862   VA25
Brown, W. - Co. A 30th Virginia Aug. 6, 1864   VA25
Brown, W.B. - Co. B 24th Georgia May 1, 1862   VA25
Brown, W.J. - Co. A 7th Louisiana May 4, 1862   VA25
Brown, W.L. - 15th Alabama April 21, 1862   VA25
Brown, W.R. - Lynchburg Virginia Aug. 14, 1862   VA25
Brown, W.W. - Adjutant- 4th Texas   July 18. 1864   VA25
Brown, Wesley - Co. G 30th North Carolina   VA11
Brown, William - Co. K 10th Georgia Infantry   VA08
Brownelson, G.W. - Co. I 19th South Carolina June 1864   VA25
Browning, ____ - Artillery   July 8, 1862   VA25
Browning, A.S. - Co. F 8th North Carolina July 20, 1864   VA25
Browning, M.N. - Co. H 14th Alabama May 31, 1862   VA25
Browning, R.M. - Co. G 10th Alabama Jan. 27, 1863   VA25
Browning, W. - Co. A 66th North Carolina July 9, 1864 VA25
Broy, J. -   VA06
Broyer, J.F. - Co. B 12th Alabama Oct. 15, 1861   VA25
Bruce, __ - Lt. - "state unknown"   VA18
Bruce, A. - Co. C 45th Georgia March 2, 1865   VA25
Bruce, G.C. - Co. G 30th North Carolina July 8, 1864 VA25
Bruce, T.J. - Co. I 38th Georgia Nov. 18, 1862   VA25
Bruison, F. - Co. H 66th North Carolina July 2, 1864 VA25
Bruison, J.F. - Co. K 37th South Carolina Aug. 9, 1863 VA25
Bruister, J.N. - 18th Georgia Aug. 29, 1861   VA25
Bruitt, T.W. - March 20, 1863   VA25
Brumble, J. - Co. A 10th Georgia Battalion Aug. 31, 1864   VA25
Bruner, W. - Co. C 44th North Carolina July 9, 1864 VA25
Brunson, J. - Co. B 13th Alabama July 8, 1862   VA25
Brunswick, ____ - Co. H 13th Georgia Sept. 9, 1862   VA25
Bruten, S.W. - 20th Georgia Battalion   June 17, 1864   VA25
Bryan, ____ - June 27, 1862 VA25
Bryan, George D. - POW - Federal Soldier Died June 17, 1862   VA19

Bryan, J.C. - Co. H 54th North Carolina May 20, 1863 VA25
Bryan, J.J. - Co. G 6th Georgia May 24, 1864 VA25
Bryan, T.S. - 13th Alabama VA11
Bryan, W.L. - Corp. - Co. B 27th North Carolina   VA28
Bryan, W.O. - Co. G 3rd North Carolina June 11, 1864 VA25
Bryant, I.I. - Co. G 5th North Carolina   VA11
Bryant, J. - Co. D 7th Louisiana Dec. 16, 1862   VA25
Bryant, J.B. - Co. K 8th Georgia June 17, 1862   VA25
Bryant, J.W. - Co. F 45th Georgia March 29, 1865   VA25
Bryant, N. - Co. D 7th North Carolina Oct. 24, 1864 VA25
Bryant, O. - Co. D 15th Louisiana Jan. 28, 1863   VA25
Bryant, P. - Co. G. 18th Mississippi Nov. 8, 1862 VA25
Bryant, R. - Co. B 2nd Florida June 27, 1862   VA25
Bryant, T.R. - 11th Mississippi Nov. 8, 1862   VA25
Bryant, Thos. B. - 18th Virginia Bat. Died April 19, 1865
    VA27
Bryant, W. - Co. D 11th Alabama Aug. 28, 1862   VA25
Bryant, __ - Co. F 2nd Louisiana Jan. 5, 1863   VA25
Bryon, J.T. - Co. K 14th Alabama April 26, 1862   VA25
Buchanan, R.N. - Co. D 13th Alabama Aug. 31, 1861   VA25
Bucher, Robert F. - Sgt. - Co. F 5th Virginia - Apparently a
    veteran. Died in Augusta County (Virginia) before
    June 1882 - Headstone reads: " Co. L 5th Virginia"
    VA28
Buckanon, W.C. - Co. D 33rd North Carolina July 16, 1864
    VA25
Buckart, J.W. - Co. I 27th North Carolina Sept. 22, 1864
    VA25
Buckhanan, M.F. - Co. k 5th South Carolina June 9, 1864
    VA25
Bucknell, J.M. - South Carolina   VA20
Buckner, D. - Co. D 14th North Carolina July 8, 1862 VA25
Buckner, M.J. - Co. I 19th Georgia June 8, 1862   VA25
Budd, J.H. - Co. G 8th Georgia July 22, 1864   VA25
Budd, W.H. - 8th Georgia VA18
Buddin, A.F. - Co. K 23rd South Carolina July 8, 1864 VA25

Buffington, G.A. - Co. I 63rd Georgia May 15, 1865   VA25
Buffington, J.H. - 15th Georgia May 20, 1864   VA25
Buffington, O.M. - Cobb's Legion (Georgia)   July 18, 1862
   VA25
Bufford, __ - 3rd Alabama 1861   VA25
Bugg, J. - Co. C 28th Georgia July 18, 1864   VA25
Bull, W.T. - Co. I 61st Virginia May 21, 1864   VA25
Bullard, J. - Co. I 10th Alabama Sept. 9, 1862   VA25
Bullard, M.J. - Co. E 5th North Carolina March 18, 1862
   VA25
Bullarson, M. - Co. H 21st Georgia June 17, 1863   VA25
Bulling, R.E. - Co. F 11th North Carolina Died Sept 15, 1861
   VA23
Bullis, W. - Co. C 26th North Carolina March 16, 1865
   VA25
Bullock, A.D. - Co. G 30th Virginia May 30, 1864   VA25
Bullock, B. - Co. E 32nd North Carolina June 2, 1864 VA25
Bullock, R.W. - Co. B 4th Alabama Aug. 17, 1862   VA25
Bullock, S.T. - Co. F 14th Mississippi July 6, 1863   VA25
Bumgardner, A.G. - Co. G 37th North Carolina June 23, 1862
   VA25
Bumley, J.W. - Co. G 11th South Carolina June 16, 1864
   VA25
Bunn, A. - Co. E 6th Louisiana Dec. 5, 1862   VA25
Bunn, J. - Alabama "Cooper's Residence"   1861 VA25
Bunn, J. - Co. C 25th Virginia Feb. 16, 1864   VA25
Bunn, J.M. - Co. B 3rd Georgia June 4, 1864   VA25
Bunn, R. - Wake County N.C. Sept. 4, 1862   VA25
Bunn, W.B. - Co. B 24th Georgia May 1, 1862   VA25
Bunn, W.J. - Co. H 22nd North Carolina May 20, 1862 VA25
Bunning, J. B. - Co. I 45th North Carolina Jan. 10, 1864
   VA25
Burch, E.C. - July 12, 1861 VA25
Burch, J.H. - 5th Texas Nov. 26, 1862   VA25
Burch, Wm. B. - "Killed by Explosive Shell" Jan. 18, 1866
   age 29   VA19

Burdess, W.H. - Co. F 1st South Carolina June 10, 1862 VA25
Burger, W.F. - 5th Alabama VA18
Burges, W. - Pvt. - Co. A 18th South Carolina Died June 28, 1865 VA26
Burgess, __ - Lt. - Paul's Battalion June 6, 1862 VA25
Burgess, C. - Co. A 37th North Carolina Nov. 1, 1864 VA25
Burgess, E. - Georgia July 20, 1861 VA25
Burgess, H. - Louisiana June 5, 1862 VA25
Burgess, R.M. - Co. I 25th South Carolina May 30, 1864 VA25
Burgess, W. - Co. F 1st South Carolina June 29, 1862 VA25
Burgess, W. - April 27, 1863 VA25
Burgory, ____ - Aug. 5, 1862 VA25
Burgory, H.C. - 4th Georgia Nov. 1, 1862 VA25
Burintine, Sam'l. - 18th Virginia VA18
Burke, F.M. - Co. H 15th Georgia Aug. 18, 1862 VA25
Burke, H.W. - Co. B 3rd Alabama Aug. 25, 1862 VA25
Burke, J. - 18th Georgia Aug. 31, 1861 VA25
Burke, Jim - Co. B 26th North Carolina Nov. 24, 1864 VA25
Burke, Jno. T. - Capt. - Co. D 17th Virginia Infantry VA10
Burke, John William - Co. B 9th Virginia Cavalry - Veteran Died May 20, 1899 VA28
Burke, R. B. - 31st Georgia Dec. 23, 1862 VA25
Burke, Thomas J. - VA12
Burke, W.E. - Co. I 14th Alabama Aug. 7, 1862 VA25
Burke, W.M. - Co. C 3rd North Carolina June 26, 1864 VA25
Burket, J.W. - 1st North Carolina VA18
Burkett, J.M. - Co. E 60th Georgia VA11
Burkett, W.B. - Co. C 50th Georgia March 17, 1863 VA25
Burkley, Wm. - Co. D 10th Louisiana May 26, 1863 VA25
Burnett, D.B. - Co. C 26th North Carolina Oct. 30, 1864 VA25
Burnett, Daniel - Co. E 27th South Carolina VA11
Burnett, George W. - see Bennett, George W. VA28
Burnett, Jordon A. - Co. A 22nd South Carolina VA11

Burney, Addison G. - Pvt. - Co. G 11th Mississippi Died May 12, 1864   VA28
Burns, Chas. - Confederate Navy   VA24
Burns, D.S. - Orr's Rifles (South Carolina)   June 29, 1862   VA25
Burns, L. - 22nd North Carolina June 10, 1862   VA25
Burns, Micheal - shot by a sentinel April 1, 1863   VA19
Burns, W.C. - 9th Louisiana VA18
Burnsides, J.S. - 9th Georgia   VA18
Burras, J.S. - Kentucky   VA20
Burrell, J. - Co. B 26th Mississippi June 10, 1864   VA25
Burrough, E.W. - Co. A 5th North Carolina   VA11
Burroughs, Dent   Lt. - Moody's Light Artillery (Madison Light Artillery) (Louisiana) Died May 10 (12), 1 VA28
Burroughs, Thomas M. - Pvt. - Co. C 54th North Carolina DOD near Fredericksburg - April 7, 1863   VA28
Burruss, J. - Co. H 45th Georgia June 5, 1862   VA25
Burruss, J. - Co. C 26th North Carolina Sept. 28, 1864   VA25
Burruss, P. - Co. C 23rd North Carolina July 17, 1864   VA25
Burruss, W. - South Carolina May 3, 1862   VA25
Burton, J.J. - Pvt. - Virginia April 9, 1865   VA22
Burton, J.J. - 15th Georgia Sept. 10, 1861   VA25
Burton, John - Co. D 38th Virginia June 17, 1862   VA25
Burton, John - Co. G 46th North Carolina May 21, 1864 VA25
Burton, Nathaniel - 19th Mississippi   VA18
Burton, R.E. - Co. D 6th Alabama June 3, 1862   VA25
Burton, V.B. - 5th Alabama June 30, 1862   VA25
Burtrice, M.A. - Co. D 5th Georgia May 15, 1863   VA25
Burweigh, D. - Lt. - Madison Artillery   This soldier's name is listed in Napier Bartlett's *Military Record of Louisiana*, however he is not listed in the cemetery's burial records. VA28
Burwell, G.H.   2nd Virginia Infantry   VA06
Burwell, Nathaniel - Co. C 2nd Virginia DOW - 2nd Manassas - Sept. 5, 1862   VA06

Burwell, Robert P. - Lt. - Stuart's Horse Artillery DOW - Battle of Brandy Station - 1863 age 19   VA06
Busbey, T.A. - Ten   VA20
Bush, B. - Co. E 3rd Alabama   VA11
Bush, Geo. - July 31, 1861 VA25
Bush, J.A. - Co. B 16th Mississippi March 16, 1863 VA25
Bush, M. - Co. I 21st Georgia July 22, 1862   VA25
Bushfield, F.M. - 27th Virginia VA18
Bushong, D. - VA12
Bushong, Franklin J. - VA12
Busty, J. - Co. A 17th Virginia Jan. 18, 1863   VA25
Buswell, A. - VA12
Butler, D. - Corp. - Co. C 12 Alabama June 30, 1862 VA25
Butler, "Rebel" - Virginia - KIA Spotsylvania C. H. - interred Aug. 24, 1996   VA28
Butler, A.R. - Co. F 49th North Carolina Nov 19, 1862 VA25
Butler, C. - Co. C 25th Virginia Oct. 12, 1863   VA25
Butler, C. - Oct. 11, 1863 VA25
Butler, C.A. - Corp. - 2nd Florida May 31, 1862   VA25
Butler, D. - Texas Nov. 11, 1862   VA25
Butler, H.H. - Sgt.- Co. C 3rd Georgia   VA23
Butler, J.E. - Co. D 12th ___ Artillery July 31, 1862   VA25
Butler, J.L. - Pvt. - Co. C 45th Georgia KIA - Fredericksburg - May 13, 1862 VA28
Butler, J.T. - Co. C 15th Virginia April 11, 1865   VA25
Butler, M. - Wise Legion   June 19, 1862   VA25
Butler, T. - 5th Alabama May 20, 1862   VA25
Butler, T. - Co. B 19th Georgia May 17, 1862   VA25
Butler, T.C. - Co. A 7th Georgia June 7, 1862   VA25
Butler, Thomas F. - Co. L ___ South Carolina Feb. 23, 1863 - disinterred   VA19
Butler, W.H. - 15th Virginia June 24, 1862   VA25
Butler, W.H. - Co. B 38th Alabama Oct. 8, 1863   VA25
Butman, J.S. - Co. K 51st North Carolina April 12, 1865   VA25

Butt, J.A. - Lt. - Co. D 60th Alabama Sept. 9, 1864 VA25
Butt, Wilson A. - Co. C 16th Virginia KIA Spotsylvania
    C. H. May 12, 1864 VA28
Butter, __ - Virginia Aug. 16, 1864 VA25
Butter, T.P. - Co. D 11th North Carolina June 14, 1864
    VA25
Butterman, R.J. - Corp. - Co. F 25th North Carolina Aug. 5,
    1864 VA25
Butts, S.T. - Co. C 7th Georgia Sept. 6, 1861 VA25
Buzhardt, Abner M. - 11th South Carolina VA04
Byerly, W.T. - C.S. Navy May 7, 1865 VA25
Byers, H.L. - Co. H 56th North Carolina Nov. 2, 1864
    VA25
Byers, R.H. - 22nd Georgia Sept. 11, 1862 VA25
Byers, W.D. - Co. F 11th Georgia June 1, 1863 VA25
Byers, W.N. - Co. E 14th North Carolina Aug. 17, 1864
    VA25
Byne, G.W. - 8th Virginia July 15, 1861 VA25
Bynums, B.S. - Co. I 27th North Carolina Oct. 3, 1864
    VA25
Byrd, B. - Co. D 19th Louisiana May 31, 1862 VA25
Byrd, B. - Co. B 22nd North Carolina May 30, 1862 VA25
Byrd, D. - Co. A 17th Mississippi May 4, 1863 VA25
Byrd, E. - Co. F 51st North Carolina June 2, 1864 VA25
Byrd, H.C. - Letcher Artillery Dec. 9, 1863 VA25
Byrd, J. - Co. K 56th North Carolina June 25, 1864 VA25
Byrd, J.G. - 16th Georgia Sept. 5, 1862 VA25
Byrd, M.J. - North Carolina Feb. 10, 1863 VA25
Byrd, P.B. - Major - 6th Florida Battalion June 5, 1864
    VA25
Byrd, T. - Oct. 26, 1863 VA25
Byrd, W.H. - Co. B 49th North Carolina May 9, 1865
    VA25
Byrd, W.W. - 4th South Carolina VA18
Byrne, W. - Co. A 51st North Carolina Sept. 9, 1862 VA25
C____, W.G. - Co. G 57th Georgia Feb. 24, 1864 VA25

C __ , D __ - Lt. - Co. D 16th North Carolina   VA11
C __ , G.N. - Co. C 4th Georgia July 15, 1863   VA25
Cabbage, __ - Co. K 7th Virginia July 20, 1862   VA25
Cabball, J.C. - Co. I 57th North Carolina Jan. 24, 1863
    VA25
Cabell, William H. - KIA   VA19
Cabell, William Henry - Sgt. - VMI Cadet -KIA - Battle of
    New Market - May 15, 1864 - Buried at Hollywood
    Cemetery   VA21
Cabinis, J.S. - Co. F 9th Louisiana Jan. 8, 1863   VA25
Caddle, J.N. - Co. H 26th North Carolina April 26, 1864
    VA25
Cader, S. - Co. I 16th Georgia   Sept. 1861   VA25
Cadgett, D.R. - Co. E 18th North Carolina   VA11
Cadwell, Joel D. - Co. G 49th Georgia   VA11
Cagart, J.L. - Co. I 56th North Carolina   March 4, 1865
    VA25
Cahoon, J. - Co. D 22nd Georgia   Oct. 24, 1864   VA25
Caker, W.H. - Artillery   May 26, 1862   VA25
Calden, J.J. - Co. G 2nd Georgia July 1, 1862   VA25
Calder, H.C. - Co. I 1st Texas   May 28, 1862   VA25
Caldwell, William C. - Sgt. - Co. F 16th Mississippi Died
    May 12, 1864   VA28
Calhoun, B. - Co. B 23rd Georgia July 8, 1864   VA25
Calhoun, B.N. - Cobb's Legion (Georgia) Aug. 9, 1862
    VA25
Calhoun, J.W. - Co. E 28th Georgia   Sept. 3, 1864   VA25
Calhoun, Jas. C. - Co. B 11th North Carolina Died Sept __,
    1861   VA23
Calhoun, John - Co. G 17th Georgia   Oct. 9, 1864   VA25
Calhoun, T.W. - 13th Alabama   Sept. 3, 1861   VA25
Call, G.W. - Major - 2nd Florida.   May 31, 1862   VA25
Call, George - June 3, 1862 VA25
Callan, W.F. - Co. I 55th Virginia   Sept. 4, 1862   VA25
Callender, M.J.B. - Mississippi   March 18, 1863   VA25

Callicott, M. - Co. K 34th North Carolina June 30, 1862 VA25
Calliford, J.H. - Co. E 23rd North Carolina June 11, 1864 VA25
Callins, Thos. - July 20, 1861 VA25
Calmes, M. - Clark Cavalry VA06
Caltrain, D.F. - North Carolina June 13, 1862 VA25
Calven, A.J. - Co. E 24th Virginia VA11
Calvert, George R. - VA15
Calvert, John S. - VA12
Calvin, C.P. - Lt. - Co. G 15th Georgia Oct. 13, 1864 VA25
Calvin, J.J. - Co. G 2nd Georgia July 1, 1864 VA25
Calvin, John - Co. K 2nd Louisiana May 17, 1862 VA25
Calwell, H. - Co. F 48th Georgia June 5, 1864 VA25
Camden, George Nelson - Vol. - South Carolina VA18
Camerson, T.D. - Co. G 6th Georgia VA11
Cammeron, J.W. - Co. I 26th North Carolina July 16, 1864 VA25
Camp, I. Martin - POW - Federal Soldier Died Dec. 21, 1861 VA19
Camp, J.C. - Co. F 16th Georgia May 22, 1864 VA25
Camp, Jalws - POW - Federal Soldier Died Dec. 25, 1861 VA19
Camp, R.B. - Co. F 35th Georgia June 23, 1864 VA25
Camp, S. - Co. C 34th North Carolina June 14, 1862 VA25
Camp, W.A. - 21st Georgia July 4, 1863 VA25
Campbell, __ - Aug. 20, 1861 VA25
Campbell, __ - Virginia July 8, 1862 VA25
Campbell, A. - Pvt. - Co. B 18th Virginia Died June 3, 1865 VA26
Campbell, A.A. - Pvt. - Co. F 1st South Carolina April 6, 1865 VA24
Campbell, B.B. - Co. K 8th Georgia Sept. 20, 1861 VA25
Campbell, B.H. - Co. H 35th Georgia June 15, 1864 VA25
Campbell, H. - Co. F 11th Louisiana May 14, 1862 VA25

Campbell, H.A. - Co. D 46th North Carolina July 26, 1864
    VA25
Campbell, H.H. - Co. B 37th North Carolina July 17, 1864
    VA25
Campbell, J. - Co. G 38th Georgia June 22, 1862 VA25
Campbell, J. - Co. D 13th South Carolina June 12, 1864
    VA25
Campbell, J.A. - 8th South Carolina VA18
Campbell, J.C. - Co. K 1st South Carolina Engineer Corps
    July 12, 1864 VA25
Campbell, J.P. - Co. I 14th South Carolina Aug. 8, 1864
    VA25
Campbell, J.W. - Co. I 14th Georgia June 9, 1864 VA25
Campbell, R. - Co. F 11th Georgia July 6, 1862 VA25
Campbell, V. - Co. A 56th North Carolina July 22, 1864
    VA25
Campbell, W. - Co. H 4th Mississippi May 6, 1862 VA25
Campbell, W. - Co. H 4th North Carolina Sept. 6, 1862
    VA25
Campbell, W.J. - Co. K 1st South Carolina July 8, 1862 VA25
Campbell, W.P. - Co. F 44th North Carolina July 30, 1864
    VA25
Campbell, W.T. - Co. B 22nd South Carolina Sept. 4, 1862
    VA25
Camps, __ - June 15, 1862 VA25
Campton, T.H. - Co. F 14th South Carolina July 17, 1862
    VA25
Can, H. - 6th North Carolina VA18
Cance, P. - Co. C 10th North Carolina Nov. 1, 1864 VA25
Candle, G. - Co. D 27th Georgia May 7, 1862 VA25
Cane, C. - 2nd Florida May 16, 1862 VA25
Cane, J.A. - Co. I 17th South Carolina Sept. 11, 1864 VA25
Cane, J.A. - Co. I 9th Louisiana May 25, 1863 VA25
Cane, W.F. - Co. F 11th Florida Oct. 19, 1864 VA25
Cane, W.F. - Co. C 26th South Carolina July 27, 1864 VA25
Canfield, W.T. - Co. E 17th Mississippi. July 5, 1862 VA25

Canley, ____ - May 29, 1862 VA25
Canliffe, H.M. - 8th Louisiana Jan. 22, 1862 VA25
Canner, __ - Co. I 25th North Carolina July 25, 1862 VA25
Canner, F.C. - Co. C 10th Florida Sept. 24, 1864 VA25
Cannie, J.M. - DOD Nov. 11, 1862 VA19
Cannon, Caspers Bowman - Pvt. - Co. A 3rd South Carolina Battalion Died May 8, 1864 Headstone reads: "A Battery VA28
Cannon, J.C. - South Carolina July 24, 1864 VA25
Cannon, W. - Co. I 24th Georgia Feb. 19, 1865 VA25
Cannon, William - Co. H 3rd North Carolina name also spelled: " Von Kannon" and "Vuncannon" VA28
Canon, S. - Georgia Aug. 1, 1861 VA25
Canon, W. - Co. H 13th North Carolina May 18, 1864 VA25
Canon, W.R. - Co. I 25th North Carolina July 22, 1862 VA25
Cantrell, C.M. - Co. A 13th South Carolina June 28, 1864 VA25
Caphart, H.R. - Co. B 2nd South Carolina Sept. 29, 1862 VA25
Caphart, J. - Co. F 4th Georgia Dec. 23, 1862 VA25
Caphart, J.W. - Co. F 4th Georgia Dec. 20, 1862 VA25
Capps, J.M. - Co. G 12th South Carolina June 9, 1862 VA25
Capps, J.N. - Co. I 6th North Carolina Jan. 12, 1865 VA25
Capps, P. - Co. I 6th North Carolina Jan. 12, 1865 VA25
Capps, W. - Co. G 3rd North Carolina June 25, 1863 VA25
Capps, W.G. - 9th Alabama Cavalry May 31, 1862 VA25
Cardwell, A.P. - Co. C 26th South Carolina July 3, 1864 VA25
Carey, J.M. - 14th Louisiana. Infantry - KIA - Battle of Williamsburg - May 5, 1862 VA02
Carithers, D. - Co. H 23rd North Carolina July 22, 1864 VA25
Carld, V. - Co. F 57th North Carolina VA11
Carle, V. - 57th North Carolina VA11
Carley, R.J. - Georgia VA20
Carlton, E. - Holcombe's Legion (Georgia) VA25

Carlton, J.L. - Co. E 17th North Carolina June 26, 1865 VA25
Carlton, J.S. - Co. E 52nd North Carolina Oct. 26, 1864 VA25
Carlton, J.T. - Co. B 27th North Carolina Dec. 2, 1864 VA25
Carlyle, H. - 8th North Carolina Aug. 29, 1862 VA25
Carlyle, J. - Co. C 21st Mississippi May 8, 1863 VA25
Carlyle, R.E. - Co. A 2nd South Carolina Aug. 29, 1862 VA25
Carlyle, W.M. - Co. I 13th Alabama June 15, 1862 VA25
Carmichiall, J.B. - 27th South Carolina June 12, 1864 VA25
Carmickle, D.H. - Co. K 26th Alabama March 4, 1865 VA25
Carnes, W.A. - Co. G 28th Georgia July 5, 1862 VA25
Carney, C. Pvt. - South Carolina Aug. 21, 1864 VA22
Carney, D. - Louisiana June 25, 1863 VA25
Carney, E. - Co. B 22nd North Carolina Sept. 2, 1864 VA25
Caron, J. - Co. B 28th Alabama June 20, 1862 VA25
Carpenter, A. - Co. B 8th Georgia Battalion March 23, 1865 VA25
Carpenter, C. - C.S. Navy Nov. 29, 1863 VA25
Carpenter, G.L. - DOD Nov. 18, 1862 VA19
Carpenter, H. - Co. H 45th Virginia VA08
Carpenter, L.J. - Co. A 38th North Carolina June 14, 1863 VA25
Carpenter, P.A. - Co. B 5th North Carolina Aug. 10, 1863 VA25
Carper, James M. - Co. C 7th Georgia VA11
Carper, R.B. - 11th Virginia Infantry - KIA - Battle of Williamsburg - May 5, 1862 VA02
Carr, D.C. - Co. B 12th Mississippi June 23, 1862 VA25
Carr, Everett T. - Pvt. - Co. F 20th North Carolina MW May 9, 1864 Died May 15(16?), 1864 VA28
Carr, J. - C.S. Navy April 28, 1865 VA25
Carr, James - Co. C 1st North Carolina July 8, 1862 VA25
Carr, John O. - Co. B 6th Virginia Cavalry KIA Spotsylvania C. H. May 1864 VA28
Carr, M.J. - Jeff. Davis's Artillery Aug. 7, 1862 VA25

Carr, M.L. Sgt. - Co. K 49th Georgia   May 20, 1864   VA25
Carr, S. - 4th Alabama Aug. 7, 1862   VA25
Carr, W.A. - 13th Alabama Sept. 15, 1861   VA25
Carraker, William - 15th Alabama VA11
Carraway, ___ - Co. F 6th Alabama May 26, 1864   VA25
Carrihan, C. - 12th Virginia Cavalry   VA18
Carrington, E. - Co. E 20th Georgia May 31, 1862   VA25
Carrol, Hamilton - see Carroll, Hamilton   VA28
Carroll, A. - Palmetto Sharp Shooters (South Carolina) July 5, 1862   VA25
Carroll, D. - Pvt. - Co. C 53rd North Carolina .Died May 9, 1865   VA26
Carroll, D. - Nov. 19, 1862 VA25
Carroll, Hamilton - Pvt. - Co. B 31st Virginia KIA - Spotsylvania Court House Headstone reads: "Carrol" VA28
Carroll, J.S. - Virginia   VA20
Carroll, W.F. - Co. B 51st North Carolina Aug. 12, 1864 VA25
Carroway, W.D. - Lexington Guards (Texas) Aug. 10, 1861 VA25
Carsley, J.F. - Co. A 14th Virginia July 13, 1862   VA25
Carson, C.F. - "54", Virginia   VA20
Carter, ___ - 16th North Carolina Nov. 4, 1862   VA25
Carter, ___ - Mosby's Virginia Cavalry Hung while POW - Sept 23, 1864   VA23
Carter, ___ - 1862   VA25
Carter, ___ - Nov. 5, 1862 VA25
Carter, A.J. - Tennessee   VA20
Carter, A.J. - Co. A 17th South Carolina Aug. 9, 1864 VA25
Carter, A.P. - Mosby's Cavalry (Virginia) Jan. 23, 1864 VA25
Carter, Asa - Co. C 15th ___   VA28
Carter, E.T. - 56th Virginia June 30, 1862   VA25

Carter, Elijah A. - Lt. - Co. A 37th North Carolina MW May 12, 1864 Died May 13, 1864 Headstone reads: "Sgt." VA28
Carter, G. - Co. E 37th North Carolina Oct. 17, 1863 VA25
Carter, G.W. - Co. A 2nd Virginia Cavalry May 30, 1864 VA25
Carter, G.W. Virginia June 15, 1862 VA25
Carter, G.W. - Co. K 45th Georgia June 29, 1862 VA25
Carter, G.W. - Co. G 15th South Carolina Aug. 18, 1862 VA25
Carter, Geo. - Capt.- Ten VA20
Carter, H. - Co. K 6th Georgia June 30, 1862 VA25
Carter, H.B. - 7th Virginia VA18
Carter, J.A. - Co. F 54th North Carolina March 17, 1863 VA25
Carter, J.J. - Co. G 27th Georgia Aug. 17, 1864 VA25
Carter, J.J. - Co. E 18th North Carolina Sept. 3, 1864 VA25
Carter, J.M. - Nov. 8, 1862 VA25
Carter, J.W. - Co. F 27th Georgia Aug. 12, 1864 VA25
Carter, John - 10th Fla. VA04
Carter, Julian - VA06
Carter, L.F. - Capt. - June 6, 1863 VA25
Carter, O. - Co. E 61st North Carolina Sept. 5, 1864 VA25
Carter, R. - Co. D 10th Georgia June 20, 1863 VA25
Carter, R.A. - Co. H 38th Virginia Aug. 10, 1862 VA25
Carter, S. - Co. E 17th Georgia Aug. 8, 1864 VA25
Carter, S.C. - Co. G 57th Virginia May 1865 VA25
Carter, S.G. - Co. E 27th South Carolina Aug. 10, 1864 VA25
Carter, W. - Co. E 34th North Carolina Aug. 3, 1864 VA25
Carthy, G.B. - Co. I 32nd North Carolina Oct. 4, 1864 VA25
Cartrell, T. - Co. I 1st Mississippi Cavalry July 27, 1863 VA25
Carty, W.N. - 5th Texas Jan. 2, 11862 VA25
Carver, __ - Co. K 6th Alabama July 26, 1862 VA25
Carver, __ - Co. G 15th North Carolina Oct. 8, 1862 VA25

Carver, J.N. - Co. II 2nd North Carolina Battalion June 8, 1865   VA25
Cary, C.G. - Co. F 38th Virginia Jan. 19, 1862   VA25
Cary, G.M. - Gloucester Cavalry June 26, 1862   VA25
Cary, I.M. - POW - Federal Soldier Died Jan. 5, 1862   VA19
Casbry, P.A. -Louisiana Feb. 12, 1862   VA25
Cascadon, Thos. - Co. C 48th North Carolina Dec. 17, 1863   VA25
Case, J.L. - 20th Georgia VA18
Casey, J.E. - Kentucky   VA20
Casey, J.F. - Co. F 10th Alabama Dec. 3, 1863   VA25
Casey, L. - Co. D 23rd North Carolina June 1864   VA25
Casey, O.J. - Georgia Oct. 15, 1861   VA25
Cash, B. - Co. E 13th Alabama June 16, 1862   VA25
Cash, J.T. - Co. D 40th Mississippi May 30, 1864   VA25
Cash, J.T. - Co. D 40th Mississippi May 30, 1864   VA25
Cash, R. - Co. K 37th Georgia Sept. 6, 1862   VA25
Cash, W. - Co. D 47th North Carolina Sept. 18, 1864   VA25
Cash, W.J. - Price's Artillery   May 17, 1862   VA25
Cash, Wyatt - Corp. - Co. I 49th Virginia DOW June 6, 1864 (MW May 18, 1864)   VA28
Cashand, __ - Co. D 26th Georgia July 1, 1852   VA25
Caskie, J. - Co. D 5th South Carolina June 30, 1862 VA25
Caslind, __ - July 8, 1862 VA25
Cason, A.G. - Co. G 10th Virginia June 5, 1863   VA25
Cason, J.D. - Co. F 6th Virginia May 28, 1864   VA25
Cason, M.T. - Co. B 50th Georgia   VA11
Casson, J.H. - Sgt. - Co. E 55th North Carolina Oct. 9, 1864   VA25
Castello, D. - Co. B 8th Florida March 17, 1863   VA25
Castillio, T. - Co. I 9th Georgia July 4, 1862   VA25
Castle, F.L. - Co. H 31st Georgia Aug. 5, 1862   VA25
Castleberry, H.C. - Co. H 7th Georgia July 8, 1862   VA25
Castleberry, W.D. - Lt. - Co. K 2nd Mississippi   Oct. 14, 1864   VA25
Castleman, C.D. - VA06

Castleman, Wm. - VA06
Castly, J.J. - Co. F 48th Georgia   VA11
Caston, S. - Co. G 2nd Florida May 20, 1863   VA25
Cates, F.C. - Co. D 1st North Carolina May 18, 1863 VA25
Cates, J.W. - Co. E 56th North Carolina Sept. 11, 1864   VA25
Cates, M.A. - 13th Alabama Oct. 30, 1861   VA25
Cates, P.N. - Co. G 44th North Carolina July 6, 1964 VA25
Cates, W.A. - Co. C 17th Mississippi July 14, 1862   VA25
Cathcart, J.B. - Sgt. - Co. K 26th North Carolina   Nov. 26, 1864   VA25
Catlett, T.J. - 28th Virginia VA18
Cato, C.T. - Co. E 19th Georgia July 23, 1864   VA25
Cato, J. - Co. E 19th Georgia July 18, 1864   VA25
Cato, J.G.F. - Co. F 28th Georgia Aug. 31, 1864   VA25
Cato, M.L. - Co. F 28th Georgia Aug. 31, 1864   VA25
Cato, W.R. - Co. D 28th Georgia Oct. 5, 1864   VA25
Caton, S. - Co. D 53rd North Carolina Oct. 28, 1864   VA25
Cator, R.E. - 2nd South Carolina Aug. 31, 1861   VA25
Catts, W.H. - Co. I 46th North Carolina Dec. 31, 1864   VA25
Caudle, W.H. - Co. F 11th North Carolina Died Oct 3, 1861   VA23
Caugham, Wm. - North Carolina July 3, 1862   VA25
Caughlin, E. - Mississippi Sept. 6, 1861   VA25
Caughman, G.E. - Co. F 1st South Carolina 1862   VA25
Cauley, __ - DOD Nov. 22, 1862   VA19
Caulston, __ - Co. B 24th Georgia July 5, 1862   VA25
Caun, W.E. - 2nd Florida July 8, 1862   VA25
Causey, H.. - Co. D 4th South Carolina Feb. 25, 1865 VA25
Caut, J.M. - Sgt. - 2nd Florida July 2, 1862   VA25
Cauthorn, __ - Co. K 5th South Carolina Aug. 29, 1862 VA25
Cauthorn, H. - Co. B 5th South Carolina Aug. 29, 1862 VA25
Cauthorn, W.B. - Co. B 53rd Georgia March 9, 1863   VA25
Cavaugh, A.A. - Co. B 5th Louisiana Dec. 24, 1862   VA25
Cavauton, T. - Co. F 53rd North Carolina March 29, 1865   VA25
Cave, J.J. - 60th Virginia VA08

Cawley, J. - Sgt. - Co. C 66th North Carolina. June 14, 1864 VA25
Cecil, R. - Lt. - Co. K 1st Virginia Cavalry June 23, 1864 VA25
Center, Archer - 24th North Carolina VA05
Cevens, A.H. - 17th Mississippi VA18
Chalfin, J. - Washington Artillery Sept. 17, 1861 VA25
Chalkley, C.B. - Co. C 32nd Virginia Nov. 30, 1862 VA25
Chamberlain, Samuel - Pvt. - Co. H 4th North Carolina Died May 12, 1864 Headstone reads: " Chamberlin" VA28
Chamberlin, Samuel - see Chamberlain, Samuel VA28
Chambers, E.A. - Co. C 11th Alabama June 17, 1865 VA25
Chambers, G.W. - Virginia Artillery June 16, 1864 VA25
Chambers, M.C. - Co. I 19th Georgia May 31, 1862 VA25
Chambers, Thomas J. - Pvt. - Co. A 14th Alabama VA28
Chambers, William - Nov. 17, 1862 VA19
Chambliss, J. - Co. G 9th Louisiana Jan. 9, 1862 VA25
Chameron, G.W. - Co. I 26th South Carolina Oct. 5, 1864 VA25
Champion, J. - Co. F 47th North Carolina March 7, 1865 VA25
Champlier, __ - Lt. - Co. I 1st South Carolina Jan. 2, 1863 VA25
Chandler, C. - Co. F 14th North Carolina July 7, 1862 VA25
Chandler, H. - Co. A 13th North Carolina June 2, 1864 VA25
Chandler, S.W. - Co. D 7th South Carolina Aug. 3, 1864 VA25
Chandler, W. - Co. B 20th Mississippi Aug. 31, 1864 VA25
Chaning, W.A. - 17th Virginia Oct. 20, 1861 VA25
Chanley, Thos. - May 24, 1861 VA25
Chapell, __ Died May 22, 1864 age 18 VA19
Chapell, R. - Co. I 6th North Carolina June 23, 1862 VA25
Chaplin, J.C. - 5th South Carolina VA18
Chapman, B.M. - Co. H 6th South Carolina Oct. 9, 1864 VA25
Chapman, H.D. - Co. C 17th Georgia Aug. 15, 1864 VA25

Chapman, J.M. - Pvt. - Co. E 6th North Carolina Died June 8, 1865   VA26
Chapman, J.W. - Co. K 2nd Georgia July 8, 1862   VA25
Chapman, L.J. - Pvt. - Co. G 37th North Carolina .Died May 8, 1865   VA26
Chappal, __ - KIA May 22, 1864   VA19
Charing, L. - Co. F 3rd North Carolina April 23, 1864   VA25
Chase, E. - Lt. - Co. H 40th Virginia Aug. 5, 1862   VA25
Chastian, G.A. - Co. I 17th Mississippi May 20, 1862   VA25
Chatt, Jesse - 21st Georgia VA18
Cheatham, W.T. - Co. G 1st South Carolina Aug. 9, 1863   VA25
Cheatmon, __ - Co. B 4th North Carolina Aug. 10, 1863   VA25
Cheely, P.P. - Virginia   VA20
Cheenery, S.G. - Died Jan. 26, 1863   age 36   VA19
Cheeney, Lemuel - 44th North Carolina   VA04
Cherry, J. - Co. A 17th North Carolina Aug. 9, 1864 VA25
Cheshire, W. - Co. H 45th Georgia June 1, 1863   VA25
Chesnut, D. - Co. A Huger Artillery July 5, 1864 VA25
Chesnut, G.R. - Co. A 38th Georgia July 6, 1862   VA25
Chesnut, W. - Co. F 5th Alabama Aug. 17, 1862   VA25
Chester, __ - Co. K 22nd North Carolina Sept. 3, 1862   VA25
Chester, J.R. -   VA28
Chester, J.W. - Capt. - Co. E 3rd Alabama Aug. 12, 1864   VA25
Chester, M. - Co. H 11th North Carolina Jan. 12, 1865   VA25
Chester, S. - Co. K 32nd North Carolina Sept. 2, 1862   VA25
Chestnut, J.R. - 9th Louisiana VA18
Chevis, J.T. - Co. I 22nd South Carolina Aug. 4, 1864 VA25
Chewing, J.T. - Co. I 3rd Georgia July 20, 1862   VA25
Chi_well, H.J. - Pvt. - Co. C 11th Florida Died May 6, 1865   VA26
Chichester, J. Conway - 1st Virginia Cavalry   VA10
Childress, __ -Virginia July 5, 1862   VA25

Childress, J. - Co. C 27th South Carolina June 29, 1864 VA25
Childress, J. - Co. E 17th South Carolina Aug. 7, 1862 VA25
Childress, T.J. - Co. I 12th Virginia July 8, 1862   VA25
Childress, T.T. - Hampton Legion (South Carolina) Aug. 7, 1862   VA25
Childress, W.W. - Co. B 12th South Carolina June 15, 1862 VA25
Chilton, J. - Co. G 14th North Carolina Jan. 24, 1864   VA25
Chisholm, A. - Co. E 36th North Carolina Oct. 9, 1864 VA25
Chisman, F.E. 15th Alabama July 1, 1864   VA25
Chisman, R. - Co. A 32nd Virginia May 12, 1864   VA25
Chitwood, P. - Co. A 23rd Georgia Oct. 30, 1862   VA25
Chity, W. - Co. G 3rd Virginia Aug. 18, 1862   VA25
Chounacy, T. - Co. F 7th Louisiana Sept. 9, 1864   VA25
Chrisp, William G. - Lt. (Sgt.?) - Co. F 30th North Carolina VA28
Christian, __ - Virginia June 2, 1862   VA25
Christian, E.J. - Major - 23rd North Carolina   1862   VA25
Christian, William Thompson - Veteran - Feb. 12, 1836 - Jan.. 21, 1891
Christy, H. - Co. I 7th Virginia Aug. 16, 1862   VA25
Christy, M.G. - Co. I 7th North Carolina Aug. 5, 1862 VA25
Chucheris, __ - 38th Georgia April 16, 1862   VA25
Chum, W. - Co. B 4th North Carolina June 13, 1862 VA25
Chumblee, Earl - Co. H 2nd South Carolina Rifles name also spelled: "Chumbler" VA28
Chumbler, Earl - see Chumblee, Earl   VA28
Churchill, __ - Lt. - July 2, 1862   VA25
Churets, Wm. - Co. F 13th North Carolina Sept. 4, 1864 VA25
Churl, M. - Co. C 38th Georgia   VA11
Cider, Jacob - Died March 17, 1863   age 23   VA19
Ciscal, G. - Virginia   VA20
City, J.H. - Virginia Artillery   May 12, 1862   VA25
Clamants, R.A. - Co. F 18th Virginia June 30, 1862   VA25

Clarck, A. - Co. G 49th Virginia June 10, 1862   VA25
Clardy, L.G. - Co. D 18th South Carolina July 1, 1864 VA25
Clarence, __ - 20th Georgia April 20, 1862   VA25
Clark, A.J. - Co. F 4th South Carolina Cavalry   March 25, 1865   VA25
Clark, A.W. - Co. G 38th Alabama April 28, 1865   VA25
Clark, Andrew F. - Pvt. - Co. C 20th Georgia name on headstone - "Clarke"   VA28
Clark, C.F. - POW - Federal Soldier Died Nov. 18, 1861   VA19
Clark, G.E. - 16th North Carolina Sept. 19, 1864   VA25
Clark, G.V. - Co. B 37th Virginia July 10, 1864   VA25
Clark, G.W. - Co. B 37th Virginia June 3, 1864   VA25
Clark, G.W. - Co. C 15th Georgia May 25, 1862   VA25
Clark, George William - Pollock's / Fredericksburg Artillery (Virginia) Veteran Died Sept. 14, 1925   VA28
Clark, H. - Co. F 1st Louisiana June 17, 1864   VA25
Clark, H.J. - Co. I 20th Georgia March 18, 1863   VA25
Clark, J. - 4th Texas Nov. 5, 1862   VA25
Clark, J. - Cobb's Legion (Georgia)   Sept. 1861   VA25
Clark, J.C. - Co. D 11th North Carolina March 13, 1865   VA25
Clark, J.D. - Pvt. - Co. K 54th North Carolina Died May 17, 1865   VA26
Clark, J.M. - 5th North Carolina April 14, 1862   VA25
Clark, J.W. - Co. E 28th Georgia July 13, 1864   VA25
Clark, James E. - April 18, 1863   VA19
Clark, James S. - see Clarke, James S.   VA28
Clark, M.J. - Feb. 26, 1865 VA19
Clark, Nevin - Capt. - Co. E 28th North Carolina   VA28
Clark, S. - Co. C 6th Georgia Feb. 23, 1863   VA25
Clark, T.C. - July 4, 1862 VA25
Clark, W. - Co. F 5th Louisiana Nov. 25, 1862   VA25
Clark, W.C. - Co. B 53rd North Carolina June 10, 1864   VA25
Clark, W.H. - Co. E 7th South Carolina Oct. 5, 1864 VA25

Clark, W.R. - Capt. - Co. K 12th Mississippi Aug. 20, 1864
   VA25
Clark, W.T. - Aug. 15, 1862 VA25
Clark, W.T. - Hampton's Pilot (Virginia) Aug. 15, 1862
   VA25
Clarke, Andrew F.- see Clark, Andrew F.   VA28
Clarke, George W. - Pvt. - Co. K 1st North Carolina Died May
   8, 1864   VA28
Clarke, James S. - Pvt. - Co. E 15th South Carolina Died May
   8, 1864 Headstone reads: "Clark"   VA28
Clarkson, R. - Kentucky June 17, 1865   VA25
Clarkson, Thomas U. - Co. A 30th North Carolina   VA11
Clarrett, __ - 19th Mississippi July 8, 1862   VA25
Clary, R.M. - Co. C 27th Georgia July 1864   VA25
Clay, C. - 17th Georgia Dec. 2, 1862   VA25
Clay, T.K. - Sgt. - Co. C 49th Georgia March 14, 1865
   VA25
Clayton, G.R. - Co. K 4th Georgia   VA11
Clayton, J. - Pvt. - Co. F 1st South Carolina Artillery Died
   May 12, 1865 VA26
Clayton, Wm. - Artillery June 20, 1862   VA25
Cleaveland, W.B. - Co. I 2nd Virginia June 6, 1863   VA25
Cleek, Elijah G. - Pvt. - Co. D 37th Virginia   VA28
Cleghom, P. - 13th Alabama   Sept. 16, 1861   VA25
Clelland, D. - Orr's Rifles (South Carolina)   May 21, 1864
   VA25
Clem, Jacob H. - VA12
Clem, William - Grave not marked   VA15
Clemants, J.C. - Co. B 49th South Carolina June 15, 1862
   VA25
Clemby, G.M. - Died Oct. 23, 1861   VA19
Clemens, A. - Co. I 24th Georgia Nov. 12, 1862   VA25
Clemhern, M. - Pvt. - 6th South Carolina Aug. 22, 1864
   VA22
Clemmons, A. - Co. A 5th Virginia April 1, 1865   VA25
Clemmons, E. - Tennessee April 20, 1865   VA25

Clenly, G.W. - POW - Federal Soldier Died Oct. 23, 1861 VA19

Clerry, A. - Co. B 46th North Carolina Sept. 29, 1864   VA25

Clery, Olvey - Co. M Palmetto Sharpshooters -South Carolina Died June 2, 1863   VA03

Client, B.H. - Co. D 12th Georgia Artillery Feb. 17, 1865 VA25

Clifton, Charles H. - Pvt. - Co. D 9th Louisiana Died May 10, 1864   VA28

Cline, J.A. - Co. C 48th North Carolina Dec. 22, 1864   VA25

Cline, Philip M. (MD) - medical doctor   VA12

Clinedinst, John W. - VA12

Clipper, S.C. - Co. G 4th Alabama June 10, 1862   VA25

Clodfeller, David C. - see Clodfelter, David C.   VA28

Clodfelter, David C. - Pvt. - Co. I 14th North Carolina Died May 10, 1864 Headstone reads: " Clodfeller"   VA28

Clontz, James M. - Pvt. - Co. B 11th North Carolina Died June 14, 1865   VA26

Clopton, John - Co. E 19th Mississippi July 3, 1862   VA25

Closin, A. - Co. F 38th North Carolina Oct. 4, 1864 VA25

Cloud, Alexander H. - Pvt. - Co. I 4th Georgia MW May 12, 1864   VA28

Cloud, J.D. - Co. D 18th Mississippi July 12, 1862   VA25

Cloud, M.L. - Georgia   VA20

Clousa, S.C. - Co. H 26th Alabama May 5, 1863   VA25

Clouts, J.W. - Co. I 6th __   VA08

Cluart, A.D. - Co. D 53rd Virginia June 2, 1863   VA25

Clyoen, J.A. - Virginia   VA20

Coates, J.D. - 13th Mississippi July 1862   VA25

Coates, J.H. - Co. B 41st Virginia Nov. 8, 1862   VA25

Cobb, C. - Co. I 5th North Carolina March 20, 1865   VA25

Cobb, H.A. - Orr's Rifles (South Carolina) June 26, 1864 VA25

Cobb, J. - Co. E 56th North Carolina July 2, 1864 VA25

Cobb, Rankin - Pvt. - Co. A 53rd North Carolina DOW VA28

Cobb, S.W. - Co. G 45th North Carolina Oct. 5, 1864 VA25
Cobb, T.C. - Co. F 23rd North Carolina Jan. 15, 1863   VA25
Cobb, W. - Co. F 14th North Carolina July 3, 1862   VA25
Coblier, J.B. - Co. F 1st North Carolina July 12, 1863 VA25
Cochran, J.L. - Co. D 45th Georgia July 1, 1862   VA25
Cock, L.G. - Co. A 4th Texas June 23, 1862   VA25
Cocke, Jackson - Virginia   VA20
Cockerham, John E. - Co. H 11th North Carolina Died Dec 6, 1861   VA23
Cockran, J. - Co. I 10th Alabama June 3, 1862   VA25
Cockran, M. - 6th Alabama July 8, 1862   VA25
Codison, C.A. - Co. H 44th North Carolina Nov. 15, 1864   VA25
Coffee, L.W. - Co. F 52nd Georgia July 28, 1863   VA25
Coffee, Robert H. - Pvt. - Co. I 49th Virginia   MW Spotsylvania C. H.   Name also spelled "Coffey"   VA28
Coffen, James - Co. G 12th South Carolina June 2, 1862   VA25
Coffer, J.W. Capt. - H.L. Artillery (South Carolina)   Oct. 22, 1862   VA25
Coffey, Robert H. - see Coffee, Robert H.   VA28
Coffin, W.F. - Co. I 13th South Carolina June 26, 1862   VA25
Coffin, W.N. - Orr's Rifles (South Carolina) July 4, 1862   VA25
Coffman, M.D. - VA15
Coffray, J.N. - Co. B 19th Georgia   Sept. 7, 1863   VA25
Coffrey, A.B. - Sgt. - Co. A 22nd North Carolina   Oct. 1864   VA25
Cogbern, J.H. - Co. F 14th South Carolina June 21, 1862   VA25
Cogburn, B.J. - Pvt. - Co. A 7th South Carolina KIA Fredericksburg - Dec. 13, 1862   VA28
Cogg, M.W. - Co. C 3rd North Carolina Sept. 19, 1864   VA25

Coggin, H. - Co. I 13th South Carolina Aug. 13, 1862   VA25
Coggin, J.L. - Co. I 13th South Carolina Aug. 11, 1862   VA25
Coggin, J.M. - Co. C 23rd North Carolina Aug. 7, 1862 VA25
Coggin, W.A. - Co. K 34th North Carolina July 19, 1862   VA25
Coggin, Wm. F. - Co. I 13th South Carolina June 26, 1862   VA25
Cohen, Henry - KIA - June 29, 1864   VA17
Cohen, I. - Hampton's Legion - South Carolina   VA17
Cohen, Jacob A. - Captain - Co. A 10th Louisiana. KIA - 2nd Manassas Aug. 30, 1862 - age 33   VA17
Cohen, James - Co. B 22nd North Carolina April 21, 1862   VA25
Coker, B.G. - Co. H 9th Louisiana Dec. 8, 1862   VA25
Coker, H.R. - Co. K 17th Mississippi July 5, 1862   VA25
Coker, J. - Co. I 28th South Carolina July 17, 1864   VA25
Coker, J.T. - Co. G 9th South Carolina Oct. 13, 1861 VA25
Coker, J.T. - 28th Virginia Nov. 17, 1862   VA25
Coker, W.P. - Co. I 22nd Georgia Nov. 16, 1862   VA25
Colbert, A. - 20th Georgia VA18
Colbert, V.W. - Co. G 15th South Carolina Feb. 24, 1864   VA25
Cole, __ - Co. D 53rd Georgia Oct. 20, 1862   VA25
Cole, Ben. J. - 8th __   VA18
Cole, J. - Co. B 44th Georgia July 3, 1865   VA25
Cole, J. - Co. H 35th Georgia Aug. 3, 1864   VA25
Cole, J.H. - Co. K 42nd Mississippi July 27, 1862   VA25
Cole, J.W. - Co. K 25th North Carolina Nov. 19, 1862   VA25
Cole, M.B. - 12th North Carolina July 1862   VA25
Cole, M.M. - June 20, 1862 VA25
Cole, T. - Co. B 13th South Carolina Nov. 9, 1862 VA25
Coleman, J.B. - Lt. - 16th Mississippi Aug. 18, 1864 VA25
Coleman, J.C. - Arkansas Battalion   May 28, 1862   VA25
Coleman, M.B. - Co. K 19th Georgia Dec. 18, 1862   VA25
Coleman, P. - Co. D 7th Louisiana April 3, 1862   VA25

Coleman, R.H. - Co. B 40th Virginia June 20, 1864   VA25
Coleman, S.F. - Co. G 4th South Carolina March 25, 1865   VA25
Coley, B. - Co. H 14th North Carolina June 30, 1862   VA25
Coley, J.H.L. - Co. G 44th Alabama March 17, 1863   VA25
Colley, John T. - Lt. - Co. D 12th Georgia DOW May 14, 1864 (MW May 10, 1864) VA28
Colley, John T. - Sgt. - Co. B 13th Georgia Died May 12, 1864   VA28
Collier, H.R. - Co. F 21st Mississippi June 4, 1862   VA25
Collier, J. - May 6, 1864 VA25
Collier, J. - Co. C 17th North Carolina Oct. 4, 1864 VA25
Collier, J.D. - Co. G 14th Alabama July 16, 1862   VA25
Collier, P.S. - Co. D 13th Georgia July 4, 1862   VA25
Collim, Andrew - see Collins, Andrew   VA28
Collin, J.J. - Co. G 62nd North Carolina March 18, 1865   VA25
Collin, W.W. - Co. C 34th North Carolina Feb. 28, 1865   VA25
Collins, A.A. - Co. E 44th North Carolina Aug. 15, 1864   VA25
Collins, Andrew - Co. E 22nd Georgia name on headstone - "Collim"   VA28
Collins, G.W. - "63" , Virginia   VA20
Collins, J.A. - Co. H 1st South Carolina May 29, 1864 VA25
Collins, J.G. - Latham's Bat. (Virginia)   VA18
Collins, J.T. - Co. F 48th Mississippi Nov. 19, 1864   VA25
Collins, James - July 14, 1861 VA19
Colmbs, A.H. - Co. A 47th Virginia Dec. 31, 1862   VA25
Colney, J.R. - 1st Texas April 29, 1862   VA25
Colquitt, __ - Co. A 24th North Carolina July 5, 1862 VA25
Colrain, __ - July 8, 1862 VA25
Colton, J. - 21st Georgia VA18
Coltran, J.L. - Co. A 17th North Carolina June 30, 1865   VA25
Coltran, John - Co. A 6th North Carolina July 9, 1862 VA25

Coltrane, D.F. - June 13, 1862 VA25
Coltrane, J.W. - July 7, 1862 VA25
Colvart, A.J. - Co. I 1st Engineer Corps July 14, 1864   VA25
Colville, John R. - Pvt. - Co. F 15th North Carolina Died near Fredericksburg - Dec. 27, 1862   VA28
Colwell, __ - KIA - Battle of New Market - May 15, 1864 VA15
Colwell, S. - VA12
Combs, L. - POW - Federal Soldier Died Dec. 8, 1861   VA19
Combs, S.E. - Co. I 35th North Carolina July 20, 1862   VA25
Comby, W.A. - Co. F 22nd North Carolina April 3, 1865 VA25
Cometry, P. - Wheat's Battalion April 4, 1862   VA25
Comina, A.B. - Co. H 15th Alabama June 25, 1862   VA25
Comlow, T. - 51st North Carolina   VA24
Compton, F. - Co. G 4th North Carolina Nov. 26, 1864 VA25
Compton, M. - 18th Virginia VA18
Compton, M. - 13th North Carolina   VA18
Concords, B. - Feb. 10, 1865 VA25
Conday, G. - Co. B 35th North Carolina June 24, 1864   VA25
Condor, __ - Lt. - Co. F 3rd Florida June 1, 1862   VA25
Cone, J.A. - Co. B 3rd South Carolina Nov. 9, 1862 VA25
Cone, W.T. - Co. I 18th Georgia Sept. 2, 1861   VA25
Coner, W.T. - Cobb's Legion (Georgia)   May 8, 1863 VA25
Coney, G.B. - Georgia Battalion   Sept. 2, 1864   VA25
Conley, W.L. - Co. E 7th North Carolina Oct. 4, 1864   VA25
Connall, J. - 5th Alabama July 7, 1862   VA25
Connelly, John - Co. A 15th Louisiana July 3, 1864   VA25
Conner, E. - Co. C 28th Georgia July 15, 1862   VA25
Conner, H. - Co. H 46th North Carolina July 17, 1864   VA25
Conner, J.A. - Co. E 61st Georgia March 12, 1863   VA25
Conner, J.B. - Co. H 9th Louisiana Dec. 29, 1863   VA25
Conner, W.O. - Co. K 19th Georgia Oct. 1861   VA25
Connoly, Timothy - 8th Louisiana VA18
Connor, S.O. - C.S. Navy Aug. 1865   VA25
Conor, J. - C.S. Navy   Nov. 9, 1862   VA25

Conray, S.P. - 15th South Carolina July 5, 1862   VA25
Converse, William - POW - Federal Soldier Died Feb. 14, 1862   VA19
Conway, J. - VA12
Conyers, J. - 9th South Carolina Vols.   VA18
Conyers, J.M. - Co. E 15th Georgia May 23, 1864   VA25
Cook, A. - Co. K 18th Georgia Oct. 2, 1861   VA25
Cook, A. - Co. F 11th South Carolina Aug. 4, 1864 VA25
Cook, A. - Co. A 27th Georgia June 10, 1862   VA25
Cook, C. - Co. K 18th Georgia June 4, 1862   VA25
Cook, Champ G. - KIA June 29, 1862   VA19
Cook, G.W. - Co. C 4th Georgia May 6, 1864   VA25
Cook, G.W. - Cobb's Legion (Georgia)   May 29, 1863 VA25
Cook, G.W. - Co. B 46th North Carolina July 27, 1864   VA25
Cook, Isaac F. - Sgt. - Co. G 13th Alabama   VA28
Cook, J. - Lt. - Co. G 3rd Alabama   May 14, 1863   VA25
Cook, J. - Co. E 2nd South Carolina   VA25
Cook, J. - Co. A 8th North Carolina March 7, 1865 VA25
Cook, J.A. - Co. A 27th Georgia June 10, 1862   VA25
Cook, J.B. - Pvt. - Co. A 34th Virginia Died June 18, 1865   VA26
Cook, J.C. - Pvt. - Georgia April 23, 1865   VA22
Cook, J.H. - Co. F 10th Alabama Feb. 8, 1863   VA25
Cook, J.J. - 3rd Alabama 1864   VA25
Cook, J.N. - Co. F 10th Alabama Oct. 29, 1864   VA25
Cook, J.T. - Co. F 19th Georgia Aug. 31, 1862   VA25
Cook, Jeremiah - Pvt. - Co. B 4th Georgia Died Jan. 13, 1863 in Ferguson's Hospital (Virginia) "J. Cook"   VA28
Cook, S. - Co. K 5th Texas Aug. 11, 1862   VA25
Cook, S.C. - Sgt. - 28th Mississippi Cavalry   1864 VA25
Cook, Simear - Virginia   VA20
Cook, W.P. - Co. D 15th North Carolina Feb. 10, 1865   VA25
Cook, Wm. - 7th Alabama Aug. 31, 1861   VA25
Cooke, John R. - General - Infantry   1833 - 1891   VA25
Cooksey, J.H. - Co. I 2nd Louisiana Aug. 7, 1862   VA25
Cooley, __ - Co. D 35th Georgia Sept. 17, 1862   VA25

Cooley, L. - Co. D 38th North Carolina June 14, 1864   VA25
Coombs, C. - Virginia March 5, 1864   VA25
Coonts, Edwin - Co. H 15th Virginia March 6, 1865
    Cemetery roster lists this soldier as "E. Coontz."
    VA24
Coontz, E. - See Edwin Coonts   VA24
Coontz, K. - Virginia   VA22
Cooper, A. - Co. I 61st Virginia June 13, 1865   VA25
Cooper, A.O. - Co. F 64th Georgia Jan. 24, 1864   VA25
Cooper, D. - Aug. 31, 1861 VA25
Cooper, G. - Co. A 43rd North Carolina May 27, 1864 VA25
Cooper, G. - Co. E 3rd North Carolina May 23, 1863 VA25
Cooper, G.W. - Co. H 17th Mississippi April 20, 1862 VA25
Cooper, H.A. - Ten   VA20
Cooper, Haley A. - Sgt. - Co. F 57th Virginia   VA28
Cooper, J.N. - Virginia July 8, 1864   VA25
Cooper, J.T. - Co. A 14th Georgia April 23, 1864   VA25
Cooper, L.T. - 21st __   VA18
Cooper, O.F. - Capt. - Co. C 2nd North Carolina Sept. 9, 1864
    VA25
Cooper, S.G. - South Carolina Jan. 17, 1865   VA25
Cooper, T. - Co. K 33rd North Carolina May 23, 1863 VA25
Cooper, T.W. - Co. I 47th Virginia Aug. 20, 1862   VA25
Cooper, W.H. - Co. K 54th Georgia Nov. 16, 1864   VA25
Coots, W. - Co. D 18th Virginia Cavalry   May 2, 1865
    VA25
Copeland, __ - POW - Federal Soldier Died June 16, 1862
    VA19
Copeland, A.H. - 5th Alabama Dec. 29, 1862   VA25
Copeland, David - 6th North Carolina   VA11
Copeland, J. - Co. B 17th Georgia Oct. 1, 1864   VA25
Copeland, R. - Co. F 28th North Carolina Aug. 3, 1862 VA25
Copeland, Robert - Nelson's Battery   VA28
Copenhaver, W.C. - 2nd Virginia Infantry   VA06
Coppla, N. - Co. G 1st Georgia March 1, 1865   VA25
Copwnnaver, M. - VA06

Corbert, V. - 1st Engineering Corps. Jan 23, 1864 VA25
Corbett, R.E. - Co. D 17th Virginia Infantry VA10
Corbin, __ - Co. A 1st South Carolina May 20, 1862 VA25
Corbin, G.B. - 9th Georgia VA18
Corbin, J.D. - Co. A 1st South Carolina Jan. 1, 1862 VA25
Corbin, J.W. - Co. H 1st Virginia Battalion 1865 VA25
Corbin, J.W. - Co. I 1st Virginia May 1, 1865 VA25
Corcoran, Dennis - Co. B Tiger Rifles (Wheat 1st Special Louisiana Battalion) - Executed Dec 9, 1861 VA16
Cord, G. - Co. D 18th Georgia Dec. 25, 1864 VA25
Cordell, S.I. - Pvt. - Co. A __North Carolina Died June 19, 1865 VA26
Cordla, T. - 45th North Carolina Aug. 1, 1863 VA25
Coreley, M. - Co. D 8th North Carolina Oct. 5, 1864 VA25
Cornbow, Thomas - Pvt. - North Carolina Aug. 21, 1864 VA22
Cornell, S. - Co. G 14th Tennessee Sept. 4, 1862 VA25
Cornett, C. - Co. C 21st Georgia May 21, 1862 VA25
Corney, C. - 21st South Carolina VA24
Cornwall, F.M. - Co. E 12th North Carolina - A farmer in Cleveland County, North Carolina, before the war. VA28
Corranter, __ - 12th Mississippi July 8, 1862 VA25
Correll, Jno. - Co. H 15th Alabama Died Jan 12, 1862 VA23
Correll, Rufus - Co. C 15th Alabama Died Nov 18, 1861 VA23
Cosbell, H. - Co. E 21st North Carolina May 5, 1864 VA25
Cosby, J.E. - Co. C 10th Virginia Artillery Battalion Oct. 27, 1864 VA25
Cosman, Wm. - Co. E 26th Georgia Aug. 16, 1862 VA25
Coster, D.D. - 8th Georgia VA18
Costner, J. - Co. H 37th North Carolina VA11
Coston, Frank - Co. E 7th Georgia Died Jan 6, 1862 VA23
Cotter, J. - Co. F 14th Alabama Aug. 18, 1862 VA25
Cotter, J.W. - Co. G 45th Georgia May 24, 1863 VA25
Cotton, Benjamin - 8th Louisiana VA18

Counts, P.W. - Co. H 13th South Carolina July 16, 1862 VA25
Courtney, D.S. - June 25, 1862 VA25
Courtney, W.B. - Co. I 5th Alabama July 29, 1862   VA25
Cover, C.L. - Co. D 14th South Carolina Nov. 19, 1862   VA25
Covington, B. - Co. G 9th Louisiana Dec. 17, 1862   VA25
Covington, G.T. - Co. E 57th North Carolina July 30, 1864 VA25
Covington, R.B. - Co. H 43rd North Carolina Feb. 25, 1864 VA25
Cowan, Robert W. - DOW July 7, 1862   VA19
Coward, __ - 8th South Carolina Oct. 8, 1862   VA25
Coward, A. - 9th Louisiana VA18
Cowart, __ - Co. M 16th North Carolina June 12, 1862 VA25
Cowen, J. - Co. B 22nd North Carolina May 14, 1862 VA25
Cowhart, J.T. - Virginia Artillery   1864   VA25
Cowley, __ - Capt. - Rifle Co.   May 28, 1862   VA25
Cowne, T. - Corp. - Co. E 28th South Carolina   Oct. 15, 1864 VA25
Cowsart, J.W. - Co. G 35th Georgia June 2, 1864   VA25
Cox, A.F. - 1st Texas June 2, 1862 VA25
Cox, D. - Co. D 22nd South Carolina Dec. 20, 1864   VA25
Cox, E. -   Virginia   VA20
Cox, Edward M. - Pvt. - Co. H Hampton's Legion Died June 23, 1865   VA26
Cox, Gambriel - 1st North Carolina   VA04
Cox, J.B. - 1st South Carolina June 14, 1862   VA25
Cox, J.F. - Co. H 14th North Carolina   VA11
Cox, J.H. - Co. B 6th Virginia June 17, 1862   VA25
Cox, J.S. - Co. E 3rd South Carolina Battalion   Sept. 6, 1862 VA25
Cox, J.S. - Co. E 3rd South Carolina Battalion Sept. 6, 1862 VA25
Cox, James - VA04
Cox, L.D. - Co. G 25th South Carolina Oct. 23, 1864   VA25

Cox, M.D. - Co. F 4th South Carolina June 20, 1864 VA25
Cox, S.J. - Co. H 4th Virginia Dec. 15, 1863   VA25
Cox, S.W. - Co. K 27th North Carolina Nov. 15, 1864   VA25
Cox, S.Y. - Co. A 10th Alabama July 5, 1862   VA25
Cox, W. - Co. G 38th Virginia May 31, 1862   VA25
Cox, W.A. - Co. B 24th North Carolina June 5, 1862 VA25
Cox, W.C. - Co. D 11th Mississippi Aug. 2, 1862   VA25
Cox, W.D. - 9th Alabama   VA18
Cox, W.H. - Lt. - Co. A 18th Alabama   March 12, 1865   VA25
Cox, Wm. - Co. C 37th North Carolina July 17, 1862   VA25
Crabtree, S. - Co. G 27th North Carolina Oct. 25, 1864   VA25
Craddock, D. - Georgia Artillery April 27, 1865   VA25
Craddock, H.A. - Lt. - Co. B 3rd South Carolina   May, 29, 1862   VA25
Craddock, H.M. - Co. H 13th South Carolina July 7, 1862   VA25
Craddock, R.J. - Co. I 3rd Virginia March 23, 1865   VA25
Craft, Irvin - Virginia   VA20
Craft, Jas. - Pvt. - Co. D 12th South Carolina July 31, 1864   VA22
Crafton, D. - Co. K 61st North Carolina Aug. 10, 1863   VA25
Crafton, J.W. - C.S. Navy   May 3, 1865   VA25
Craigg, __ - Aug. 12, 1864 VA25
Craigg, J.W. - Co. F 1st North Carolina Dec. 26, 1862 VA25
Craily, J.C. - 11th Virginia Infantry - KIA - Battle of Williamsburg - May 5, 1862   VA02
Crain, M. - Died Nov. 12, 1862   VA19
Crane, J.H. - 8th Louisiana June 26, 1862   VA25
Crann, W.F. - Co. F 13th Alabama Dec. 2, 1864   VA25
Cranor, C.C. - Co. D 4th Mississippi July 25, 1863   VA25
Craps, T.E. - Co. K 15th South Carolina July 8, 1862 VA25
Crason, E.R. - Co. H 4th Virginia Cavalry June 12, 1864   VA25
Craven, P.F. - 22nd North Carolina Sept. 2, 1862   VA25
Craver, J. - Co. B 53rd North Carolina Dec. 21, 1864   VA25

Craver, J.W. - Co. I 51st North Carolina July 29, 1864   VA25
Craw, G.W. - Co. C 18th Mississippi July 9, 1862   VA25
Crawford, C. - C.S. Navy   Nov. 8, 1864   VA25
Crawford, C.A. - Co. G 14th Alabama Feb. 16, 1862   VA25
Crawford, C.C. -   May 1, 1865   VA25
Crawford, G.B. - Pvt. - Co. B 12th Alabama   VA28
Crawford, George W. - Co. H 17th Georgia   VA11
Crawford, H. - South Carolina April 25, 1862   VA25
Crawford, H. - Co. K 8th Georgia May 16, 1862   VA25
Crawford, J.M. - Co. C 48th North Carolina Nov. 17, 1862   VA25
Crawford, Jas. - Georgia   VA20
Crawford, Jno. - Co. D 4th North Carolina June 14, 1862   VA25
Crawford, John - Co. F 7th Georgia June 2, 1864   VA25
Crawford, R. - 14th Louisiana. Infantry - KIA - Battle of Williamsburg - May 5, 1862   VA02
Crawford, R.C. - Co. K 48th Georgia Aug. 27, 1864   VA25
Crder, John - DOW March 17, 1863   age 23   VA19
Creacy, B. - Co. F 42nd Virginia June 20, 1863   VA25
Cready, W.P.M. - Co. C 18th Tennessee April 21, 1865   VA25
Creamer, J.W. - Co. F 12th Georgia   VA28
Creasu, T. - Co. C 21st North Carolina   VA11
Credle, Hezekiah - Co. F 23rd North Carolina   VA11
Creekman, L.H. - Co. H 8th Florida May 21, 1865   VA25
Cregg, J.W. - 15th Alabama Jan. 30, 1862   VA25
Creighton, H. - Co. D 26th Mississippi June 18, 1864   VA25
Creighton, Tom - Co. A 28th North Carolina June 20, 1862   VA25
Crenshaw, H.N. - Co. C 1st South Carolina Jan. 5, 1863 VA25
Crenshaw, J. - Co. F 24th Georgia June 1, 1862   VA25
Crew, A. - Co. F 12th Virginia July 5, 1862   VA25
Crew, A.M. - Georgia Jan. 8, 1863   VA25
Crews, Q.R. - Co. K 13th Alabama May 20, 1862   VA25
Cribbs, J.W. - 3rd North Carolina July 30, 1861   VA25

Cried, J. - Co. H 50th Georgia July 27, 1864   VA25
Criggs, J.D. - Co. D 40th Virginia May 24, 1863   VA25
Crim, John William - VA15
Crima, G.W. - Co. I 54th North Carolina Sept. 28, 1863
    VA25
Crimes, B.F. - Co. A 18th Mississippi July 5, 1862   VA25
Crin, J.J. - Co. I 18th Georgia Aug. 26, 1864   VA25
Crippini, J.J. - Co. C 17th Mississippi April 21, 1863 VA25
Crismond, Joseph Patrick Henry - Co. A 36th Virginia
    Cavalry   VA28
Crist, Joseph - VA12
Cristo, W.J. - Co. H 38th North Carolina June 20, 1862
    VA25
Crite, G.W. - Co. E 38th Georgia June 4, 1864   VA25
Crittard, W.L. - Co. B 51st Virginia Sept. 9, 1864   VA25
Crockett, Charles Gay - VMI Cadet -KIA - Battle of New
    Market - May 15, 1864 -Buried at VMI   VA21
Crockett, W.V. - Co. A 1st Tennessee May 10, 1863   VA25
Cromer, J.S. - Co. F 20th South Carolina Dec. 28, 1864
    VA25
Croner, P.F. - 22nd North Carolina Sept. 3, 1862   VA25
Cront, J.T. - Co. K 20th South Carolina   VA11
Crooke, P.O. - Virginia   VA20
Crooker, J.B. - Orr's Rifles (South Carolina)   May 25, 1864
    VA25
Croom, J. - Co. H 8th North Carolina March 31, 1865   VA25
Croom, William - Co. C 1st North Carolina   VA28
Crosby, P.S. - Co. K 5th Florida Sept. 29, 1862   VA25
Crosey, C.- 18th Virginia May 26, 1865   VA25
Cross, J.B. - Miller's Battalion April 7, 1865   VA25
Cross, J.W. - Co. B 11th Georgia Died Dec. 20, 1861 (?)
    VA23
Cross, R.J. - Capt. - Co. I 15th North Carolina   Sept. 26, 1864
    VA25
Cross, T. - Co. E 33rd North Carolina May 28, 1864 VA25
Cross, T.M. - Co. B 42nd Virginia Nov. 8, 1862   VA25

Cross, W.C. - Mississippi Oct. 30, 1862   VA25
Crouch, B. - Co. C 2nd North Carolina Sept. 2, 1862 VA25
Crouch, E. - Co. C 5th South Carolina Oct. 4, 1861 VA25
Crouch, L. - Co. G 37th North Carolina June 10, 1863   VA25
Crouch, M. - Co. F 31st Virginia June 4, 1864   VA25
Crow, D. - Co. E 1st South Carolina July 4, 1862 VA25
Crow, Michael - Co. I 11th Virginia   VA10
Crow, W.T. - Co. I 9th Alabama   VA11
Crowell, G.L. - Carroll County, Virginia   Oct. 5, 1861   VA25
Crowell, J.T. - Co. G 18th North Carolina May 29, 1863   VA25
Crowes, R. - Co. I 61st North Carolina July 11, 1864   VA25
Crowley, Michael - Co. D 17th Virginia Infantry   VA10
Cruber, W.B. - Corp. - Palmetto Sharp Shooters (South Carolina)   March 26, 1865   VA25
Cruise, R.T. - Co. E 26th North Carolina   VA11
Cruise, W.S. - Pvt. - Co. E 13th Alabama Died June 10, 1865 VA26
Crumby, W.C. - Co. G 16th Georgia May 23, 1864   VA25
Crumel, Z.R. - Lt. - Co. G 25th North Carolina July 25, 1862 VA25
Crumley, J. - Richmond Light Guard (Virginia) April 8, 1865 VA25
Crump, C. - Co. A 10th Alabama Aug. 17. 1862   VA25
Crump, D. - Co. F 11th Virginia Sept. 2, 1862   VA25
Crump, J.W. - 5th Alabama Sept. 3, 1861   VA25
Crump, R.G. - Co. I 10th Alabama April 14, 1863   VA25
Crumpley, R.M. - Co. C 56th North Carolina June 24, 1864 VA25
Crunch, D. - Co. G 9th Virginia Oct. 18, 1863   VA25
Crutchfield, R.D. - Co. B 35th North Carolina Aug. 2, 1862 VA25
Cual, F.H. - Burgess's Battery (Florida) Aug. 10, 1862   VA25
Culbert, __ - Co. K 7th Virginia Aug. 7, 1862   VA25
Culbert, J. - Co. I 38th Virginia June 2, 1862   VA25
Culbert, M.B. - Co. K 16th Virginia Aug. 7, 1862   VA25

Culbert, P. - Co. G 2nd Georgia Aug. 18, 1862   VA25
Culbertson, J.W. - Co. E 16th North Carolina June 4, 1864   VA25
Culbertson, J.W. - South Carolina Jan. 10, 1863   VA25
Culburth, H.L. - 5th South Carolina Nov. 30, 1862   VA25
Cullars, S. - Co. I 14th Tennessee Aug. 7, 1862   VA25
Culleck, G.W. - Co. H 37th North Carolina June 9, 1862   VA25
Cullen, M. - Co. D 18th Virginia   VA08
Cullens, __ - Camp Lee - Virginia Aug. 8, 1862   VA25
Culler, J.H. - Co. I 21st North Carolina Nov. 6, 1862 VA25
Cumings, F.W. - Co. K 11th South Carolina Aug. 31, 1864   VA25
Cumings, J. - Corp. - Co. H 48th Mississippi Oct. 19, 1864   VA25
Cumings, J. - Co. E 27th South Carolina Sept. 14, 1862   VA25
Cumings, W.F. - North Carolina Artillery June 9, 1864   VA25
Cumings, W.T. - Co. K 14th Alabama   May 29, 1862   VA25
Cumley, __ - 8th Alabama Nov. 1, 1862   VA25
Cumley, J. - Patterson's Artillery   May 20, 1862   VA25
Cumming, John - 7th Louisiana VA18
Cumpton, L.H. - Co. C 6th South Carolina July 17, 1864   VA25
Cunch, B. - Co. C 2nd North Carolina Sept. 3, 1862 VA25
Cundiff, G.W. - Pvt. - Co. B 10th Virginia Bat .Died May 25, 1865   VA26
Cune, __ - 10th Louisiana 1862   VA25
Cungham, Jan - POW - Federal Soldier Died Dec. 11, 1861   VA19
Cunningham, A.J. - Capt. - Co. H 4th South Carolina July 3, 1864   VA25
Cunningham, __ - Co. K 45th Georgia July 1862   VA25
Cunningham, E. - Virginia July 9, 1862   VA25
Cunningham, G.M. - Died Nov. 20, 1862   VA19
Cunningham, J. - Co. A 14th Alabama Jan. 26, 1863   VA25

Cunningham, James - POW - Federal Soldier Died Oct. - 22, 1861   VA19
Cunningham, James - 5th South Carolina May 26, 1864   VA25
Cunningham, James W. - Co. I 33rd Virginia   VA28
Cunningham, Jo. Tho. - Died July 11, 1862   VA19
Curl, A. - Co. E 31st North Carolina Oct. 8, 1863 VA25
Curles, ____ - M. Artillery   Oct. 8, 1862   VA25
Curran, A. - Co. F 66th North Carolina June 24, 1864   VA25
Currella, C. - 11th Georgia Oct. 24, 1862   VA25
Currie, J.C. - "Doctor" - Kentucky Aug. 26, 1863   VA25
Curry, __ - Co. I 5th Florida Nov. 7, 1862   VA25
Curry, B. - Co. C 6th Florida June 27, 1864   VA25
Curry, F.P. - see Curry, J.R. .   VA28
Curry, J.K. - see Curry, J.R. .   VA28
Curry, J.R. - Co. C 16th Mississippi Died May 12, 1864
    Headstone reads: "F.P. Curry" service record reads: "T.K. Curry"VA28
Curry, N.W. - Co. A 6th South Carolina Aug. 8, 1864 VA25
Curry, W.F. - 15th Georgia VA18
Curtis, __ - Co. H 15th North Carolina Nov. 4, 1862 VA25
Cussack, W. - Co. K 1st Kentucky April 7, 1862   VA25
Cutchings, O.B. - 41st Virginia Aug. 7, 1862   VA25
Cuthbertson, Wm. S. - Pvt. - Co. K 5th North Carolina Died June 28, 1865   VA26
Cutley, A.P. - Co. F 20th South Carolina Aug. 18, 1864   VA25
Cutter, W.H. - Co. C 2nd Alabama March 26, 1863   VA25
D____, J.B. - 61st Georgia Aug. 1862   VA25
D____, J.B. - Co. I 67th Georgia Dec. 22, 1862   VA25
D____, M.B. - 4th Texas Dec. 22, 1862   VA25
Dacus, D.U.M. - Co. F Hampton's Georgia Legion   May 15, 1864   VA25
Dailey, __ Capt. - Co. A 1st Louisiana July 1862   VA25
Dailey, J.J. - Co. F 6th Alabama Aug. 30, 1862   VA25
Dailey, J.L. - Georgia Sept. 26, 1862   VA25

Dailey, P. - Co. B 35th Georgia Sept. 22, 1862   VA25
Dainback, J. - Co. I 2nd North Carolina Feb. 26, 1865 VA25
Daisy, John 8th Alabama Infantry - KIA - Battle of
    Williamsburg - May 5, 1862   VA02
Dale, J. - Co. B 21st Georgia Nov. 16, 1862   VA25
Dale, J.C. - Co. G 42nd North Carolina Nov. 7, 1864 VA25
Dale, J.N. - 13th Georgia VA18
Dale, T.J. - Co. B 33rd North Carolina Nov. 6, 1862 VA25
Dale, W.P. - Co. K 28th Georgia May 12, 1862   VA25
Dale, W.W. - Co. C 48th North Carolina June 26, 1862
    VA25
Dale, W.N. - Co. B 3rd North Carolina May 27, 1864 VA25
Dalton, J.W. - Co. F 51st Virginia   VA11
Dalton, S.C. - 47th Virginia VA18
Dalty, D.C. - Co. C 46th Virginia June 18, 1862   VA25
Dampeer, Stephen W. - Sgt. - Co. B 16th Mississippi Died
    May 12, 1864 Headstone reads: "Dampier"   VA28
Dampier, John W. - Pvt. - Co. C 26th Georgia Died Jan. 6,
    1864   VA28
Dampier, Stephen W. - see Dampeer, Stephen W.   VA28
Dance, D.H. - Co. G 25th North Carolina Dec. 22, 1862
    VA25
Daniel, A.M. - Co. I 1st South Carolina   VA28
Daniel, I.B. - Co. C 35th Georgia April 17, 1865   VA25
Daniel, J.B. - Co. C 35th Georgia April 19, 1865   VA25
Daniel, J.L. - Pegram's Battery July 23, 1864   VA25
Daniel, J.L. - Jones' Light Artillery   March 23, 1863   VA25
Daniel, J.R. - Co. G 30th Georgia July 27, 1862   VA25
Daniel, R.A. - 3rd South Carolina Feb. 8, 1863   VA25
Daniel, T.S. - Co. C 35th Georgia Sept. 4, 1862   VA25
Daniel, T.S. - Co. C 32nd Georgia Sept. 4, 1862   VA25
Daniel, W. - Co. H 4th Georgia June 19, 1862   VA25
Daniel, W. - Co. C 28th North Carolina June 24, 1862   VA25
Daniel, W.M. - 13th North Carolina   VA18
Daniel, Z. - Corp. - Co. B 2nd Georgia Battalion   Nov. 5,
    1862   VA25

Dansley, W.H.R. - Lt. - Co. A 9th Louisiana April 23, 1865 VA25

Dantler, Q. - 2nd South Carolina May 29, 1864   VA25

Danty, A. - Co. I 67th Georgia Feb. 25, 1865   VA25

Danville, __ - Kemper's Battery   VA10

Darby, J.J. - Co. F 23rd South Carolina Aug. 26, 1862   VA25

Darden, Henry J. - Pvt. - Co. D 6th Georgia Died April 3, 1863 VA28

Darden, T.R. - Virginia - age 63   VA25

Dargan, P. - 8th Alabama Infantry - KIA - Battle of Williamsburg - May 5, 1862   VA02

Dargin, J. - Co. C 60th Virginia July 4, 1862   VA25

Darley, C. - Co. F 1st Louisiana June 25, 1862   VA25

Darlton, J. - Co. A 24th South Carolina Oct. 23, 1862   VA25

Darlton, S. - Co. D 24th Virginia June 17, 1865   VA25

Darlton, W. - Sumpter Artillery (South Carolina) June 3, 1862 VA25

Darnett, F.P. - Co. F 1st South Carolina Jan. 1, 1863 VA25

Darold, W.H. - VA20

Darpsey, L. - Co. A 14th Georgia April 16, 1865   VA25

Darrow, J.B. - Co. D 28th North Carolina Jan. 11, 1863 VA25

Dartson, W.C. - 7th Virginia VA18

Dashier, John W. - Virginia   VA28

Dason, __ - 1st Texas July 5, 1862   VA25

Daton, M.B. - Co. G 13th South Carolina July 8, 1862 VA25

Datson, A.C. - Co. A 37th North Carolina May 14, 1863 VA25

Daugherty, J. -   VA06

Daughty, Elias - Co. K 12th Georgia name on headstone - "Doharty"   VA28

Dav (?), H. - Co H 8th ____ Died March 1862   VA23

Davenport, __ - Sgt. DOW Aug. 7, 1862 age 21   VA19

Davenport, J. - Co. H 17th North Carolina Nov. 7, 1864 VA25

Davenport, J.M. - Co. C 23rd South Carolina Feb. 13, 1865 VA25

Davenport, Martha - "C.S.A." Dec. 27, 1862   VA25
Davenport, S. - 3rd Georgia July 3, 1864   VA25
David, F.M. - 16th Georgia Oct. 5, 1863   VA25
David, H. - 6th South Carolina Oct. 3, 1862   VA25
David, J. - Surgeon - Co. C 12th Georgia July 16, 1864   VA25
Davidson, J. - Lt. - Co. H 31st Georgia   Sept. 6, 1862   VA25
Davidson, J.M. - Co. H 15th North Carolina July 20, 1864   VA25
Davidson, R.B. - Co. E 37th North Carolina June 8, 1864   VA25
Davidson, R.J. - Co. I 35th Georgia June 8, 1864   VA25
Davidson, T. J. - Colonel - 3rd Mississippi   1862   VA25
Davidson, T.J. - Co. C 13th Mississippi Aug. 8, 1862   VA25
Davidson, W. - Co. B 7th Louisiana Dec. 27, 1862   VA25
Davidson, W.B. - Co. G 9th Louisiana. Dec. 20, 1862   VA25
Davis, A. - Co. A 44th North Carolina Oct. 2, 1864 VA25
Davis, A. - Co. H 55th Virginia June 12, 1862   VA25
Davis, Addison - Mosby's Cavalry   VA10
Davis, Barlett - Lt. - Co. K 32nd North Carolina Died May 12, 1864   VA28
Davis, C. - 35th Georgia June 10, 1862   VA25
Davis, C. - Co. D 48th North Carolina Nov. 12, 1862   VA25
Davis, E.J. - 11th Alabama Aug. 13, 1861   VA25
Davis, E.T. - Mosby's Cavalry   VA10
Davis, E.W. - Co. K 40th North Carolina May 27, 1865 VA25
Davis, F. - Co. I 4th North Carolina May 26, 1862   VA25
Davis, F. - Co. K 5th South Carolina Aug. 2, 1862 VA25
Davis, G.D. - Hardaway's Batt. July 28, 1862   VA25
Davis, G.H. - Co. I 12th __ May 26, 186_   VA25
Davis, H. - 11th North Carolina July 1864   VA25
Davis, H.A. - Pvt. - North Carolina April 24, 1864   VA22
Davis, H.T. - Co. I 17th Georgia July 24, 1862   VA25
Davis, I.L. - Co. A 50th Georgia May 24, 1863   VA25
Davis, J. - VA06
Davis, J. - Pvt. - Co. F 9th Georgia Died June 23, 1865   VA26

Davis, J. - Co. A 63rd North Carolina Dec. 3, 1863 VA25
Davis, J. - Co. I 25th North Carolina Aug. 23, 1864   VA25
Davis, J.A. Sumpter Artillery (South Carolina)   May 21, 1862 VA25
Davis, J.C. - Co. B 46th Virginia Battalion   May 12, 1865 VA25
Davis, J.C. - 30th North Carolina Dec. 26, 1863   VA25
Davis, J.E. - Co. C 13th South Carolina March 3, 1865   VA25
Davis, J.G. - Orr's Rifles (South Carolina) Aug. 24, 1862 VA25
Davis, J.H. - Co. I 21st South Carolina Aug. 12, 1864   VA25
Davis, J.H. - Co. K 30th North Carolina March 13, 1865 VA25
Davis, J.L. - Sgt. - Co. C 18th Georgia Died June 12, 1865 VA26
Davis, J.P. - Co. K 1st North Carolina Oct. 25, 1864 VA25
Davis, J.R. - Co. C 8th Georgia Died Feb. 25, 1862 VA23
Davis, J.R. - Co. B 13th North Carolina Jan. 25, 1863   VA25
Davis, J.R. - 2nd Virginia June 5, 1862   VA25
Davis, J.R. - Co. I 27th Georgia June 5, 1862   VA25
Davis, J.S. - Corp. - Co. B 2nd South Carolina Rifles Died April 5, 1863   VA03
Davis, J.T. - Co. G 21st Georgia March 13, 1863   VA25
Davis, J.W. - Co. D 14th Alabama Aug. 6, 1862   VA25
Davis, Jefferson - President of the Confederacy - 1808 - 1889 VA25
Davis, Jno. - South Carolina Artillery   May 4, 1862 VA25
Davis, John - see Davis, William A. J.
Davis, John B. - Mosby's Cavalry   VA10
Davis, John Bennet - Partisan ranger (Virginia)   VA04
Davis, Joseph - son of Jefferson Davis - President of the Confederacy VA25
Davis, M. - Co. H 26th North Carolina May 16, 1863 VA25
Davis, N.G. - 10th Louisiana Sept. 30, 1861   VA25
Davis, R. - Co. I 2nd North Carolina May 15, 1863 VA25
Davis, R.P. - Co. E 35th Georgia July 13, 1862   VA25

Davis, Robert W. - Pvt. - Co. E 5th Virginia Cavalry KIA at Todd's Tavern - May 7, 1864   VA28
Davis, S.C. - Feb. 13, 1863 VA25
Davis, T. - Co. D 14th Virginia Aug. 26, 1862   VA25
Davis, W. - Co. D 25th North Carolina Aug. 1, 1864 VA25
Davis, W.J. - 11th Mississippi   VA18
Davis, W.M. - Co. B 2nd North Carolina Feb. 20, 1863 VA25
Davis, William A. J. - Co. C 4th Georgia Other records list this soldier as "John Davis" VA28
Davis, Wm. - Co. K 14th Alabama Aug. 26, 1862   VA25
Davis, Wm. J. - Co. I 57th Virginia Died May 5, 1863 VA03
Davison, O.C. - Co. H 5th Alabama Aug. 20, 1862   VA25
Davison, Robert E. - Sgt. - Co. F 21st Mississippi MW May 8, 1864 Died May 16, 1864 Born in Tennessee   VA28
Davrils, C. - North Carolina Aug. 12, 1863   VA25
Daw, J. - Co. B 44th North Carolina Oct. 22, 1863   VA25
Daw, J.W. - Co. D 15th South Carolina May 22, 1864 VA25
Dawdy, E.N.G. - May 16, 1863 VA25
Daws, E. - 2nd Florida Aug. 31, 1861   VA25
Dawson, Adam P. - Pvt. - Co. B 15th Georgia Died May 10, 1864   VA28
Dawson, R.H. - Co. E 2nd Maryland April 24, 1865   VA25
Dawson, T. - Co. A 23rd South Carolina Sept. 2, 1864   VA25
Dawson, W. - Battle's Brigade (Alabama)   VA28
Dawson, W.H. - Co. K 19th Georgia Infantry   VA10
Dawson, W.H. - Co. H 19th Georgia May 19, 1864   VA25
Dawson, W.R. - Co. C 44th Alabama Sept. 2, 1864   VA25
Day, Conrad E. - Jeff Davis Legion   VA18
Day, I.B. - Co. F 12th South Carolina Dec. 21, 1863   VA25
Day, W.W. - 21st Virginia VA18
Dayhart, George - Co. F 37th North Carolina June 10, 1863   VA25
Dayley, J.H. - Co. C 35th Georgia June 20, 1862   VA25
Dayton, _ - July 2, 1862 VA25
De Saussure, H. - Lt. - 6th South Carolina   VA25
De Watt, __ - VA25

De Watt, N.B. - VA25
Deal, __ - Co. A 5th Alabama June 27, 1862 VA25
Deal, M.M. - Co. K 46th North Carolina July 22, 1864 VA25
Deal, S.C. - Co. F 2nd South Carolina May 22, 1862 VA25
Deal, Thos. - Co. G 2nd North Carolina May 21, 1862 VA25
Dean, H. - Co. F 19th Alabama Aug. 17, 1862 VA25
Dean, J.W. - Co. E 19th Georgia Aug. 14, 1862 VA25
Dean, W.V. - Co. F 13th Alabama June 25, 1862 VA25
Deapt, __ - Co. B 5th Alabama July 2, 1862 VA25
Dearmont, J. - Clark Cavalry VA06
Deason, W. - Co. C 1st Texas July 3, 1862 VA25
Deaton, A.S. - Co. I 7th North Carolina May 10, 1863 VA25
Deaver, T. - Co. I 62nd North Carolina May 27, 1865 VA25
Debman, T.R. - Co. G 44th North Carolina Aug. 8, 1864
    VA25
Debo, W.L. - 28th Virginia April 23, 1862 VA25
Debode, Jno. - Alabama Oct. 27, 1862 VA25
DeBouse, J.F. - Pvt. - 18th North Carolina Infantry DOW
    June 21, 1862 VA09
Debtor, C. - Co. F 23rd North Carolina May 23, 1862 VA25
Debtor, J. - 2nd Virginia Infantry VA06
Debusk, Andrew J. - Pvt. - Co. F 37th Virginia Cavalry Died
    May 12, 1864 VA28
Dechard, David M. - see Deckerd, David M. VA28
Deckerd, David M. - Capt. - Co. A 4th Texas KIA -
    Wilderness - May 6, 1864 Headstone reads: "Co. E -
    Dechard" VA28
Dees, Joel - Kelly's Light Artillery (South Carolina) Died
    June 7, 1863 VA03
Defenback, Wilhelmina - Civilian - Killed in explosion of C.S.
    Laboratory - March 15, 1863 age 15 VA19
Degaffenreed, Major - Georgia VA22
Deitz, Jacob - POW - Federal Soldier Died Oct. 27, 1861
    VA19
DeJarnett, James P. - Co. G 3rd Alabama Died May 12, 1864
    VA28

Delbridge, A.W. - Co. B 3rd Alabama Aug. 30, 1862   VA25
Delbridge, T. - 33rd Alabama Aug. 29, 1862   VA25
Delvuch, M. - Co. A 15th North Carolina Aug. 22, 1864   VA25
Demperge, J.W. - Sgt. - Co. H 12th Georgia July 22, 1864   VA25
Demsey, L.C. - Co. D 14th Georgia April 13, 1865   VA25
Denal, O. - Co. G 1st Virginia May 14, 1862   VA25
Denian, James - Co. I 6th Alabama April 26, 1862   VA25
Denkins, S. - 3rd South Carolina Battalion Jan. 7, 1863   VA25
Denmark, J.J. - Georgia Sept. 23, 1861   VA25
Dennard, F.M. - Co. D 18th Georgia June 12, 1862   VA25
Dennard, J.E. - Co. B 14th Georgia Oct. 27, 1864   VA25
Dennis, J.R. - Pvt. - Co. F 11th South Carolina Died June 16, 1865   VA26
Dennis, John Y. - Pvt. - Co. K 44th Georgia DOW May 18, 1864   VA28
Dennis, S. - 17th Mississippi Aug. 10, 1861   VA25
Dennis, Singleton - 6th Alabama   VA18
Dennis, W.D.T. - Co. A 12th Georgia   VA11
Dennis, W.J. - Jefferson Davis's Artillery Jan. 9, 1863   VA25
Dennon, W.T. - Co. A 27th Georgia Aug. 1, 1864   VA25
Dennyson, Andrew - POW - Federal Soldier Died Feb. 3, 1862   VA19
Denson, A. - Co. C 9th Louisiana Dec. 26, 1862   VA25
Denson, F. - Co. F 27th Georgia July 17, 1862   VA25
Dent, E.L. - 15th Georgia Sept. 30, 1861   VA25
Dent, J.J. - Co. G 15th Georgia Dec. 7, 1862   VA25
Dent, W. - Co. H 48th Georgia May 18, 1863   VA25
Derrer, Marcus - Pvt. - South Carolina May 13, 1865   VA22
Deshields, G. - Co. B 7th North Carolina Sept. 2, 1864   VA25
Desmaret, James - Co. F 8th Louisiana July 23, 1862   VA25
Detson, J. - Co. H 14th North Carolina May 12, 1864   VA25
Devenport, C. - Co. C 19th Georgia June 4, 1862   VA25

Devereur, Wm. J. - POW - Federal Soldier Died Dec. 4, 1861 VA19
Dews, A. - Co. H 26th Georgia July 28, 1863   VA25
Dews, J. - Co. D 8th Alabama June 1, 1863   VA25
Dial, J.J. - Co. G 35th Georgia Dec. 7, 1863   VA25
Dial, P.T. - Co. C 51st North Carolina July 22, 1864   VA25
Dickens, E. - Co. C 21st North Carolina June 3, 1864 VA25
Dickerson, D.A. - Co. I 28th North Carolina Jan. 24, 1865 VA25
Dickerson, M. - Co. D 4th South Carolina Oct. 27, 1862 VA25
Dickerson, W. - Co. F 47th North Carolina July 24, 1863 VA25
Dickey, John - Co. A 3rd Georgia Oct. 1, 1862   VA25
Dickhard, W.F. - Aug. 14, 1861 VA25
Dickson, D.W. - Co. K 15th Georgia Nov. 18, 1862   VA25
Dickson, H. - 14th Georgia Aug. 1862   VA25
Dickson, J.W. -   VA20
Dickson, William Irvine - Lt. - Co. C Orr's Rifles (South Carolina) Headstone reads: "1st South Carolina Rifles" VA28
Dight, A.L. - Co. H 38th North Carolina Aug. 13, 1864   VA25
Dillard, J. - Co. K 35th Tennessee March 10, 1865   VA25
Dillard, S.H. - Co. D 1st North Carolina March 8, 1865 VA25
Dillard, S.J. - 14th Alabama Aug. 4, 1862   VA25
Dillard, T.J. - Co. C 13th South Carolina Aug. 7, 1862 VA25
Dillion, Henry - VA12
Dilph, A.H. - North Carolina Cavalry July 4, 1864 VA25
Dingler, Miles M. - Pvt. - Co. H 4th North Carolina KIA Fredericksburg VA28
Dinkle, C.A. - Co. C 5th Virginia April 25, 1865   VA25
Dinsdla, J. - Co. K 64th Georgia Oct. 10, 1864   VA25
Diser, __ - Co. B 6th Alabama July 5, 1862   VA25
Dishman, L. - 2nd Virginia Infantry   VA06
Dishman, Robert L. - Co. A 15th Virginia Cavalry Died May 7, 1864 VA28

Dison, Leroy - POW - Federal Soldier Died Apr. 18, 1862 VA19
Divers, H. - Co. D 16th Virginia VA11
Divine, J.M. - Co. D 14th North Carolina Sept. 9, 1862 VA25
Dix, James H. - son of James H. and Catharine C. Dix of Accomak May 3, 1849 - Sept. 9, 1861 VA02
Dixen, S.H. - Co. F 8th North Carolina Infantry VA08
Dixon, _ - Artillery July 6, 1862 VA25
Dixon, A.B. - 2nd Florida Sept. 31, 1861 VA25
Dixon, A.J. - Co. G 14th North Carolina Sept. 6, 1862 VA25
Dixon, H. - Co. D 20th South Carolina Oct. 15, 1864 VA25
Dixon, J. - July 28, 1861 VA25
Dixon, J.C. - Co. K 7th Mississippi July 11, 1862 VA25
Dixon, J.G. - 4th Texas June 1, 1862 VA25
Dixon, J.H. - Co. E 27th Georgia June 5, 1862 VA25
Dixon, J.J. - Co. D 14th North Carolina Aug. 18, 1862 VA25
Dixon, J.L. - Georgia VA20
Dixon, J.M. - Pvt. - Co. D 18th Virginia Artillery Died May 23, 1865 VA26
Dixon, T. - VA12
Dixon, T.J. - Co. C 14th Georgia Jan. 13, 1863 VA25
Dixon, W.K. - Co. A 21st Georgia June 25, 1862 VA25
Dobbin, J.J. - VA06
Dobins, J. - Co. I 28th North Carolina May 27, 1863 VA25
Dobson, James - Co. H 4th North Carolina July 4, 1862 VA25
Dockerty, M. - Co. F 14th Louisiana June 16, 1862 VA25
Dodcets, __ - South Carolina Aug. 7, 1861 VA25
Dodd, G.W. - 4th South Carolina VA18
Dodd, Jas. - Co. I 24th Georgia May 26, 1862 VA25
Dodd, John B. - Died May 17, 1864 age 12 VA19
Dodson, E.E. - Co. H 14th Louisiana Aug. 25, 1862 VA25
Dodson, R.A. - Co. H 14th Alabama Aug. 6, 1862 VA25
Doggett, G. - 3rd Georgia Aug. 12, 1862 VA25
Doggett, T. - 5th Georgia VA18
Doharty, Elias - see Daughty, Elias VA28

Doity, M.J. - Sgt. - Co. A 20th South Carolina Jan. 1, 1865 VA25

Doles, T.J. - Georgia   VA20

Dolin, J. - 3rd Washington Artillery   VA18

Domiricky, D.H.J. - Co. A 1st Louisiana June 8, 1863   VA25

Donahoe, W.M. - Co. G 35th Georgia May 13, 1863   VA25

Donahue, S.R. - Sgt. - Co. H 6th North Carolina Died May 21, 1865   VA26

Donald, John A. - McGregor's Artillery   VA28

Donald, P.B. - Co. G 8th Virginia June 5, 1862   VA25

Donald, P.O. - Co. I 17th Mississippi July 24, 1863   VA25

Donaldson, W.F. - Co. F __th Kentucky Aug. 7, 1861   VA25

Donell, W. - 1st Louisiana May 15, 1862   VA25

Donerve, W.A. - Co. H 6th North Carolina Jan. 10, 1865 VA25

Donman, D.A. - Co. H 1st Florida Aug. 4, 1864   VA25

Donn, A.O. - Co. C 1st South Carolina June 15, 1863 VA25

Donohoe, __ - Co. K 6th Louisiana May 16, 1862   VA25

Donohoe, W. - Co. H 18th Georgia July 31, 1862   VA25

Donwood, W.C. - Co. C 20th Virginia July 28, 1865   VA25

Dood, John B. - KIA May 7, 1864 age 12   VA19

Dooley, John - Co. A 26th Mississippi Dec. 2, 1864   VA25

Doraty, John - age 24 KIA Oct. 7, 1864   VA19

Dore, J.M. - 8th South Carolina   VA18

Dorman, __ - 5th North Carolina Nov. 6, 1862   VA25

Dorn, J. - Corp. - Co. K 15th South Carolina June 27, 1864 VA25

Dorns, J.B. - Confederate Guards   Oct. 13, 1863   VA25

Dornwood, H.C. - Co. C 28th Virginia July 28, 1864   VA25

Dorsay, W.A. - Co. H 3rd Georgia May 24, 1862   VA25

Dorsey, B. - Co. C 13th Alabama July 16, 1862   VA25

Dorsey, R. - Co. F 66th North Carolina July 5, 1864 VA25

Doty, M.J. - Sgt. - Co. A 20th South Carolina Jan. 1, 1865 VA25

Doughlass, John E. - POW - Federal Soldier Died June 8, 1862   VA19

Doughtry, R. - Co. F 2nd North Carolina VA11
Douglas, J.O.J. - Co. K 37th North Carolina VA11
Douglass, E. - Co. G 2nd Louisiana Sept. 4, 1862 VA25
Douglass, J.R. - Co. H 6th Georgia June 15, 1862 VA25
Douglass, Jackson - Georgia VA20
Douglass, L. - Co. C 31st Georgia Feb. 20, 1865 VA25
Douglass, W.H. - Co. B 3rd South Carolina Sept. 9, 1862 VA25
Dounger, William - Died Oct. 26, 1861 VA19
Dove, A. - Co. D 17th Virginia Infantry VA10
Dove, M.H. - Co. G 53rd Virginia June 12. 1862 VA25
Dover, F.P. - Co. D 14th North Carolina May 23, 1862 VA25
Dowden, J.D. - Co. G 28th Virginia July 1, 1864 VA25
Dowden, John - Co. B 5th North Carolina April 25, 1862 VA25
Dowdy, Z. - Sgt. - Co. D 5th North Carolina Jan. 20, 1863 VA25
Downan, R.S. - Co. C 1st Tennessee Dec. 11, 1864 VA25
Downey, C. - 16th North Carolina March 14, 1862 VA25
Downey, G.D. - 4th North Carolina Sept. 22, 1864 VA25
Downing, J.F. - Co. K 1st Ten Aug. 11, 1862 VA25
Downs, R.S. - Co. G 1st North Carolina Aug. 17, 1862 VA25
Dowry, G.W. - Co. K 46th North Carolina Sept. 22, 1864 VA25
Doylass, D.P. - Co. F 12th South Carolina July 5, 1862 VA25
Doyle, J.J. - Co. B 9th Louisiana May 24, 1863 VA25
Doyle, R.G.D. - Co. A 4th Texas July 7, 1862 VA25
Dozier, John A. - Pvt. - Co. F 12th Georgia Died May 10, 1864 VA28
Drake, T. - Co. K 28th Georgia July 30, 1864 VA25
Drees, W.C. - Co. G 7th South Carolina July 6, 1862 VA25
Drew, R. - Co. I 7th South Carolina Dec. 22, 1862 VA25
Drewry, I.H. - 13th Virginia May 12, 1864 VA25
Drigens, H. - Co. C 11th South Carolina June 6, 1864 VA25
Driggins, J.A. - Co. G 23rd South Carolina Aug. 30, 1862 VA25

Driggs, P. - Co. G 23rd North Carolina Aug. 29, 1862   VA25
Drink, S. - Phillips' Legion (Georgia) Dec. 24, 1862   VA25
Drinkard, J.P. - Co. H 13th South Carolina July 8, 1862 VA25
Drinkard, W.A. - Co. A 2nd South Carolina Aug. 17, 1862   VA25
Drinkens, H.K. - Co. K 1st South Carolina Sept. 19, 1863   VA25
Driscoe, Jno. - Co. F 14th Louisiana July 2, 1862   VA25
Driven, W. - Co. E 7th North Carolina Sept. 30, 1864   VA25
Driver, William Giles - Corp. - Co. A 13th Georgia DOW May 13, 1864 (MW May 12, 1864) VA28
Drum, D. - Co. G 37th North Carolina Aug. 15, 1862   VA25
Drum, W.J. - Co. G 2nd South Carolina Aug. 5, 1863 VA25
Drummon, __ - Died Nov. 22, 1862   VA19
Drustly, Margaret - Civilian -Killed in explosion of C.S. Laboratory - March 15, 1863 age 16   VA19
Dubberly, William W. - Pvt. - Co. B 61st Georgia KIA - Fredericksburg Dec. 13, 1862 VA28
Duchamp, Arthur - Ensign - Co. C 8th Louisiana Died May 11, 1864   VA28
Dudenheim, Albert - Co. B 8th Louisiana   This soldier's name is listed in Napier Bartlett's *Military Record of Louisiana*, however he is not listed in the cemetery's burial records. VA28
Dudley, M.P. - Pvt. - Co. H 57th Virginia Died June 2, 1865   VA26
Duett, J. - Co. C 26th South Carolina July 24, 1864   VA25
Duffeys, M. - Co. K 6th Louisiana May 22, 1863   VA25
Duffy, F. - Georgia   VA20
Duffy, Rosen M. - Co. I 6th South Carolina Died May 13, 1863 VA03
Dugger, T.J. - Co. C 5th Florida Sept. 22, 1862   VA25
Duke, __ - Cobb's Legion (Georgia) July 1, 1862   VA25
Duke, __ - 26th Georgia July 1862   VA25
Duke, A.G. - Co. H 27th Georgia Sept. 9, 1862   VA25
Duke, E. - Georgia   VA20

Duke, H. - Sgt. - Co. F 21st South Carolina Aug. 8, 1864 VA25
Duke, M.O. - Co. I 13th Alabama March 1863 VA25
Duke, Nathan T. - Co. I 15th Alabama VA11
Duke, R.W. - Co. H 27th Georgia Sept. 9, 1862 VA25
Duke, T.S. Virginia - Killed at Harper's Ferry - July 28, 1862 VA25
Duke, William W. - Pvt. - Co. H 59th Georgia Died May 10, 1864 VA28
Dukery, J. - Co. A 3rd Georgia Nov. 17, 1862 VA25
Dulany, D. French - Mosby's Cavalry VA10
Dumbar, James - Co. E 6th South Carolina VA11
Dumfry, A.J. - Co. B 14th Georgia June 15, 1863 VA25
Dun, John - Co. D 5th North Carolina VA11
Duncan, B. - Co. C 1st South Carolina May 24, 1862 VA25
Duncan, B.C. - Co. I 7th South Carolina Aug. 30, 1862 VA25
Duncan, J. Pvt.- Co. B 31st Virginia VA28
Duncan, J. - VA12
Duncan, J.C. - Pvt. - North Carolina Aug. 9, 1864 VA22
Duncan, J.C. 1st South Carolina July 7, 1864 VA25
Duncan, M.P. - Co. E 10th Georgia Sept. 22, 1864 VA25
Dunford, __ - Co. G 23rd South Carolina Nov. 18, 1862 VA25
Dunigan, J. - Co. F 49th Georgia July 6, 1862 VA25
Dunlap, R.M. - Co. H 5th South Carolina Aug. 24, 1862 VA25
Dunlap, William - Co. A 41st North Carolina VA11
Dunlop, __ - Sgt. - July 10, 1862 VA25
Dunlop, J.W. - Co. A 6th South Carolina Sept. 17, 1864 VA25
Dunlop, W.G. - Georgia Sept. 30, 1861 VA25
Dunn, __ - Co. H 37th North Carolina July 29, 1863 VA25
Dunn, D. - Co. C 12th South Carolina July 30, 1864 VA25
Dunn, D. - Co. D 56th North Carolina July 20, 1865 VA25
Dunn, E.T. - Co. F 14th North Carolina VA28
Dunn, Elijah - Lt. - Co. I 4th North Carolina VA28
Dunn, H. - 37th North Carolina Aug. 19, 1862 VA25

Dunn, I. - Co. D 1st North Carolina   VA11
Dunn, J. - VA12
Dunn, J.W. - Co. K 26th Alabama July 8, 1862   VA25
Dunn, M. - Co. A 46th North Carolina Nov. 21, 1863   VA25
Dunn, M.A. - Co. A 1st North Carolina May 30, 1862 VA25
Dunn, S.Y. - Corp. - Co. A Palmetto Sharp Shooters (South Carolina) July 24, 1862   VA25
Dunn, T.J. - 12th Alabama Aug. 4, 1861   VA25
Dunn, W.T. - Co. G 60th Georgia May 3, 1863   VA25
Dunston, F.J. - Virginia   VA07
Dupane, Edgar - VA12
Dupin, T. - 8th Louisiana Dec. 26, 1862   VA25
Dupree, D. - 23rd Georgia July 1, 1864   VA25
Durat, A.L. - Co. K Palmetto Sharp Shooters (South Carolina) July 1864 VA25
Durham, A. - Lt.- Co. C 8th Louisiana   This soldier's name is listed in Napier Bartlett's *Military Record of Louisiana*, however he is not listed in the cemetery's burial roster. VA28
Durham, G. - Co. I 16th Louisiana Nov. 19, 1864   VA25
Durham, J.A. - Capt. - Co. D 49th Georgia   May 11, 1864   VA25
Durham, J.W. - North Carolina April 7, 1864   VA25
Durham, T.J. - Pvt. - North Carolina March 26, 1865   VA22
Durham, W.D. - Sgt. - Co. K ___ Georgia   Oct. 23, 1863   VA25
Durham, W.H. - Co. K 18th North Carolina July 2, 1862   VA25
Durham, W.J. - Co. G 28th North Carolina Sept. 30, 1864   VA25
Durkin, James - Co. C 9th Alabama May 18, 1862   VA25
Durry, John - 11th Mississippi   VA18
Durwith, S. - 1862 VA25
Duval, F.L. - Co. F 13th Georgia June 29, 1864   VA25
Dyall, __ - Co. D 50th Georgia March 21, 1865   VA25
Dycus, R.Y. - Co. I 1st Tennessee April 3, 1865   VA25

Dye, J. - Alabama Dec. 24, 1862   VA25
Dye, J.C. - Corp. - Nov. 18, 1862   VA25
Dye, S. - 6th South Carolina   VA18
Dyer, A.L. - Lt. - Co. C 16th Georgia June 6, 1864   VA25
Dyer, E.J. - Co. H 38th North Carolina Aug. 13, 1864   VA25
Dyer, J. - Co. C 26th Alabama July 14, 1862   VA25
Dyer, J.A. - Co. G 46th Mississippi June 6, 1864   VA25
Dyer, J.M. - Co. D 13th Alabama June 24, 1862   VA25
Dyer, J.T. - Co. D 9th Georgia Nov. 7, 1862   VA25
Dyer, N. - Co. I 5th South Carolina June 21, 1862 VA2
Dykes, J. - VA18
Dyser, B. - Co. H 51st Georgia Oct. 30, 1862   VA25
Eachard, C.B. - Co. C 15th South Carolina Oct. 24, 1863   VA25
Eader, Wm. - Co. H 11th North Carolina Died Sept __, 1861   VA23
Eadridge, J. - 48th Virginia VA18
Eads, A. - Co. B 10th Georgia June 24, 1864   VA25
Eagles, Lorenzo Dow - Lt. - Co. F 30th North Carolina   VA28
Eakin, J.D. - Co. F - Holcombe's Legion (Georgia)   March 25, 1865   VA25
Earles, J.J. - Washington Artillery Died Apr 23, 1862   VA23
Earles, M.S. - Co. D 55th North Carolina June 25, 1864   VA25
Earley, J. - Capt. White's Company   May 22, 1862 VA25
Earley, J.G. - Co. K 8th Virginia Feb. 20, 1862   VA25
Early, J.S. - Co. H 14th North Carolina July 22, 1864   VA25
Earnhart, E.D. - Capt. - Co. I 42nd North Carolina   March 20, 1863   VA25
Earnhart, P. - Co. D 42nd North Carolina Oct. 3, 1864 VA25
Earnheart, Alexander A. - Pvt. - Co. A 20th North Carolina   MW May 19, 1864   VA28
Earvin, A.J. - Co. H 2nd Louisiana June 22, 1864   VA25
Earvin, W. - Co. E 23rd Virginia May 30, 1864   VA25

Eashing, Anthony - "a prisoner" Co. D 8th Virginia Feb. 27, 1863   VA19

Eason, W. - Co. A 9th Louisiana Dec. 8, 1862   VA25

Eason, W. - Co. H 5th North Carolina July 14, 1862 VA25

East, J.H.L. - Co. F 3rd South Carolina Jan. 5, 1865 VA25

Eastwood, B. - Sgt. - Co. F 23rd North Carolina June 19, 1862   VA25

Eastwood, G.W. - Co. E 3rd Georgia July 29, 1862   VA25

Eastwood, J. - Co. E 13th Alabama May 26, 1862   VA25

Eatier, John - 4th Louisiana. Battalion age 16   Oct. 17, 1861   VA25

Eaton, James M. - Pvt. - Co. H 60th Georgia KIA - Fredericksburg Dec. 13, 1862 VA28

Ecard, J. - Co. B 41st North Carolina July 21, 1865   VA25

Echart, J.R. - 21st Virginia July 22, 1865   VA25

Echols, J.A. - Co. A 38th Georgia Jan. 29, 1863   VA25

Eckford, W.J. - Capt. - Co. B 13th Mississippi   1862 VA25

Eddelman, W.B. - Co. B 53rd Georgia June 22, 1863   VA25

Edder, J.W. - Co. B 12th South Carolina June 15, 1862   VA25

Edge, A.H. - Co. C 6th North Carolina Sept. 23, 1861   VA25

Edge, H. - 28th Georgia Sept. 20, 1862   VA25

Edinger, J.R. - Co. B 48th North Carolina Sept. 14, 1864   VA25

Edison, J.W. - Co. C 48th North Carolina   VA11

Edmunds, __ - Co. I 53rd Georgia Nov. 1862   VA25

Edmunds, A.F. - Co. A 35th North Carolina Nov. 1, 1862   VA25

Edmunds, D. - 28th North Carolina Sept. 2, 1862   VA25

Edmunds, G.H. - Virginia Sept. 7, 1863   VA25

Edmunds, J.M. - Co. I 53rd Georgia Nov. 1862   VA25

Edmunds, W. - Co. I 50th Georgia Feb. 10, 1863   VA25

Edmunds, W. - Co. D 2nd Florida June 13, 1862   VA25

Edmundson, William H. - Asst. Surgeon - 52nd Virginia Died May 10, 1864 Headstone reads: " " Wm. H.F. Inlanson". Old records list this soldier as: " Wm. H. F. Inlandson" VA28

Edwards, D. - Co. C 45th North Carolina Nov. 12, 1863 VA25

Edwards, I.C. - Virginia   VA07

Edwards, J.A. - 15th Virginia Cavalry Jan. 19, 1864 VA25

Edwards, J.B. - Co. K 6th Georgia Aug. 8, 1864   VA25

Edwards, J.D. - Co. F 44th North Carolina June 5, 1864 VA25

Edwards, J.J. - Co. E 27th Virginia Sept. 17, 1864   VA25

Edwards, J.W. - Co. H 5th Florida Sept. 21, 1862   VA25

Edwards, L.B. - Co. G 35th Georgia April 23, 1863   VA25

Edwards, M.P. - Tennessee   VA20

Edwards, Mathew M. - Sgt. - Co. G 37th North Carolina VA28

Edwards, W.A. - 1863   VA25

Edwards, W.R. - Co. G 44th North Carolina Jan. 24, 1865 VA25

Efford, T.J. - Lt. - Co. G 48th Virginia   Oct. 13, 1864   VA25

Efrid, S.S. - Co. H 14th North Carolina July 17, 1862   VA25

Efton, A. - Co. I 5th South Carolina Sept. 2, 1864 VA25

Eggleston, Benjm. - Died - Sept. 27, 1862 - age 23   VA19

Eggleston, G.A. - Co. F 42nd Virginia July 27, 1862   VA25

Eggleston, John Cary - Pvt. - Anderson's Company Light Artillery (Richmond Howitzers) DOW May 27, 1864 MW Spotsylvania Court House VA 28

Eggleston, William B. - May 30, 1863 VA19

Eiseman, G. - Corp. - 12th Mississippi   VA17

Elam, J.F. - Louisiana. Artillery June 16, 1865   VA25

Elder, J.B. - Co. C 14th Alabama Aug. 5, 1862   VA25

Elder, James E. 25th Tennessee   VA04

Elder, M.B. - Co. I 9th South Carolina Oct. 15, 1861 VA25

Elder, M.V. - 9th Louisiana Oct. 16, 1861   VA25

Eldridge, Jo. - POW - Federal Soldier Died Feb. 28, 1860 (sic) VA19

Elkins, Wm. - Pvt. - Co. I 5th South Carolina Died May 20, 1865   VA26
Ellen, E.J. - 8th South Carolina Oct. 15, 1861   VA25
Ellen, J.B. - Co. D 42nd North Carolina Aug. 12, 1864   VA25
Ellen, Moses - Co. D 23rd North Carolina   VA11
Ellenton, D.P.   21st North Carolina Feb. 9, 1865   VA25
Ellington, D. - 8th South Carolina   VA18
Ellington, Henry B. - Resident of Confederate Soldiers Home Died Jan. 22, 1909 age 61   VA19
Elliott, E. - 27th Georgia VA18
Elliott, H. - Co. D 45th North Carolina July 17, 1864   VA25
Elliott, J.D. - 24th Georgia Infantry   VA08
Elliott, L. - Co. H 49th Virginia July 9, 1862   VA25
Elliott, R.E. - Capt. - 2nd South Carolina June 7, 1864   VA25
Elliott, S.D. - Co. F 52nd North Carolina May 26, 1865 VA25
Elliott, W.A. - Co. D 5th Alabama Aug. 24, 1862   VA25
Ellis, A.C. - Co. B 2nd Florida July 6, 1862   VA25
Ellis, C. - Co. B 4th Alabama July 23, 1862   VA25
Ellis, E.P. - Co. G 1st North Carolina March 19, 1865   VA25
Ellis, H. - Artillery   May 1, 1862   VA25
Ellis, J. - Pvt. - Virginia April 27, 1865   VA22
Ellis, J. - Lt. - Co. G 23rd Arkansas   March 10, 1865 VA25
Ellis, J. - Co. B 46th North Carolina Dec. 12, 1863   VA25
Ellis, J.F. - Co. D 33rd North Carolina June 21, 1862   VA25
Ellis, J.L. - Co. I 1st Alabama Nov. 1, 1861   VA25
Ellis, J.R. - Co. E 47th Alabama July 3, 1862   VA25
Ellis, James C. - Pvt. - Co. J 58th Virginia Vols. DOW May 30, 1863 age 24   VA19
Ellis, M.A. - Pvt. - Co. G 48th Georgia Died June 7, 1865   VA26
Ellis, M.A. - VA25
Ellis, N.A. - Co. G 12th South Carolina Jan. 21, 1863   VA25
Ellis, R.A. - POW - Federal Soldier Died Dec. 16, 1861   VA19
Ellis, R.B. - Co. G 17th Georgia Dec. 4, 1864   VA25
Ellis, R.M. - Co. H 5th North Carolina May 16, 1863 VA25

Ellis, R.R. - Co. I 19th Mississippi May 26, 1862   VA25
Ellis, Rev. R.A. - Chaplain - 13th Georgia Died May 12, 1864 headstone reads "Co. C 80th Georgia"   VA28
Ellis, W.A. - Co. C 13th Alabama May 30, 1864   VA25
Ellison, H.J. - Co. C 14th Tennessee July 1, 1862   VA25
Ellison, J. - Co. B 35th North Carolina June 18, 1864   VA25
Ellison, J.M. - Co. D 42nd Mississippi Oct. 30, 1861   VA25
Ellison, W.D. - Co. H 44th North Carolina Oct. 21, 1863   VA25
Ellison, William H. - Sgt. - Co. C 25th Virginia KIA Fredericksburg Dec. 13, 1862   VA28
Elms, A. - 12th Alabama Sept. 20, 1861   VA25
Elrand, B. - Co. B 22nd North Carolina Oct. 12, 1864   VA25
Elridge, W.H. - Co. A 6th South Carolina June 22, 1864   VA25
Elrod, S. - 5th Alabama Infantry   VA08
Elsington, D.R. - Pvt. - Co. E 1st North Carolina July 30, 1864   VA22
Elta, F.T. - 2nd Maryland May 23, 1865   VA25
Elvens, J.W. - Co. I 25th South Carolina July 8, 1864   VA25
Embrey, Amos M. - Corp. - Co. C 49th Virginia KIA Spotsylvania C. H.   VA28
Emerson, William H. - Pvt. - Co. I 5th Virginia MW Spotsylvania C. H. May 19, 1864 DOW the next day   VA28
Emory, J. - Co. B 7th Georgia April 26, 1862   VA25
England, Abner V. - KIA Oct. 13, 1862 age 26   VA19
English, __ - 1862   VA25
English, John - 28th Virginia   VA18
English, W.T. - Co. E 13th Alabama June 10, 1862   VA25
Engrain, W.H. - Co. A 7th North Carolina July 1, 1863   VA25
Ennis, Charles H. - Sgt. - Cooke's Co. Stafford Light Artillery (Virginia)   VA28
Epps, H. - Co. E 17th South Carolina Aug. 1862   VA25
Epps, J. - Co. K 1st Tennessee July 1, 1863   VA25
Epps, J.W. - Co. B 14th North Carolina June 30, 1862   VA25
Ernis, James - Co. D 28th Georgia Died Jan 4, 1862   VA23

Ervins, __ July 11, 1862 VA25
Erwine, John - Baltimore Artillery   VA18
Eskridge, Henry - KIA June 6, 1862   VA19
Estep, Raphael - VA12
Ester, N. - Co. G 9th South Carolina Oct. 9, 1861 VA25
Ester, W.F. - Co. A 22nd North Carolina Dec. 28, 1862
    VA25
Esters, E. - Co. D 5th South Carolina Oct. 18, 1864 VA25
Estis, A.C. - Co. C 18th South Carolina Aug. 6, 1864 VA25
Estis, E.A. - Co. D 1st North Carolina April 31, 1864   VA25
Estis, J.B. - Co. C 56th Virginia Aug. 9, 1863   VA25
Estis, N.M. - Co. C 26th Alabama June 10, 1862   VA25
Estlow, Godfrey - Co. K 6th Artillery   VA11
Estor, W.L. - Co. G 2nd Mississippi July 15, 1862   VA25
Etheredge, W.B. - North Carolina Died Jan. 4, 1863   VA03
Etheridge, James S. - Pvt. - Co. C 6th Georgia Last name also
    spelled "Ethridge".   VA28
Ethridge, Edward - 6th Georgia   VA28
Ethridge, J.C. - Sgt. - Co. K 12th Alabama April 20, 1863
    VA25
Ethridge, J.E. - 5th Fla.   VA18
Ethridge, James S. - see Etheridge, James S.
Eubank, J.H. - Co. C 27th Georgia June 16, 1862   VA25
Eur, B. - Co. D 5th North Carolina April 7, 1865 VA25
Evans, __ - Alabama Nov. 12, 1861   VA25
Evans, B.A. - Co. E 2nd South Carolina May 16, 1862 VA25
Evans, C.W. - Co. I 25th South Carolina Aug. 3, 1864 VA25
Evans, D. - Navy Brigade   Sept. 29, 1862   VA25
Evans, E. - Co. F 1st Georgia Oct. 5, 1864   VA25
Evans, E.M. - Co. C 34th Virginia Battalion   VA11
Evans, G.P. - Co. B 2nd Florida April 27, 1865   VA25
Evans, Harding - 11th North Carolina   VA18
Evans, Isaac L. - Pvt. - Co. A 5th Virginia Cavalry KIA
    Spotsylvania C. H   VA28
Evans, J. - Co. I 14th Georgia May 24, 1864   VA25
Evans, J. - Co. E 44th Virginia July 11, 1862   VA25

Evans, J. - 12th Alabama Nov. 12, 1862   VA25
Evans, J.A. - Co. K 14th Georgia May 28, 1864   VA25
Evans, J.C. - Co. A 13th Alabama May 26, 1863   VA25
Evans, J.H. - Co. A 53rd North Carolina June 22, 1864 VA25
Evans, J.J. - Co. G 49th Georgia Sept. 4 , 1862   VA25
Evans, J.R. - Co. F 13th North Carolina May 30, 1864 VA25
Evans, J.W. - Co. K 3rd North Carolina April 13, 1864   VA25
Evans, N. - Co. D 12th Georgia Battalion   1864   VA25
Evans, S. - VA12
Evans, S. - Co. G 14th South Carolina Jan. 15, 1863   VA25
Evans, S.B. - Co. B 27th Georgia June 23, 1864   VA25
Evans, T.H. - Co. G 14th South Carolina Aug. 22, 1862 VA25
Evans, W. - Co. H 5th Florida Nov. 22, 1862   VA25
Evans, W.J. - 3rd Georgia "C.G."   1862   VA25
Evans, W.T. - Co. K 4th North Carolina Oct. 23, 1862 VA25
Everett, A. - Co. I 17th North Carolina Oct. 5, 1862 VA25
Everett, J.A. - Co. E 17th North Carolina Sept. 14, 1864 VA25
Everett, W.P. - 9th Alabama Infantry - KIA - Battle of Williamsburg - May 5, 1862   VA02
Evergate, S.H. - Co. H 11th Georgia June 10, 1862   VA25
Everhart, J. - VA06
Everhart, R. - Co. A 57th North Carolina July 13, 1864 VA25
Everick, H. - Co. E 19th North Carolina Aug. 5, 1864 VA25
Everson, J.M. - Co. D 42nd Mississippi Oct. 28, 1862. VA25
Evins, R. - Co. K 11th Alabama June 24, 1862   VA25
Ewing, W.A. - 10th Mississippi   VA18
Ezell, G.J. - Co. B 50th Georgia June 6, 1864   VA25
Ezzell, J. - Co. I 46th North Carolina Sept. 16, 1864   VA25
F __ , H.W. - Co. G 6oth Georgia Jan. 7, 1863   VA25
Fadely, Samuel - 10th Virginia VA18
Fafford, A.W. - Co. D 40th North Carolina Aug. 13, 1864 VA25

Fagan, Marcus Friley - Sgt. - Co. G 1st North Carolina Died
   May 10, 1864   VA28
Fail, M.M. - Co. C 5th Florida Sept. 14, 1862   VA25
Fail, M.N. - Co. I 17th South Carolina Sept. 15, 1862   VA25
Fail, S. - Co. D 1st South Carolina Nov. 2, 1864 VA25
Faint, __ - KIA June 28, 1862 age 27   VA19
Fair, K.C. - Pvt. - Co. H 13th Georgia - Died May 12, 1864
   Name on headstone - "Faire" VA28
Fairchild, J. - Co. G 9th Louisiana April 20, 1862   VA25
Faircloth, H. - Co. C 45th Georgia Aug. 29, 1864   VA25
Faircloth, J. - Co. A 59th Georgia Jan. 26, 1865   VA25
Faircloth, J. - Co. I 46th North Carolina May 10, 1864 VA25
Faircloth, W.R. - 15th Alabama VA18
Faire, K.C. - see Fair, K.C.   VA28
Fairfax, R. - Lt. - C.S. Navy July 8, 1862   VA25
Fairling, J.J. - Co. G 7th Virginia May 20, 1861   VA25
Fallon, Thomas - Sgt. - Co. C 1st Georgia   VA28
Falsen, G.W. - Sept. 3, 1862 VA25
Fant, Henry - DOW May 28, 1863 age 21   VA19
Farcloth, C.S. - 59th Georgia VA18
Faries, Henry - 6th North Carolina   VA18
Farinton, C.C. - June 15, 1862 VA25
Farland, George - POW - Federal Soldier Died Nov. 15, 1861
   VA19
Farlow, H. - Co. A 9th Virginia Artillery April 27, 1862
   VA25
Farlow, J. - 32nd North Carolina April 23, 1862   VA25
Farmer, E. - Co. F 13th South Carolina July 8, 1862 VA25
Farmer, J. - Co. E 23rd Mississippi June 3, 1862   VA25
Farmer, J. - Co. D 1st Louisiana June 28, 1863   VA25
Farmer, J.H. - Co. A 27th Tennessee Aug. 15, 1863   VA25
Farmer, M. - Co. I 17th South Carolina Sept. 9, 1862   VA25
Farmer, Sidney T. - Lt. - Co. G 38th Georgia - "Co. C" on
   headstone Died May 10, 1864   VA28
Farrant, __ - July 8, 1862 VA25
Farrant, W.F. - Co. A 13th South Carolina July 8, 1862 VA25

Farrar, C.S. - Co. G 38th Virginia   VA08
Farrell, J.S. - Co. I 12th South Carolina June 25, 1864   VA25
Farrell, S. - Co. G 28th Georgia Oct. 3, 1863   VA25
Farris, C.W. - 9th Virginia Cavalry   VA18
Farris, J.A. - Co. F 61st Georgia Jan. 11, 1863   VA25
Farris, O.A. - Co. G 18th South Carolina Jan. 7, 1865 VA25
Fate, H.C. - Georgia   VA22
Faulk, W.G. - Co. F 7th North Carolina Oct. 14, 1864 VA25
Faulkner, G.P. - Virginia   VA20
Faulkner, Sam'l - 6th South Carolina   VA18
Faulkner, T.M. - 16th Georgia Sept. 5, 1861   VA25
Faulkner, W. - 15th North Carolina July 5, 1862   VA25
Faulks, G.L. - Co. E 38th Georgia July 16, 1862   VA25
Featherston, W.A. - Co. H 37th North Carolina July 12, 1864   VA25
Fells, T.J. - Co. E 14th North Carolina July 1, 1862 VA25
Felmount, O.W. - Co. F 36th North Carolina July 16, 1862   VA25
Felt, A.H. - 2nd South Carolina July 16, 1862   VA25
Felton, C. - 17th North Carolina July 28, 1864   VA25
Felton, John E. - Jeff Davis Legion   VA18
Felts, S.J. - Co. F 45th Georgia Feb. 8, 1863   VA25
Felts, T.J. - Co. F 48th Georgia Jan. 9, 1863   VA25
Fender, T.B. - Co. G 1st South Carolina Feb. 10, 1865 VA25
Fenn, G.W. - Co. G Phillip's Legion (Georgia) Feb. 26, 1865   VA25
Fennell, H. - Co. G 22nd South Carolina Aug. 4, 1864 VA25
Fennelly, John - Adjutant. - Co. F 14th Louisiana MW May 19, 1864 Died June 1, 1864   VA28
Fepps, Lucius - POW - Federal Soldier Died Dec. 13, 1861   VA19
Fergin, J.M. - Co. C 45th North Carolina March 2, 1865   VA25
Ferguson, J.H. - Co. C 4th South Carolina Cavalry   VA24
Ferrell, W.G. - Co. G 22nd North Carolina July 1, 1864 VA25
Ferrell, W.H. - Corp. - Co. F 53rd Georgia   VA28

Few, Alex - Co. H 15th Alabama Died Mar 3, 1862   VA23
Fields, F. C. - see Fields, James Clark   VA28
Fields, J. - Lt. Colonel - March 12, 1863   VA25
Fields, J. - Co. H 64th Georgia Aug. 13, 1864   VA25
Fields, J. - Co. I 27th Georgia May 14, 1862   VA25
Fields, J.B. - Co. G 48th North Carolina Nov. 16, 1864   VA25
Fields, J.C. - Co. I 21st Mississippi Feb. 13, 1863   VA25
Fields, James Clark - Pvt. - Co. H 14th Tennessee Headstone reads: "F.C. Fields"   VA28
Fields, M. - Co. G 48th North Carolina Sept. 4, 1864   VA25
Fields, W.C. - Pvt. - Co. B 10th Virginia Battery Died May 19, 1865   VA26
Figer, H.F. - 11th North Carolina June 25, 1864   VA25
Figgens, J.M. - Co. G 23rd Georgia   VA11
Figgs, __ - June 4, 1862 VA25
Filton, J.B. - Co. H 6th South Carolina June 25, 1864 VA25
Filtzmyers, Jacob - Co. G 33rd Virginia   VA28
Fincannon, John - Co. B 11th North Carolina Aug. 18, 1864   VA25
Finch, Edward T. - Killed by explosion of detonating powder June 13, 1861 age 38   VA19
Finch, J.M. - Alabama May 24, 1862   VA25
Finch, M.H. - Co. E 16th Mississippi Aug. 20, 1862   VA25
Fincher, A.S. - Co. E 22nd South Carolina April 7, 1865   VA25
Fincher, W.F. - Co. F 1st Louisiana March 20, 1863   VA25
Finck, P.A. - Lt. - Co. F 57th North Carolina March 20, 1863   VA25
Finham, B. - Co. D 49th Virginia June 18, 1862   VA25
Fink, J.D. - Sgt. - Co. A 28th Virginia June 27, 1862   VA25
Fink, Simon Peter - 4th North Carolina Cavalry KIA - Upperville - June 21, 1863   VA07
Finley, J. - Adjutant - 14th Louisiana This soldier's name is listed in Napier Bartlett's *Military Record of Louisiana*, however he is not listed in the cemetery's burial roster.   VA28

Finley, J.H. - Graham' Battery (North Carolina) Feb. 6, 1864 VA25
Finley, J.H. - Co. C 1st South Carolina Nov. 7, 1862 VA25
Finley, J.H. - 11th Georgia July 7, 1862 VA25
Finley, J.M. - 47th Alabama Feb. 5, 1863 VA25
Finley, J.R. - 4th Texas Jan. 31, 1862 VA25
Finley, S.D. - Co. B Holcombe's Legion (Georgia) Nov. 21, 1864 VA25
Finn, H.F. - Co. E ____ VA28
Finnel, __ - Pvt. - South Carolina 1864 VA22
Finney, H. - Co. F 28th North Carolina Jan. 7, 1865 VA25
Finney, T. - Virginia Oct. 26, 1863 VA25
Finnis, J.P. - 23rd Georgia April 19, 1862 VA25
Firtich, Charles - 25th South Carolina VA04
Fish, M.G. - 9th Virginia July 5, 1862 VA25
Fish, T.G. - Sgt. - Co. I 4th Georgia May 23. 1863 VA25
Fishard, J. - 52nd Virginia April 21, 1865 VA25
Fisher, __ - Lt. - Co. G 10th Alabama Feb. 7, 1863 VA25
Fisher, __ - Aug. 1, 1861 VA25
Fisher, J. - C.S. Navy May 10, 1865 VA25
Fisher, T.M. - Holcombe's Legion (Georgia) March 5, 1865 VA25
Fitch, J.D. - Virginia Sept. 5, 1864 VA25
Fitchett, R.E. - Co. B 18th Georgia Sept. 30, 1861 VA25
Fitzgerald, __ - 1st Engineer Corps - CSA March 24, 1865 VA25
Fitzgerald, J.B. - Co. A 49th Georgia Aug. 5, 1862 VA25
Fitzgerald, W.G. - Co. I 19th Mississippi Nov. 15, 1864 VA25
Fitzgerald, Wiliam J. - Pvt. - Co. H 45th Georgia Died May 12, 1864 VA28
Fitzpatrick, A. - April 20, 1862 VA25
Fitzpatrick, John - Civilian -Killed in explosion of C.S. Laboratory - Feb. 6, 1862 age 17 VA19
Fizer, Samuel - Virginia VA20
Flack, R.F. - Co. K 45th North Carolina June 15, 1864 VA25

Flagg, C.S. - Capt. - 2nd Florida June 18, 1862   VA25
Flaken, J.F. - Georgia Feb. 6, 1864   VA25
Flannagan, A.H. - Co. A 2nd Mississippi Sept. 19, 1863
    VA25
Flannagan, J.F. - Co. H 42nd Mississippi Sept. 22, 1862 VA25
Fleet, J.B. - Co. D 53rd Georgia Aug. 3, 1862   VA25
Fleming, G.S. - 2nd Florida Infantry - KIA - Battle of
    Williamsburg - May 5, 1862   VA02
Fleming, H.L.E. - 25th South Carolina   VA04
Fleming, P. - Co. H 27th North Carolina July 13, 1864   VA25
Fleming, R.H. - Co. A 8th Alabama Feb. 3, 1862   VA25
Fleming, R.J. - Co. D 18th South Carolina July 20, 1864
    VA25
Fleming, J.F. - Co. K 7th Louisiana Oct. 13, 1863   VA25
Flentiff, W.D. - Co. D 11th North Carolina Nov. 9, 1864
    VA25
Fletcher, __ - 8th South Carolina Aug. 8, 1862   VA25
Fletcher, J. - 1st South Carolina Rifles July 14, 1862   VA25
Fletcher, J.M. - 8th Georgia Aug. 7, 1861   VA25
Fletcher, John - Co. K 53rd Virginia July 2, 1862   VA25
Fletcher, O. - Co. I 53rd South Carolina Dec. 23, 1862   VA25
Fletcher, S.I. - July 6, 1862 age 19   VA19
Fletcher, Wesley - Co. B 8th Virginia   VA11
Flick, J.H. - 10th Virginia VA18
Flick, W.J. - 22nd North Carolina Nov. 19, 1863   VA25
Flington, Jerry - 18th Mississippi   VA18
Flinn, J.F. - Co. I 8th Virginia Infantry   VA08
Flinn, W.G. - 6th Louisiana VA18
Flint, T. - Virginia Reserves Feb. 20, 1865   VA25
Flon, D.N. - May 25, 1861 VA25
Flournoy, __ - Georgia Sept. 22, 1862   VA25
Flournoy, M.A. - Co. I 12th Alabama June 5, 1862   VA25
Flowers, James - 15th Alabama Died Nov 19, 1861   VA23
Flowers, John - 9th Louisiana VA18
Flowers, William W. - Pvt. - Co. B 2nd North Carolina Died
    May 12, 1864   VA28

Floyd, B. - Co. B 11th South Carolina Oct. 6, 1864 VA25
Floyd, G.F. - Co. A 49th North Carolina Nov. 21, 1863 VA25
Floyd, J.B. - Co. G 46th South Carolina Sept. 14, 1864   VA25
Floyd, J.M. - Co. E 1st Georgia Died Jan 8, 1862   VA23
Floyd, J.M. - Co. D 3rd South Carolina July 13, 1864 VA25
Floyd, James - North Carolina Aug. 5, 1862   VA25
Floyd, S.H. - Co. E 50th Georgia July 17, 1864   VA25
Floyd, W. - Co. A 18th Mississippi Jan. 21, 1863 VA25
Floyd, W.A. - Co. C 12th North Carolina   VA28
Floyd, W.W. - Lt. Colonel 17th Tennessee   May 19, 1864 VA25
Fluke, W.C. - VA12
Fodge, W.G. - Co. D 47th Virginia July 11, 1862   VA25
Fogg, D. - Capt. "Sailor" (C.S. Navy?) Aug. 7, 1863 VA19
Foley, David - Pvt. - Co. A 57th North Carolina Died June 16, 1865   VA26
Folke, P. - 15th Alabama VA18
Folsom, J.W. - Corp. - Co. D 20th Georgia Cavalry   Sept. 4, 1864   VA25
Folson, R.W. - Colonel - 14th Georgia   May 24, 1864 VA25
Foltz, John P. - VA15
Foltz, T. - 16th Mississippi   VA17
Foot, J. - Co. H 25th North Carolina Aug. 8, 1864 VA25
Forbes, ____ - Colonel - KIA - July 17, 1862   VA19
Forbes, A.R. - Co. F 54th North Carolina Jan. 5, 1863 VA25
Forbes, A.W. - Co. H 5th North Carolina Sept. 11, 1864 VA25
Forbes, G.V.H. - Colonel - DOD Sept. 24, 1861 "disinterred and conveyed to Natchez, Mississippi - Dec. 5, 186 VA19
Forbes, T.M. - Co. K 9th Virginia Dec. 29, 1862   VA25
Forbes, W.A. - Colonel - KIA 2nd Manassas   VA19
Ford, C.E. - Lt. - Stuart's Artillery (Virginia)   May 31, 1862 VA25
Ford, Chas. E. - Major - Stuart Horse Artillery   VA10

Ford, George - Co. F 23rd South Carolina   VA11
Ford, George W. - Co. F 23rd South Carolina   VA11
Ford, H. - 12th South Carolina June 20, 1862   VA25
Ford, J. - Co. G 14th South Carolina April 4, 1863   VA25
Ford, J.H. - Co. H Cobb's Legion (Georgia)   Oct. 11, 1863
   VA25
Ford, J.H. - Co. G 36th North Carolina 1865   VA25
Ford, J.J. - Co. I 5th North Carolina June 17, 1862 VA25
Ford, J.W. - Co. F 40th Virginia July 8, 1862   VA25
Ford, J.W. - Co. I 44th Georgia Sept. 3, 1862   VA25
Ford, R. -   VA08
Ford, S. - Co. G 50th Georgia July 5, 1864   VA25
Ford, W.W. - Co. B 61st Georgia Sept. 7, 1862   VA25
Ford, Walter S. - Co. D 17th Virginia Infantry   VA10
Fore, H. - Georgia Aug. 29, 1862   VA25
Fore, Wm. - Co. A 35th Georgia Aug. 30, 1862   VA25
Forloin, G.D. - Co. I 38th Virginia Aug. 9, 1862   VA25
Formly, J.W. - 8th Georgia May 25, 1861   VA25
Forrest, Joseph C. - Pvt. - Co. F 13th South Carolina Died
   May 12, 1864   VA28
Forrest, L. Irby - Lt. - Co. K 37th Virginia KIA Spotsylvania
   C. H   VA28
Forsyth, James - 8th Virginia Infantry   VA10
Forte, A. - 17th Mississippi   VA18
Forton, J. - Co. F 66th North Carolina Sept. 30, 1864   VA25
Fortune, P.S. - Co. F 18th North Carolina Jan. 7, 1863 VA25
Fortune, V.E. - 2nd Mississippi Battalion June 20, 1862
   VA25
Foster, __ - July 3, 1862 VA25
Foster, __ - May 17, 1862 VA25
Foster, __ - July 1, 1862 VA25
Foster, A. - Co. C 26th North Carolina March 16, 1865
   VA25
Foster, A. - Co. A 42nd North Carolina Jan. 12, 1865   VA25
Foster, A. - Co. C 5th South Carolina May 16, 1862 VA25
Foster, B.C. - Lt. - Co. I 5th Alabama June 10, 1864   VA25

Foster, J. - 22nd South Carolina   VA18
Foster, J.B. - 18th Alabama July 3, 1862   VA25
Foster, J.F. - Co. F 42nd Mississippi Sept. 12, 1862 VA25
Foster, P.R. - 6th Alabama May 1863   VA25
Foster, Powhatan T. - Co. E 9th Cavalry Veteran - Died Aug. 17, 1914   VA28
Foster, Z.M. - Co. K 21st Mississippi July 8, 1862   VA25
Fountain, N. - Co. B 44th North Carolina Oct. 9, 1864 VA25
Fourts, J.J. - Co. G 42nd North Carolina July 24, 1864   VA25
Fowler, C.A. - Co. D 25th North Carolina Jan. 3, 1863 VA25
Fowler, G.W. - 16th Georgia VA23
Fowler, J. Pvt. - Co. F 18th Virginia .Died May 25, 1865   VA26
Fowler, John - 12th Alabama Dec. 3, 1864   VA25
Fowler, S.D. - "M.D." - Maryland July 7, 1862   VA25
Fowler, S.D. - 17th Virginia Nov. 26, 1862   VA25
Fowler, Samuel - 11th Georgia VA18
Fowler, W. - Co. D 45th Georgia July 18, 1864   VA25
Fox, C.J. - Pvt. - Co. F 11th Virginia Died June 12, 1865   VA26
Fox, Frank - Mosby's Cavalry   VA10
Fox, G.N. - Co. G 46th North Carolina Jan. 23, 1865   VA25
Fox, M.M. - Co. E 14th North Carolina April 10, 1863   VA25
Fox, Miles - North Carolina   VA20
Foy, J.R. - Co. E 7th South Carolina Oct. 2, 1864 VA25
Frailey, W.H. - Co. B 58th Virginia Aug. 5, 1862   VA25
Fraley, John T. - Lt. - Co. E 2nd North Carolina Died May 15, 1864   VA28
Fralie, Wm. J. - Sgt. - 25th South Carolina   VA04
France, F. - Co. F 60th Virginia May 21, 1861   VA25
France, G. - Co. B 40th Virginia Aug. 5, 1862   VA25
Francis, E. - Co. I 25th Virginia Feb. 23, 1863   VA25
Frank, J. - Georgia   VA17
Frank, J.W. - Co. E 3rd South Carolina   VA11
Frank, J.W. - Co. B 48th Georgia Sept. 22, 1862   VA25
Franklin, J.G. - Alabama   VA28

Franklin, W.M. - Co. H 7th South Carolina Battalion Dec. 24, 1861   VA25
Frasa, __ - 6th North Carolina July 1862   VA25
Fraser, S. - Co. D 10th Virginia Sept. 10, 1863   VA25
Frasier, J. - Lathan Co. (North Carolina) June 6, 1862   VA25
Frasier, J. - Sumpter Artillery (South Carolina) May 14, 1862   VA25
Frasier, Jas. - Co. I 13th North Carolina July 8, 1862 VA25
Frasier, L.B. - Co. F 46th North Carolina July 17, 1864   VA25
Frasier, L.T. - Co. B 12th North Carolina May 30, 1864 VA25
Fravers, __ - 1862   VA25
Frazier, Daniel V. - Corp. - 7th South Carolina   VA04
Frazier, Steven - Co. K 55th North Carolina Died June 25, 1863   VA03
Freeland, J. - Co. C 2nd South Carolina Aug. 8, 1864   VA25
Freeman, Benjamin - 13th South Carolina   VA11
Freeman, Chas. A. - Georgia   VA20
Freeman, Hugh - Pvt. - Co. B 2nd North Carolina Battalion Died May 14, 1864 VA28
Freeman, I. - Corp. - Co. I 10th Virginia Died Nov. 11, 1862   VA06
Freeman, J. - Co. F 64th North Carolina Jan. 19, 1865   VA25
Freeman, J. - Co. C 13th North Carolina Nov. 14, 1864   VA25
Freeman, J. - Co. C 2nd South Carolina Aug. 8, 1864 VA25
Freeman, J.E. - Co. C 1st Texas July 5, 1862   VA25
Freeman, J.H. - Cobb's Legion (Georgia)   May 24, 1862   VA25
Freeman, J.W. - Co. F 28th North Carolina Sept. 5, 1862   VA25
Freeman, Joseph - Co. D 17th Virginia Infantry   VA10
Freeman, Joseph W. - Pvt. - Co. I 8th South Carolina Died May 8, 1864   VA28
Freeman, S.A. - 18th Georgia Sept. 12, 1861   VA25
Freeze, D. - Co. B 46th North Carolina Aug. 9, 1864   VA25

Fresen, J. - Hampton's Legion (South Carolina) April 8, 1863 VA25
Friddell, T.F. - F.P. Phillip's Legion - Cavalry VA18
Fridgo, R.R. - Capt. - Co. K 11th Georgia Oct. 7, 1864 VA25
Frith, B.C. - 6th Virginia VA18
Fritter, T. - Co. C 38th Virginia Nov. 22, 1862 VA25
Fross, E.A. - Co. C 24th Georgia July 8, 1864 VA25
Frount, L. - Co. D 14th North Carolina July 11, 1864 VA25
Fruzeland, Jacob - Pvt. - Co. A 30th North Carolina Died June 14, 1865 VA26
Fry, A.W. - Co. D 42nd North Carolina Aug. 1, 1864 VA25
Fry, Eli. - Pvt. - Co. G 2nd Virginia VA28
Fryar, J. - Pvt. - North Carolina May 31, 1865 VA22
Fugle, L. - Corp. - Co. F 37th Georgia Sept. 20, 1864 VA25
Fulban, P.H. - Co. I 3rd Virginia June 18, 1862 VA25
Fulbright, M.W. - Co. E 60th Georgia Dec. 23, 1862 VA25
Fuller, H.L. - Co. E 18th North Carolina July 7, 1862 VA25
Fuller, J. - Co. K 8th Alabama Aug. 14, 1862 VA25
Fuller, J.D. - Co. G 22nd Georgia Aug. 23, 1864 VA25
Fuller, J.M. - Co. E 28th Georgia June 2, 1862 VA25
Fuller, L.D. - 27th N.C. Sept. 20, 1864 VA25
Fuller, T.E. - Co. B 11th Alabama June 30, 1862 VA25
Fuller, W.S. - see Fuller, Uriah S. VA28
Fuller, William L. - Lt. - Co. E 6th Virginia Cavalry DOW May 7, 1864 (Todd's Tavern) VA28
Fuller. Uriah S. - Pvt. - Co. G 49th Georgia KIA Dec. 13, 1862 at Fredericksburg Headstone reads - headstone reads - "W.S. Fuller" VA28
Fullers, H.A. - Co. A 22nd South Carolina Oct. 9, 1864 VA25
Fullers, H.C. - Co. B 38th Virginia Aug. 5, 1862 VA25
Fullerston, John - 2nd South Carolina VA18
Fullerton, A.M. - Co. A 26th Alabama June 7, 1862 VA25
Fulton, W. - Co. G 21st North Carolina June 30, 1865 VA25
Fulwood, J.T. - Co. A 3rd Georgia Cavalry March 23, 1865 VA25

Fumley, W. - 9th Alabama July 3, 1862   VA25
Furgerson, J.T. - Pvt. - North Carolina Oct. 1, 1864   VA22
Furguson, B.F. - Co. C 22nd Georgia July 8, 1862   VA25
Furguson, D. - July 11, 1862 VA25
Furguson, D. - Co. G 13th Mississippi July 1862   VA25
Furguson, J. - Co. I 26th North Carolina Aug. 12, 1864   VA25
Furguson, J.H. - Pvt. - South Carolina Aug. 1, 1864   VA22
Furguson, J.W. - Co. A 42nd Mississippi Aug. 21, 1862   VA25
Furguson, T.J. - Co. D 13th Georgia March 15, 1865   VA25
Furgusson, R.P. - DOD - Dec 22, 1862   VA19
Furlough, T. - Co. H 8th Louisiana March 24, 1862   VA25
Furlow, __ 2nd Mississippi Oct. 28, 1862   VA25
Furlow, H. - Co. E 3rd Virginia Aug. 24, 1862   VA25
Furlwright, M. - Page's Artillery (Virginia) July 12, 1864   VA25
Furquit, W. - Co. G 44th Georgia May 27, 1863   VA25
Fuster, D. - Co. A 16th North Carolina May 13, 1863 VA25
Futner, W.J. - Co. F 12th South Carolina July 11, 1864   VA25
Futral, H. - 13th North Carolina Aug. 30, 1861   VA25
Futress, __ - Co. D 12th Georgia Jan. 5, 1863   VA25
G __ , T.J. - Co. I 1st Texas Aug. 7, 1862   VA25
Gabriel, A. Alonzo - Pvt. - Co. K 23rd North Carolina Died May 09, 1864   VA28
Gabrith, J.N. - Washington Artillery (Louisiana.)   Sept. 20, 1864   VA25
Gaddy, J.N. - Co. E 30th North Carolina   Oct. 27, 1863   VA25
Gage, D. - Letcher Artillery (Virginia)   March 10, 1862   VA25
Gailers, Jno. - Co. D 16th Georgia   Oct. 8, 1861   VA25
Gain, C.S. - 8th South Carolina   VA18
Gaines, H. - Co. E 24th North Carolina July 20, 1864   VA25
Gaines, H.H. - Co. C 52nd Virginia June 15, 1864   VA25
Gaines, J.B. - Co. A 49th Virginia July 17, 1863   VA25

Gaines, J.W. - Co. C 13th South Carolina Oct. 18, 1864 VA25

Gaines, __ - Allan's Battery (Virginia) July 9, 1862   VA25

Gaines, Joseph B. - Co. L 53rd Virginia   VA11

Gales, R. - Co. A 13th South Carolina June 3, 1862 VA25

Galett, A. - Sgt. - Co. G 15th Georgia   May 28, 1863   VA25

Galetts, A.J. - Co. F 15th Georgia May 2, 1862   VA25

Gallion, A.W. - Died Dec. 16, 1862   VA19

Gallong, F. - 13th Alabama Aug. 2, 1861   VA25

Galloway, A.A. - North Carolina Aug. 12, 1863   VA25

Galloway, W.T. - Co. D 42nd Mississippi Sept. 29, 1862 VA25

Galoway, J.S. - Co. A 44th Georgia June 1, 1864   VA25

Galtney, A.D. - 31st North Carolina Dec. 6, 1864   VA25

Galveston, G.W. - 16th North Carolina May 28, 1864   VA25

Galveston, J.C. - Co. H 7th North Carolina May 30, 1864 VA25

Gamball, F. - Co. B 28th North Carolina   1862   VA25

Gamball, P.H. - Co. A 54th North Carolina Jan. 18, 1863 VA25

Gamball, T.W. - Co. B 28th North Carolina Sept. 1, 1862 VA25

Gamball, W. - Co. H 1st South Carolina June 10, 1862 VA25

Gamble, A. - Co. K 60th Georgia   VA11

Gambol, J.H. - Co. K 30th North Carolina Jan. 19, 1864 VA25

Gambrell, John E. - Pvt. - Co. K Orr's Rifles (South Carolina) KIA - Chancellorsville - May 3, 1863. Headstone reads: " 1st South Carolina Rifles" VA28

Gamlin, R. - Dec. 11, 1862   VA25

Gannon, A.H. - Co. H 3rd South Carolina   Sept. 21, 1864 VA25

Gannon, J.B. - Co. A 51st Virginia   May 21, 1864   VA25

Gantree, J. - C.S. Navy April 16, 1865   VA25

Gantz, O. - Co. F 34th North Carolina   VA28

Gany, J. - Co. E 5th Florida. June 13, 1863   VA25

Garbird, Jno. - Virginia   VA20
Gardiner, J. - South Carolina   VA22
Gardner, C. - Co. A 2nd Florida. Aug. 28, 1861   VA25
Gardner, Elijah T. - Sgt. - Co. E 2nd South Carolina Died May 12, 1864   VA28
Gardner, J. C. - Co. H 7th South Carolina Cavalry Feb. 17, 1865   VA25
Gardner, J. J. - Sumpter Artillery (South Carolina)   May 4, 1862   VA25
Gardner, J.M. - Co. F 7th South Carolina Oct. 30, 1862 VA25
Gardner, James - Pvt. - 15th South Carolina Dec. 11, 1864   VA24
Gardner, R. - Co. K 3rd Alabama Infantry   VA08
Gardner, W.R. - Co. G 17th Mississippi Jan. 30, 1863   VA25
Garlick, A.J. - Co. B 4th Virginia March 9, 1863   VA25
Garlin, R. - CSA Artillery Jan. 5, 1862   VA25
Garlington, J.P. - Co. B 1st Louisiana Aug. 6, 1864   VA25
Garman, M.H. -   April 1, 1862   VA25
Garner, W.D. - Co. B 6th Alabama Oct. 16, 1862   VA25
Garnes, P. - Co. A 6th Georgia Jan. 1, 1862   VA25
Garnett, B.F. - Co. E 14th Alabama May 22, 1863   VA25
Garnett, Jas. A. - Sgt. - Co. I 8th Virginia June 27, 1862   VA25
Garnett, W.T. - Co. B 9th Georgia July 1, 1862   VA25
Garrant, W.A. - Co. B 3rd Georgia June 27, 1862   VA25
Garrett, C. - 42nd Virginia Aug. 26, 1862   VA25
Garrett, G. - Co. E 35th North Carolina May 27, 1865 VA25
Garrett, H. - Georgia Oct. 15, 1861   VA25
Garrett, Henry T. - Pvt. - Co. E 8th Georgia KIA Dec. 13, 1862 at Fredericksburg VA28
Garrett, J. - May 6, 1864 VA25
Garrett, James M. - Pvt. - Co. D 35th Georgia DOW May 15, 1864   VA28
Garrett, P. - 13th Alabama March 3, 1862 VA25
Garrett, S.V.   Alabama Dec. 16, 1862   VA25
Garrett, W. - Co. E 13th South Carolina May 18, 1862 VA25

Garrick, J.W. - Co. D 2nd Georgia Jan. 18, 1863   VA25
Garrison, J.H. - 1st South Carolina Oct. 9, 1861   VA25
Garrison, R. - 47th Virginia July 3, 1862   VA25
Garter, Vinson - 2nd South Carolina   VA18
Garth, H. - 2nd Virginia Cavalry   VA23
Gary, J. - Co. A 5th South Carolina Sept. 18, 1864   VA25
Gaskins, A. - Co. I 31st North Carolina July 29, 1864   VA25
Gassett, W. - Co. D 42nd Alabama Oct. 13, 1862   VA25
Gastin, J.W. - 48th Mississippi Nov. 10, 1862   VA25
Gates, C. - C.S.N. Jan. 31, 1865   VA25
Gates, L. - Co. F 7th South Carolina July 14, 1864 VA25
Gatewood, __ - Co. P (sic) 13th North Carolina Sept. 8, 1861   VA25
Gatewood, T. - 1st Alabama Nov. 12, 1862   VA25
Gatewood, W. - 16th Georgia Nov. 12, 1862   VA25
Gatkins, G. - Co. K 43rd North Carolina July 4, 1864 VA25
Gatlin, J.H. - Co. A 1st Mississippi July 29, 1863   VA25
Gay, Edwin - VA15
Gay, G.W. - Co. M 16th Alabama May 20, 1862   VA25
Gay, J. - Co. H 14th Georgia June 21, 1864   VA25
Gay, J. - Co. G 44th Georgia June 4, 1864   VA25
Gay, J.T. - Lt. - Co. B 4th Georgia April 28, 1865   VA25
Gay, P.S. - Co. G 44th Georgia June 29, 1864   VA25
Gay, W.C. - Co. C 6th Georgia Aug. 6, 1864   VA25
Gay, W.R. - Co. E 27th North Carolina Sept. 9, 1864   VA25
Gay, Wm. - 13th North Carolina   VA18
Gearing, Jas. - VA06
Geary, James - Pvt. - Co. G Hampton's Legion Died May 28, 1865   VA26
Gee, A.J. - Co. H Palmetto Sharp Shooters July 19, 1864   VA25
Gefpeys, B. - Co. C 27th South Carolina March 20, 1865   VA25
Gelkin, J. - Co. E 3rd North Carolina Sept. 4, 1862 VA25
Genhan, __ - May 15, 1862 VA25

Gentry, A.V. - Co. H 34th North Carolina Aug. 12, 1863
    VA25
Gentry, Andrew - Pvt. - 37th North Carolina Infantry DOW
    June 14, 1862   VA09
Gentry, D. - Co. G 45th Georgia June 7, 1864   VA25
Gentry, F.G. - Co. B 37th North Carolina July 2, 1862 VA25
Gentry, W. Pvt. - Virginia April 5, 1865   VA22
Gentry, W.C. - Co. E 22nd Georgia Aug. 12, 1864   VA25
Gentry, Watkins L. - KIA July 6, 1864 age 23   VA19
George, __ - Co. F 12th North Carolina June 13, 1861
    VA25
George, A. - 47th North Carolina Dec. 9, 1863   VA25
George, J.L. - Co. A 7th Georgia Cavalry   March 12, 1865
    VA25
George, P. - Co. K 30th North Carolina Jan. 8, 1862 VA25
Gerald, B. - 7th South Carolina July 13, 1861   VA25
Germin, A.H. - Co. H 3rd North Carolina Sept. 21, 1864
    VA25
Gerrald, Simon - POW - Federal Soldier Died Oct. 17, 1861
    "of Boon County"   VA19
Gersberg, Henry - Salem, Virginia KIA - June 2, 1864   VA17
Gesham, W.C. - Co. H 9th Alabama May 24, 1862   VA25
Gibb, A.J. - Co. G 3rd Georgia Nov. 9, 1862   VA25
Gibbs, C.C. - Co. E 2nd Florida July 12, 1864   VA25
Gibbs, D.C. - Co. K 19th Georgia May 10, 1862   VA25
Gibbs, F. - Co. F 10th Georgia Aug. 31, 1861   VA25
Gibbs, J.S. - Pvt. - Co. D 34th Georgia Died May 28, 1865
    VA26
Gibbs, Wm. - POW - Federal Soldier Died Dec. 6, 1861
    VA19
Gibley, J.W. - 8th South Carolina   VA18
Gibson, A.J. - 6th Alabama   VA11
Gibson, D.K. - Co. H 2nd Mississippi Battalion June 17, 1862
    VA25
Gibson, G.W. - Co. B 4th North Carolina July 24, 1864 VA25
Gibson, Isaac S. - DOW July 18, 1862   VA19

Gibson, J.F. - Co. H 1st Texas May 12, 1862 VA25
Gibson, J.J. - Co. C 37th North Carolina July 3, 1862 VA25
Gibson, J.W. - 2nd South Carolina VA18
Gibson, W. - Clark Cavalry VA06
Gibson, W.J. Georgia March 28, 1863 VA25
Gibson, W.P. - Co. E 44th Georgia July 9, 1862 VA25
Gibson, W.S. - Hampton's Legion (Georgia) July 6, 1864 VA25
Giddens, James H. - Pvt. - Co. L 26th Georgia Died May 10, 1864 name also spelled "Gidiedins" VA28
Giddins, James H. - see Giddiedens, James H. VA28
Gies, __ - Conscript C.S.A. March 12, 1863 VA25
Gilbert, __ - 3rd Alabama July 3, 1862 VA25
Gilbert, A.H. - Co. A 6th Louisiana May 26, 1864 VA25
Gilbert, B. - 3rd Alabama Dec. 29, 1862 VA25
Gilbert, J.F. - Co. A 22nd North Carolina June 25, 1862 VA25
Gilbert, J.G. - Co. F 59th Georgia Nov. 19, 1862 VA25
Gilbert, L. - Co. D 17th North Carolina Aug. 31, 1864 VA25
Gilder, J. - Co. I 47th Georgia May 30, 1863 VA25
Gile, W.H. - Virginia VA20
Giles, A. - Co. D 14th North Carolina June 8, 1862 VA25
Giles, H.H. - Co. C 59th Georgia Aug. 17, 1864 VA25
Giles, William A. - Pvt. - Co. H 49th Virginia KIA Fredericksburg Dec. 13, 1862 VA28
Gill, A.M. - Co. F 44th N.C. Dec. 7, 1863 VA25
Gill, Jas. - VA06
Gilles, C. - Co. B 7th Georgia Cavalry April 15, 1865 VA25
Gillespie, A. - Co. E 20th South Carolina Dec. 25, 1864 VA25
Gillespie, John N. - Fry's Battery - Orange Artillery (Virginia) KIA - Spotsylvania Court House May 12, 1864 VA28
Gillespie, L.P. - Co. H 22nd Georgia Aug. 8, 1864 VA25
Gillespie, W.D. - Co. H 28th North Carolina July 17, 1862 VA25

Gillespie, W.L. - Co. C 1st South Carolina Cavalry June 24, 1864   VA25
Gilliam, C.W.   Virginia Feb. 10, 1863   VA25
Gilliam, J. - July 12, 1861 VA25
Gilliam, J.S. - Sgt. - Kemper's Battery (Virginia)   1864   VA25
Gilliam, J.W. - Co. A 15th N.C. Nov. 1, 1863   VA25
Gilliland, J.W. - Kentucky   VA20
Gilling, H. - Co. E 44th North Carolina   March 7, 1865   VA25
Gillispie, John N. - see Gillespie, John N.   VA28
Gilmore, __ - July 1862   VA25
Gilmore, A. - Co. F 29th Virginia May 18, 1864   VA25
Gilmore, H.A. - Georgia   VA20
Gilmore, I. - Co. B 7th North Carolina Sept. 1, 1862 VA25
Gilmore, J. - Co. I 27th North Carolina April 23, 1864   VA25
Gilmore, J. - Co. D 10th Georgia March 28, 1863   VA25
Gilmore, R.M. - Co. H 11th Alabama Oct. 19, 1863   VA25
Gilstrope, E. - Co. F 22nd South Carolina Aug. 27, 1864   VA25
Girdman, E. - Co. C 2nd North Carolina   VA11
Givens, Lewis C. - Virginia   VA20
Gladden, H.G. - Co. H 49th North Carolina Jan. 12, 1862   VA25
Gladden, John - 2nd Florida Aug. 11, 1861   VA25
Glance, James H. - Pvt. - Co. H 2nd North Carolina Battalion   Died May 19, 1864 Headstone reads: "Gland" VA28
Glanton, C.R. - Co. B 6th South Carolina Oct. 22, 1864 VA25
Glass, P.M. - Co. D 44th Georgia July 20, 1862   VA25
Glass, R.C. - 1st Maryland Artillery   Nov. 7, 1863 VA25
Glasscock, Charles B. - Co. B 20th Virginia Battalion   VA11
Glasscock, E.A. - Co. A 8th Louisiana Dec. 11, 1862   VA25
Glassgall, C.M. - Co. C 21st North Carolina May 21, 1864   VA25
Glea, H. - Co. A 2nd Mississippi June 27, 1862   VA25
Gleaton, A.B.T. - Co. F 59th Georgia Oct. 22, 1864   VA25

Gleeny, T.A. - I3 (sic) Alabama Oct. 25, 1862   VA25
Glener, E. - Co. B 12th Georgia April 8, 1864   VA25
Glenn, A.W. - North Carolina Artillery July 14, 1864   VA25
Glenn, B. - Co. B 14th Georgia July 28, 1862   VA25
Glenn, Ed. - Died Aug 12, 1862   age 19   VA19
Glenn, J.D. - Co. I 3rd North Carolina Sept. 21, 1862   VA25
Glenn, R.D. - Co. K 6th Georgia July 2, 1863   VA25
Glenn, R.J. - Co. B 26th North Carolina July 20, 1864   VA25
Gliscal, D.A. - Georgia   VA20
Glond, A.S. - Co. I 18th Mississippi June 19, 1862   VA25
Glover, H.H. - Co. B 62nd Georgia Died Jan. 20, 1863   VA03
Glover, J.D. - Co. G 17th Georgia Aug. 1, 1862   VA25
Glover, William A. - see Glover, William Hocker   VA28
Glover, William Hocker - Sgt. - Co. H 2nd Virginia Cavalry KIA Spotsylvania C. H. May 8, 1864   Other records state "Co. A 2nd Virginia Infantry"   VA28
Gochenour, Jacob - VA12
Gochenour, John - VA14
Godard, E.E. - Co. E 44th Georgia   VA11
Goddin, J.M. - Co. D 30th North Carolina Aug. 30, 1862   VA25
Godding, J.W. - Pvt. - 14th North Carolina Infantry Died June 9, 1862   VA09
Godsey, A.H. - Co. H 19th Mississippi June 19, 1862   VA25
Gody, H.W. - Co. I 43rd North Carolina July 17, 1864   VA25
Goff, W.A. - Co. A 8th Florida June 16, 1863   VA25
Goiner, James - Co. B 25th Virginia   VA08
Gold, J.P. - Co. K 3rd Alabama July 8, 1862   VA25
Gold, Marion B. - Co. E 12th North Carolina Inf. DOW (Malvern Hill) July 8, 1862 VA25
Golden, M. - Co. G 5th Louisiana June 27, 1862   VA25
Golden, O.P. - 10th Alabama VA18
Golden, W.H. - Co. E Orr's Rifles (South Carolina)   March 12, 1865   VA25

Golight, W.B. - Co. F 13th South Carolina July 13, 1862 VA25

Golightly, H. - Co. B 8th Alabama July 13, 1862 VA25

Gollum, Martin - 18th Mississippi VA18

Gond, W. - 9th Louisiana May 3, 1862 VA25

Gont, J.F. - Co. C 2nd North Carolina March 12, 1863 VA25

Good, J.T. - Virginia VA20

Good, Madison - Grave not marked VA15

Good, R.W. - Kentucky VA20

Goodbye, H.S. - Kentucky VA20

Goode, J. - Co. H 44th North Carolina Jan. 31, 1865 VA25

Goodin, J.T. - Co. K 45th Georgia Aug. 7, 1862 VA25

Gooding, W.D. - Mosby's Cavalry VA10

Goodman, __ - 4th North Carolina July 2, 1861 VA25

Goodman, A. - Co. D 27th North Carolina Jan. 31, 1864 VA25

Goodman, H. - Co. B 8th Louisiana June 22, 1862 VA25

Goodman, J.T. - Co. K 10th Alabama June 22, 1862 VA25

Goodrich, Chas. D. - Pvt. - Virginia Nov. 22, 1864 Cemetery roster lists this soldier as "Chas. O. Goodrich" VA22

Goodson, C. - 8th Alabama Oct. 27, 1862 VA25

Goodwin, __ - Co. G 12th Mississippi July 4, 1862 VA25

Goodwin, A. - Co. D 27th North Carolina June 25, 1864 VA25

Goodwin, B.A. - Co. G 1st North Carolina April 6, 1865 VA25

Goodwin, G.R. - Aug. 1, 1863 VA25

Goodwin, J.F. - Co. I 3rd Virginia June 19, 1862 VA25

Goodwin, J.G. - Co. C 53rd Georgia May 8, 1865 VA25

Goodwin, Marcellus - Pvt. - Co. E 19th Virginia Bat. Died May 24, 1865 VA26

Goodwin, Mardis Gale - Corp. - Co. G 44th Alabama Died May 8, 1964 VA28

Goodwin, Thos. - Pvt. - Co. A 30th Georgia Died June 9, 1865 VA26

Goodwood, G. - Pvt. - Georgia April 6, 1865 VA22

Goody, J.N. - Co. E 30th North Carolina Oct. 27, 1863   VA25
Gooven, J.W. - Co. H 5th Alabama April 26, 1862   VA25
Gorday, A. - Co. G 27th Georgia July 3, 1864   VA25
Gorden, J. - Co. C 51st Georgia May 18, 1863   VA25
Gorden, J.R. - Co. C 14th Alabama May 29, 1862   VA25
Gorden, James - Co. D 51st Georgia   VA11
Gordon, B.F. - Co. A 24th Georgia May 14, 1862   VA25
Gordon, C. - Co. F 66th North Carolina Nov. 25, 1864   VA25
Gordon, J.C. - July 25, 1862   VA25
Gordon, J.W. - Co. E 23rd Virginia Aug. 23, 1864   VA25
Gordon, Thomas Churchill - Sgt. - Co. D 30th Virginia
    Veteran Died July 25, 1906   VA28
Gordon, W. - Co. I 44th North Carolina Oct. 2, 1864 VA25
Gordon, William W. - Pvt. - 13th North Carolina Infantry
    Died 1862   VA09
Gore, M. - Co. G 20th North Carolina March 24, 1865   VA25
Gorman, C. - Oct. 30, 1862 VA25
Gosling, Henry - Co. K 19th Georgia Infantry   VA10
Gossett, __ - North Carolina Aug. 30, 1861   VA25
Gossip, E.M. - 13th South Carolina July 8, 1862   VA25
Gough, James - Co. C 2nd North Carolina   VA11
Goulsby, W.T. - Alabama   VA20
Gounts, D. - Co. C 53rd Georgia Dec. 23, 1862   VA25
Goutz, J.F. - March 23, 1863   VA25
Gowen, William B. - POW - Federal Soldier - New York
    Regt. - Died Oct. 5, 1861   VA19
Grace, M.S. - Co. K 6th Alabama Aug. 7, 1862   VA25
Grace, T.T. - Co. B 10th Georgia Feb. 24, 1863   VA25
Graddick, __ - Co. F 64th Georgia Sept. 6, 1864   VA25
Grady, B.F. - Co. B 3rd North Carolina July 22, 1862 VA25
Grady, C.J. - Pvt. - Co. H 46th Georgia Died May 27, 1865
    VA26
Grady, F. - 21st Mississippi July 5, 1862   VA25
Grady, Henry C. - Capt. - Co. D 27th North Carolina Died
    May 12, 1864   VA28
Grady, J.B. - 7th South Carolina June 29, 1864   VA25

Grady, T. - Clark Cavalry VA06
Graham, F.M. - Co. A 7th Georgia June 25, 1864   VA25
Graham, G.G. - Co. H 10th Georgia June 23, 1864   VA25
Graham, H.L.F. - Co. I 26th South Carolina Sept. 24, 1864   VA25
Graham, J. - Ritter's Battery (Virginia) Aug. 10, 1862   VA25
Graham, L. - Co. B 5th Florida Nov. 25, 1862   VA25
Graham, S.W. - Co. H 30th North Carolina Aug. 14, 1862   VA25
Graham, Wm. - Co. C 24th Virginia Oct. 7, 1862   VA25
Grainger, W. - 1st South Carolina May 15, 1863   VA25
Gramers, W.D. - Allan's Battery (Virginia) June 10, 1862   VA25
Grandy, P.H. - Lt. - Co. D 1st North Carolina June 26, 1862   VA25
Granger, L.B. - Co. D 18th Alabama July 23, 1862   VA25
Granger, W. - Co. A 22nd North Carolina June 22, 1864   VA25
Grant, __ - 1st South Carolina July 11, 1862   VA25
Grant, G.G. - 13th Georgia July 22, 1862   VA25
Grant, J. - Co. F 2nd South Carolina July 9, 1864   VA25
Grant, J.T. - 1st North Carolina Cavalry Dec. 7, 1863   VA25
Grant, W. - 9th South Carolina Oct. 24, 1862   VA25
Grantland, J.Q. - Co. A 40th North Carolina April 7, 1865   VA25
Grathan, S. - Co. I 12th Mississippi July 14, 1862   VA25
Graver, P. - Co. K 12th South Carolina July 16, 1862   VA25
Graverly, B. - Co. D 55th North Carolina Sept. 27, 1864   VA25
Graves, B. Frank - VA15
Graves, J.C. - Co. A 13th South Carolina July 6, 1862 VA25
Gravitt, J. - Co. E 23rd Georgia Nov. 24, 1862   VA25
Grawl, L. - Co. D 20th Georgia June 26, 1864   VA25
Gray, A.W. - Co. A 53rd Virginia July 9, 1862   VA25
Gray, A.W. - 53rd Georgia Aug. 9, 1862   VA25
Gray, B. - Co. D 27th North Carolina June 15, 1864   VA25

Gray, B.A. - Co. H 43rd North Carolina June 11, 1864   VA25
Gray, C. - Co. G 54th North Carolina July 6, 1865 VA25
Gray, Daniel L. - Pvt. (Lt. On headstone) - Co. K 61st
   Georgia Died May 12, 1864   VA28
Gray, Geo. - Co. E 3rd Virginia April 18, 1862   VA25
Gray, J. - Co. A 44th Georgia June 4, 1864   VA25
Gray, J. J. - April 8, 1863   VA25
Gray, Jno. - Co. A 2nd Arkansas June 20, 1862   VA25
Gray, Thos. - Corp. - Co. A 21st Mississippi July 13, 1862
   age 23   VA25
Gray, W. - Co. B 9th South Carolina   Oct. 9, 1861 VA25
Gray, William H. - Pvt. - Co. B 58th Virginia KIA
   Spotsylvania C. H. - May 18, 1864   VA28
Grayson, R.O. - Lt. - Co. F 8th Virginia June 27, 1862   VA25
Greeman, F. - Co. F 1st Texas June 1, 1862   VA25
Green, __ - Texas Aug. 3, 1861   VA25
Green, __ - Lt. - May 13, 1863   VA25
Green, A.M. - Co. H 41st Tennessee July 20, 1863   VA25
Green, C.H. - Co. C 8th Florida Oct. 30, 1862   VA25
Green, D.L. - Co. C 4th North Carolina Cavalry May 21, 1862
   VA25
Green, E. - Lt. - Co. C 20th North Carolina June 1862   VA25
Green, E. - Lt. - Co. C 20th North Carolina June 1862   VA25
Green, Elbridge - Pvt. - 14th Alabama Died in 1862 in either
   Dumfries (Virginia) or Fredericksburg (Virginia
   VA28
Green, G.W. - Co. H 47th North Carolina Oct. 3, 1864 VA25
Green, Geo. - Co. D 18th Mississippi July 9, 1862   VA25
Green, H. - Co. D 2nd Florida Aug. 8, 1862   VA25
Green, H. - Virginia   VA20
Green, J. - Co. H 5th North Carolina Oct. 7, 1862 VA25
Green, J. - Co. I 32nd Virginia   Nov. 18, 1862   VA25
Green, J.J. - Texas   VA20
Green, J.L. - Co. A 13th Georgia Feb. 25, 1865   VA25
Green, J.W. - 11th Georgia VA18
Green, Jno. - Waggoner -July 1, 1862   VA25

Green, M.J. - Co. B 13th South Carolina July 8, 1862 VA25
Green, O. - VA06
Green, S. - Co. B 2nd Florida Battalion June 18, 1864 VA25
Green, S.L. - Co. D 13th Georgia Feb. 14, 1865 VA25
Green, T - Co. H 5th North Carolina Oct. 17, 1862 VA25
Green, T. 9th Louisiana Aug. 31, 1861 VA25
Green, T. - Co. H 13th South Carolina July 9, 1862 VA25
Green, T.G. - Co. D 57th North Carolina Nov. 19, 1863 VA25
Green, W.N. - 8th Georgia Sept. 13, 1861 VA25
Greenwell, G.A. - Co. F 22nd North Carolina June 10, 1862 VA25
Greenwell, J. - Virginia Artillery Sept. 7, 1862 VA25
Greenwood, W.R. - Co. C 47th Virginia March 19, 1865 VA25
Greenwood, William B. - Pvt. - Co. H 54th North Carolina DOD near Fredericksburg - May 13, 1863 VA28
Greeson, H.C. - Co. A 13th North Carolina VA11
Gregory, David - Pvt. - Co. F 41st Alabama Died June 17, 1865 VA26
Gregory, J.F. - Sgt. - Co. C 27th Georgia June 28, 1864 VA25
Gregory, R. - Co. B 38th Virginia June 1, 1862 VA25
Gregory, R.D. - Co. B 32nd Virginia June 3, 1862 VA25
Gregory, R.L. - 24th Virginia Oct. 27, 1861 VA25
Gregory, R.P. - June 17, 1862 VA25
Gregory, S.P. - Co. G 13th North Carolina July 16, 1864 VA25
Gregory, Sam'l. - 18th Virginia VA18
Gregory, W. - 14th North Carolina Aug. 21, 1861 VA25
Grenn, __ July 9, 1862 VA25
Greven, J.M. - Co. A 12th South Carolina June 8, 1862 VA25
Grewsham, E.H. - Capt. Smith's Co. Oct. 10, 1861 VA25
Grewsham, G.W. - Co. G 23rd North Carolina June 17, 1862 VA25

Grewsham, H.B. - Co. D 13th South Carolina July 1, 1862 VA25
Grey, Thomas P. - Rockbridge Artillery VA11
Grier, William B. - DOD Nov. 25, 1862 VA19
Griffin, A. - Nov. 16, 1862 VA25
Griffin, A.C. - Sgt. - Co. C 4th South Carolina Cavalry July 4, 1864 VA25
Griffin, B. - 5th Alabama June 27, 1862 VA25
Griffin, B.F. - Co. I 8th Alabama Nov. 24, 1862 VA25
Griffin, Cornelius O. - Co. D 14th North Carolina VA28
Griffin, G.D. - Co. B 3rd Alabama Aug. 28, 1862 VA25
Griffin, G.W. - Co. G 26th Alabama June 10, 1862 VA25
Griffin, H. - 9th Georgia Nov. 21, 1862 VA25
Griffin, Henry - Co. H 12th Alabama July 5, 1862 VA25
Griffin, J.L. - Co. I 13th South Carolina Aug. 5, 1862 VA25
Griffin, J.R. - Co. G 1st South Carolina Sept. 1, 1862 VA25
Griffin, J.R. - Co. G 1st North Carolina Sept. 1, 1862 VA25
Griffin, J.S. - Hampton's Legion (Georgia) Aug. 14, 1862 VA25
Griffin, John - Co. H 12th Virginia July 5, 1862 VA25
Griffin, L.G. - Co. B 29th Alabama April 22, 1865 VA25
Griffin, M.H. - Co. H 14th Georgia June 18, 1862 VA25
Griffin, P. - Co. K 53rd North Carolina March 7, 1865 VA25
Griffin, P.J. - Alabama VA20
Griffin, R. - Co. K 37th North Carolina June 16, 1862 VA25
Griffin, R.M. - Co. E 48th North Carolina April 29, 1864 VA25
Griffin, T. - 12th Mississippi July 5, 1862 VA25
Griffin, W. - Co. H 14th Alabama June 17, 1862 VA25
Griffin, W. - Co. G 22nd Alabama May 2, 1865 VA25
Griffin, W.A. - Co. I 6th Alabama March 4, 1863 VA25
Griffith, R.W. - Co. B 55th Georgia Sept. 2, 1863 VA25
Griffith, W. - Co. A 2nd Ark Sept. 17, 1862 VA25
Grifin, J.C. - Pvt. - Alabama Oct. 14, 1864 VA22
Grigg, A.D. - Co. B 21st South Carolina Nov. 13, 1864 VA25

Griggs, D.H. - Co. G 34th North Carolina Nov. 9, 1864 VA25
Griggs, H. - Co. C 19th Virginia June 25, 1862   VA25
Griggs, T.J. - Co. C 20th Georgia July 2, 1863   VA25
Grigsby, J. - 9th Alabama VA18
Grimes, C.W. - Co. G 12th Georgia   VA28
Grimes, F. - Co. K 28th Georgia May 13, 1862   VA25
Grinder, W.M. - Co. G 37th North Carolina June 14, 1863
    VA25
Grinsford, G. - Co. C 47th North Carolina Nov. 7, 1864 VA25
Grinsley, W. - North Carolina Sept. 19, 1864   VA25
Grisard, A.B. - Co. K 1st Kentucky March 14, 1862   VA25
Grisworld, R.C.N. - Co. C 17th Mississippi May 14, 1862
    VA25
Grizzle, John P. - Lt. - Texas Oct. 17, 1864   VA22
Grodrey, Samuel - Co. E 15th South Carolina   VA11
Grog, W.C. - VA12
Groham, G. - Co. G 6th Alabama May 22, 1862   VA25
Groham, J.E. - Co. C "H.L." (Georgia) [Hampton's Legion?]
    July 31, 1864   VA25
Grooms, A. - Co. E 2nd South Carolina July 16, 1861   VA25
Gross, H. - Louisiana. Battalion July 31, 1861   VA25
Gross, W. - Co. I 28th North Carolina June 29, 1864   VA25
Gross, William - Virginia   VA22
Grossen, W. - Lt. - 14th Louisiana May 27, 1863   VA25
Grove, Henry H. - VA12
Grove, J.B. - 35th Georgia Aug. 8, 1862   VA25
Grubb, St. - Lt. - 2nd Virginia Infantry   VA06
Grubbs, J.M. - 2nd Virginia Infantry   VA06
Grubbs, John - Co. D 8th Virginia Oct. 10, 1862   VA25
Grubbs, L.B. - Co. B 38th Virginia July 22, 1862   VA25
Grubbs, Leon R. - Corp. - Co. A 23rd Virginia KIA
    Spotsylvania C. H. May 12, 1864   VA28
Grubbs, N.T. - Co. I 1st South Carolina May 20, 1864 VA25
Grubbs, Pam - 2nd Virginia Infantry   VA06
Grubbs, William W. - Corp. - Co. A 47th Alabama Died May
    8, 1864   VA28

Grubbs, Wm. - 2nd Virginia Infantry   VA06
Grue, Albert - 1st Georgia Regt.   VA18
Grussell, Samuel - Co. A 1st __ VA18
Guard, J.A. - Co. D 51st Virginia July 22, 1864   VA25
Guess, B.E. - Louisiana   VA20
Guess, W.B. - Lt. - Co. A 2nd Louisiana July 8, 1862 VA25
Guile, J.M. - Co. B 25th Virginia Aug. 12, 1864   VA25
Guill, Charles - Pvt. - Co. F 53rd Virginia Died July 4, 1865   VA26
Guinn, __ - Co. F 3rd North Carolina Infantry   VA08
Guira, N. - 15th Louisiana Sept. 1, 1862   VA25
Guire, P. - Co. A 27th Georgia Aug. 17, 1862   VA25
Guire, T. - July 14, 1862 VA25
Guiron, W.H. - Co. F 42nd Mississippi June 25, 1863   VA25
Gullery, W.Y. - Co. H 15th Georgia June 22, 1862   VA25
Gullick, G.W. -   VA25
Gum, G. - VA12
Gum, W.J. - VA12
Gumley, John - Texas Aug. 30, 1861   VA25
Gunn, __ - 14th Alabama 1862   VA25
Gunn, __ - July 8, 1862 VA25
Gunn, A.J. - 16th Georgia Oct. 10, 1861   VA25
Gunn, C.G. - Co. I 15th South Carolina April 4, 1864   VA25
Gunnell, J.J. - Co. F 3rd Alabama June 12, 1862   VA25
Gunnell, J.W. - 8th Virginia Infantry   VA10
Gunsey, Council - Holcomb Legion   VA18
Gurkins, J.A. - Co. E 55th North Carolina June 2, 1864 VA25
Gurvin, B.C. - Co. K 6th Alabama June 9, 1863   VA25
Gussin, A. - Co. H 35th Georgia Oct. 4, 1864   VA25
Gust, J.T. - Cobb's Legion (Georgia)   May 8, 1863 VA25
Guthrie, James L. - Pvt. - Co. D 19th Virginia Bat. Died June 16, 1865   VA26
Guy, G.H. - VA12
Guy, W.H. - 2nd Mississippi Oct. 13, 1864   VA25
Guy, Wm. - VA20

Gwathmey, A.S. - Co. F 27th North Carolina Dec. 12, 1863 VA25
H __ , G.W. - Co. A 13th Mississippi Sept. 6, 1862 VA25
H __ , J.G. - Co. H 5th South Carolina Aug. 9, 1864 VA25
H __ , L.D. - April 20, 1862 VA25
H __ , P.L. - 60th Georgia May 7, 1862 VA25
Hackeman, Gerhard D. - Pvt. - 18th North Carolina Infantry DOW June 1, 1862 VA09
Hackett, John - Co. E 60th Georgia VA11
Haden, A.A. - 5th Alabama Aug. 10, 1862 VA25
Haden, C. - Co. H 40th Virginia April 5, 1861 VA25
Hagan, __ - 12th Mississippi VA18
Hagan, R.P. - Co. G 52nd North Carolina Nov. 24, 1864 VA25
Haggard, C. - Louisiana. Artillery July 8, 1864 VA25
Haines, __ - March 28, 1864 VA25
Haines, J. - Co. C 9th Louisiana Nov. 19, 1861 VA25
Haines, J.R. - VA28
Haines, Jos. D. - POW - Federal Soldier Died June 19, 1862 VA19
Haira, J.O. - Co. I 15th Louisiana July 31, 1863 VA25
Haithcox, Joshua - see Hathcox, Joshua
Halbert, F.M. - Co. K 22nd South Carolina Sept. 7, 1862 VA25
Hales, L.F. - Corp. - Co. A 16th Mississippi Died May 12, 1864 VA28
Haley, B.H. - Co. C 4th North Carolina June 11, 1862 VA25
Haley, J.W. - Co. F 42nd Virginia May 24, 1863 VA25
Haley, John -Died Feb. 24, 1862 VA19
Halfhill, F.M. - 19th Mississippi May 26, 1861 VA25
Hall, __ - VA06
Hall, __ -1862 VA25
Hall, A. - Co. C 38th North Carolina Jan. 16, 1865 VA25
Hall, A.J. - Co. E 28th Virginia May 1, 1864 VA25
Hall, B. - June 5, 1862 VA25
Hall, D.J. - Co. K 35th North Carolina July 3, 1864 VA25

Hall, F. - Co. D 48th Georgia   Sept. 5, 1864   VA25
Hall, H. - 2nd Alabama Sept. 22, 1862   VA25
Hall, H. - Citizen - Sept. 9, 1864   VA25
Hall, H.F. - Co. D 27th North Carolina Sept. 20, 1862   VA25
Hall, I. - Co. B 2nd Mississippi April 20, 1862   VA25
Hall, J. - 13th South Carolina July 10, 1862   VA25
Hall, J. - Co. I 57th North Carolina Jan. 14, 1863   VA25
Hall, J. - Co. K. 16th North Carolina Oct. 4, 1864   VA25
Hall, J. T. - Co. I 3rd Virginia   Sept. 24, 1862   VA25
Hall, J.C. - Co. K 5th Florida March 1, 1862   VA25
Hall, J.H. - Co. F 13th South Carolina July 21, 1862   VA25
Hall, J.M. Pvt. - Co. H 13th Georgia   MW May 12, 1864   VA28
Hall, James - POW - Federal Soldier Died Feb. 27, 1862   VA19
Hall, L. - Co. A 6th Alabama June 19, 1862   VA25
Hall, L.H. - Co. A 28th North Carolina Aug. 25, 1864   VA25
Hall, Lindsey - Pvt. - Co. H 38th Georgia Died April 15, 1863 Headstone reads - "Lyndsey Hall"   VA28
Hall, Lyndsey - see Hall, Lindsey   VA28
Hall, R.H. - Cobb's Legion (Georgia) June 18, 1862   VA25
Hall, S.H. - 48th Georgia VA18
Hall, T.B. - Co. B 14th Virginia   VA11
Hall, Thos. - Pitt County North Carolina   Sept. 6, 1862   VA25
Hall, W.B. - Co. H 38th Georgia June 7, 1864   VA25
Hall, W.W. - Co. A 15th Georgia July 28, 1862   VA25
Hall, Wiley M. - Co. B 15th Alabama   VA11
Hall, Z. - Pvt. - Virginia March 19, 1865   VA22
Hallen, H. - June 6, 1862 VA25
Halley, R.T. - 49th Virginia Infantry   VA10
Hallfield, J.S. - Co. B 11th Georgia Nov. 14, 1864   VA25
Hallingsworth, A. - Co. G 49th Virginia July 10, 1862   VA25
Hallon, John A. - Co. E 2nd North Carolina   VA11
Halloway, J.T. - Co. F 26th North Carolina July 8, 1862 VA25
Halmer, J.H. - 8th Georgia July 16, 1864   VA25

Halsonser, J.Q. - Co. C 48th North Carolina Oct. 30, 1863 VA25

Halstead, J.K. - 2nd Signal Corps Oct. 2, 1864 VA25

Halt, E.R. - 1st Virginia Cavalry May 18, 1862 VA25

Halt, J. - Co. C 5th North Carolina Oct. 17, 1864 VA25

Haltewanger, J.G. - Co. C 20th South Carolina VA11

Halty, J. - McNeil's Co. Aug. 9, 1862 VA25

Ham, W.F. - Co. A 47th Alabama June 25, 1864 VA25

Hambee, J. - Co. G 12th South Carolina July 27, 1862 VA25

Hambleton, H.W. - Co. B 3rd Alabama Jan. 22, 1863 VA25

Hame, J.B. - Hampton's Legion VA18

Hamer, C.W. - Co. C 30th Georgia June 15, 1864 VA25

Hamers, T. - 4th Arkansas Sept. 9, 1862 VA25

Hamilton, James H. - Pvt. - Co. B 42nd Virginia DOW May 30, 1864 (MW Spotsylvania C. H. May 12, 1864) Headstone reads:" Co. B 2nd Virginia Infantry" VA28

Hamilton, Joseph - 6th Alabama VA18

Hamlet, L.B. - 4th Virginia Cavalry May 7, 1862 VA25

Hamlet, L.B. - Sumpter Artillery (South Carolina) May 7, 1862 VA25

Hamlin, Jacob - Co. G 57th North Carolina Died April 22, 1865 VA27

Hammel, James - 3rd Georgia Battalion VA18

Hammer, D.W. - Co. B 48th Alabama Jan. 2, 1863 VA25

Hammet, C.B. - Hampton's Legion (South Carolina) Aug. 26, 1862 VA25

Hammington, ___ - July 3, 1862 VA25

Hammock, Albert J. - Pvt. - Co. C 4th Georgia Died May 10, 1864 VA28

Hammock, J.H. - Co. B 24th North Carolina Sept. 1, 1862 VA25

Hammock, Lewis - Jackson's Horse Artillery (Virginia) VA11

Hammon, ___ - North Carolina VA07

Hammond, A.H. - Co. D 26th Mississippi May 31, 1865 VA25
Hammond, C.D. - Co. D 12th South Carolina June 13, 1864 VA25
Hammond, C.G. - Co. K 13th Alabama Oct. 19, 1864   VA25
Hammond, G.N. - Capt. - Co. B 1st Virginia Cavalry May 17, 1864   VA25
Hammond, J. - Co. D 12th South Carolina Aug. 2, 1862 VA25
Hammond, J.W. - Co. I 7th Georgia July 9, 1862   VA25
Hammond, L.H. - April 10, 1861   VA25
Hammond, M. - Co. H 6th South Carolina   VA28
Hammond, O.F. - Co. I 12th Virginia Aug. 26, 1863   VA25
Hammond, W.T. - Sgt. Major - Clark Cavalry   VA06
Hamner, D.L. - Co. I 14th Alabama June 14, 1862   VA25
Hampleton, __ - Co. H 59th Georgia Oct. 17, 1864   VA25
Hampleton, G.W. - 2nd Georgia Aug. 9, 1861   VA25
Hampton, R. - Co. I 24th Georgia May 23, 1861   VA25
Hampton, R.F. - Co. B 27th North Carolina July 28, 1864 VA25
Hampton, S.P. - 11th Georgia VA18
Hampton, W. - 1st South Carolina Aug. 23, 1861   VA25
Hampton, W.F. - Co. E 18th Virginia   May 10, 1862   VA25
Hampton, W.H. - 7th South Carolina Cavalry Aug. 11, 1861 VA25
Hamrick, Reuben - Sgt. - Co. D 55th North Carolina Died May 14, 1863   VA03
Hancock, A.M. - Co. C 6th Virginia Cavalry June 5, 1864 VA25
Hancock, E.S. - Co. A 5th Alabama July 5, 1862   VA25
Hancock, F.J. - Co. H 20th South Carolina   VA11
Hancock, J. - Co. E 48th Virginia Jan. 30, 1865   VA25
Hancock, J. - Sgt. - Co. C 27th Georgia Dec. 4, 1864   VA25
Hancock, James E. - Co. B 8th South Carolina   VA28
Hancock, John - Co. B 13th Georgia Feb. 19, 1865   VA25
Hancock, W.B. - Virginia   VA20
Hand, G.W. - Co. D 13th Virginia May 17, 1865   VA25

Hand, J.M. - Co. C 42nd Mississippi June 17, 1864 VA25
Hand, T.A. - Sgt. - Co. F 8th Georgia Oct. 10, 1864 VA25
Handerson, W. - 19th Georgia VA18
Hanes, Jacob H. - Corp. - Co. G 4th North Carolina Died May 12, 1864 VA28
Hanes, W.G. - Georgia Battalion Dec. 20, 1864 VA25
Haney, C.G. - Co. F 18th South Carolina Oct. 10, 1862 VA25
Haney, H. - Co. H 37th North Carolina Dec. 4, 1864 VA25
Hangen, J.F. - Co. G 52nd North Carolina June 24, 1864 VA25
Hankins, G.G. - Died Nov. 27, 1862 VA19
Hanks, Samuel - VA20
Hanley, J.A. - Co. D 8th Alabama Oct. 9, 1863 VA25
Hanley, J.F. - Co. C 42nd Virginia Nov. 12, 1862 VA25
Hanley, W.C. - Co. C 3rd Georgia Sept. 13, 1864 VA25
Hanna, G.W. - Co. G 45th Georgia Sept. 9, 1862 VA25
Hannah, J.W. - Co. E 28th Georgia Oct. 7, 1862 VA25
Hannah, Josiah P. - Phillip's Legion - Cavalry VA18
Hannah, T.R. - 9th Louisiana VA18
Hannon, G.W. - Corp. - 8th Alabama Aug. 8, 1862 VA25
Hanret, W.O. - Pvt. - Virginia April 5, 1865 VA22
Hanshaw, W.H. - VA08
Hanson, J. - Co. C 30th Virginia March 23, 1863 VA25
Hapel, A. - Pvt. - Virginia July 2, 1864 VA22
Happler, L. - Co. D 68th Virginia July 3, 1862 VA25
Harald, L. - Co. D 18th North Carolina Oct. 10, 1863 VA25
Hardee, J.W. - Co. D 27th North Carolina Sept. 11, 1864 VA25
Hardee, W.L. - Capt. - Virginia VA11
Harden, A. - Co. B 5th South Carolina Cavalry April 20, 1862 VA25
Harden, A. - Co. F 4th Texas June 7, 1862 VA25
Harden, J. - 44th North Carolina Nov. 15, 1864 VA25
Harden, J.F. - 22nd Mississippi Oct. 22, 1864 VA25
Harden, J.R. - Co. F 15th Alabama VA11
Harden, J.R. - 37th North Carolina Aug. 6, 1862 VA25

Harden, Robert T. - Pvt. - Co. G 15th Georgia Died at Guinea Station in 1863   VA28
Hardiman, Francis - POW - Federal Soldier Died Oct. 14, 1861   VA19
Hardin, Thomas J. - Colonel - Co. I 19th Mississippi Died May 12, 1864 born in Monroe County, Kentucky, on July 7, 1829   VA28
Harding, C.B. - Virginia Infantry   VA08
Harding, W. - 8th Georgia April 2, 1861   VA25
Harding, W. - Alabama   VA20
Hardister, James L. - Co. I 5th North Carolina   VA11
Hardwick, S. - Virginia   VA20
Hardy, A.F. - Cobb's Legion (Georgia)   VA18
Hardy, H.R. - Co. H 3rd Alabama July 14, 1862   VA25
Hare, G.W. - Co. H 43rd North Carolina March 20, 1865   VA25
Hare, John - Co. C 7th North Carolina July 30, 1864 VA25
Hargrove, F. - Co. F 12th Alabama Nov. 5, 1861   VA25
Hargrove, J. - Co. H 3rd Virginia Nov. 12, 1862   VA25
Harigan, P. - Co. B 1st Virginia March 18, 1861   VA25
Harmack, __ - Co. K 4th Georgia June 25, 1862   VA25
Harman, A. - Co. A 14th Louisiana Nov. 1, 1861   VA25
Harman, H. - 2nd Florida Sept. 7, 1862   VA25
Harman, H.T. - Co. D 17th Virginia Infantry   VA10
Harmett, __ - 1862   VA25
Harmon, M. - Co. E 24th Virginia   Sept. 7, 1862 VA25
Harold, H.B. - Co. G 25th North Carolina Sept. 3, 1864   VA25
Harold, L. - Co. E 17th North Carolina Aug. 24, 1864   VA25
Harold, W.P. - Co. I 5th North Carolina June 6, 1864 VA25
Harp, David - 3rd South Carolina   VA18
Harper, __ - July 18, 1862   VA25
Harper, George W. - Pvt. - Co. B 47 Alabama   VA28
Harper, J.B. - Co. H 3rd Georgia July 7, 1862   VA25
Harper, John - Phillip's Legion (Georgia) May 8, 1863   VA25

Harper, M.R. - Co. K Orr's Rifles (South Carolina) July 10, 1862   VA25
Harper, Thaddeus - Co. B 15th Alabama   VA11
Harper, W. - Co. G 20th North Carolina   Sept. 23, 1862   VA25
Harper, W. T. - Mobile Cavalry (Alabama) July 6, 1863   VA25
Harrell, A. - Co. A 2nd North Carolina. Aug. 18, 1862   VA25
Harrell, A.J. - 2nd Florida Aug. 22, 1861   VA25
Harrenger, __ - 1862   VA25
Harriett, J. - Co. A 10th Louisiana May 2, 1863   VA25
Harrington, __ - Richmond City Battalion (Virginia)   May 28, 1864   VA25
Harrington, D.B. - Co. A 25th North Carolina Dec. 28, 1863   VA25
Harrington, M.M. - Co. E 3rd Georgia Aug. 15, 1864   VA25
Harris, A. - Co. C 61st North Carolina Oct. 19, 1864   VA25

Harris, A. - Cobb's Legion (Georgia) July 28, 1862   VA25
Harris, A.A. - Co. A 17th North Carolina March 6, 1865   VA25
Harris, A.L. - Co. A 14th Alabama Aug. 1, 1862   VA25
Harris, A.S. - Co. C 14th Alabama Aug. 3, 1862   VA25
Harris, B. - Co. F Palmetto Sharp Shooters   Nov. 1864   VA25
Harris, C.B. - 4th Kentucky May 22, 1861   VA25
Harris, D. - Co. E 15th North Carolina Sept. 22, 1862   VA25
Harris, D. - Co. B Cutt's Battalion (Georgia) Aug. 23, 1864   VA25
Harris, D. G. - Co. F 7th Georgia   Oct. 3, 1864   VA25
Harris, D. M. - Co. F 53rd Georgia   May 20, 1863   VA25
Harris, D.H. - Pvt. - Co. F 60th Georgia Died Dec. 13, 1862   VA28
Harris, E.E. - Co. E 4th North Carolina   VA11

Harris, Frank - Pvt. - Co. I 3rd South Carolina DOD in
 Fredericksburg - April 3, 1863   VA28
Harris, G.B. - Co. C 12th North Carolina June 5, 1864 VA25
Harris, G.O. - Montgomery Blues (Alabama)Aug. 1, 1862
 VA25
Harris, George H. - Died Apr. 1, 1862   VA19
Harris, H. - Co. G 5th North Carolina June 2, 1864 VA25
Harris, H. - Co. H 15th Georgia   Sept. 26, 1862 VA25
Harris, J. - Co. F 20th North Carolina Aug. 7, 1862 VA25
Harris, J. - Co. D 4th North Carolina May 17, 1863 VA25
Harris, J. W. - Batt. Oct. 22 VA25
Harris, J. H. - Troop Artillery (Georgia) July 14, 1864   VA25
Harris, J.C. - Mississippi Aug. 7, 1861 VA25
Harris, J.Q. - Co. D 24th North Carolina Sept. 27, 1864
 VA25
Harris, J.R. - Co. G 66th North Carolina June 25, 1864   VA25
Harris, J.R. - Co. B 12th Georgia July 22, 1864   VA25
Harris, J.T. - Co. A 14th South Carolina Jan. 28, 1865   VA25
Harris, James D. - POW - Federal Soldier Died June 19, 1862
 VA19
Harris, Joel - Virginia   VA20
Harris, John - Pvt. - Co. E Navy B.N.C. Died June 30, 1865
 VA26
Harris, John M.V. - Sgt. - Co. K 47th Alabama MW in the
 Battle of the Wilderness VA28
Harris, L.A. - Cobb's Legion (Georgia) Dec. 9, 1864 VA25
Harris, M.D. - Co. A 13th South Carolina Aug. 7, 1862 VA25
Harris, M.V. - Co. A 3rd Alabama Aug. 24, 1862   VA25
Harris, P. - Co. C 20th North Carolina Sept. 26, 1862   VA25
Harris, R. - VA12
Harris, R.C. - Co. B 59th Georgia July 24, 1864   VA25
Harris, R.T. - 24th Georgia Jan. 2, 1863   VA25
Harris, Robert H. - "a prisoner" Co. D 8th Virginia Feb. 26,
 1863   VA19

Harris, Samuel N. - Corp. - Co. D 3rd South Carolina
Battalion Died May 8, 1864 Headstone reads: "3rd
South Carolina Infantry" VA28
Harris, T. - South Carolina July 30, 1862 VA25
Harris, T. - Co. B 3rd South Carolina Aug. 7, 1862 VA25
Harris, T. - Nov. 10, 1864 VA25
Harris, T.J. - Co. F 42nd Mississippi Oct. 26, 1862 VA25
Harris, W. - 18th North Carolina May 28, 1864 VA25
Harris, W. - Co. I 31st Virginia VA08
Harris, W.A. - Co. D 11th Georgia Aug. 1, 1864 VA25
Harris, W.H. - VA28
Harris, W.H. - Co. H 53rd Georgia May 20, 1863 VA25
Harris, W.T. - Co. G 20th Georgia March 18, 1863 VA25
Harris, W.W. - Co. C 13th Louisiana May 17, 1862 VA25
Harrison, A. - Co. A 21st Georgia Sept. 29, 1862 VA25
Harrison, A.S. - 8th Virginia Infantry VA10
Harrison, David W. - VA15
Harrison, E.G. - Winchester (Virginia) Nov. 8, 1862 VA25
Harrison, Edmond Carter - KIA age 59 VA19
Harrison, H.C. - Co. D 63rd Tennessee May 19, 1864 VA25
Harrison, J. - Co. E 31st North Carolina Aug. 9, 1862 VA25
Harrison, Jno. - Co. D 40th Virginia July 31, 1862 VA25
Harrison, R.M. - Alabama VA20
Harrison, Richard S. - Pvt. - Co. E 12th Virginia Died during
the Summer of 1864 VA28
Harrison, Rob. - Virginia VA20
Harrison, T.W. - Co. B 31st Georgia Sept. 26, 1862 VA25
Harrison, W.H. - July 5, 1861 VA25
Harrison, W.M. - Co. D 31st Georgia Aug. 8, 1862 VA25
Harrold, J.W. - Co. F 6th Georgia May 29, 1861 VA25
Harrold, S.W. - Co. B 6th Georgia May 31, 1861 VA25
Harry, S.D. - 2nd South Carolina VA18
Hart, F.E. - Co. I 19th Georgia May 23, 1861 VA25
Hart, J. - Co. F 27th Georgia Sept. 1, 1864 VA25
Hart, J.M. - Gordon's Batt. Oct. 16, 1864 VA25
Hart, Jno. - Co. A 17th Virginia July 13, 1862 VA25

Hart, O. - Co. C 30th North Carolina Sept. 29, 1863   VA25
Hart, T.H. - Cobb's Legion (Georgia) June 26, 1864   VA25
Hartford, S.G. - Lt. - Co. B 7th Georgia Nov. 16, 1864
    VA25
Harthorne, J.J. -Lt. - Co. A 13th Mississippi July 16, 1862
    VA25
Harthorne, R. - Co. B 14th Georgia July 19, 1864 VA25
Hartie, A.D. - Co. C 13th Alabama Feb. 9, 1863   VA25
Hartley, H.S. - Co. C 8th Louisiana Dec. 17, 1863   VA25
Hartley, J.L. - Co. C 15th South Carolina June 12, 1864
    VA25
Hartley, W.B. - Co. H 14th North Carolina June 14, 1862
    VA25
Hartsfield, Ava Curtis - VMI Cadet - MW - Battle of New
    Market - May 15, 1864 DOW June 26, 1864 - DOW
    June 26, 1864 - Buried at Petersburg, Virginia
    VA21
Hartsfield, D.W. - Co. I 19th Arkansas May 28, 1863   VA25
Hartwell, J. - Co. B 7th North Carolina July 14, 1862 VA25
Hartzog, I.C.- Lt. - Co. A 37th North Carolina Aug. 7, 1862
    age 35   VA25
Harvey, B.G. - Co. C 10th Georgia Oct. 7, 1862   VA25
Harvey, J.C. - Co. D 42nd Virginia Nov. 12, 1862   VA25
Harvey, John - Co. H 1st Texas May 19, 1862   VA25
Harvey, L.H. - Co. H 59th North Carolina Oct. 16, 1864
    VA25
Harvey, L.J. - Co. A 1st South Carolina   Oct. 19, 1864
    VA25
Harvey, R. - Co. B 64th Georgia July 24, 1864   VA25
Harvey, R.F. - Co. E 8th Georgia Aug. 29, 1862   VA25
Harvey, T. - Co. B 8th Virginia Aug. 24, 1862   VA25
Harwell, J.W. - Co. E 51st North Carolina Nov. 2, 1864
    VA25
Harwell, J.W. - Co. G 16th Georgia   Sept. 4, 1861 age 45
    VA25

Harwell, William Thomas - Corp. - Co. D Jeff Davis Legion (Mississippi) - KIA near Shady Grove on May 8, 1864 VA28

Harwood, P.E. - Co. A 5th Alabama June 5, 1862   VA25

Haskins, J.J. - Died Nov. 26, 1862   VA19

Haslett, R.E. - Capt. - Wise Legion (Maryland) Aug. 27, 1863 VA25

Haslip, V.S. - 11th Georgia VA18

Hassebank, F. - Pvt. - Co. B Huger's Battery Artillery Died May 11, 1865   VA26

Hastell, J. - 9th Louisiana VA18

Hastin, T.W. - Co. E 37th North Carolina   Sept. 8, 1862 VA25

Hatcher, B.G. - Latham's Artillery (North Carolina)   VA11

Hatcher, Clinton - Co. F 8th Virginia Regt. 1840-1861   VA01

Hatcher, T.S. - Co. F 44th Georgia July 25, 1862   VA25

Hatcher, W. - Florida Aug. 16, 1861   VA25

Hathaway, H.C. - Co. A 7th Virginia Cavalry   Sept. 7, 1862 VA25

Hathcock, J. - Co. B 14th North Carolina Jan. 2, 1862   VA25

Hathcox, Joshua - Pvt. - Co. H 4th North Carolina DOD - Fredericksburg - April 7 (8), 1862 Headstone reads VA28

Hatihcox, Joshua - see Hathcox, Joshua

Hatson, M. - Co. E 38th North Carolina   Sept. 12, 1862 VA25

Hatton, G.E. - Virginia June 14, 1862   VA25

Hatton, J.H. - Co. K 37th Alabama   March 12, 1865 VA25

Hatton, R.H.S. - Md. Horse Artillery   VA18

Hattoway, A. - Co. D 10th Georgia   Oct. 16, 1864   VA25

Hattoway, J. - Co. H 42nd North Carolina July 25, 1864 VA25

Haupt, G.B. - Lt. - Co. G 2nd Maryland   Oct. 14, 1864 VA25

Havener, J.R. - Co. D 14th North Carolina   March 16, 1863 VA25

Hawis, N.C. - Co. C 23rd North Carolina   VA11
Hawkins, E.R. - Lt. - Co. C 8th Virginia Dec. 27, 1864   VA25
Hawkins, J. - Co. D 26th Alabama July 16, 1862   VA25
Hawkins, James - Lt. - Co. I 24th Georgia KIA Battle of the Wilderness May 6, 1864   VA28
Hawkins, P.W. - Co. F 2nd South Carolina Feb. 19, 1865   VA25
Hawks, N. -Virginia   VA20
Hawks, P.H. - Co. D 51st Virginia July 24, 1865   VA25
Hawle, M. - Co. C Hampton's Legion (Georgia) June 5, 1862   VA25
Hawners, J.B. - Co. F 1st Tennessee   Nov. 23, 1862 VA25
Haws, J. - Co. C 1st Virginia Artillery   Oct. 17, 1861   VA25
Haws, W. - Co. K 28th North Carolina April 2, 1862   VA25
Hawson, A.M. - Co. C 4th Louisiana April 16, 1865   VA25
Hawthman, H.S. - Co. K 13th South Carolina Oct. 5, 1864   VA25
Hawthorn, W.B. - 53rd Georgia March 16, 1863   VA25
Hawze, J.C. - Sgt. - Co. I 5th Alabama July 25, 1862   VA25
Hawze, J.S. - Co. B Cobb's Legion (Georgia) July 22, 1862   VA25
Hay, William - Surgeon - CSA - Died Stanton (sic), Virginia - June 30, 1864   VA06
Haycock, Edgar - Co. K 6th Virginia   VA10
Hayes, A. - Co. K 48th Georgia Sept. 29, 1862   VA25
Hayes, A.B. - Co. A 48th North Carolina June 17, 1864   VA25
Hayes, H.H. - 51st Georgia Nov. 8, 1862   VA25
Hayes, J. - Co. K 34th North Carolina March 19, 1863   VA25
Hayes, J. - Co. D 15th South Carolina June 17, 1864   VA25
Hayes, J.B. - Co. B 37th North Carolina Sept. 30, 1864   VA25
Hayes, J.G. - Nov. 9, 1861 VA25
Hayes, J.J. - Co. G 49th North Carolina Sept. 9, 1864   VA25
Hayes, J.V.S. - Co. B 16th Georgia July 24, 1863   VA25

Hayes, L. - Co. G 47th North Carolina July 1, 1864 VA25
Hayes, Thos. - June 5, 1862 VA25
Hayes, W. - 6th Alabama July 27, 1863 VA25
Haygood, Thomas - Phillip's Georgia Legion VA18
Hayne, E.S. - 1st South Carolina 1862 VA25
Hayne, J.W. - Co. C 5th North Carolina Dec. 26, 1862 VA25
Hayne, W.G. - Co. I 19th Louisiana May 31, 1861 VA25
Haynes, B. - Co. D 3rd North Carolina Aug. 13, 1864 VA25
Haynes, C.E. - Pvt. - Co. H 13th Georgia Died May 7, 1865 VA26
Haynes, John - Co. H 25th South Carolina April 10, 1863 VA25
Haynes, Luther Cary - VMI Cadet - MW - Battle of New Market - May 15, 1864 DOW June 15, 1864 Buried at his home "Sunny Side" in Essex County, Virginia. VA21
Haynes, Willie C. - POW - Federal Soldier Died Oct. 8, 1861 VA19
Hays, Benj. F. - Co. I 42nd Mississippi Died April 29, 1863 VA03
Hays, Erastus W. - 25th South Carolina VA04
Hays, S. - Virginia Artillery May 27, 1862 VA25
Hays, W. - 14th North Carolina June 3, 1862 VA25
Hayser, G. - Co. E 24th North Carolina May 21, 1863 VA25
Hayslip, J.G. - Prince Co. June 4, 1862 VA25
Hayslip, T. - June 7, 1862 VA25
Hayward, B. - Co. G 3rd Georgia June 10, 1862 VA25
Hayward, J.R. - Co. C 23rd North Carolina June 11, 1862 VA25
Hayward, L.G. - Co. G 2nd North Carolina March 20, 1863 VA25
Haywood, Thos. - 1st Virginia Artillery Aug. 27, 1862 VA25
Hazel, F.M. - Co. D 13th Georgia Oct. 6, 1863 VA25
Hazelwood, J.L. - Co. C 9th Alabama May 14, 1862 VA25
Head, __ - 53rd Georgia Sept. 7, 1862 VA25

Head, C.T. - Co. I 7th Georgia July 9, 1862   VA25
Head, J.P. - Co. E 13th South Carolina May 14, 1862 VA25
Head, T. - 11th Alabama Aug. 2, 1861   VA25
Head, W.H. - Co. C 42nd Virginia   VA23
Head, Wm. - 3rd Georgia Sept. 26, 1862   VA25
Headbeth, __ - Co. I 28th North Carolina Jan. 7, 1863 VA25
Heaen, J.G. - Co. G 7th Georgia Died Feb 25, 1862   VA23
Heath, A. - Co. B Wise's Legion (Virginia) April 27, 1861
    VA25
Heath, G. - Co. C 6th North Carolina Jan. 17, 1864 VA25
Heath, J.W. - 13th Alabama Sept. 19, 1861   VA25
Heatwold, B.T. - Co. F 13th Virginia   VA11
Heck, L. - Co. K 12th Mississippi July 15, 1862   VA25
Heddly, J.B. - Co. E 40th Virginia June 9, 1862   VA25
Hedgcock, A. - Co. G 66th North Carolina Aug. 12, 1864
    VA25
Hedrick, B. - Tennessee   VA20
Heflin, T. - Capt. - Co. I 47th Virginia May 24, 1863
    Headstone reads: "Corp. Thomas Heflin"   VA25
Heflin, Thomas - see Heflin, T.   VA25
Hefner, R.P.- Lt. - Co. G 26th Virginia Battalion   VA11
Heller, H.J. - Co. H 40th North Carolina Aug. 7, 1864 VA25
Helly, J.M. - 57th North Carolina   VA11
Helms, J.F. - Co. K 5th Alabama May 10, 1862   VA25
Helton, Ira - Virginia   VA20
Henderson, __ - May 30, 1862 VA25
Henderson, __ - July 1, 1862 VA25
Henderson, C. - 25th Virginia VA08
Henderson, C.A. - Co. F 31st Georgia Feb. 12, 1863   VA25
Henderson, C.C. - Alabama   VA20
Henderson, C.F. - Co. F 13th South Carolina July 1, 1864
    VA25
Henderson, J.C. - 7th South Carolina   VA18
Henderson, J.F. - Co. C 6th South Carolina July 29, 1864
    VA25

Henderson, J.M. - Co. F 2nd South Carolina June 1, 1863 VA25

Henderson, J.W. - Co. D 5th South Carolina July 4, 1862 VA25

Henderson, L.F. - Co. A 6th North Carolina Dec. 16, 1861 VA25

Henderson, M.F. - Sgt. - Co. G 50th Georgia May 21, 1863 VA25

Henderson, M.M. - Co. F 27th South Carolina Jan. 19, 1865 VA25

Henderson, M.R. - 1st Georgia Legion VA25

Henderson, P. - Co. I 3rd Virginia Cavalry May 10, 1862 VA25

Henderson, T. - Sept. 9, 1862 VA25

Henderson, Thos. - Sept. 9, 1862 VA25

Henderson, W. - Co D ___ Alabama Died Dec 11, 1862 VA23

Henderson, W.H. - Co. C 14th South Carolina May 23, 1864 VA25

Henderson, W.H. - Co. E 22nd Georgia Oct. 19, 1864 VA25

Henderson, Wm. P. - KIA Aug. 7, 1863 "disinterred and taken to South Carolina- Jan. 16, 1864" VA19

Hendricks, __ - Co. B 5th Alabama July 7, 1862 VA25

Hendricks, __ - Co. H 15th North Carolina Sept. 9, 1864 VA25

Hendricks, __ - 1862 VA25

Hendricks, A. - Co. H 19th Georgia Aug. 23, 1864 VA25

Hendricks, A.J. - Co. G 22nd Virginia June 9, 1863 VA25

Hendricks, D. - 9th Georgia Sept. 15, 1861 VA25

Hendricks, D.H. - Co. C 15th North Carolina Aug. 10, 1864 VA25

Hendricks, F.W. - 12th Louisiana 1865 VA25

Hendricks, G.A. - Capt. - Co. E 2nd South Carolina Dec. 19, 1864 VA25

Hendricks, J. - Co. F 16th Alabama Sept. 7, 1862 VA25

Hendricks, J.C. - Co. H 6th North Carolina June 14, 1862
    VA25
Hendricks, J.H. - Co. B 48th North Carolina Sept. 17, 1864
    VA25
Hendricks, J.T. - Co. B 14th Alabama July 7, 1862   VA25
Hendricks, James - Co. I 53rd Georgia March 9, 1863   VA25
Hendricks, L.W. - Co. C 15th South Carolina Aug. 11, 1862
    VA25
Hendricks, N. - Co. K 48th North Carolina June 5, 1864 VA25
Hendricks, P.F. - Co. B 56th North Carolina July 30, 1864
    VA25
Hendricks, P.H. - 9th Georgia VA18
Hendricks, S.C. - Co. I 38th Virginia July 5, 1862   VA25
Hendricks, W.J. - 2nd Florida Aug. 27, 1861   VA25
Henkel, C. Polybius - VA15
Henkel, C.C. (M.D.) - medical doctor   VA15
Henkel, John E. - VA15
Henkel, L.P. - VA15
Henkel, Luther M. - VA15
Henley, F.E. - Co. I 10th Mississippi May 24, 1865 VA25
Henright, Thos. - Virginia Aug. 8, 1861   VA25
Henry, B.D.R. - Co. F 12th South Carolina July 8, 1862 VA25
Henry, D. - C.S. Navy Dec. 24, 1864   VA25
Henry, F. - Co. K 3rd Tenn. May 22, 1865   VA25
Henry, George W. - Pvt. - Co. D 49th Virginia MW May 12,
    1864 Other records list this soldier as KIA at Fisher's
    Hill VA28
Henry, J.W. - 5th South Carolina July 19, 1862   VA25
Henry, Jas. F. - Died Nov. 17, 1862   VA19
Henry, W.A. - Co. E 13th Mississippi July 23, 1862   VA25
Hensley, F. - Co. K 5th North Carolina   VA11
Hensley, J. - Sept. 9, 1862 VA25
Hensley, J.H. - Co. D 22nd North Carolina March 29, 1865
    VA25
Herby, W.H. - Lt. - Co. I 11th Virginia   VA10
Herky, J. - Aug. 20, 1864 VA25

Herman, C.A. - Co. K 13th South Carolina Oct. 20, 1864 VA25

Hermicle, J.R. - Pvt. - Co. K 32nd North Carolina Died June 15, 1865 VA26

Hernden, M. - 4th North Carolina Aug. 29, 1862 VA25

Herndern, __ - Kershaw's Battery (South Carolina) June 26, 1862 VA25

Herndon, __ - Wise's Artillery (Virginia) May 27, 1862 VA25

Herndon, Thomas M. - Sgt. - Co. E 59th Georgia Died May 13, 1864 VA28

Herndon, W.J. - Co. I 11th Georgia VA25

Herrick, J.W. - Co. B 51st North Carolina Aug. 6, 1864 VA25

Herrin, John D. - Pvt. - Co. D 26th Georgia Died May 10, 1864 VA28

Herring, A.A. - Co. G 4th North Carolina Sept. 7, 1862 VA25

Herring, A.A. - Co. G 48th Georgia Sept. 7, 1862 VA25

Herring, B.F. - Co. I 18th Georgia Aug. 28, 1861 VA25

Herring, G. - Co. B 66th North Carolina July 24, 1864 VA25

Herring, J.W. - Co. I 24th Georgia June 1, 1862 VA25

Herring, M. - 5th Alabama VA18

Herring, T.D. - Letcher Artillery (Virginia) May 3, 1862 VA25

Herring, V. - Aug. 20, 1861 VA25

Herringer, E.S. - Jeff. Davis's Legion May 23, 1861 VA25

Herrod, John - Pvt. - Co. G 5th Alabama Died May 11, 1864 VA28

Herron, G.S. - 7th South Carolina VA04

Herron, G.W. - 8th__ VA18

Hessberg, I. - Caroline Co. VA17

Hester, J. - 28th North Carolina Nov. 26, 1862 VA25

Heter, A. - VA12

Heth, G.L. - 9th South Carolina Nov. 19, 1861 VA25

Hevner, G. - VA12

Hewith, A. - Co. E 12th Georgia Dec. 12, 1864 VA25

Hewitt, Edward - Co. G 20th North Carolina   VA11
Hewson, G.A. - Co. G 23rd Georgia July 23, 1862   VA25
Heyman, A. - Georgia   VA17
Hibp, J.M. - 9th South Carolina Died Dec 21, 1861 (?)   VA23
Hickey, J.M. - Co. H 42nd Mississippi Aug. 17, 1862   VA25
Hickman, H. - 2nd Florida July 22, 1862   VA25
Hicks, A. - Co. D 21st North Carolina Feb. 8, 1862 VA25
Hicks, A.J. - 5th Texas Nov. 12, 1861   VA25
Hicks, B.F. - Alabama   VA20
Hicks, D. - Aug. 9, 1862 VA25
Hicks, J. - Co. E 8th Alabama Feb. 6, 1863   VA25
Hicks, J.B. - Co. F 12th North Carolina June 18, 1862 This appears to be James B. Hicks of Co. E 12th North Carolina Infantry. He Died of "fever" on June 17, 1862.   VA25
Hicks, Jno. - Virginia   VA20
Hicks, T. - Co. H 12th South Carolina June 1862   VA25
Hicks, W. - 13th Alabama July 30, 1862   VA25
Hicks, W.H. - 25th Virginia Battalion   March 5, 1864   VA25
Higginbotham, John Carlton - Colonel - Co. B 25th Virginia KIA Spotsylvania C. H. May 10, 1864   VA28
Higginbottam, F. - Co. F 8th Louisiana Jan 4, 1864   VA25
Higginbottam, J.R. - Co. E 8th Louisiana Jan 26, 1861   VA25
Higgins, F. - Co. G 2nd North Carolina Feb. 19, 1865   VA25
Higgins, F. - Co. H 7th Alabama   March 8, 1865   VA25
Higgins, J.D. - 5th Alabama VA18
Higgins, J.H. - Co. E 1st South Carolina June 20, 1863   VA25
Higgins, Thomas - 4th North Carolina Cavalry - 1863   VA07
Higgins, W.S. - Nov. 2, 1861 VA25
Higginson, J. - Jones' Bat. May 6, 1862   VA25
Higgs, J.F. - Co. B 5th Louisiana Dec. 12, 1862   VA25
Higgs, S. - VA12
Highsmith, J.E. - 26th Georgia July 27, 1862   VA25
Hight, W.J. - Co. H 44th North Carolina June 11, 1864   VA25

Hightoun, J.C. - 15th Alabama July 25, 1862   VA25
Higler, H. - Co. A 5th Alabama Feb. 5, 1863   VA25
Higner, J. - Co. E 24th North Carolina Feb. 22, 1865   VA25
Hill, __ - South Carolina Oct. 8, 1862   VA25
Hill, __ - Co. A 47th Virginia July 1, 1862   VA25
Hill, A. - Co. G 48th Georgia June 1864   VA25
Hill, A.P. (Ambrose Powell) - General - 3rd Army Corps 1825 - April 2, 1865 - KIA at Petersburg - Remains moved in 1892 to his monument at the site were he received his commission as Brigadier General. VA25
Hill, A.V. - Co. A 24th Georgia July 6, 1864   VA25
Hill, F. - Co. F 22nd North Carolina April 20, 1862   VA25
Hill, F.P. - Co. B 26th North Carolina Nov. 24, 1864   VA25
Hill, H.H. - 2nd Georgia   VA18
Hill, H.M. - 14th South Carolina Aug. 27, 1862   VA25
Hill, Hillman, R.S. - Co. F 61st Georgia Aug. 7, 1862   VA25
Hill, J. - Corp. - Co. G 26th South Carolina Aug. 5, 1864   VA25
Hill, J. - Co. E 27th Georgia July 5, 1862   VA25
Hill, J.A. - Co. A 8th Florida Nov. 13, 1862   VA25
Hill, J.A. - Cooper's Rifles   Nov. 10, 1861   VA25
Hill, J.B. - Co. E 1st Georgia Reserves   March 1, 1865   VA25
Hill, J.C. - Co. C 14th North Carolina June 3, 1862 VA25
Hill, J.C. - Co. K 33rd North Carolina June 2, 1863 VA25
Hill, J.C. - Co. I 5th Texas April 20, 1861   VA25
Hill, J.D. - Co. H 13th Mississippi May 2, 1863   VA25
Hill, J.D. - Pitt County (North Carolina)   Sept. 11, 1862   VA25
Hill, J.L. - Co. I 19th Georgia Dec. 26, 1862   VA25
Hill, J.W. - Co. E 11th North Carolina Sept. 2, 1864   VA25
Hill, L.P. - Co. D 1st Virginia Reserves Feb. 25, 1865   VA25
Hill, L.W. - Co. G 14th Georgia Jan. 10, 1863   VA25
Hill, M.A. - July 4, 1862 VA25
Hill, O. - 61st Virginia VA18
Hill, P. - 6th Alabama June 3, 1862   VA25

Hill, R.T. - 13th Mississippi   VA18
Hill, T.G. - Co. G 6th Alabama June 3, 1862   VA25
Hill, T.H.A. - Jeff Davis Legion   VA18
Hill, W.A. - Co. A 12th South Carolina Sept. 2, 1862   VA25
Hill, W.J. - Co. C 49th North Carolina July 24, 1864   VA25
Hill, W.J. - Co. F 9th Louisiana Sept. 4, 1862   VA25
Hill, W.L. - 13th Alabama Aug. 31, 1861   VA25
Hill, William A. - Co. B 6th Virginia   VA08
Hillard, J. - Co. H 6th Alabama June 5, 1862   VA25
Hilleary, W.M. - 1st Maryland Artillery June 27, 1862 VA25
Hilley, J.P. - Co. H 27th Georgia June 13, 1864   VA25
Hillhouse, E. - Co. D 28th Georgia June 8, 1862   VA25
Hilliard, J. - Cobb's Legion (Georgia) July 18, 1862   VA25
Hillman, R.S. - Co. F 61st Georgia Aug. 7, 1862   VA25
Hillwright, A. - Co. K 26th North Carolina Aug. 27, 1864
    VA25
Hilton, G.W. - Co. B 16th Mississippi Sept. 2, 1862 VA25
Hindman, R.A. - 9th Alabama   VA18
Hinds, George W. - see Hines, George W.   VA28
Hines, A.L. - 1st South Carolina Oct. 16, 1864   VA25
Hines, E.B. - 21st Georgia May 6, 1862   VA25
Hines, George W. - Pvt. - Co. H 5th Alabama Died May 12,
    1864 Name also spelled "George W. Hinds"   VA28
Hines, J. - Co. E 61st North Carolina July 30, 1864   VA25
Hines, J. - C.S. Navy April 2, 1865   VA25
Hines, J. D. - Co. E 61st North Carolina July 25, 1864   VA25
Hines, J.H. - Co. C 10th Georgia May 13, 1862   VA25
Hines, L. - Co. H 22nd North Carolina March 8, 1862   VA25
Hines, L.A. - Co. H 1st South Carolina Oct. 16, 1864 VA25
Hines, L.H.D. - Co. E 13th South Carolina June 25, 1862
    VA25
Hines, P. - Corp. K 5th Louisiana June 29, 1864 VA25
Hines, R.B. - Co. H 2nd North Carolina Nov. 8, 1862 VA25
Hines, W. - Co. H 2nd North Carolina July 5, 1862 VA25
Hinnant, John C. - Pvt. - Co. C 1st North Carolina Died May
    10, 1864   VA28

Hinson, William J. - Pvt. - Co. H 18th North Carolina Died May 13, 1864 VA28
Hinwell, W. - Georgia VA28
Hissant, Wm. - Davis Battalion May 17, 1862 VA25
Hit, J.W. - Co. G 49th Virginia June 2, 1863 VA25
Hitchcock, D. - Co. I 59th Georgia Sept. 2, 1864 VA25
Hitchcock, F.H. - Co. C 7th South Carolina Battalion D Aug. 4, 1864 VA25
Hite, Fon - Clark Cavalry VA06
Hite, Irwine - Clark Cavalry VA06
Hite, Thomas J. - Cutshaw's Light Artillery (Virginia) KIA Spotsylvania Court House May 12, 1864 - This soldier also served in the Jackson Artillery and the Allegheny Artillery. VA28
Hite, W.H. - Clark Cavalry VA06
Hix, Jackson - Co. A 15th Alabama VA11
Hix, Wm. - 24th Georgia May 18, 1862 VA25
Hixi, W.J. - Co. H 11th South Carolina March 5, 1865 VA25
Hizer, Daniel - KIA - Battle of New Market - May 15, 1864 VA15
Hobbs, E. - Co. B 12th Virginia Artillery June 14, 1862 VA25
Hobbs, E.M. - Virginia VA20
Hobbs, F. - Co. B __ North Carolina Artillery June 25, 1862 VA25
Hobbs, J.D. - Co. K 5th Texas June 11, 1862 VA25
Hobbs, John - Co. H __ Maryland Battalion Aug. 15, 1862 VA25
Hobbs, L.C. - Virginia VA20
Hobbs, M.D. - 9th Alabama July 8, 1862 VA25
Hobby, J.A. - Co. I 13th South Carolina Dec. 26, 1862 VA25
Hobby, Wm. - Co. F 49th Georgia July 4, 1862 VA25
Hodell, H.D. - Co. G __th South Carolina VA11
Hodge, J.A. - Wise's Legion (Virginia) Jan. 22, 1861 VA25

Hodge, T.W. - Co. A 12th South Carolina March 2, 1862 VA25
Hodge, Wm. - Co. C 17th Mississippi June 22, 1862 VA25
Hodges, A.L. - Co. F 6th Georgia July 8, 1864 VA25
Hodges, Catharine - Co. K 5th Louisiana April 7, 1862 VA25
Hodges, H. - Co. A 28th North Carolina Aug. 20, 1864 VA25
Hodges, H.F. - Co. A 30th Alabama May 30, 1864 VA25
Hodgins, H. - Co. E 4th North Carolina June 21, 1862 VA25
Hodgins, J. - Co. I 13th Alabama June 25, 1862 VA25
Hoffman, T.H. - Lt. and Adjutant- 31st Virginia June 2, 1864 VA25
Hogan, J.R. - 10th Alabama Oct. 7, 1861 VA25
Hogan, John - Co. A 20th North Carolina VA28
Hoge, C.A. - Co. F 2nd Maryland Oct. 2, 1864 VA25
Hogg, L. - Co. A 4th Georgia May 20, 1863 VA25
Holcomb, C.J. - Co. G 44th Georgia Aug. 15, 1863 VA25
Holcomb, Martin - 17th Mississippi VA18
Holcombe, J.W. - Co. G 31st Georgia Feb. 17, 1863 VA25
Holcome, J.H. - Georgia VA20
Hold, G.W. - Co. F 48th Georgia Aug. 5, 1864 VA25
Holden, B. - Mauley's Batt. (North Carolina) July 15, 1864 VA25
Holden, D. - Co. A 49th Georgia June 5, 1864 VA25
Holden, J.T. - Co. C 28th North Carolina Nov. 29, 1864 VA25
Holden, W.H. - Co. G 27th North Carolina July 9, 1864 VA25
Holder, S. - Co. B 37th North Carolina July 26, 1862 VA25
Holder, W.H. - Co. C 4th North Carolina VA11
Holiday, S.W. - Co. B 6th Alabama May 22, 1861 VA25
Holiday, W.H. - Co. A 2nd Maryland June 3, 1864 VA25
Hollaman, D. - Florida Nov. 19, 1862 VA25
Holland, G. - Co. B 5th Louisiana June 6, 1863 VA25
Holland, J. - Aug. 5, 1864 VA25
Holland, J. C. - Sgt. - Co. H 28th North Carolina June 18, 1864 VA25

Holland, J. W. - C.S. Navy   Nov. 18, 1864   VA25
Holland, J.G. - Co. K 19th Georgia Sept. 11, 1862   VA25
Holland, J.W. - Pvt. - Co. A 18th Virginia Died May 14, 1865   VA26
Holland, N. - Co. H 4th North Carolina June 6, 1863 VA25
Holland, S.T. - Co. C 57th Virginia Dec. 7, 1861   VA25
Holland, T.R. - Co. F 7th South Carolina Aug. 27, 1864 VA25
Holland, W.D. - South Carolina   VA07
Hollifield, W.H. - Co. F 18th North Carolina   VA11
Hollingshead, T.A. - Co. B 12th Alabama   Sept. 22, 1862   VA25
Hollingsworth, J. - Co. C 43rd North Carolina Dec 25, 1863   VA25
Hollingsworth, J. J. - Mississippi Artillery Aug. 1862   VA25
Hollingsworth, J. W. - Mississippi Aug. 28, 1862   VA25
Hollins, James F. - Pvt. - Co. B 59th Alabama Died April 30, 1865   VA26
Holloway, __ - Major - Florida   Oct. 17, 1864   VA25
Holloway, J. - Co. F 22nd North Carolina July 6, 1864 VA25
Holloway, J.M. - Arkansas July 8, 1861   VA25
Holly, __ - Aug. 12, 1862 VA25
Holly, G. - 14th North Carolina May 24, 1861   VA25
Holly, R. - Co. E 2nd North Carolina June 25, 1863 VA25
Hollyhead, A. - Co. B 14th Alabama April 21, 1861   VA25
Holme, __ - South Carolina July 10, 1862   VA25
Holmes, A.H. - Co. C 2nd North Carolina Sept. 2, 1864 VA25
Holmes, A.L. - Co. B 43rd North Carolina June 11, 1864   VA25
Holmes, B. - Co. D 3rd North Carolina Dec. 26, 1862 VA25
Holmes, E. - Co. H 24th Georgia June 25, 1862   VA25
Holmes, G. - Co. C 17th Mississippi July 29, 1862   VA25
Holmes, G.W. - Co. G 15th Georgia April 26, 1862   VA25
Holmes, Henry - Pvt. - Co. E 64th Georgia Died May 28, 1865   VA26
Holmes, J.H. - Co. I 1st North Carolina June 22, 1864 VA25
Holmes, R. - Co. F 14th Tennessee July 7, 1862   VA25

Holmes, W.C. - Co. C 4th South Carolina July 18, 1862 VA25
Holmes, W.C. - June 25, 1862 VA25
Holmes, W.N. - Co. B Tucker's Cavalry July 26, 1864 VA25
Holmes, W.T. - Co. A 11th North Carolina Oct. 24, 1864 VA25
Holsenbach, H. - 15th South Carolina Nov. 12, 1862 VA25
Holt, __ - Colonel 8th Georgia Infantry VA08
Holt, C. - Co. H 47th North Carolina June 6, 1864 VA25
Holt, J. - Aug. 9, 1862 VA25
Holt, J. C. - Co. C 49th Georgia Nov. 19, 1862 VA25
Holt, L.B. - Artillery Sept. 23, 1863 VA25
Holt, R. Augustus - Capt. - Co. K 14th GA. MW May 12, 1864 (Died May 14, 1864) VA28
Holt, William H. Dec. 19, 1862 "disinterred and taken to North Carolina " VA19
Holtsclaw, G.H. - Pvt. - Co. C 22nd South Carolina Died May 9, 1865 VA26
Home, L.H. - Co. C 35th North Carolina July 28, 1862 VA25
Home, W.H. - Co. C 14th Virginia VA11
Homer, W.H. - Co. D 9th Georgia Nov. 16, 1862 VA25
Honac, W.D. - Co. F 16th Georgia May 8, 1863 VA25
Honsick, __ - July 7, 1862 VA25
Hood, A.J. - South Carolina VA07
Hood, B. - Co. C 12th South Carolina June 25, 1862 VA25
Hood, G.L. - Co G 1st Maryland Died Oct 6, 1861 VA23
Hood, W. - Co. E 64th Georgia Aug. 19, 1864 VA25
Hoode, J.T. - Co. B 4th Alabama Aug. 1862 VA25
Hooe, Alfred - 8th Virginia Infantry VA10
Hook, John - Co. F 48th Georgia May 21, 1863 VA25
Hooker, David H. - Pvt. - Co. B 1st South Carolina KIA - Wilderness - May 6, 1864 VA28
Hooker, F.F.M. - Co. B 1st South Carolina VA28
Hooks, J. - 28th Georgia VA18
Hooks, J. - Co. D 42nd North Carolina July 3, 1864 VA25

Hooks, John Pvt. - Co. I 3rd Georgia Died May 14, 1864 VA28

Hooks, W.H. - Co. I 15th North Carolina July 17, 1864   VA25

Hooks, W.L. - Co. C 14th Alabama July 7, 1862   VA25

Hooper, F.M. - Co. A 44th Alabama April 27, 1865   VA25

Hooser, J.H. - 11th Alabama VA18

Hoover, A.V. - Co. F 28th North Carolina Aug. 7, 1864 VA25

Hoover, B. - VA12

Hoover, H. - Co. F 10th Virginia July 22, 1862   VA25

Hoover, J.M. - Lt. - Co. K 46th North Carolina July 6, 1864 VA25

Hoover, Samuel R. - VA12

Hope, __ - July 7, 1862 VA25

Hope, B.A. - Co. E 12th North Carolina July 15, 1864 This soldier is not listed in this unit's roster.   VA25

Hope, J. - Co. D 1st North Carolina Aug. 7, 1862 VA25

Hopkins, D.A. - Co. H __th Georgia June 6, 1862   VA25

Hopkins, J.H. - Pvt. - Co. B 22nd South Carolina Died June 24, 1865   VA26

Hopkins, John E. - VA12

Hopkins, L. - June 7, 1862 VA25

Hoppell, C. - 5th Alabama Aug. 13, 1861   VA25

Hopson, J.W. - 8th Georgia VA18

Hora, M.O. - Co. E 15th Louisiana Sept. 1, 1864   VA25

Horan, Nanie - Civilian -Killed in explosion of C.S. Laboratory - March 15, 1863 age 14   VA19

Horn, E.V.P. - Georgia Feb. 10, 1865   VA25

Horn, G. - Lt. - Co. B 14th Texas June 18, 1864   VA25

Horn, J. - Co. D 8th South Carolina June 19, 1862 VA25

Horn, O.W. - Co. A 25th North Carolina Dec. 1, 1862 VA25

Horn, T.W. - Co. A 33rd North Carolina Aug. 15, 1862 VA25

Horne, J. - Co. I 12th Virginia July 1, 1862   VA25

Horne, John - Co. G 3rd Virginia May 6, 1862   VA25

Horner, Wm. - Co. H 1st Texas Jan. 2, 1862   VA25

Horseman, S.E. - 8th Virginia Infantry   VA10

Horton, A.R. - Co. G 64th Georgia Oct. 10, 1864   VA25
Horton, C. - Co. H 31st North Carolina Oct. 5, 1864 VA25
Horton, C.C. - Co. A 17th North Carolina July 20, 1864
   VA25
Horton, D.F. - 25th North Carolina June 13, 1864   VA25
Horton, J.R. - Co. G 53rd Georgia April 20, 1863   VA25
Horton, John - Co. H 16th North Carolina Aug. 19, 1862
   VA25
Horton, R.F. - Co. F 48th North Carolina July 3, 1864 VA25
Horton, R.M. - Co. K 18th Mississippi Nov. 19, 1862 VA25
Horton, S.H. - Co. I 11th Alabama June 16, 1864   VA25
Hothrington, P. - Co. E 21st Mississippi Aug. 4, 1862   VA25
House, A. - Cobb's Legion (Georgia) June 19, 1864   VA25
House, A. W. - Capt. A. Davis's Co. (Virginia) Aug. 10, 1861
   VA25
House, H. - 38th North Carolina   VA18
House, M.C. - Pvt. - Co. I 3rdArkansasDied June 9, 1865
   VA26
House, S.M. - Co. C 24th Georgia June 20, 1864   VA25
Houseley, H. - Stewart's Artillery July 29, 1863   VA25
Houston, A.A. - Texas Batt. Aug. 4, 1861   VA25
Howard, A.D. - Co. G 4th Texas Nov. 27, 1861   VA25
Howard, A.S. - Co. C 52nd Georgia July 28, 1863   VA25
Howard, C. - Co. K 1st Georgia June 25, 1864   VA25
Howard, C.J. - C.S. Navy   March 23, 1863   VA25
Howard, I.S. - Co. H 48th Alabama   VA11
Howard, J. - 21st Mississippi June 19, 1862   VA25
Howard, J.H. - Co. C 18th Mississippi May 8, 1863   VA25
Howard, N. - 1st Engineer Corps Aug. 18, 1864   VA25
Howard, O.A. - Co. B 24th Virginia Cavalry April 22, 1865
   VA25
Howard, Robert J. - Pvt. - Co. B 4th Texas Died May 12, 1864
   VA28
Howard, T. - Co. C 42nd Mississippi Sept. 4, 1862 VA25
Howard, W. - Co. K 28th North Carolina Sept. 21, 1864
   VA25

Howard, W. - Co. E 66th North Carolina Aug. 17, 1864 VA25
Howard, W. - Co. B 49th Georgia April 1, 1863   VA25
Howard, W.A. - Co. G 49th North Carolina Aug. 5, 1864 VA25
Howard, Wm. - 8th North Carolina Aug. 30, 1861   VA25
Howchens, W. - Co. H 22nd North Carolina   May 11, 1862 VA25
Howe, __ - 3rd North Carolina Aug. 1, 1861   VA25
Howe, E. - Virginia   May 7, 1864   VA25
Howe, S. - Pvt. - South Carolina Nov. 15, 1864   VA22
Howell, A.J. - Cooper's Rifles   Oct. 5, 1861   VA25
Howell, B.A. - Co. D 35th North Carolina Cavalry June 7, 1864   VA25
Howell, D.A. - Georgia   VA20
Howell, J.D. - Corp. - Co. F 9th Louisiana July 12, 1863 VA25
Howell, Jesse M. - Pvt. - Co. A 6th Georgia Died at Fredericksburg, Virginia   VA28
Howell, John - Co. B 11th North Carolina Died Sept 19, 1861 VA23
Howell, M.C. - Cobb's Legion (Georgia)   1862   VA25
Howell, R.A. - Co. C 57th Virginia Aug. 5, 1864   VA25
Howell, Thos. - Co. G 49th North Carolina Aug. 22, 1864 VA25
Hownen, L. - June 6, 1862 VA25
Hoyle, G. - Co. K 34th North Carolina Oct. 19, 1864   VA25
Hoys, A.S. - 1st South Carolina July 3, 1862   VA25
Hoyts, G.D. - Co. I 47th North Carolina Dec. 13, 1863   VA25
Hubbard, __ - Lt. July 8, 1862   VA25
Hubbard, J.A. - Co. B 43rd North Carolina July 18, 1864 VA25
Hubbard, R.C. - Co. H 18th Virginia June 1, 1862   VA25
Hubert, V. - Artillery Aug. 13, 1862   VA25
Hucabee, J.J. - Co. B 14th Alabama Aug. 1, 1862   VA25
Hucaby, A.J. - Co. B 45th Georgia May 27, 1864   VA25

Huckery, A.J. - Co. B 45th Georgia May 24, 1865   VA25
Huckstop, __ - Nov. 3, 1861 VA25
Huddleston, J.W. - Co. C 4th North Carolina Artillery June 25, 1862   VA25
Huddleston, W.H. - Co. D 13th Mississippi Jan. 30, 1863   VA25
Hudgens, Samuel - Pvt. - Co. A 10th Virginia Died July 2, 1865   VA26
Hudgins, A.L. - Georgia Oct. 7, 1862   VA25
Hudgins, B.B.   1st Virginia June 4, 1862   VA25
Hudgson, A.J. - Co. I 9th Louisiana May 26, 1862   VA25
Hudsack, L.R.M. - Co. F 26th North Carolina Nov. 15, 1864   VA25
Hudson, D. - Co. B 18th Georgia Sept. 18, 1861   VA25
Hudson, G. - Co. B 9th Louisiana May 8, 1862   VA25
Hudson, H. - Wise's Legion (Virginia)   May 13, 1862   VA25
Hudson, J.C. - Co. C 15th Georgia July 8, 1862   VA25
Hudson, J.W. - Co. G 14th North Carolina Sept. 6, 1862   VA25
Hudson, L.B. - Co. I 19th Virginia Sept. 6, 1862   VA25
Hudson, R.M. - Pvt. - Co. D 19th Virginia Died June 12, 1865   VA26
Hudson, Z.J. - Co. C 15th Georgia Sept. 18, 1861   VA25
Hues, W.H.T. -   VA28
Huff, __ - 17th Virginia Sept. 7, 1862   VA25
Huff, B.A. - Co. C 27th Georgia Oct. 26, 1864   VA25
Huff, J. - Co. K 44th North Carolina Oct. 4, 1864 VA25
Huff, J.R. - Lt. - Co. E Hampden's Legion June 20, 1864   VA25
Huff, T. - Co. K 12th North Carolina April 21, 1865   VA25
Huff, T.C. - Co. K 48th Georgia Sept. 7, 1862   VA25
Huff, W.H. - Co. H 15th North Carolina June 24, 1864   VA25
Huffman, __ - March 3, 1862 VA25
Huffman, J.D. - Co. D 45th North Carolina June 9, 1864   VA25

Huffman, J.R. - Pvt. - Co. I 1st Virginia Died June 16, 1865 VA26
Huffman, J.W. - 18th Mississippi Aug. 1, 1862   VA25
Huffman, Jno. - Co. B 15th Alabama Died Jan 25, 1862 VA23
Huffman, L.T. - Co. E 57th North Carolina Nov. 23, 1862 VA25
Huffman, L.W. - Co. G 18th Mississippi July 31, 1862   VA25
Huffman, T. - April 14, 1862   VA25
Huffman, W.A. - Mississippi   VA18
Huflander, J.H. - Co. G 35th Georgia June 18, 1864   VA25
Hufley, J. - 14th Louisiana July 2, 1862   VA25
Hugan, R.D. - Co. B 22nd North Carolina July 16, 1862 VA25
Huger, J.H. - Co. G 55th North Carolina May 2, 1864 VA25
Huger, M.G. - Co. I 1st Texas Nov. 12, 1862   VA25
Huggins, C.J. - Co. B 12th South Carolina Aug. 4, 1862 VA25
Hughes, __ - Sept. 7, 1862 VA25
Hughes, __ - Co. F 22nd North Carolina April 20, 1862 VA25
Hughes, A. - Co. G 56th North Carolina July 12, 1864   VA25
Hughes, A.F. - Texas Aug. 27, 1861   VA25
Hughes, Holly - Pvt. - Co. B 3rd Alabama Died May 10, 1864   VA28
Hughes, J. - Co. G 27th North Carolina June 17, 1864   VA25
Hughes, J.L. - 18th Virginia June 5, 1862   VA25
Hughes, J.W. - Co. A 10th Alabama June 30, 1862   VA25
Hughes, M.H. - Capt. - Co. A 56th North Carolina June 14, 1864   VA25
Hughes, R. - Co. E 6th North Carolina Feb. 19, 1865 VA25
Hughes, S.W. - Pvt. - Co. F 34th Georgia Headstone reads: "Hughs"   VA28
Hughins, J.H. - Co. B 11th Georgia June 6, 1862   VA25
Hughs, S.W. - see Hughes, S.W.   VA28
Hulcking, W.S. - Co. E 8th Georgia Sept. 14, 1864   VA25
Huley, H. - Co. A 35th Georgia April 25, 1864   VA25

Hulf, B. - Sept. 4, 1862 VA25
Hulin, N.A. - Co. D 23rd North Carolina June 5, 1863 VA25
Hull, J.W. - Co. K 35th Georgia Sept. 4, 1862   VA25
Hullet, D. - Co. C 38th North Carolina May 2, 1864 VA25
Hult, Geo. - July 15, 1862 VA25
Hult, W. - Georgia   VA20
Humden, W.F. - Virginia Feb. 10, 1864   VA25
Hume, J.F. - Co. A 21st Mississippi July 13, 1862 VA25
Humes, __ -VA12
Humphreys, A.J. - Capt. - Co. A 17th Virginia - KIA - Battle of Williamsburg - May 5, 1862   VA02
Humphreys, B.B. - Co. I 34th North Carolina July 10, 1864 VA25
Humphreys, John - Lt. - Alexandria, Virginia - KIA - Battle of Williamsburg - May 5, 1862   VA02
Humphreys, P.C. - Co. C 15th North Carolina May 4, 1864 VA25
Humphreys, Richard H. - see Humphries, Richard H.   VA28
Humphries, E.E. - Lt. - Co. A 2nd Florida July 5, 1862 VA25
Hundle, E.L. - Co. K 6th North Carolina March 8, 1865 VA25
Hunley, R.S. - 7th Virginia VA18
Hunnicutt, J.B. - Co. G 12th South Carolina June 27, 1864 VA25
Hunnicutt, L.M. - Co. F 1st South Carolina Rifles   Sept. 28, 1864   VA25
Hunnycutt, W.H. - Virginia VA20
Hunphries, Richard H. - Pvt. - Co. F 8th Louisiana VA28
Hunston, H.L. - Co. C 37th North Carolina May 23, 1863 VA25
Hunt, __ - POW - Federal Soldier Died June 10, 1862 VA19
Hunt, Benjamin - Pvt. - Co. A Cobb's Legion Died May 8, 1865 VA26
Hunt, D.C. - Co. F 38th Georgia Nov. 15, 1864   VA25
Hunt, J.C. - Kentucky   VA20

Hunt, J.C. - Co. F 2nd North Carolina July 12, 1863 VA25
Hunt, S. - Co. E 17th Georgia April 26, 1862   VA25
Hunt, Solomon - Co. K 6th North Carolina   VA11
Hunt, Z.T. - Co. A 23rd Georgia July 6, 1864   VA25
Hunter, H.E. - Co. E 42nd Georgia   VA11
Hunter, Thos. - Co. E 11th North Carolina Died Sept 26, 1861
    VA23
Hunter, W. - Co. D 13th North Carolina May 23, 1864 VA25
Hunter, W.D. - Co. H 24th Georgia   May 30, 1862   VA25
Hunter, W.J. - Co. I 3rd North Carolina Cavalry June 20,
    1864   VA25
Hunton, Eppa - General - CSA - 1823-1908   VA25
Hunton, T.W. - Rice's Battery June 6, 1864   VA25
Hupp, C.T. -   VA12
Hurbert, F.W. - Co. K 12th Georgia Sept. 7, 1862   VA25
Hurdell, J.A. - Co. D 18th Georgia June 4, 1862   VA25
Hurdnall, J. - Co. D 18th Georgia June 3, 1862   VA25
Hurdon, J. - Co. H 35th Georgia Aug. 28, 1862   VA25
Hurley, J.M. - Co. C 58th Virginia July 23, 1862   VA25
Hurley, J.R. - 7th South Carolina May 27, 1864   VA25
Hurley, M. - Co. A 1st Virginia Cavalry   May 12, 1865
    VA25
Hurly, M. - Co. A 1st Virginia May 12, 1865   VA25
Hurt, J. - Co. I 19th Georgia May 13, 1862   VA25
Hurt, James - 6th South Carolina Nov. 22, 1861   VA25
Hurt, L. - Co. B 8th South Carolina Nov. 19, 1862 VA25
Hurt, R.K. - Co. C 23rd North Carolina June 24, 1862   VA25
Huser, Jos. C. - 11th North Carolina Died Sept 2, 1861 VA23
Huser, Nich. - 11th North Carolina Died Oct 12, 1861 VA23
Husker, R. - Co. I 5th South Carolina Oct. 6, 1864 VA25
Hutcheison, R. - Co. H 22nd North Carolina June 11, 1862
    VA25
Hutchers, L.F. - 22nd North Carolina Aug. 20, 1862   VA25
Hutcherson, __ - Georgia Battalion   Sept. 11 1864   VA25
Hutcherson, A. - Co. E 54th North Carolina July 18, 1865
    VA25

Hutcherson, G.W. - Co. F 18th North Carolina Aug. 9, 1862 VA25

Hutcherson, J.W. - Co. H 53rd North Carolina June 15, 1864 VA25

Hutcheson, G.B.L. - Co. C 14th Tennessee May 28, 1864 VA25

Hutcheson, G.W. - Co. F 18th South Carolina Sept. 7, 1862 VA25

Hutcheson, T.L. - Co. F 1st Engineers June 14, 1864 VA25

Hutchins, C. - Co. H 22nd North Carolina May 29, 1862 VA25

Hutchins, J. - Co. C 23rd North Carolina June 25, 1862 VA25

Hutchins, P. - Co. H 22nd North Carolina Aug. 27, 1862 VA25

Hutchinson, C.H. - 8th Virginia Infantry VA10

Hutchinson, J.L. - 8th Virginia Infantry VA10

Hutchison, J. - Co. H 22nd North Carolina May 26, 1861 VA25

Hutt, A.B. - 9th Virginia Cavalry June 13, 1862 VA25

Hutt, M. - Co. D 62nd Georgia July 25, 1864 VA25

Huttle, G.T. - 1st Texas Dec. 26, 1862 VA25

Hutto, A. - 15th Alabama Dec. 7, 1861 VA25

Hutto, A.P. - 5th Alabama VA18

Hutton, Wiliam B. - Lt. - Co. A 5th Battalion KIA - Chancellorsville - May 3, 1863 VA28

Hutts, B.F. - Sgt. - Co. I 27th Georgia Sept. 5, 1864 VA25

Hyde, J. - Co. G 1st Texas July 17, 1862 VA25

Hymon, C.J. - Co. H 8th South Carolina Sept. 20, 1861 VA25

Idison, R.R. - 27th Georgia VA18

Inack, __ - Co. F 1st South Carolina July 6, 1862 VA25

Incher, J.J. - 11th Alabama VA18

Ingle, L.M. - Co. H 28th North Carolina June 11, 1863 VA25

Ingold, A.A. - Co. A 17th North Carolina June 19, 1862 VA25

Ingold, E.P. - Sgt. - Co. F 40th North Carolina March 17, 1865   VA25
Ingraham, J. - 33rd Georgia July 4, 1862   VA25
Ingraham, J. - 2nd Louisiana July 15, 1861   VA25
Ingraham, K. - Co. C 48th North Carolina July 3, 1862   VA25
Ingraham, L.F. - Co. B 4th North Carolina Aug. 25, 1864   VA25
Ingraham, T.E. - Co. I 55th Virginia Jan. 14, 1863   VA25
Inham, T. - 1862   VA25
Inick, J.A. - Co. G 54th South Carolina July 20, 1864   VA25
Inlandson, W.H.F. - old cemetery records entry for Edmundson, William H.   VA28
Iranthan, D.J. - Co. A 42nd North Carolina Aug. 26, 1864   VA25
Irby, G.W. - Co. B 6th South Carolina July 9, 1862 VA25
Irby, S.H. - 11th Mississippi July 1862   VA25
Ireland, A. - Co. I 3rd North Carolina July 7, 1863 VA25
Ireland, F.S. - Co. G 25th South Carolina May 23, 1864 VA25
Irvina, J. - Co. K 11th Alabama June 20, 1862   VA25
Irving, __ - 1862   VA25
Irving, A.B. - Co. I 38th Georgia Aug. 20, 1862   VA25
Irving, Robert W. - Pvt. - Shoemaker's Horse Artillery (Virginia) KIA at Waite's Shop - May 12, 1864   VA28
Irwin, J. - Died June 26, 1863   VA09
Irwin, Samuel - Co. B 11th North Carolina Died Sept 21, 1861   VA23
Isonhower, J.N. - Co. F 37th North Carolina Jan. 7, 1863   VA25
Isonhower, M. - Co. F 23rd North Carolina Oct. 16, 1864   VA25
Ivers, J. - Co. C 2nd Florida June 7, 1862 age 29   VA25
Ivey, B. - Co. E 1st South Carolina   Sept. 3, 1864   VA25
Ivey, J. - Corp. - Co. D 12th South Carolina 1864 VA25
Ivey, J.N. - Co. F 15th Georgia May 14, 1862   VA25

Ivey, J.W. - 15th Georgia Sept. 28, 1861   VA25
Ivey, Thomas J. - Lt. - Co. I 1st North Carolina Artillery
    VA28
Ivory, J. - 10th Georgia Sept. 10, 1861   VA25
J____ , W. - Co. F 24th Georgia Aug. 26, 1862   VA25
Jack, J.P. - Co. E 47th Alabama June 17, 1864   VA25
Jacks, J.B. - Co. D 14th Alabama Aug. 12, 1862   VA25
Jackson, __ - Co. C 53rd Georgia Dec. 22, 1862   VA25
Jackson, __ - July 1, 1862 VA25
Jackson, A. - Co. C 1st Texas April 29, 1862   VA25
Jackson, Archibald A. - Lt. - Co. H 30th North Carolina
    VA28
Jackson, B.B. - Pvt. - Jeff Davis Artillery Died June 10, 1865
    VA26
Jackson, C. - Co. A 14th North Carolina Nov. 20, 1864
    VA25
Jackson, D. - Co. E 47th North Carolina July 1, 1864 VA25
Jackson, G.M. - Co. E 24th Georgia July 3, 1862   VA25
Jackson, H. - Co. A 21st Virginia June 19, 1862   VA25
Jackson, Henry - Virginia   VA20
Jackson, J. - Co. K 13th Alabama May 10, 1862   VA25
Jackson, J.A. - Co. C 44th North Carolina July 24, 1864
    VA25
Jackson, J.H. - 13th South Carolina July 5, 1862   VA25
Jackson, J.M. - Co. D 35th Georgia April 19, 1865   VA25
Jackson, J.O. - Palmetto Sharp Shooters (South Carolina)June
    6, 1864   VA25
Jackson, J.R. - Co. D 15th Alabama Died Nov. 20, 1862
    VA23
Jackson, J.W. - 30th North Carolina Dec. 16, 1862   VA25
Jackson, James - KIA Sept. 18, 1862   VA19
Jackson, Jas. - Died Sept 17, 1862   VA19
Jackson, Jas. W. - Capt. - Kemper's Battery   VA10
Jackson, John - Co. A 8th Louisiana Dec. 17, 1862   VA25
Jackson, M.L.C. - Co. G 17th Georgia Aug. 26, 1862   VA25
Jackson, N. - Co. D 35th Georgia April 19, 1865   VA25

Jackson, N. - Co. C 21st Mississippi July 10, 1861 VA25
Jackson, Samuel - Co. D 49th North Carolina VA11
Jackson, T. - Co. F 33rd North Carolina Nov. 19, 1862 VA25
Jackson, Thomas J. - Co. G 47th North Carolina VA28
Jackson, W.A. - Co. F 18th Georgia June 6, 1862 VA25
Jackson, Wade - 6th Alabama VA18
Jacobs, H. - South Carolina VA17
Jacobs, J. Pvt. - Co. C 20th South Carolina Aug. 20, 1864 VA22
Jacobs, M. - Co. H 1st Texas June 20, 1862 VA25
Jacods, A. Pvt. - Co. F 11th Florida Died June 19, 1865 VA26
James, G.W. - Co. I 15th Alabama April 29, 1862 VA25
James, J. - Co. F 48th Georgia June 6, 1864 VA25
James, J. - Co. A 15th South Carolina July 6, 1864 VA25
James, J. - Co. C 48th North Carolina Oct. 9, 1863 VA25
James, J. - Co. K 17th North Carolina Aug. 2, 1864 VA25
James, J. - Co. B 27th North Carolina March 9, 1865 VA25
James, J.A. - Co. D 2nd Mississippi Aug. 5, 1863 VA25
James, M.M. - "C.Y.M." 1865 VA25
James, T. - Pvt. - South Carolina Aug. 21, 1864 VA22
Janard, F. - 8th Louisiana VA18
Janney, __ - Co. C 57th Virginia Oct. 6, 1861 VA25
Janney, W. - Clark Cavalry VA06
Jarvis, J. - Co. F 42nd North Carolina Aug. 30, 1864 VA25
Jarvis, J.M. - Co. H 39th North Carolina July 6, 1862 VA25
Jarvis, J.W.A. - C.S. Navy June 27, 1863 VA25
Jarvis, Ottway - KIA Sept. 22, 1864 age 27 VA19
Jarvis, P. - Co. E 3rd South Carolina Sept. 20, 1862 VA25
Jarvis, S. - Co. I 26th North Carolina Sept. 14, 1862 VA25
Jefferson, John Cox - POW - Federal Soldier Died Jan. 16, 1862 VA19
Jefferson, R. Moler - Co. D 12th Virginia VA08
Jefferson, T. - C.S. Navy June 8, 1863 VA25

Jefferson, Thomas Garland - VMI Cadet - MW - Battle of New Market - May 15, 1864 DOW May 18, 1864 - Buried at VMI VA21

Jeffery, D.G. - Lt. - Co. B 50th Georgia April 23, 1863 VA25

Jeffreys, J. - Virginia Sept. 17, 1864 VA25

Jeffreys, T.A. - Co. I 19th Mississippi April 19, 1865 VA25

Jenkins, __ - Co. B 1st Georgia March 23, 1865 VA25

Jenkins, J.S. - 13th North Carolina VA18

Jenkins, Jno. - Virginia VA20

Jenkins, Moses - Co. B 8th Artillery VA11

Jenkins, Samuel - 8th Virginia Infantry VA10

Jenkins, Tilman - Corp. - Co. C 1st North Carolina Artillery VA28

Jenkins, W. - North Carolina Died Jan. 10, 1863 VA03

Jenks, E. - 2nd South Carolina VA18

Jenks, W.P. - Co. F 8th South Carolina June 18, 1862 VA25

Jennings, A. - Co. A 3rd South Carolina May 25, 1854(sic) VA25

Jennings, D. - Co. D 17th North Carolina Aug. 16, 1864 VA25

Jennings, G.N. - Troop Artillery (Georgia) July 25, 1862 VA25

Jennings, H. - Co. B 53rd Virginia July 17, 1862 VA25

Jennings, H.L. - 8th Virginia Nov. 26, 1863 VA25

Jennings, P. - 2nd North Carolina June 19, 1862 VA25

Jennings, W. - Co. K 61st Virginia Aug. 6, 1863 VA25

Jennings, W.J. - Capt. - 14th Tennessee July 16, 1862 VA25

Jenny, J. - Co. C 57th Virginia Dec. 4, 1861 VA25

Jenny, S.G. - 22nd Georgia Dec. 8, 1862 VA25

Jermin, W. - June 5, 1862 VA25

Jerwan, S.D. - Co. A 43rd North Carolina Nov. 24, 1863 VA25

Jestive, L. - Pvt. - Co. F 56th North Carolina Aug. 21, 1864 VA22

Jett, J. - 2nd Battalion (Virginia) Feb. 10, 1865 VA25

Johns, D.S. - Co. K 5th Florida Aug. 26, 1862   VA25
Johns, J.R. - Sgt. - Co. D 21st Georgia   VA11
Johnson, __ - VA25
Johnson, __ - 35th Georgia 1862   VA25
Johnson, __ - 3rd North Carolina July 17, 1862   VA25
Johnson, __ - Co. C 14th Alabama June 19, 1862   VA25
Johnson, __ - Co. A 13th South Carolina June 9, 1862 VA25
Johnson, A. - Capt. - 10th Louisiana   VA25
Johnson, A. - Crenshw's Battery (Virginia) June 17, 1862
     VA25
Johnson, A. J. - Co. B 9th Georgia Artillery Dec. 6, 1864
     VA25
Johnson, A.D. - 3rd Alabama Aug. 16, 1862   VA25
Johnson, A.V. - Co. C 14th Alabama June 20, 1862   VA25
Johnson, Alice - Civilian -Killed in explosion of C.S.
     Laboratory - March 14, 1863 age 14   VA19
Johnson, B. - Co. C 11th South Carolina Nov. 8, 1862 VA25
Johnson, Benjamin L. - Pvt. - Co. H 7th Georgia Died May 8,
     1864   VA28
Johnson, C. - Co. C 38th Georgia June 3, 1862   VA25
Johnson, C.A. - Co. C 1st North Carolina June 15, 1862 VA25
Johnson, C.C. - Co. L 15th Alabama   VA11
Johnson, D.A. - Co. H 46th North Carolina June 29, 1864
     VA25
Johnson, D.B. - Co. K 14th South Carolina May 30, 1864
     VA25
Johnson, D.B. - Co. E 2nd South Carolina May 12, 1863
     VA25
Johnson, D.D. - Co. G 14th Georgia Aug. 25, 1864   VA25
Johnson, D.J. - Co. D 18th Georgia July 30, 1864   VA25
Johnson, E.A. - 20th Georgia VA18
Johnson, E.A. - Co. B 2nd Louisiana July 3, 1862   VA25
Johnson, E.H. - North Carolina   VA20
Johnson, Edward - Major General - 1816 - 1873   VA25
Johnson, Edward D. - Corp. - Co. F 1st North Carolina MW
     May 10, 1864 (Died May 15, 1864)   VA28

Johnson, Elias J. - Pvt. - Co. D 32nd North Carolina Died May 10, 1864 VA28

Johnson, Ezekiel - see Johnson, Ezeriel VA28

Johnson, Ezeriel - Pvt. - Co. F 7th South Carolina Died in Fredericksburg Headstone reads: "Ezekiel" VA28

Johnson, F. - Co. E 1st South Carolina June 15, 1862 VA25

Johnson, G.A. - Co. K 51st North Carolina July 29, 1864 VA25

Johnson, G.B. - Co. B 3rd Alabama Jan. 7, 1863 VA25

Johnson, G.W. 7th South Carolina VA18

Johnson, H.T. - Co. K 42nd Mississippi Sept. 1862 VA25

Johnson, J. - Co. G 28th Virginia Nov. 26, 1862 VA25

Johnson, J. - Co. H 54th North Carolina Jan. 10, 1863 VA25

Johnson, J. - Co. A 37th North Carolina Jan. 12, 1863 VA25

Johnson, J. - Co. B 15th North Carolina May 11, 1863 VA25

Johnson, J. - 28th North Carolina Jan. 26, 1865 VA25

Johnson, J. - Co. E 13th Georgia July 19, 1862 VA25

Johnson, J.A. - Pvt. - Virginia March 20, 1865 VA22

Johnson, J.A. - Co. B 17th Alabama Oct. 4, 1861 VA25

Johnson, J.A. - Co. K 4th Texas May 11, 1863 VA25

Johnson, J.C. - Co. A 15th North Carolina May 27, 1864 VA25

Johnson, J.D. - Co. H 2nd South Carolina July 27, 1862 VA25

Johnson, J.H. - Co. B 48th North Carolina Nov. 17, 1863 VA25

Johnson, J.H. - Co. I 2nd North Carolina June 5, 1862 VA25

Johnson, J.J. - Co. G 38th Georgia Aug. 9, 1862 VA25

Johnson, J.S. 3rd Georgia Bat. VA18

Johnson, J.S. - Co. G 16th Georgia Sept. 29, 1861 VA25

Johnson, J.T. - Co. F 5th Alabama May 23, 1863 VA25

Johnson, J.V. - Pvt. - North Carolina May 6, 1865 VA22

Johnson, J.W. - Co. I 14th Alabama Aug. 9, 1862 VA25

Johnson, J.W. - Co. B 1st Louisiana May 23, 1864 VA25

Johnson, J.Y. - Co. K 11th North Carolina Sept. 27, 1864 VA25

Johnson, Jabez - Pvt. - Virginia April 24, 1865 VA22

Johnson, L.D. - Co. K 7th Georgia Aug. 13, 1864   VA25
Johnson, M. J. - Halifax (Virginia)   1864   VA25
Johnson, N. - Co. F 12th North Carolina June 25, 1862   VA25
Johnson, P.C. - Pvt. - North Carolina April 3, 1865 Cemetery roster lists this soldier as "P.G. Johnson". VA22
Johnson, P.G. - see Johnson, P.C. VA22
Johnson, P.L. - Co. H 5th Texas June 5, 1862   VA25
Johnson, P.M. - Pvt. - Co. I 41st Alabama Died June 23, 1865   VA26
Johnson, R. - Co. E 21st Mississippi May 31, 1862   VA25
Johnson, R.A. - Co. I 24th North Carolina July 1, 1864 VA25
Johnson, R.A. - Co. A 52nd North Carolina May 3, 1864   VA25
Johnson, S.A. - Co. E 12th South Carolina Nov. 9, 1863 VA25
Johnson, T. - Co. D 15th Georgia Dec. 8, 1862   VA25
Johnson, T. - Co. G 49th Georgia Sept. 1862   VA25
Johnson, T. - Co. B 11th North Carolina July 6, 1864 VA25
Johnson, T.M. - Co. F 10th Alabama Feb. 14, 1863   VA25
Johnson, T.W. - Pvt. - Co. H 46th Virginia Died June 2, 1865   VA26
Johnson, W. - Louisiana Jan. 29, 1863   VA25
Johnson, W. - Co. B 46th North Carolina Dec. 3, 1863 VA25
Johnson, W. - Co. K 42nd Mississippi Aug. 9, 1862   VA25
Johnson, W. - North Carolina June 25, 1862   VA25
Johnson, W. - Co. K 45th Georgia June 15, 1862   VA25
Johnson, W.E. - Jan. 2, 1864 "Shot by Reb. Guard"   VA19
Johnson, W.E. - Mississippi Sept. 10, 1861   VA25
Johnson, W.M. - Co. E 13th South Carolina May 27, 1864   VA25
Johnson, W.P. - 17th Georgia VA18
Johnson, William - Pvt. - Co. E 12th South Carolina KIA May 12, 1864 (Grave not marked) VA28
Johnson, William N. - Co. G 15th South Carolina   VA28
Johnson, William S. - Corp. - Co. G 59th Georgia Died May 10, 1864   VA28

Johnston, George A. - 1st Lt. - 18th North Carolina Infantry DOW June 9, 1862   VA09
Johnston, H. - June 5, 1862 VA25
Johnston, J.T. - Corp. - Co. K 2nd South Carolina Sept. 1864 VA25
Johnston, James - Co. E 4th North Carolina   VA11
Joice, __ - 22nd North Carolina   1862   VA25
Joice, B. - Co. F 1st North Carolina Aug. 8, 1864   VA25
Joice, T.H. - Co. H 22nd North Carolina May 18, 1862 VA25
Joiner, B.F. - Co. H 12th North Carolina   VA11
Joiner, J.E. - Virginia   VA22
Jolly, A. - Co. H Palmetto Sharp Shooters (South Carolina) 1864   VA25
Jolly, H. - Artillery Aug. 10, 1864   VA25
Jolly, P.B. - Co. A 11th Alabama Died April 22, 1865 VA27
Jonburt, E. - VA18
Jones, __ - Lt. - Co. G 18th Georgia July 17, 1862   VA25
Jones, __ - April 29, 1862   VA25
Jones, __ - 5th Texas   1862   VA25
Jones, A. - C.S. Navy Jan. 16, 1865   VA25
Jones, A. - Capt. - Co. I 10th Louisiana May 22, 1863 VA25
Jones, A. - Co. H 40th Virginia May 31, 1862   VA25
Jones, A. - 2nd South Carolina May 13, 1863   VA25
Jones, A.A. - Co. C 5th Texas July 5, 1862   VA25
Jones, A.B. - Co. C 48th Alabama 1863   VA25
Jones, B. - 47th Virginia Aug. 20, 1862   VA25
Jones, B. - Co. A 47th North Carolina March 12, 1865   VA25
Jones, B. - Alabama Aug. 20, 1862   VA25
Jones, Ben W. - Georgia   VA20
Jones, C.S. - Co. K 38th Georgia May 28, 1864   VA25
Jones, D. - Co. F 13th South Carolina July 9, 1862 VA25
Jones, D.S. - Co. K 5th Florida Aug. 26, 1862   VA25
Jones, D.S.C. - 11th Virginia Infantry - KIA - Battle of Williamsburg - May 5, 1862   VA02

Jones, David L. - Mosby's Virginia Cavalry shot while POW
- Sept 23, 1864 VA23
Jones, E. - 28th Virginia VA18
Jones, E.C. - Livingston Guards (Texas) Aug. 9, 1861 VA25
Jones, E.S. - Co. E 4th North Carolina Nov. 8, 1862 VA25
Jones, Edmund L. - Lt. - Co. D 45th North Carolina VA28
Jones, Giles - Kentucky VA20
Jones, Henry - Died Nov. 10, 1862 VA19
Jones, Henry Jenner - VMI Cadet -KIA - Battle of New
Market - May 15, 1864 - Buried at VMI VA21
Jones, J. - "G" South Carolina VA24
Jones, J. - Virginia Feb. 14, 1863 VA25
Jones, J. - Co. G 4th South Carolina July 21, 1864 VA25
Jones, J. - Co. I 18th Alabama Oct. 14, 1861 VA25
Jones, J. - 3rd South Carolina Oct. 29, 1861 VA25
Jones, J. - 4th Louisiana Feb. 6, 1862 VA25
Jones, J. - Co. G 4th South Carolina Cavalry July 21, 1864
VA25
Jones, J. - Co. K 9th Georgia May 1, 1862 VA25
Jones, J. - Co. H 6th Georgia Nov. 9, 1864 VA25
Jones, J. - Co. B 2nd Georgia Sept. 23, 1861 VA25
Jones, J. H. - Co. H 60th Virginia Aug. 29, 1862 VA25
Jones, J.A. - Co. A 34th North Carolina Nov. 6, 1864 VA25
Jones, J.F. - Lt. - Co. K 5th Texas July 8, 1862 VA25
Jones, J.F. - Doctor -Black Horse Cavalry (4th Virginia
Cavalry). April 26, 1864 VA25
Jones, J.F. - Co. A 1st South Carolina July 5, 1862 VA25
Jones, J.H. - Co. D 46th North Carolina May 23, 1864 VA25
Jones, J.J. - Co. A 2nd North Carolina May 23, 1863 VA25
Jones, J.L. - 9th Louisiana VA18
Jones, J.P. - 24th Virginia VA18
Jones, J.R. - Co. G 14th North Carolina VA11
Jones, J.R. - Co. B 1st Tennessee Aug. 9, 1862 VA25
Jones, J.R. - Co. D 1st Tennessee Sept. 20, 1862 VA25
Jones, J.V. - Co. G 2nd South Carolina June 16, 1862 VA25
Jones, J.W. - Co. H 48th Alabama July 4, 1862 VA25

Jones, James - see Jones, Joseph S. VA28
Jones, James - POW - Federal Soldier Died Oct. 19, 1861 VA19
Jones, James W. - Pvt. - Georgia Died May 14, 1864 VA28
Jones, John - KIA March 4, 1864 VA19
Jones, John - Co. C 27th North Carolina Dec. 19, 1863 VA25
Jones, John A.B. - Co. G 14th North Carolina VA28
Jones, John F. - Pvt. - Co. E 3rd Virginia VA28
Jones, John H. - Pvt. - Co. I 2nd North Carolina MW - Spotsylvania Court House VA28
Jones, Joseph S. - Sgt. - Co. K 12th Virginia MW Spotsylvania C. H. May 12, 1864 Headstone reads: Headstone reads:" James Jones" VA28
Jones, L. - Co. F 56th North Carolina Aug. 18, 1864 VA25
Jones, L.C. - Co. I 20th South Carolina Aug. 17, 1864 VA25
Jones, M. - Pvt. - Co. D 18th Virginia Died June 2, 1865 VA26
Jones, M. April 13, 1863 VA25
Jones, M. - Co. K 14th Georgia June 11, 1862 VA25
Jones, M. - Co. E 31st Georgia July 17, 1862 VA25
Jones, M. - Louisiana July 10, 1861 VA25
Jones, M. - Co. C 4th North Carolina June 18, 1862 VA25
Jones, M.D. - 10th Alabama VA18
Jones, Mathew - Co. D 2nd South Carolina VA11
Jones, N.H. - Co. B 11th Alabama Feb. 6, 1862 VA25
Jones, R. - Co. F 45th Georgia May 22, 1863 VA25
Jones, R. - Co. A 11th Mississippi Jan. 22, 1862 VA25
Jones, R. - Co. C 2nd North Carolina July 25, 1862 VA25
Jones, R. - Co. A 55th North Carolina April 12, 1865 VA25
Jones, R.S. - Elizabeth City (Virginia) Dec. 8, 1862 VA25
Jones, S. - 9th Virginia Cavalry June 12, 1862 VA25
Jones, S.B. - Sgt. - Co. D 56th Virginia April 27, 1865 VA25
Jones, Samuel W. - Lt. Colonel - Co. F 13th Georgia Died May 12, 1864 VA28

Jones, T. - King William Artillery (Virginia)   March 10, 1863   VA25
Jones, T. - Co. B 14th North Carolina Nov. 9, 1862 VA25
Jones, V. - Co. F 1st South Carolina July 14, 1864 VA25
Jones, W.A. - Co. I 14th Louisiana June 30, 1862   VA25
Jones, W.E. - Sgt. KIA Jan. 29, 1864   VA19
Jones, W.E. - Co. B 33rd North Carolina Aug. 9, 1862 VA25
Jones, W.G. - Co. A 25th North Carolina Nov. 4, 1862 VA25
Jones, W.H. - Pvt. - Co. B 30th North Carolina Died June 22, 1865   VA26
Jones, W.H. - Moore's Artillery June 16, 1863   VA25
Jones, W.J. - Co. A 35th North Carolina   VA11
Jones, W.M. - Major - 9th Georgia   Oct. 26, 1864 age 26   VA25
Jones, W.M. - Lt. - Co. C 18th Georgia   VA25
Jones, W.M. - Co. E 48th Alabama Sept. 9, 1862   VA25
Jones, W.M. - Major - 9th Georgia Oct. 26, 1864 age 24   VA25
Jones, W.M. - Co. A 1st South Carolina Oct. 11, 1864 VA25
Jones, W.S. - Co. H 6th South Carolina May 5, 1865 VA25
Jonson, W.F. - Georgia   VA20
Jont, A. - Capt. - Co. I 10th Louisiana May 22, 1863   VA25
Jordan, __ - 2nd Alabama July 5, 1862   VA25
Jordan, A. - Co. I 27th North Carolina Sept. 4, 1864   VA25
Jordan, B.A. - Co. C 4th Texas Dec. 29, 1862   VA25
Jordan, C. - Co. A 7th Georgia July23, 1864   VA25
Jordan, D.F. - Co. B 10th Georgia March 14, 1863   VA25
Jordan, F.J. - Co. G 38th Georgia Oct. 7, 1862   VA25
Jordan, F.M. - Co. F 15th North Carolina Nov. 10, 1864   VA25
Jordan, F.M. - Co. C 8th Georgia June 1, 1863   VA25
Jordan, J.H. - Sgt. - Co. D 61st North Carolina June 15, 1864   VA25
Jordan, J.J. - 3rd Virginia Artillery June 18, 1862 VA25
Jordan, J.W. - Co. G 26th Alabama Aug. 8, 1862   VA25
Jordan, S. - 55th North Carolina Jan. 4, 1865   VA25

Jordan, T. - 1st Texas Aug. 20, 1862   VA25
Jordan, W.H. - Co. B 51st Georgia July 1864   VA25
Jordan, W.S. - 1st South Carolina Sept. 21, 1861   VA25
Jordan, Wm. - Cottom's Artillery June 25, 862   VA25
Josey, J.R. - Co. C 21st South Carolina July 11, 1864   VA25
Joy, __ - May 13, 1861   VA25
Joyner, A.J. - Co. K 45th North Carolina June 14, 1863   VA25
Joyner, Alsey M. - Co. I 30th North Carolina 1835 - 1864   VA28
Joyner, L.B. - Co. I 30th North Carolina Aug. 10, 1862   VA25
Joyner, P.H. - Co. F Palmetto Sharp Shooters (South Carolina) Oct. 1861   VA25
Joyner, R.H. - Co. D 1st North Carolina March 10, 1865   VA25
June, O.C. - Co. F 16th Mississippi Dec. 10, 1864   VA25
Justice, J. - Co. B 11th North Carolina May 30, 1864 VA25
Justice, L. - Co. B 46th North Carolina Aug. 19, 1864   VA25
Justice, W.M. - Killed on Central Railroad July 29, 1862   VA25
Kabbfleish, John - Pvt. - Co. D 22nd Georgia Died May 20, 1865   VA26
Kadle, Silas - Co. I 16th Georgia Sept. 8, 1861   VA25
Kagey, D.F. - VA15
Kaldy, M. - Co. A 14th Louisiana Oct. 11, 1863   VA25
Kaler, A.W. - Co. E 25th Georgia June 14, 1862   VA25
Kalley, J.L. - Co. H 5th Florida Sept. 29, 1862   VA25
Kamp, J.G. - Co. E 7th North Carolina Aug. 1, 1862 VA25
Kamp, J.J. - Co. G 59th Georgia June 26, 1864   VA25
Kane, __ - June 1862   VA25
Kane, Bridget - Killed by "Explosion (of) Magazine" April 5, 1865 age 53   VA19
Kane, J.W. - Co. I 16th Georgia Sept. 3, 1863   VA25
Kann, Thos. - Co. D 9th Louisiana July 12, 1863   VA25
Kannon, B. - 1862   VA25

Karan, J. - Co. D 15th North Carolina May 3, 1863 VA25
Karr, D.A. - Co. C 58th Virginia May 21, 1863   VA25
Karr, D.J. - Co. D 49th North Carolina July 3, 1862 VA25
Kaughman, Neil - POW - Federal Soldier Died Dec. 10, 1861
    VA19
Kay, D.M. - Co. H 1st South Carolina July 8, 1862 VA25
Kayes, J. - Co. E 24th Georgia Sept. 12, 1863   VA25
Keasler, James T. - Pvt. - Co. H 5th Alabama Died May 12,
    1864   VA28
Keath, E. - Co. E 1st South Carolina June 8, 1862 VA25
Keath, L.L. - Capt. - Co. G 61st North Carolina   Oct. 5, 1864
    VA25
Keath, R.B. - Co. H 34th North Carolina Oct. 16, 1864   VA25
Keath, T.J. - Co. F 1st South Carolina Aug. 9, 1862 VA25
Keating, James - 17th Virginia Infantry - KIA - Battle of Williamsburg - May 5, 1862   VA02
Kee, James G. - Sgt. - W. Virginia (sic) Feb. 17, 1865
    VA22
Keeler, D. - Lt. - 2nd Virginia Infantry   VA06
Keeling, Robert - KIA June 2, 1862   VA19
Keen, F.D. - Co. D 44th Georgia March 14, 1865   VA25
Keen, T.J. - Co. F 3rd Virginia March 29, 1865   VA25
Keever, Daniel A. - Sgt. - 25th South Carolina   VA04
Kehac, P. - Virginia Aug. 3, 1861   VA25
Kehely, A.J. - Co. C 15th Alabama   VA11
Kein, William - POW - Federal Soldier Died June 9, 1862
    VA19
Kell, C.R. - Co. C 32nd North Carolina March 15, 1865
    VA25
Kellam, J.W. - Co. I 6th South Carolina March 1, 1865 VA25
Keller, R. - Co. D 13th Alabama May 26, 1862   VA25
Kelley, J.M. - Co. G 19th Georgia Feb. 25, 1865   VA25
Kelley, Joseph H. - Pvt. - Co. D 13th South Carolina Died
    May 18, 1864   VA28
Kelley, William J. - see Kelly, William J.   VA28
Kells, E.C. - Co. I 4th South Carolina Nov. 8, 1865 VA25

Kelly, __ - 12th Mississippi 1862   VA25
Kelly, A.A. - Co. E 47th Alabama July 3, 1863   VA25
Kelly, A.O. - Co. F 1st South Carolina July 11, 1863 VA25
Kelly, E. - Pvt. - Co. E 2nd South Carolina Died May 16, 1865   VA26
Kelly, J.T. - Co. G 19th Georgia May 21, 1862   VA25
Kelly, M. - Co. A 14th Louisiana May 3, 1863   VA25
Kelly, M.F. - Co. E 44th North Carolina Oct. 13, 1864   VA25
Kelly, N. - 8th Alabama June 30, 1862   VA25
Kelly, R. - Virginia   VA20
Kelly, S.G. - Co. B 3rd Alabama Dec. 13, 1863   VA25
Kelly, W.W. - Co. I 20th Alabama July 25, 1862   VA25
Kelly, William J. - Pvt. - Co. D 13th South Carolina Died May 12, 1864 Headstone reads: "Kelley"   VA28
Kemer, J. - Co. F 47th Virginia May 24, 1862   VA25
Kemp, Asa - 12th Mississippi   VA18
Kemp, J.A.J. - Co. F 17th Georgia June 18, 1862   VA25
Kemp, Jno. - 8th Louisiana VA18
Kemp, L. - VA12
Kemp, T. - Virginia   VA20
Kemp, W.B. - Pvt. - Virginia 1864   VA22
Kenabick, J.M. - Sgt. - Co. J 15th Georgia Died Jan 24, 18__   VA23
Kenard, A.A. - Co. I 23rd North Carolina June 25, 1862   VA25
Kenard, A.C. - Co. I 4th Texas Nov. 28, 1861   VA25
Kenard, A.M. - Co. F 35th Mississippi July 30, 1863   VA25
Kendrick, J.C. - Co. D 14th Mississippi June 25, 1862   VA25
Kendrick, P.F. - Co. B 56th North Carolina July 20, 1864   VA25
Kenneday, A.W. - Co. H 17th North Carolina Nov. 23, 1862   VA25
Kennedy, E.D. - Co. F 8th Georgia July 18, 1864   VA25
Kennedy, W.H. - Co. C 48th North Carolina June 23, 1864   VA25

Kennerley, L.H. - Co. B 2nd North Carolina Cavalry Nov. 29, 1862 VA25

Kenney, H. - Co. C 2nd North Carolina March 5, 1865 VA25

Kennison, Edwin - see Kerrison, Edwin VA28

Kenny, A.G. - Co. A 42nd North Carolina Aug. 8, 1864 VA25

Kenny, T. - Co. G 35th Alabama Aug. 19, 1862 VA25

Kent, J.E. Pvt. - Co. E Cobb's Legion Died June 14, 1865 VA26

Kent, J.F. - Co. G 16th Alabama Oct. 11, 1863 VA25

Kent, J.P. - Co. I 31st Georgia Jan. 14, 1863 VA25

Keplinger, George - Pvt. - Co. I 33rd Virginia Headstone reads: "Kiplinger" VA28

Kerby, Reynold M. - Died July 30, 1861 - age 21 VA19

Kerfoot, D. - 2nd Virginia Infantry VA06

Kerlin, F.M. - Co. A 24th Virginia Sept. 14, 1862 VA25

Kerns, P. - Co. H 14th Louisiana Dec. 25, 1863 VA25

Kerr, J. - Co. F 49th North Carolina May 14, 1865 VA25

Kerrison, Edwin - Pvt. - Co. I 2nd South Carolina Died May 8, 1864 Memorial stone in Magnolia Cemetery in VA28

Kersey, John - Charleston Guards (South Carolina) Aug. 3, 1861 VA25

Kersh, A.J. - Co. G 1st (Haygood's) South Carolina Died May 30, 1863 VA03

Kersler, J.R. - Co. K 19th Mississippi Jan. 19, 1863 VA25

Kesler, G.T. - Co. E 57th Virginia May 30, 1862 VA25

Kesler, J. - VA12

Kesley, P.S. - July 30, 1863 VA25

Kespy, W.O. - Co. I 30th North Carolina May 22, 1862 VA25

Kessick, W.F. - Co. B 3rd South Carolina May 3, 1863 VA25

Kessucker, J.W. - Co. E 2nd Virginia VA11

Kester, W.M. - Co. E 28th North Carolina Feb. 19, 1864 VA25

Kevan, M. - Co. A 23rd North Carolina Dec. 7, 1863 VA25

Kevan, T. - Co. F 52nd North Carolina April 26, 1864 VA25

Key, C.H. - Pvt. - Co. G 34th Virginia Died June 24, 1865 VA26

Key, R.H. - Co. B 1st Maryland Cavalry Sept. 29, 1864 VA25

Kidd, N.B. - Cobb's Legion (Georgia) Sept. 30, 1861 VA25

Kilber, M.M. - Co. G 2nd North Carolina Cavalry July 1, 1864 VA25

Kile, J. - Co. C 32nd Virginia Aug. 7, 1864 VA25

Kile, W.L. - Co. H 13th North Carolina May 26, 1862 VA25

Kiles, W.W. - Co. K 24th Georgia Aug. 9, 1862 VA25

Killand, J.W. - Co. I 6th South Carolina Feb. 28, 1865 VA25

Killer, E. - Co. B 37th North Carolina Oct. 7, 1864 VA25

Killer, W.W. - Co. I 26th Alabama Aug. 1, 1862 VA25

Killheart, H. - Co. C 10th North Carolina Feb. 19, 1864 VA25

Killkelly, __ - Nov. 8, 1861 VA25

Kimball, J.D. - Co. E 1st Texas Sept. 2, 1862 VA25

Kimble, H. - Co. G 13th North Carolina June 15, 1862 VA25

Kimble, J.G. - Co. I 44th Georgia May 8, 1862 VA25

Kimble, J.S. - Co. C 46th North Carolina Feb. 19, 1864 VA25

Kimble, Wm. - Co. E 13th South Carolina June 10, 1862 VA25

Kimbro, W.B. - Co. B 3rd Georgia VA28

Kimbrough, ____ - Lt. - Co. D 47th Alabama Aug. 8, 1864 VA25

Kimbrough, A.A. - Mississippi Sept. 17, 1862 VA25

Kimbrough, M.A. - Co. I 34th North Carolina June 19, 1864 VA25

Kimbrough, William J. - Sgt. - Co. G 4th Virginia Cavalry Died May 9, 1864 VA28

Kincheloe, William A. - Co. A 49th Virginia VA28

King, A.F. - 5th North Carolina Cavalry DOW - 1863 VA07

King, A.J. - Co. B 18th North Carolina Jan. 14, 1863 VA25

King, Andrew J. - Sgt. - Co. E 26th Georgia KIA - Petersburg, Virginia - June 18, 1864 VA28

King, D.R. - Co. F 3rd Alabama Died May 7, 1862   VA23
King, Franklin - POW - Federal Soldier - Kentucky - Died
    Feb. 21, 1863   VA19
King, G.D. - Co. C 6th Alabama June 18, 1862   VA25
King, J. - March 1863   VA25
King, J.C. - Co. I 3rd North Carolina Jan. 12, 1865 VA25
King, J.M. - Co. H 11th North Carolina Oct. 16, 1864   VA25
King, J.R. - Co. B 42nd Mississippi Nov. 18, 1862   VA25
King, J.W. - South Carolina   VA20
King, J.W. - Co. E 16th Georgia March 17, 1865   VA25
King, James A. - McGregor's Artillery   VA28
King, L.J. - Co. C 61st North Carolina July 6, 1864 VA25
King, T.J. - Co. G 27th Georgia May 21, 1862   VA25
King, W.A. - Co. E 13th North Carolina June 13, 1863   VA25
King, W.R. - 2nd South Carolina Aug. 3, 1864   VA25
King, Wiliam - Pvt. - North Carolina March 25, 1865 VA22
Kingberry, F. - Hospital Guard Aug. 24, 1862   VA25
Kingsallie, M. - Co. H 6th Alabama Sept. 23, 1863   VA25
Kink, S. - 16th North Carolina June 14, 1862   VA25
Kink, S.A. - Co. E 24th Virginia 1862   VA25
Kinn, R. - North Carolina 1865   VA25
Kinner, M. - C.S. Navy   March 29, 1865   VA25
Kinney, B.R. - Corp. - Co. D 14th North Carolina Died May
    12, 1864   VA28
Kiplinger, George - see Keplinger, George   VA28
Kirby, Ed - Lt. Colonel - KIA Chickahominy   VA19
Kirby, J. - Co. C 7th South Carolina May 25, 1862 VA25
Kirby, J.M. - Co. C 49th Virginia April 20, 1862   VA25
Kirby, T.J. - Co. I 13th North Carolina June 2, 1862 VA25
Kirk, E.H. - 6th North Carolina May 30, 1864   VA25
Kirk, K. - Co. I 5th North Carolina Jan. 14, 1863 VA25
Kirkland, J. - Co. A 66th Virginia June 26, 1864   VA25
Kirkland, J.H. - Co. C 15th Georgia Nov. 8, 1862   VA25
Kirkland, T. - Co. I 37th North Carolina May 14, 1865 VA25
Kirkman, J.M. - Sgt. - Co. E 2nd North Carolina June 5, 1864
    VA25

Kirkmeyer, W. - Virginia Artillery July 20, 1862   VA25
Kirkpatrick, S.P. - Co. C 5th Alabama July 22, 1862   VA25
Kirline, J. - Co. E 27th Georgia Sept. 7, 1862   VA25
Kisty, J. - Co. G 5th North Carolina Jan. 6, 1862 VA25
Kittle, George A. - Co. A 62nd Virginia Cavalry KIA -
    Berry's Ferry - July 19, 1864   VA06
Kleeper, W.H. - POW - Federal Soldier Died June 19, 1862
    VA19
Klouty, A. - Co. G 42nd North Carolina Sept. 25, 1864
    VA25
Knapp, Miles M. - Co. F 58th North Carolina Headstone
    reads: "Knupp"   VA28
Knettel, Louis - Pvt. - Co. K 30th Virginia Died June 10,
    1865   VA26
Knier, W.W. - Pvt. - Co. F 49th North Carolina Died May 24,
    1865   VA26
Knight, A.M. - Co. K 12th S.C. Sept. 9, 1864   VA25
Knight, J.J. - 6th North Carolina May 30, 1862   VA25
Knight, John - Cobb's Legion (Georgia) June 10, 1862   VA25
Knight, John - Co. B 7th Tenn. Aug. - 11,1862   VA25
Knight, John - Co. H 2nd Virginia 1862   VA25
Knight, L.A. - 14th Alabama June 5,1862   VA25
Knight, Wm. - Co. C 3rd Alabama Jan. 27,1863   VA25
Knotts, S. - Co. C 6th Alabama Aug. - 11,1862   VA25
Knowlan, T. - Co. B 8th Alabama 1862   VA25
Knox, J. - Co. F 15th South Carolina May 30, 1864 VA25
Knox, J. - Co. C 17th North Carolina May 3, 1863 VA25
Knox, William - 2nd South Carolina   VA18
Knox, Wm. - Co. H 61st North Carolina July 1, 1864 VA25
Knupp, Miles M. - see Knapp, Miles M.   VA28
Koker, J.H. - Sgt. Major - 59th Alabama June 23, 1864
    VA25
Koler, S. - Cobb's Legion (Georgia)   Sept. 9, 1861   VA25
Koon, Lyman - Co. D 17th Virginia Infantry   VA10
Koonce, P.M. - Tennessee   VA11
Kork, C.O. - Co. C 10th Alabama May 24, 1862   VA25

Kruser, T.J. - 1st Georgia VA18
Kutty, P.S. - April 7, 1862 VA25
Lacery, M.J. - Co. B 37th North Carolina June 15, 1862
    VA25
Lack, D.B. - Co. A 1st South Carolina July 14, 1862 VA25
Lack, J.B. - Co. K 6th Alabama May 3, 1862   VA25
Lack, J.F. - Co. A 12th South Carolina July 18, 1862   VA25
Lackey, James M. - Pvt. - Co. E 13th North Carolina Died
    May 21, 1864 VA28
Lackey, T.O. - Co. C 37th North Carolina June 12, 1862
    VA25
Lacoure, L. - Co. A 2nd Louisiana Oct. 2, 1864   VA25
Lacra, J.R. - 55th Virginia Nov. 4, 1862 VA25
Lacy, John - Co. B 28th Virginia (Courtney's Virginia
    Artillery) Died Feb 27, 1862   VA23
Lafanar, __ - Sgt. - Co. I 46tyh North Carolina July 15, 1864
    VA25
Lafsey, H.T. - Lt. - Co. C 27th Georgia June 2, 1864   VA25
Lagg, A.C. - Co. F 21st Virginia June 27, 1864   VA25
Lake, H. - June 20, 1862 VA25
Lake, W.T. - 3rd South Carolina June 1, 1862   VA25
Lallards, E. - Kentucky   VA20
Lam, Charles - POW - Federal Soldier Died June 11, 1862
    VA19
Lamb, R. - Co. C 18th South Carolina July 27, 1862   VA25
Lambden, T.T. - 1862   VA25
Lambert, Abram M. - Pvt. - Co. C 5th Virginia Died May 12,
    1864   VA28
Lambert, Geo. - March 1863   VA25
Lambert, J.L. - Co. E 26th North Carolina March 2, 1864
    VA25
Lambert, R.J. - Co. B 4th Texas May 5, 1865   VA25
Lambert, R.P. - Co. E 26th North Carolina Oct. 22, 1864
    VA25
Lambert, W.A. - Co. D 1st Georgia Reserves Feb. 26, 1865
    VA25

Lamma, Frank -VA15
Lampie, M. - Corp. - Co. A 14th North Carolina   VA28
Lampkin, A.N. - Co. I 26th North Carolina July 16, 1864
    VA25
Lampkin, G.M. - Co. C 47th Virginia July 27, 1862   VA25
Lanbrum, G.M. - Kentucky   VA20
Lancaster, A.O. - Co. A 14th Alabama June 17, 1862   VA25
Lancaster, B.S. - Co. K 46th North Carolina May 1, 1864
    VA25
Lancaster, M.D. - Co. A 44th North Carolina Sept. 28, 1864
    VA25
Lancaster, T. - Co. D 12th Alabama June 18, 1862   VA25
Lancaster, W.H. - Died Jan. 28, 1863   VA19
Lancaster, W.H. - DOW Jan 28, 1863   VA19
Lancaster, W.W. - Co. F 12th North Carolina June 18, 1862
    VA25
Lancy, W.A. - Co. F 27th North Carolina Oct. 31, 1865   VA25
Land, J. - Co. B 11th North Carolina July 9, 1865 VA25
Land, L.L. - Co. B 2nd North Carolina Dec. 22, 1863 VA25
Land, R. - Co. E 49th Georgia July 8, 1862   VA25
Land, W.H. - Co. B 2nd Florida May 20, 1862   VA25
Land, Wm. - Hampton's Legion July 30, 1862   VA25
Landes, E. - VA12
Landford, T.P. - Palmetto Sharp Shooters (South Carolina)
    March 7, 1864   VA25
Landman, M.N. - Lloyd's Artillery April 10, 1862   VA25
Landrith, A. - Co. G 42nd Mississippi   Sept. 17, 1862   VA25
Landrum, S.L. - Co. I 14th Louisiana Dec. 21, 1864   VA25
Lane, C.P. - 1st Virginia Artillery   May 9, 1862   VA25
Lane, E.W. Pvt. - Co. C 18th Virginia Died June 11, 1865
    VA26
Lane, G.L. - Co. B 12th Georgia July 21, 1862   VA25
Lane, H. - June 7, 1862 VA25
Lane, J. - Co. G 1st South Carolina Aug. 13, 1864 VA25
Lane, J.B. - 21st South Carolina June 7, 1864   VA25
Lane, J.F. - 13th Georgia June 6, 1864   VA25

Lane, James E. - Pvt. - Co. A 11th Virginia Died June 24, 1865   VA26
Lane, W.A. - Co. G 4th North Carolina June 24, 1862 VA25
Lane, William H. - Corp. - Co. K 7th Tennessee Died May 12, 1864   VA28
Lanes, J.A. - Co. B 13th South Carolina April 23, 1862 VA25
Lanford, T. - Co. H 17th Georgia Oct. 25, 1864   VA25
Langden, J.J. - Co. E 48th Georgia July 8, 1864   VA25
Langer, B. - Co. C 66th North Carolina Aug. 27, 1864   VA25
Langford, B.B. - 17th Virginia VA18
Langford, C.M. - Co. C 13th Alabama Jan. 27, 1863   VA25
Langford, S.W. - Co. C 17th Georgia Nov. 16, 1862   VA25
Langley, J. - Co. G 33rd North Carolina July 28, 1863   VA25
Langley, J.A. - 2nd North Carolina May 29, 1863   VA25
Langley, J.V. - March 7, 1865 VA25
Langston, __ - Co. D 23rd Georgia June 19, 1862   VA25
Langston, C.C. - Co. I 51st Georgia May 25, 1863   VA25
Langston, R.F. - Co. G 35th Georgia July 13, 1862   VA25
Lanier, J.T. - Co. I 13th Alabama May 29, 1862   VA25
Lanier, R. - Co. B 51st Georgia July 8, 1864   VA25
Lankin, __ - 3rd North Carolina July 7, 1862   VA25
Lansdoun, T.B.   8th Louisiana VA18
Lard, G.M. - Co. B 35th North Carolina Dec. 29, 1861   VA25
Lard, J.E. - Co. B 35th Georgia July 2, 1862   VA25
Lard, J.L. - Co. B 43rd North Carolina Dec. 23, 1864   VA25
Lard, J.M. - Georgia   VA20
Larlton, __ - July 2, 1862 VA25
Larr, W.R. - Co. C 2nd North Carolina Jan. 3, 1863 VA25
Laseter, H. - Sumpter Artillery   May 12, 1862   VA25
Laslie, Jno. - Capt. - 2nd Virginia Cavalry   VA23
Lassater, __ - 12th Alabama VA18
Lasseter, J. - Co. I 9th Virginia Nov. 29, 1862   VA25
Lasseter, W.H. - Co. B 11th Georgia June 22, 1864   VA25
Lassiter, I.L. - Manly's Battery (South Carolina)   VA28

Lassiter, J.J. - Pvt. - Co. F 11th Florida Died May 2, 1865 VA26
Laster, J. - Co. I 5th North Carolina May 10, 1862 VA25
Laster, W.H. - 6th South Carolina Sept. 14, 1861 VA25
Lasvie, W. - Co. A 2nd Virginia July 5, 1862 VA25
Latham, D.L. - Co. H 4th North Carolina July 13, 1864 VA25
Latham, S.M. - Co. E 12th South Carolina July 21, 1862 VA25
Lathers, A.J. - Co. A 19th Mississippi July 3, 1862 VA25
Lathrop, A.L. - Co. I 40th North Carolina May 25, 1864 VA25
Latimer, A.W. - Lt. - 49th Georgia May 29, 1865 VA25
Latson, T.M. - Co. I 6th Georgia July 12, 1864 VA25
Latta, W.G. - Co. C 27th North Carolina May 15, 1864 VA25
Lattow, P.W. - Co. E 66th North Carolina Aug. 22, 1864 VA25
Latty, W. - Co. A 66th North Carolina Sept. 3, 1864 VA25
Launce, B.F. - Alabama VA20
Lavender, F.F. - Phillip's Legion - Cavalry VA18
Law, C. - Co. I 4th Georgia May 13, 1863 VA25
Lawdermilk, L. - Co. I 26th North Carolina June 12, 1864 VA25
Lawis, W.F. - North Carolina VA20
Lawless, F.M. - Co. I 24th Virginia Aug. 9, 1862 VA25
Lawner, H. - Co. E 6th North Carolina Jan. 26, 1865 VA25
Lawrance, B. - Co. A 14th North Carolina July 4, 1862 VA25
Lawrance, D. - Aug. 1, 1863 VA25
Lawrance, M. - Co. K 28th Georgia May 14, 1862 VA25
Lawrance, M.Y. - Co. C 49th Georgia July 22, 1864 VA25
Lawrance, W.A. - Co. F 9th Virginia Oct. 16, 1861 VA25
Lawrence, B.F. - Alabama VA20
Lawrence, S.R. - 20th Georgia VA18
Lawson, A. - Co. G 38th Georgia July 8, 1862 VA25
Lawson, Andrew J. - Sgt. - Co. A 21st Virginia Died June 10, 1864 (MW - Spotsylvania Court House) VA28
Lawson, E. - Co. B 15th Louisiana May 29, 1863 VA25
Lawson, J. - Co. C 57th Virginia Nov. 19, 1862 VA25

Lawson, J.M. - Hampton's Legion Feb. 22, 1864   VA25
Lawson, M. - Co. C 61st Georgia 1865   VA25
Lawson, R. - 14th Virginia Cavalry   VA11
Lay, W.J. - Co. A 5th Texas July 2, 1865   VA25
Layhorn, J.W. - Reeve's Co. Oct. 1, 1861   VA25
Layhorn, S.P. - Co. A 27th Georgia Aug. 7, 1864   VA25
Layton, J.T. - Co. C 66th North Carolina June 24, 1864
      VA25
Lazenog, R.B. - Jordan's Artillery   May 20, 1862   VA25
Leach, C. - Co. A 28th Virginia June 3, 1864   VA25
Leach, D.M. - Co. E 1st South Carolina 1864   VA25
Leach, J. - Co. D 15th North Carolina March 19, 1865   VA25
Leadbetter, S.H. - Co. G 16th North Carolina Oct. 4, 1864
      VA25
Leadcutter, W. - Co. D 55th North Carolina Jan. 6, 1864
      VA25
Leads, C. - Co. C 2nd North Carolina Aug. 23, 1864 VA25
Leary, A. - Co. I 10th Georgia April 30, 1865   VA25
Leary, Emile - Ellet's Light Artillery (Crenshaw Artillery) -
      Virginia   VA28
Leatherman, J. - Co. H 19th North Carolina May 25, 1864
      VA25
Leatherman, J.L. - 4th Georgia May 24, 1864   VA25
Leberry, James - POW - Federal Soldier Died Apr. 21, 1862
      VA19
Lechman, L. - Co. F 4th North Carolina   VA11
Ledford, L. - Co. I 48th North Carolina Aug. 8, 1864 VA25
Lee, __ - 6th Alabama June 20, 1862   VA25
Lee, A. - 22nd North Carolina May 4, 1862   VA25
Lee, A.W.- 23rd Georgia May 20, 1862   VA25
Lee, Absolom (E.) - Troop Artillery - Georgia   VA28
Lee, Andrew - Pvt. - Co. D 41st Alabama Died June 17, 1865
      VA26
Lee, Andrew J. (Sr.) - Pvt. - Co. B 16th Mississippi Died May
      12, 1864   VA28
Lee, B.B. - Co. F 34th North Carolina Sept. 29, 1864   VA25

Lee, B.T. - 7th Georgia VA18
Lee, E. - Co. E 59th Georgia Nov. 26, 1862   VA25
Lee, Fitxhugh - General 1835-1905   VA25
Lee, H. - Co. C 2nd South Carolina Nov. 15, 1865 VA25
Lee, H.S. - Co. E 15th North Carolina Jan. 28, 1863   VA25
Lee, H.T. - Co. K 26th North Carolina May 4, 1865 VA25
Lee, J. - Co. C 52nd North Carolina Oct. 14, 1864   VA25
Lee, J.B. - Co. C 59th Georgia Aug. 22, 1864   VA25
Lee, J.H. - Co. I 12th North Carolina May 24, 1864 VA25
Lee, J.W. - Lt. - Co. A 59th Georgia   Nov. 19, 1862   VA25
Lee, James - Co. A 24th North Carolina July 12, 1864   VA25
Lee, James K. - DOW - Bull Run - Aug. 4, 1861   VA19
Lee, John H. - 4th Virginia VA10
Lee, John W. - POW - Federal Soldier Died Nov. 30, 1861
    VA19
Lee, L. - Co. K 38th Georgia June 22, 1864   VA25
Lee, Nathan A. - Pvt. - Co. G 1st North Carolina Died May
    10, 1864   VA28
Lee, R.M. - Co. F 17th Virginia Infantry   VA10
Lee, S. - Co. H 20th North Carolina Aug. 2, 1862 VA25
Lee, S.B. - Co. K 30th North Carolina June 29, 1864   VA25
Lee, W. - Capt. - Co. K 40th Virginia   Oct. 9, 1864   VA25
Lee, W.C. - Pvt. - Co. I 43rd North Carolina .Died May 13,
    1865   VA26
Lee, W.H. - Co. A 8th Louisiana Nov. 19, 1862   VA25
Lee, W.J. - Co. E 1st South Carolina July 1, 1862 VA25
Leech, D.M. - Co. A 1st South Carolina   May 30, 1864
    VA25
Leffell, Jas. - Co. B 28th Virginia Died Feb 6, 1862 VA23
Leftrick, J.T. - Co. K 1st Virginia July 20, 1862   VA25
Leftwich, George - KIA Oct. 7, 1862   VA19
Legett, J.M. - Lt. Colonel - 10th Louisiana May 3, 1863
    VA25
Legett, W.H. - Co. F 6th Virginia   May 29, 1863   VA25
Legg, J.H. - 11th Georgia VA18

Leggett, Redding. - Sgt. - Co. E 4th North Carolina Died May 12, 1864   VA28
Leghorn, P.P. - 13th Virginia   May 6, 1862   VA25
Lehman, A. - South Carolina   VA17
Lehon, J. - 2nd Battalion   May 24, 1862   VA25
Leigh, B.W. - Major KIA   VA19
Leitz, C.K. - Co. K 14th Louisiana Nov. 19, 1862   VA25
Leitzsay, W. - Capt. - Co. H 13th South Carolina Aug. 22, 1864   VA25
Lemley, William A. - see Lemly, William A.   VA28
Lemly, William A. - Pvt. - Co. A 4th North Carolina KIA - Fredericksburg - Dec. 13, 1862 Headstone reads: "Lemley"   VA28
Lemmon, James - POW - Federal Soldier Died Dec. 23, 1861   VA19
Lemmons, T.H. - Co. H 12th Alabama Nov. 17, 1862   VA25
Lenant, W. - Co. G 5th North Carolina Feb. 1, 1865 VA25
Lenard, __ - June 18, 1862   VA25
Lenard, E. - Co. B 49th Georgia   VA11
Lenard, J. - Co. E 8th Virginia Oct. 31, 1865   VA25
Lenard, V. - Co. I 14th North Carolina July 5, 1862 VA25
Lenier, G.M. - Hardway's Battery (Virginia)Aug. 27, 1862   VA25
Lentz, __ - June 1, 1862 VA25
Leonard, Samuel - Sgt. - Co. D 5th Cavalry KIA Spotsylvania Court House VA28
Lepperd, J.H. - 7th Georgia VA18
Lerly, J. - Co. B 14th Georgia   Nov. 20, 1864   VA25
Leslie, J.W. - Tennessee   VA20
Leslie, Thomas G. - Co. K 10th Alabama   VA11
Lessley, G.W. - Pvt. - Co. K 25th South Carolina Aug. 25, 1864   VA22
Lester, B. - Co. I 2nd South Carolina Jan. 3, 1863 VA25
Lester, C.E. - Co. E 6th Alabama May 23, 1863   VA25
Lester, E.D. - Co. G 35th Georgia July 20, 1862   VA25

Lester, G.A. - Lt. Colonel - 8th Louisiana June 2, 1864 VA25
Lester, W. - 2nd Mississippi June 1, 1862 VA25
Lever, H. - Co. A 24th Virginia Aug. 24, 1862 VA25
Leverett, F.P. - Surgeon - 5th Texas June 4, 1864 VA25
Levers, __ - 11th Virginia July 6, 1862 VA25
Levery, H. - Co. H 2nd Virginia June 29, 1862 VA25
Levrith, D.M. - North Carolina Oct. 6, 1864 VA25
Levritt, T. - 14th North Carolina May 27, 1862 VA25
Levy, J. - Co. C 7th Louisiana VA28
Levy, J.J. - Co. G 42nd Mississippi Nov. 17, 1862 VA25
Levy, M. - Mississippi KIA - May 31, 1862 VA17
Lew, A.S. - Co. E 11th South Carolina Aug. 22, 1864 VA25
Lewis, __ - Lt. - Co. C 31st Virginia March 8, 1863 VA25
Lewis, A.S. - 18th Virginia VA18
Lewis, C. - VA12
Lewis, Chas. - Alabama VA20
Lewis, D. - Co. D 12th Virginia April 7, 1865 VA25
Lewis, F.A. - Co. C 4th North Carolina Aug. 4, 1862 VA25
Lewis, G.D. - 13th Alabama Sept. 20, 1861 VA25
Lewis, J. - Co. B 13th North Carolina Dec. 22, 1864 VA25
Lewis, J.D. - Co. I 57th Virginia May 21, 1862 VA25
Lewis, J.H. - Co. E 1st South Carolina Aug. 19, 1864 VA25
Lewis, J.M. - Died June 19, 1862 age 22 VA19
Lewis, J.W. - Co. F 20th North Carolina June 29, 1862 VA25
Lewis, James S. - Sgt. - Co. D 7th Georgia MW May 10, 1864 (Died May 13, 1864)VA28
Lewis, N. - Co. A 2nd North Carolina June 16, 1863 VA25
Lewis, T. - 2nd South Carolina VA18
Lewis, W.A. - Co. A 64th Georgia Sept. 11, 1864 VA25
Lewis, W.W. - Co. I 6th Alabama May 13, 1862 VA25
Leymore, W.H. - Lt. - Co. A 56th North Carolina April 25, 1865 VA25
Liben, R.M. - 8th Georgia Nov. 20, 1862 VA25
Liggett, E.D. - Co. H 42nd Mississippi Sept. 27, 1862 VA25
Liggons, P. - June 27, 1864 VA25

Light, Henry B. - Pvt. - Co. E 14th Georgia Died May 12, 1864   VA28
Lightfoot, Wm. - 12th Alabama Aug. 8, 1861   VA25
Ligler, S. - Co. D 52nd North Carolina May 22, 1864 VA25
Ligon, William H. - DOW Sept. 16, 1864   VA19
Liles, W.B. - Co. G 1st North Carolina   VA28
Lilly, Gabriel R. - Corp. - 18th North Carolina Infantry DOW May 27, 1862   VA09
Lilly, Thos. - Capt. - Co. K 26th North Carolina   Sept. 4, 1864   VA25
Linabrough, W.H. - 5th Alabama Battalion June 30, 1862 VA25
Linabrough, W.T. - Co. D 18th Alabama June 29, 1862 VA25
Linack, J. - Co. C 56th South Carolina Aug. 31, 1864   VA25
Linam, M.C.L. - Co. I 1st South Carolina   VA28
Linaman, D.A. - Co. E 57th North Carolina Oct. 19, 1864 VA25
Linar, T. - 17th North Carolina July 22, 1864   VA25
Lindback, A. - 33rd North Carolina March 12, 1863   VA25
Linden, T. - Co. H 5th Alabama June 5, 1862   VA25
Linder, W. - Co. I 3rd South Carolina Aug. 6, 1862 VA25
Lindsay, D.F. - 17th Mississippi   VA18
Lindsay, J.B. - Co. I 38th Virginia   VA28
Lindsay, J.H. - 3rd Tennessee VA18
Lindsey, __ - 3rd South Carolina Aug. 30, 1862   VA25
Lindsey, C. - Co. I 14th Louisiana July 25, 1862   VA25
Lindsey, J. - Pvt. - Co. I 11th Virginia Died June 10, 1865 VA26
Lindsey, Jas. - Clark Cavalry VA06
Lindsey, T.H. - Co. A 17th South Carolina June 20, 1862 VA25
Lindsey, W. - Co. A 13th South Carolina June 25, 1862 VA25
Linha, G.G. - Co. D 51st North Carolina Oct. 4, 1864 VA25
Link, G. - Co. H 14th Georgia Dec. 28, 1862   VA25

Link, J. - Virginia   VA20
Lipman, L.S. - Lt. 5th Louisiana. Died May 9, 1863   VA17
Lippy, W.H. - Co. B 7th North Carolina July 3, 1864 VA25
Lister, J.C. - 27th Georgia Sept. 9, 1862   VA25
Litten, John   -VA15
Little, Green B. - Co. H 1st North Carolina   VA11
Little, H.G. - KIA July 16, 1864   VA19
Little, J. - Washington Artillery (Louisiana) June 20, 1862   VA25
Little, J.A. - Pvt. - North Carolina Oct. 9, 1864   VA22
Little, W.R. - Co. F 30th North Carolina Sept. 7, 1862   VA25
Littlefields, __ - Co. C 17th Georgia May 24, 1864   VA25
Livingston, D. - Co. D 46th North Carolina Sept. 9, 1864   VA25
Livingston, D.M. - Sgt. - Co. I 27th North Carolina June 27, 1864   VA25
Livingston, J.H. - Co. H 14th North Carolina June 12, 1862   VA25
Livingston, John W. - Sgt. - Co. H 3rd Georgia Died May 10, 1864   VA28
Lloyd, Preston - Co. E 4th North Carolina   VA11
Lockard, M.N. - Co. D 17th Mississippi May 19, 1862   VA25
Lockart, H. - Co. H 5th North Carolina June 14, 1862 VA25
Lockart, John - Co. K 5th Texas May 31, 1862   VA25
Loftan, G. - Co. C 38th North Carolina June 29, 1864   VA25
Loftan, J.A. - Co. G 66th North Carolina July 16, 1864   VA25
Loften, J. - Co. F 8th Louisiana July 27, 1863   VA25
Loftin, R. - June 18, 1862 VA25
Logan, A.T. - Sumpter Artillery   May 6, 1862   VA25
Logan, A.W. - 9th Louisiana This soldier's name is listed in Napier Bartlett's *Military Record of Louisiana*, however he is not listed in the cemetery's burial roster. VA28
Logan, Andrew W. - Pvt. - Co. D 9th Louisiana   VA28
Logan, J.C. - May 17, 1862 VA25
Logan, J.W. - 19th Alabama May 18, 1862   VA25

Logan, S. - Co. K 8th Alabama June 25, 1862   VA25
Logan, W.E. - Pvt. - Virginia March 26, 1865   VA22
Logan, William H. - DOW Sept. 16, 1864   VA19
Logg, J. - Co. F - 4th North Carolina Nov. 14, 1863 VA25
Logue, __ - Capt. - Co. B 22nd Georgia Aug. 17, 1864
    VA25
Logue, Michl. - Co E 1st Maryland Died Dec 12, 1861   VA23
Logue, T. - Co. B 22nd Georgia Dec. 1, 1862   VA25
Lolley, J.W. - Cobb's Legion (Georgia) Sept. 4, 1861   VA25
Lomax, N.W. - Pvt. - Co. A 21st North Carolina DOD near
    Fredericksburg - March 28, 1863   VA28
Lomax, Pinkney Asbury - Pvt. - Co. A 54th North Carolina
    Died near Fredericksburg - Jan. 1, 1863 VA28
Londen, __ - Aug. 20, 1861   VA25
Lone, John - Co. D 28th North Carolina Aug. 24, 1862   VA25
Long, C.J. - Co. K 47th North Carolina Aug. 30, 1863   VA25
Long, F. - Co. I 28th North Carolina July 30, 1862   VA25
Long, G. - Co. A 28th South Carolina July 30, 1862   VA25
Long, G.W.M. - Pvt. - Co. B 7th South Carolina Died May
    15, 1864   VA28
Long, H. - Aug. 25, 1861 VA25
Long, J.C. - Co. A 6th Mississippi Oct. 17, 1861   VA25
Long, J.F. - Co. K 18th Mississippi June 23, 1864   VA25
Long, J.H. - Sgt. - Co. I 14th North Carolina   VA28
Long, J.J. - Co. I 18th South Carolina July 21, 1864   VA25
Long, J.M. - 3rd South Carolina Aug. 24, 1862   VA25
Long, John A. - Sgt. - Co. I 33rd Virginia   VA28
Long, S.P.W. - Co. D 28th Georgia Aug. 24, 1862   VA25
Long, T. - 49th Virginia July 30, 1862   VA25
Long, W.A. - Co. F 4th North Carolina   VA28
Long, W.B. - Co. A 1st Florida June 29, 1862   VA25
Long, Wallace W. - Pvt.. - 18th North Carolina Infantry
    DOW June 25, 1862   VA09
Longing, __ - 1st Texas Oct. 17, 1862   VA25
Lonnery, W. - 12th North Carolina Aug. 7, 1862   VA25

Lookable, H.M. - Co. B 37th North Carolina Dec. 24, 1862 VA25

Lookable, T. - Co. A 28th North Carolina Nov. 21, 1862 VA25

Loper, A. - 8th Louisiana May 4, 1862   VA25

Loper, William W. - Pvt. - Co. E 26th Georgia KIA Spotsylvania May 10, 1864   VA28

Loping, A. - C.S. Navy Jan. 3, 1863   VA25

Lordon, J.B. - Co. H 26th North Carolina June 12, 1864 VA25

Lotts, Cyrus - Pvt. - Co. D 5th Virginia Died May 10, 1864 VA28

Lounger, William - POW - Federal Soldier Died Oct. 26, 1861   VA19

Love, A. - Co. H 49th North Carolina June 14, 1864   VA25

Love, H. - Co. B 5th North Carolina Nov. 13, 1862 VA25

Love, J.G. - Georgia   VA20

Love, Lucien - Mosby's Virginia Cavalry shot while POW - Sept 23, 1864   VA23

Love, Robt. T. - Co. K 17th Virginia Infantry   VA10

Lovelace, J.H. - Co. G 18th Mississippi Jan. 12, 1863   VA25

Lovelace, P. - Co. I 13th North Carolina June 13, 1863   VA25

Lovett, F.M. - Co. H 31st Georgia Dec. 30, 1862   VA25

Lovett, S. - Co. K 45th North Carolina April 1, 1865   VA25

Lowe, Jno. - Co. G 7th Louisiana This soldier's name is listed in *Napier Bartlett's Military Record of Louisiana*, however he is not listed in the cemetery's burial roster. VA28

Lowe, John Co. - F 19th Mississippi June 15, 1862   VA25

Lowe, John T. - Pvt. - Co. G 7th Louisiana Died May 12, 1864   VA28

Lowry, __ - 1864   VA25

Lowry, __ - Co. C 2nd Mississippi June 5, 1862   VA25

Lowry, A.W. - Co. A 49th Georgia July 7, 1862   VA25

Lowry, J. - Co. A 2nd North Carolina Aug. 19, 1864 VA25

Lowry, J.F. - Orr's Rifles (South Carolina) July 27, 1862 VA25
Lowry, R.C. - 17th Louisiana   VA18
Loyd, J.M. - Co. A 24th Georgia May 28, 1862   VA25
Luber, J. - Sgt. - Co. K 8th Georgia   Oct. 12, 1864   VA25
Luby, T. - Pvt. - North Carolina 1864   VA22
Lucas, B. - Pvt. - Virginia April 24, 1865   VA22
Lucas, John Cary - Co. C 32nd Virginia Infantry   VA02
Lucas, W.J. - Virginia   VA20
Lucermoore, R. - Co. E 11th South Carolina May 28, 1864   VA25
Lucerne, Thomas - Lt. - Co. K __ Regt. Alabama Vols. DOW May 28, 1863 age 23   VA19
Lucious, B. - Pvt. - Co. F 28th Georgia Bat. Died June 23, 1865   VA26
Luck, B. - July 8, 1861 VA25
Luck, T. - Virginia Sept. 20, 1861   VA25
Luck, W.H. - Co. H 53rd Virginia June 30, 1862   VA25
Luck, W.J. - Artillery   May 29, 1862   VA25
Lucke, S.S. - KIA June 2, 1862 age 21   VA19
Lucket, L.W. - Co. D 8th Virginia June 2, 1862   VA25
Lucket, M.H. - Co. D 8th Virginia July 17, 1862   VA25
Luckland, M.M. - Co. A 4th Virginia June 14, 1863   VA25
Lucky, W. - March 1865   VA25
Lue, C.S. - Co. C 49th Georgia April 25, 1865   VA25
Luffman, J. - Co. A 33rd North Carolina Aug. 19, 1864   VA25
Luffman, J. - Co. C 11th Georgia May 16, 1862   VA25
Luke, J.W. - 1st South Carolina July 14, 1862   VA25
Luke, L. - Co. C 28th Georgia Oct. 8, 1864   VA25
Luker, C. - Co. F 56th North Carolina Sept. 30, 1864   VA25
Lumbrick, G.W. - Co. C 23rd North Carolina July 10, 1864   VA25
Lumpkin, W.L. - Co. H 8th Georgia Nov. 29, 1864   VA25
Lunder, G. - Co. I 13th North Carolina Dec. 22, 1862   VA25

Lunder, H.A. - Co. G 13th North Carolina Dec. 24, 1862 VA25

Lunhart, J.N. - Co. K 49th North Carolina Oct. 15, 1864 VA25

Lurry, A.W. - Co. A 49th North Carolina July 2, 1862 VA25

Luther, __ - July 8, 1862 VA25

Luther, D.A. - Sgt. - Co. I 17th South Carolina Nov. 8, 1865 VA25

Luther, J. - Co. I 19th Georgia May 29, 1862 VA25

Luther, J.B. - Co. I 25th North Carolina Sept. 13, 1864 VA25

Luther, Thomas F. - Co. C 9th Alabama VA11

Luttle, M.C. - Co. C 13th Alabama Feb. 13, 1863 VA25

Luty, D.A. - Co. B 23rd North Carolina Oct. 11, 1864 VA25

Lweis, J.M. - DOW June 19, 1862 age 22 VA19

Lyle, James - 16th Virginia May 18, 1862 VA25

Lyles, Alexander - Richardson's Battery (Virginia) VA04

Lynch, David H. - Pvt. - Co. B 3rd Georgia Died May 14, 1864 VA28

Lyne, D. - Co. E 1st Georgia March 19, 1865 VA25

Lynn, J.F. - Sgt. - 8th Virginia Infantry VA10

Lynn, Thomas W. - Co. D 17th Virginia Infantry VA10

Lynns, R.C. - Co. K 35th Georgia July 28, 1864 VA25

Lynns, W.A. - Co. I 27th North Carolina Sept. 14, 1864 VA25

Lynson, A.W. - Co. H 34th North Carolina June 11, 1864 VA25

Lyon, S.M. - Co. I 12th South Carolina Aug. 6, 1862 VA25

Lyons, R. - 11th Mississippi June 5, 1862 VA25

Lyons, W.S. - 19th Mississippi Oct. 31, 1861 VA25

Lyson, A.W. - Co. H 34th North Carolina June 11, 1864 VA25

M __, A. - Co. K 18th Georgia Oct. 14, 1861 VA25

M __, A.T. - Co. K 5th Georgia June 26, 1864 VA25

M __, G.W. - Co. H 37th North Carolina VA11

M __, J.N. - Co. K 21st North Carolina 1862 VA25

M __, W.K. - June 30, 1862 VA25

Mabe, David - VA20
Mable, J.W. - Co. H 22nd North Carolina June 18, 1862 VA25
Mabtin, G. - Lt.- Co. E Cobb's Georgia Legion Died Sept. 7, 1864 VA23
Machenheimer, J.G. - 24th Virginia Sept. 10, 1861 VA25
Machin, E.T. - 10th Alabama VA18
Mack, J.C. - Co. F 24th North Carolina March 9, 1865 VA25
Mack, J.M. - Corp. - Co. A 2nd South Carolina July 16, 1862 VA25
Mack, J.W. - Co. C 49th Virginia April 19, 1865 VA25
Mackey, G.W. - Co. G 35th Georgia June 17, 1862 VA25
Mackle, H. - Co. D 21st Mississippi June 3, 1862 VA25
Mackley, __ 21st Mississippi July 1, 1862 VA25
Madden, M. - Co. F 11th North Carolina March 16, 1865 VA25
Maddles, J.W. - 48th North Carolina Feb. 2, 1863 VA25
Maddox, A.J. - Georgia Jan. 13, 1863 VA25
Maddox, H.A. - Lt.- Co. C 60th Georgia MW May 12, 1864 (Died May 25)VA28
Maddox, J.W. - Co. A 51st Georgia June 19, 1863 VA25
Maddox, John - Co. E 48th North Carolina July 11, 1864 VA25
Maddy, J. - VA12
Madison, J.N. - Co. A 20th South Carolina July 1, 1864 VA25
Madison, R. - Co. F 35th North Carolina May 8, 1865 VA25
Madison, Wm. - 19th Virginia VA18
Mados, Jas. - Co. E 12th North Carolina June 30, 1862 VA25
Maevin, __ - Aug. 25, 1861 VA25
Maffett, P.C. - Sgt. - Co. E 18th Mississippi July 27, 1862 VA25
Magill, C. - Co. A 10th Louisiana July 24, 1862 VA25
Magingo, E.W. - Artillery May 30, 1862 VA25
Magors, B.T. - 26th Alabama June 1, 1862 VA25
Magors, D.K. - Co. F 1st South Carolina Aug. 17, 1864 VA25
Mahaffey, G.L. - Co. B 13th South Carolina July 20, 1864 VA25

Mahaffey, Q.D. - Co. C 14th South Carolina May 24, 1862 VA25

Mahaffey, T.L. - Co. D 23rd Georgia June 22, 1864 VA25

Mahaffey, W.A. - Co. A 38th North Carolina June 6, 1863 VA25

Maher, August - POW - Federal Soldier Died June 19, 1862 VA19

Mahoney, J.H. - Virginia Jan. 22, 1864 VA25

Maker, John - Co. B 41st Virginia Nov. 7, 1862 VA25

Malard, J.D. - Co. K 6th Florida Battery June 19, 1864 VA25

Malbone, James Lamb - Pvt. - Co. G 16th Virginia KIA Spotsylvania Court House -May 11, 1864 Headstone reads: "James L. Malborne" VA28

Malborne, James L. - see Malbone, James Lamb VA28

Maley, J. - Co. B 11th Mississippi June 30, 1862 VA25

Malina, P. - Sept. 9, 1864 VA25

Malkin, John P. - DOW July 26, 1862 age 20 VA19

Maloney, James A. - VA12

Malvin, A. - Corp. - Co. F 24th North Carolina Nov. 4, 1864 VA25

Manchett, Jonas - 4th South Carolina VA18

Mancley, C.D. - Co. F 55th North Carolina July 3, 1864 VA25

Manger, Bruce - Colonel - 5th Louisiana his soldier's name is listed in Napier Bartlett's *Military Record of Louisiana*, however he is not listed in the cemetery's burial roster. VA28

Manhook, R.A. - Co. A 15th North Carolina April 29, 1864 VA25

Mankin, J.E. - Virginia VA20

Manley, T. - Co. B 24th North Carolina Oct. 26, 1864 VA25

Manley, W.L. - Pvt.- Co. E 25th North Carolina Died June 17, 1865 VA26

Mann, A. - Orr's Rifles (South Carolina) July 20, 1864 VA25

Mann, C. C. - POW - Federal Soldier Died Feb. 7, 1862 VA19

Mann, H. - Co. B 5th Louisiana Dec. 20, 1862 VA25

Mann, S. - Moore's Battery Sept. 23, 1862 VA25
Mann, S. S. - March 11, 1862 VA25
Mann, W. H. - Co. H 18th Georgia May 22, 1862 VA25
Mannen, M. - POW - Federal Soldier Died Jan. 17, 1862 VA19
Manning, F. - Co. K 1st South Carolina Jan. 11, 1863 VA25
Manning, G. - Co. A 67th North Carolina Feb. 28, 1865 VA25
Manning, J. - Co. B 33rd North Carolina Aug. 23, 1862 VA25
Manning, William - Pvt. - Co. F 3rd Virginia Died at Fredericksburg - Jan. 4, 1863 VA28
Manon, James E. - 1st Virginia VA18
Mansfield, J.R. - 12th Artillery Oct. 15, 1862 VA25
Manstead, J. - Co. F 23rd North Carolina May 18, 1862 VA25
Manuel, J. - April 28, 1863 VA25
Manus, John A. - Pvt. - Co. A 50th Virginia VA28
Marbott, J.T. - Co. D 38th Georgia Feb. 25, 1865 VA25
March, I.O. - Co. G 6th Alabama Infantry VA08
Marchman, C.W. - Cobb's Cavalry (Georgia) July 29, 1862 VA25
Marinay, J. - Co. D 1st Louisiana March 14, 1865 VA25
Marion, J. - Co. H 21st North Carolina July 30, 1862 VA25
Marion, J.P. - VA20
Marion, R. - Co. F 21st Virginia April 14, 1863 VA25
Mark, D.L. - 13th Louisiana Sept. 14, 1861 VA25
Mark, G.M. - Co. B 49th Virginia April 18, 1865 VA25
Markham, J. - Co. H 26th Alabama Sept. 4, 1862 VA25
Marks, A.W. - Co. A 7th Georgia April 28, 1862 VA25
Marks, J.H. - Co. G 3rd Virginia July 6, 1862 VA25
Marks, Z. - Co. G 33rd North Carolina Aug. 23, 1864 VA25
Marles, __ - 3rd North Carolina Aug. 11, 1862 VA25
Marmaduke, __ - Fitz Lee's Cavalry - drowned at Holloway's Ford - Dec 31, 1863 VA05
Marr, J.H. - Clarksville (Tennessee) May 9, 1862 VA25
Marron, Thomas - Co. K 16th North Carolina VA11
Marrow, A. - Co. A 19th Georgia July 9, 1862 VA25
Marsh, C.W. - Cobb's Legion (Georgia) July 30, 1862 VA25

Marsh, J.E. - 43rd North Carolina Infantry VA08
Marshall, J. - Co. I 6th Alabama April 20, 1862 VA25
Marshall, J. H. - 3rd Virginia Battery April 26, 1865 VA25
Marshall, J.P. - Pvt. - Co. A 13th Georgia VA28
Marshall, J.W. - Co. H 21st North Carolina- Dec. 12, 1861 VA23
Marshall, John - Colonel- 4th Texas July 2, 1862 VA25
Marshall, S.F. - Co. G 21st North Carolina June 22, 1864 VA25
Marshall, W.L. - VA08
Marston, G. - Co. C 2nd Louisiana June 24, 1862 VA25
Martha, J. - Co. D 12th Alabama Oct. 26, 1862 VA25
Marthburn, J. - Co. E 3rd North Carolina Feb. 27, 1865 VA25
Martin, __ - POW - Federal Soldier Died Nov. 30, 1861 VA19
Martin, B.W. - Pvt. - Co. L 7th South Carolina Died May 8, 1864 VA28
Martin, C.L. - Hughes' Battery June 2, 865 VA25
Martin, D. - Co. A 6th Georgia May 20, 1862 VA25
Martin, D.J.V. - 1st Lt.- Co. H Palmetto Sharpshooters (South Carolina)VA29
Martin, E.M. - Louisiana Artillery May 17, 1862 VA25
Martin, E.R. - Co. C 24th South Carolina July 28, 1864 VA25
Martin, G.T. - Co. H 28th Georgia Nov. 3, 1862 VA25
Martin, G.W. - Co. A 12th Georgia Bat. June 16, 1864 VA25
Martin, Henry - 13th Alabama. VA18
Martin, J. - Virginia March 25, 1864 VA25
Martin, J. - Co. B 42nd North Carolina Sept. 27, 1864 VA25
Martin, J. Douglas - Co. A 6th Reg. South Carolina Vol. Dec. 17, 1845 - Sept. 18, 1861 VA10
Martin, J.A. - North Carolina VA20
Martin, J.A. - Co. E 1st South Carolina Aug. 20, 1863 VA25
Martin, J.C. - 38th North Carolina Aug. 22, 1862 VA25
Martin, J.G. - Co. H 7th North Carolina Oct. 3, 1864 VA25
Martin, J.H. - Co. I 44th Georgia June 13, 1864 VA25
Martin, J.J. - Co. D 12th Mississippi May 13, 1863 VA25
Martin, J.M. - Co. A 4th Texas May 18, 1862 VA25

Martin, J.S. - Co. K 3rd Alabama Jan. 25, 1863 VA25
Martin, J.T. - 4th Mississippi Aug. 21, 1864 VA24A
Martin, James F. - Pvt.- Co. I 54th North Carolina Died May 31, 1865 VA26
Martin, Jas. - Died Jan. 21, 1863 age 21 VA19
Martin, Josiah N. - Louisiana VA11
Martin, L.E. - Co. F 22nd Georgia July 29, 1862 VA25
Martin, L.Q.C. - Lt. - Co. H 28th Georgia Died Jan 28, 1862 VA23
Martin, Overstreet - 8th Virginia VA18
Martin, Patrie - Louisiana VA20
Martin, R. - Co. I 24th Georgia Sept. 22, 1861 VA25
Martin, R. - 4th Texas Nov. 15, 1861 VA25
Martin, S. - Co. K 1st Florida Feb. 10, 1863 VA25
Martin, S. - Co. K 28th South Carolina March 9, 1864 VA25
Martin, S.V. - Co. D 27th South Carolina June 25, 1864 VA25
Martin, W.A. - Co. A 22nd North Carolina May 29, 1863 VA25
Martin, W.H. - 24th Virginia VA18
Martin, W.H. - North Carolina Nov. 12, 1861 VA25
Martin, William H. - Pvt. - Co. D 53rd North Carolina MW - Spotsylvania Court House - Died June 1, 1864 VA28
Marvin, __ - Aug. 25, 1861 VA25
Masais, Daniel - Co. E 7th North Carolina VA11
Mason, __ - 49th Virginia July 3, 1862 VA25
Mason, A.J. - Co. A 4th North Carolina Nov. 24, 1862 VA25
Mason, Charles T. - Pvt. - Co. G 10th Georgia VA28
Mason, G. - Co. I 14th Virginia July 21, 1862 VA25
Mason, J. - Co. I 14th South Carolina June 9, 1864 VA25
Mason, J.P. - Co. A 49th North Carolina Nov. 21, 1863 VA25
Mason, Randolph F. - Surgeon - CSA VA10
Mason, W.E. - Co. A 6th Tennessee March 11, 1862 VA25
Mason, W.H. - Co. G 18th Virginia Nov. 26, 1862 VA25
Mason, W.T. - Co. I 18th Georgia Aug. 26, 1864 VA25
Mason, Wm. - Pvt. - Virginia April 15, 1865 VA22
Masser, J.S. - Co. A 35th Georgia Oct. 17, 1862 VA25

Massett, J. - Co. C 13th Alabama Sept. 22, 1862 VA25
Massey, __ - June 29, 1862 VA25
Massey, J.K. - Co. H 28th North Carolina Sept. 12, 1862 VA25
Massie, G.W. - Co. D 45th Virginia VA11
Massie, R. - 9th Louisiana Dec. 23, 1862 VA25
Massilott, J. - Co. C 42nd North Carolina March 23, 1865 VA25
Massingilt, P. - Co. H 2nd North Carolina May 20, 1863 VA25
Masters, John - Co. I 47th Virginia June 27, 1862 VA25
Masters, W.A. - May 14, 1862 VA25
Mathburn, J. - Co. E 3rd North Carolina Feb. 27, 1865 VA25
Matheson, J.L. - North Carolina VA20
Matheson, L.D. - Co. D 25th North Carolina VA11
Matheway, A.L. - Co. K 27th North Carolina July 22, 1864 VA25
Mathews, Walter - KIA Dec. 16, 1862 age 16 VA19
Matlock, E.F. - Co. G 18th Mississippi May 23, 1862 VA25
Matlock, L. - Co. G 18th Mississippi June 2, 1862 VA25
Matson, George -27th North Carolina VA11
Matthews, A.J. - Co. E 6th Georgia Aug. 4, 1864 VA25
Matthews, E.A. - Co. I 26th South Carolina Aug. 20, 1864 VA25
Matthews, H. - Co. I 50th Georgia Feb. 10, 1863 VA25
Matthews, J. - Co. H 39th Georgia July 27, 1863 VA25
Matthews, P. - Co. K 6th Louisiana June 3, 1863 VA25
Matthews, S.A. - Co. E 57th North Carolina July 3, 1863 VA25
Matthews, W. - Co. D 64th Georgia Oct. 8, 1864 VA25
Matthews, W.C. 8th Georgia June 12, 1862 VA25
Matthews, W.J. - Co. G 5th Alabama July 6, 1864 VA25
Matthews, W.S. - Co. H 48th Mississippi Oct. 13, 1864 VA25
Matthws, J.F. - Co. H 26th Alabama May 20, 1862 VA25
Mauldin, Issac N. - Pvt. - Co. B 15th Georgia Died May 10, 1864 VA28

Maury, Henry - Pvt. - Co. A 13th Georgia DOD at Hamilton's Crossing on May 21, 1863 VA28
Maxey, T.J. - Pvt. - Co. A 19th Mississippi Died May 10, 1864 VA28
May, A. - Co. A 37th Georgia Oct. 6, 1862 VA25
May, C. - Pvt. - North Carolina March 26, 1865 VA22
May, E.R. - Co. H 1st North Carolina Sept. 16, 1862 VA25
May, J.F. - DOW Oct. 13, 1862 VA19
May, John - Co. K 9th Alabama Sept. 6, 1862 VA25
May, M. - Co. I 13th Alabama July 13, 1862 VA25
May, N.L. - Co. K 5th Alabama July 13, 1862 VA25
May, N.L. - Co. K 5th North Carolina 1862 VA25
May, O.M.M. - Jeff. Davis's Artillery Feb. 1, 1862 VA25
May, P.H. - Co. K 17th North Carolina Sept. 22, 1864 VA25
May, R.S. - Co. G 1st Eng'r Corps Oct. 15, 1862 VA25
May, Thos. - July 4, 1861 VA25
May, W.A. - Lt.- 4th Virginia Artillery June 23, 1862 VA25
May, W.H. - Co. B 12th Alabama VA25
May, W.J. - 22nd North Carolina June 2, 1863 VA25
Maycock, __ - 13th Alabama Aug. 11, 1862 VA25
Mayer, J. - Co. K 10th Louisiana May 24, 1863 VA25
Mayer, Virginia A. - Civilian -Killed in explosion of C.S. Laboratory - March 16, 1863 age 12 VA19
Mayers, M.G. - 10th South Carolina Aug. 2, 1862 VA25
Mayes, __ - 4th Georgia July 1, 1862 VA25
Mayes, A.H. - Co. K 4th North Carolina July 4, 1862 VA25
Mayes, G.W. - Co. B Lumpkin's Battery July 5, 1864 VA25
Mayes, Marion - see Mays, Marion VA28
Mayes, T. - South Carolina July 24, 1862 VA25
Mayfield, J.L. - Hampton's Legion (Georgia) Aug. 9, 1864 VA25
Mayhugh, Zachariah - Mosby's Cavalry VA10
Maynard, __ - Crenshaw's Battery June 15, 1862 VA25
Maynard, J.A. - 1st Virginia Artillery June 15, 1862 VA25
Maynard, R.A. - Co. G 8th Georgia Nov. 4, 1864 VA25
Maynard, S. - Co. K 13th South Carolina June 1, 1862 VA25

Mayner, P. - Co. B 57th Virginia July 21, 1862 VA25
Mays, J.J. - VA12
Mays, Marion - Pvt. - Co. H 22nd Georgia MW May 12, 1864 last name also spelled Mayes VA28
Mays, T.S. - Co. F 5th Alabama June 7, 1862 VA25
Mayse, Geo. - 13th Virginia May 11, 1862 VA25
Mayslip, A. - May 24, 1862 VA25
McAbee, T. - 17th South Carolina Aug. 8, 1862 VA25
McAble, J.J. - 1st South Carolina Aug. 7, 1862 VA25
McAble, W.A. - Co. I 13th South Carolina Sept. 1862 VA25
McAll, __ - Co. G 13th South Carolina June 4, 1863 VA25
McAllan, J.C. - 13th Mississippi VA18
McAlley, Wm. - Co. F 14th Alabama Feb. 10, 1863 VA25
McAllister, A.T. - Louisiana Oct. 14, 1861 VA25
McArthur, A.L. - Co. H 49th North Carolina June 3, 1864 VA25
McArthur, Charles W. - Lt. Colonel - 61st Georgia Died May 12, 1864 VA28
McAuley, M. - Pvt.- Co. E 48th North Carolina Died June 1, 1865 VA26
McAvery, G.A. - 9th Alabama Aug. 2, 1861 VA25
McAvery, J.M. - 5th Virginia Oct. 24, 1862 VA25
McAvoy, W.H. - Co. I 51st Georgia Nov. 12, 1862 VA25
McBee, W.W. - Co. H 11th Mississippi July 7, 1862 VA25
McBrazer, G. - Co. E 14th Georgia May 7, 1865 VA25
McBrazers, J.F. - 12th Alabama Oct. 14, 1861 VA25
McBride, B. - Co. A 42nd Mississippi June 4, 1864 VA25
McBride, R. - Co. E 42nd Mississippi June 3, 1864 VA25
McBride, Samuel - Pvt. - Co. I 10th Georgia Died in camp at Fredericksburg - Dec. 1863 VA28
McBush, J. 24th - Virginia July 8, 1862 VA25
McCadlum, R.W. - Co. E 45th North Carolina March 10, 1865 VA25
McCain, Joseph M. - Pvt. - Co. I 45th North Carolina MW May 10, 1864 VA28
McCall, C.L. - Co. C 18th Mississippi Aug. 3, 1862 VA25

McCall, D.L. - Co. E 49th Georgia Aug. 3, 1862 VA25
McCall, W.R. - Co. I 21st Mississippi Aug. 17, 1862 VA25
McCan, J. - Co. H 9th Georgia Died Jan. 10, 1862 VA23
McCance, __ - Sgt. - 2nd Florida July 3, 1862 VA25
McCarick, C.J. - Co. E 25th North Carolina July 10, 1862 VA25
McCarley, S. - 6th Alabama Infantry - KIA - Battle of Williamsburg - May 5, 1862 VA02
McCarter, J.A. - Pvt. - North Carolina April 1, 1865 VA22
McCarter, T.C. - Co. D 51st Georgia May 21, 1863 VA25
McCarthy, E.B. - Capt. KIA June 4, 1864 age 27 VA19
McCarthy, J. - VA12
McCarthy, J. - Co. F 21st Mississippi Sept. 24, 1862 VA25
McCarthy, P.A. - Co. B 1st South Carolina June 4, 1863 VA25
McCaster, __ - Lt.- July 11, 1862 VA25
McCauley, L. - Virginia VA20
McCaw, W. - Co. H 5th Texas June 30, 1862 VA25
McClanahan, J. - Calhoun Guards - 8th Alabama July 24, 1861 VA25
McClellan, G.W. - Co. B 11th Georgia May 12, 1862 VA25
McClellen, A. - Co. K 44th Georgia July 31, 1864 VA25
McClenahan, John - Pvt.- Co. K 30th Virginia . Died May 22, 1865 VA26
McClenard, J.N. - Co. I 48th North Carolina July 11, 1864 VA25
McClenard, J.N. - Co. I 48th North Carolina July 11, 1864 VA25
McClenary, A.A. - Co. K 5th Texas June 1, 1862 VA25
McClinton, __ - Co. G 2nd North Carolina Aug. 8, 1862 VA25
McClinton, Jas. - Louisiana Nov. 23, 1862 VA25
McClure, A. - Pvt. - Virginia March 25, 1864. VA22
McClurg, James H. - POW - Federal Soldier Died Oct. 14, 1861 VA19
McCoin, __ - Aug. 9, 1862 VA25
McColor, M.C. - Georgia Nov. 21, 1862 VA25

McColough, W.H. - Alabama VA20
McComas, R.F. - Co. H 60th Georgia June 5, 1862 VA25
McCombs, W.T. - Co. C 27th North Carolina Dec. 8, 1863 VA25
McConnell, E. - Co. A 6th Georgia March 16, 1863 VA25
McConnell, J.D. - Corp. - Co. D 5th South Carolina July 22, 1862 VA25
McConnell, M. - Co. F 14th Alabama Sept. 14, 1864 VA25
McConol, G.B. - Co. G 3rd South Carolina June 28, 1864 VA25
McConrick, Pat. - 13th Louisiana Sept. 12, 1861 VA25
McConrick, S.P. - Co. E 1st South Carolina June 5, 1864 VA25
McCook, J.B. - Co. A 49th Georgia May 3, 1864 VA25
McCook, James - KIA Aug. 1, 1864 age 21 VA19
McCormick, W. - Co. D 51st North Carolina Oct. 9, 1864 VA25
McCowan, J.V. - Co. D 13th Georgia June 30, 1862 VA25
McCoy, __ - 6th North Carolina July 29, 1862 VA25
McCoy, __ - Co. F 19th Georgia May 6, 1862 VA25
McCoy, __ - 19th Georgia May 9, 1862 VA25
McCoy, H. - Capt. Smith's - Co. Oct. 15, 1861 VA25
McCoy, J.F. - Pvt. - Co. K 6th South Carolina Died May 15, 1865 VA26
McCoy, R.G. - "Guerillas" July 25, 1862 VA25
McCrakin, William A. - DOW Feb. 3, 1863 age 21 VA19
McCravers, J. - Co. F 36th North Carolina April 27, 1864 VA25
McCreary, C. - Co. I 26th North Carolina Aug. 22, 1864 VA25
McCreary, Sam'l. - Died Aug.13, 1861 VA18
McCuen, __ - 31st Virginia VA18
McCullin, J.M. - 20th Georgia Bat. June 2, 1864 VA25
McCullock, __ - Virginia Feb. 3, 1865 VA25
McCullock, J.W. - Capt. - Co. K 2nd Louisiana June 5, 1864 VA25

McCullock, R. - Co. A 21st Mississippi June 8, 1862 VA25
McCullom, C. - Co. G 28th North Carolina July 8, 1864 VA25
McCullom, W. - Co. A 6th South Carolina Jan. 3, 1865 VA25
McCullough, J. - Co. I 48th North Carolina Oct. 29, 1862
 VA25
McCullough, J.H. - Pvt. - Co. G 13th South Carolina Died May
 12, 1864 VA28
McCurdy, Isaac S. - Sgt. - Co. K 7th North Carolina VA28
McCurdy, S.C. - Co. G 38th Georgia Oct. 14, 1863 VA25
McCurin, J. - Co. G 1st Texas March 29, 1862 VA25
McCutchan, Robert M. - see McCutchin, Robert M. VA28
McCutchen, Robert M. - see McCutchin, Robert M. VA28
McCutchin, Robert M. - Pvt. - Co. B 14th North Carolina Died
 June 1, 1864 Name also spelled McCutchan.
 Headstone reads: "Sgt." VA28
McDade, W.A. - Co. G 3rd Georgia July 3, 1862 VA25
McDaniel, Andrew - 1st North Carolina Cavalry KIA -
 Upperville - June 21, 1863 VA07
McDaniel, B. - Co. E 1st Eng's Corps Sept. 7, 1864 VA25
McDaniel, E. - Co. B 22nd North Carolina May 20, 1862
 VA25
McDaniel, H. - Co. H 18th Mississippi May 17, 1862 VA25
McDaniel, Hamilton - VA12
McDaniel, J. - Co. G 15th South Carolina Sept. 29, 1862
 VA25
McDaniel, J.H. - Co. I 57th Virginia May 1, 1862 VA25
McDaniel, S. - VA12
McDaniel, Samuell. - VA15
McDary, M.A. - Co. A 14th North Carolina Oct. 15, 1862
 VA25
McDonald, __ - 49th Georgia June 30, 1862 VA25
McDonald, G.W. - 20th Georgia VA18
McDonald, J.M. - Co. G 21st North Carolina July. 26, 1863
 VA25
McDonald, J.W. - 4th Alabama Aug. 25, 1861 VA25

McDonald, P.S. - Co. E 12th North Carolina Sept. 2, 1864 VA25
McDonald, T. - Co. B 9th Alabama March 7, 1865 VA25
McDow, P. - Co. I 3rd North Carolina Aug. 17, 1862 VA25
McDowell, G.W. - Co. A 12th South Carolina Sept. 4, 1862 VA25
McDowell, H.M. - Co. I 18th Mississippi July 3, 1862 VA25
McDowell, J. - Co. K 5th South Carolina July 16, 1862 VA25
McDowell, J.W. - Co. F 15th South Carolina Sept. 29, 1864 VA25
McDowell, W.C. - Co. A 12th South Carolina July 27, 1862 VA25
McDowell, William High - VMI Cadet -KIA - Battle of New Market - May 15, 1864 - Buried at VMI VA21
McDunn, N.A. - South Carolina July 25, 1862 VA25
McEachen, J. - Co. G 23rd South Carolina Nov. 4, 1864 VA25
McElong, J.C. - Co. F 14th Alabama Sept. 11, 1862 VA25
McElray, G.W. - Co. I 13th Mississippi May 31, 1863 VA25
McElray, J.C. - Co. F 14th Alabama Sept. 11, 1862 VA25
McElwind, D. - Co. I 11th Georgia June 22, 1863 VA25
McEntire, D. - Co. B 33rd North Carolina June 13, 1864 VA25
McEwen, J. - Pvt.- Co. B 1st Eng. Regt. Died May 27, 1865 VA26
McFarlan, C. - Co. D 21st Mississippi May 18, 1862 VA25
McFarland, Robert - Co. K 53rd Virginia VA11
McFarlin, P.C. - Co. C 3rd North Carolina Cavalry June 25, 1864 age 19 VA25
McFarlin, T.A. - Co. G 9th Louisiana Nov. 12, 1861 VA25
McFee, J.F. - Co. I 25th North Carolina July 27, 1864 VA25
McFeeley, M. - see McFeeley, William VA28
McFeeley, William - Sgt. - Co. I 8th Louisiana Accidentally killed at Guinea Station May 5 (6), 1863Napi VA28
McGalliard, W.A. - Co. D 1st North Carolina Cavalry June 27, 1864 VA25
McGarther, J.H. - Co. H 20th Georgia Sept. 30, 1864 VA25

McGeary, S.P. - 5th Alabama VA18
McGee, F.F. - Co. B 11th Alabama Oct. 7, 1862 VA25
McGee, Peter - Pvt. - Co. A 25th Virginia Died May 11, 1865 VA26
McGee, T. - Palmetto Sharp Shooters (South Carolina) Feb. 11, 1865 VA25
McGee, T. - Co. A 4th South Carolina Sept. 30, 1862 VA25
McGehee, N.B. - Co. I 23rd Virginia Nov. 5, 1863 VA25
McGenner, E.V.- Phillips Legion VA25
McGigan, P. - Co. K 26th North Carolina Aug. 8, 1862 VA25
McGinness, P.B. - Hampton's Artillery June 30, 1864 VA25
McGinness, P.B. - Hampton's Legion June 2, 1864 VA25
McGinnis, J.B. - Pvt. -35th North Carolina .Died May 14, 1865 VA26
McGinnis, J.R. - 1st Maryland VA18
McGiven, Andrew - Co. K 2nd South Carolina Rifles Died March 17, 1863 VA03
McGland, __ - Co. K 14th Texas June 29, 1862 VA25
McGlenn, G. - Co. I 6th South Carolina July 15, 1864 VA25
McGoffin, W.S. - Co. F 1st South Carolina June 1, 1862 VA25
McGowen, J.W. - 5th Alabama April 29, 1862 VA25
McGraw, A. - Co. A 48th Georgia Sept. 9, 1862 VA25
McGreen, J. - C.S. Navy March 23, 1865 VA25
McGriff, W. - Georgia VA20
McGrines, G.W. - Co. C 15th North Carolina July 18, 1864 VA25
McGruder, Zeff. - KIA Dec. 16, 1862 age 23 VA19
McGuire, Benjamin Harrison - Lt.- Co. B 22nd Virginia KIA - Gettysburg - July 1, 1863 VA06
McGuire, P. - Co. B 11th Alabama Aug. 31, 1862 VA25
McGuire, Thomas - 18th Mississippi VA18
McHanager, __ - Co. B 26th Georgia June 18, 1862 VA25
McHolders, T. - Co. D 6th Alabama June 27, 1862 VA25
McIlhaney, A.H. - DOW July 22, 1862 VA19
McIntire, __ - Nov. 23, 1862 VA25

McIntosh, J.T. - 5th North Carolina Cavalry July 13, 1864 VA25

McIntosh, Robert - Co. K 12th Alabama VA11

McIntosh, W. - Co. I 25th South Carolina Oct. 9, 1864 VA25

McIntree, L.C. - Co. E 13th South Carolina Aug. 26, 1862 VA25

McIntyre, Duncan C. - Pvt. - Co. D 47th Alabama Died May 8, 1864 VA28

McJudkin, J.D. - Co. B 2nd North Carolina June 11, 1864 VA25

McKag, M.T. - 11th North Carolina VA18

Mckanan, P. R. - Co. K 3rd North Carolina June 29, 1863 VA25

McKane, G. - Virginia June 16, 1862 VA25

McKane, J.P. - Co. B 2nd Florida June 14, 1862 VA25

McKaran, J.T. - Co. A 26th South Carolina Jan. 10, 1865 VA25

McKee, E.H. - 6th Alabama VA18

McKell, __ - Sgt. Major - 48th North Carolina Sept. 30, 1864 VA25

McKell, J. - Co. G 12th Mississippi June 2, 1863 VA25

McKell, J.D. - Co. H 37th North Carolina June 3, 1863 VA25

McKell, J.L. - Co. H 37th North Carolina June 3, 1863 VA25

McKell, J.R. - Co. I 7th Georgia June 8, 1862 VA25

McKellam, D. - Sgt. - Co. I 53rd South Carolina March 2, 1865 VA25

McKenney, __ - Co. I 2nd Florida May 31, 1862 VA25

McKenney, W. - Co. C 24th Georgia Nov. 12, 1864 VA25

McKenvy, J.C. - Co. H 2nd Florida May 31, 1862 VA25

McKethan, __ - July 29, 1862 VA25

McKibber, M.A. - 30th North Carolina Sept. 22, 1862 VA25

McKillups, M.W. - Co. A 15th South Carolina Nov. 2, 1862 VA25

McKinney, J. - Pvt. - Co. B 49th North Carolina April 4, 1865 VA22

McKinney, J.T. - VA28

McKinnon, R.W. - Co. H 20th Georgia July 8, 1864 VA25
McKinsley, C- 27th Georgia May 12, 1862 VA25
McKinzie, R.H. - Co. G 23rd South Carolina VA28
McKitrick, J. - Co. B 27th South Carolina July 18, 1864 VA25
McKnauf, D.C. - Co. F 16th North Carolina June 27, 1862
 VA25
McLain, J. -VA20
McLand, J.M. - Co. G 24th North Carolina July 16, 1864
 VA25
McLane, __ - 23rd Georgia June 5, 1862 VA25
McLane, W. - Co. G 51st South Carolina March 12, 1865
 VA25
McLaughlin, __ - Co. C 6th Maryland Oct. 23, 1863 VA25
Mclaughlin, J.M. - Co. H 19th Virginia VA08
McLaughlin, S. - Co. F 6th South Carolina Dec. 28, 1864
 VA25
McLaughlin, S.D. - Co. B 4th North Carolina Cavalry June 20,
 1864 VA25
McLean, D. - see McLean, D.N..
McLean, D.N. - Corp. - Co. I
 26th Georgia Died May 12, 1864 headstone reads:' D.
 McLean"
McLean, R. - Oct. 30, 1861 VA25
McLee, D. - Co. A 17th Virginia InfantryVA10
McLemo, J.O. - Co. A 1st South Carolina Aug. 9, 1864 VA25
McLemore, M.L. - Co. H 30th North Carolina May 28, 1864
 VA25
McLendon, __ - Lt.- Co. K 26th Georgia Infantry VA08
McLendon, C.G. - Lt.- Co. B 51st Georgia June 4, 1864 VA25
McLendon, M. - Co. H 15th Alabama Sept. 6, 1862 VA25
McLeod, John - 42nd Mississippi Aug. 9, 1862 VA25
McLeskey, Joseph W. - Co. H 7th South Carolina VA28
McLind, __ - Co. G 48th Georgia Sept. 12, 1862 VA25
McLocklin, W.H. - Co. K 26th North Carolina July 10, 1862
 VA25
McLoughlan, __ - 48th Georgia Sept. 29, 1862 VA25

McLur, S.F. - Co. B 17th Mississippi July 8, 1862 VA25
McMann, M. - Co. B 25th Virginia Jan. 22, 1864 VA25
McMarlin, __ - 13th South Carolina July 5, 1862 VA25
McMartin, W.W. - Co. G 40th North Carolina March 31, 1865 VA25
McMath, W.T. - Co. A 20th Georgia June 11, 1864 VA25
McMinn, Delaware - KIA April 24, 1864 age 21 VA19
McMitchell, J.J. - DOW July 14, 1862 age 20 VA19
McMonan, R.M. - POW - Federal Soldier Died Dec. 19, 1861 VA19
McMoy, H. - 38th Georgia Aug. 7, 1862 VA25
McMoy, S.B. - Co. A 38th Georgia Aug. 18, 1862 VA25
McMullen, R. - Nov. 17, 1862 VA25
McMurray, P. - Co. K 11th Mississippi May 30, 1864 VA25
McMurray, W. - Co. H 6th Georgia July 3, 1862 VA25
McMurray, W.C. - Co. A 42nd Virginia May 17, 1862 VA25
McMurry, R. - Pvt. - Co. K 1st South Carolina Eng. Regt. Died June 7, 1865 VA26
McMurton, M. - Co. B 22nd South Carolina March 1, 1865 VA25
McNady, W.S. - Co. G 22nd North Carolina Sept. 4, 1864 VA25
McNain, Martin - Co. I 12th Georgia VA11
McNair, John - Co. H 2nd North Carolina Jan. 9, 1865 VA25
McNair, W. - Lt.- Co. C 8th Georgia Nov. 3, 1864 VA25
McNale, D. -12th Artillery Aug. 30, 1862 VA25
McNall, __ - 15th North Carolina May 30, 1862 VA25
McNeal, Charles M. - VA12
McNeal, Henry - VA12
McNeal, Henry - VA12
McNeal, J.J. Alabama - VA20
McNealy, J.B. - North Carolina Infantry - body removed VA08
McNeely, John P. - Pvt. - Co. C 20th Georgia VA28
McNeely, William M. - Co. I 7th North Carolina VA28
McNeil, D. - Co. D 12th North Carolina Oct. 17, 1862 VA25

McNeil, J. D. - Co. F 13th Mississippi July 8, 1862 VA25
McNeil, J. E. - Co. F 10th Georgia Bat. June 2, 1864 VA25
McNeil, William H. - Pvt. - 18th North Carolina Infantry
    DOW June 14, 1862 VA09
McNeil, Wm. - Virginia Feb. 20, 1864 VA25
McNeily, J. - Capt. - Hampton's Legion June 18, 1864 VA25
McNeily, J.B. - 46th North Carolina Jan. 16, 1863 VA25
McNich, J.M. - Co. F 23rd South Carolina Aug. 20, 1862
    VA25
McNich, S.M. - Co. H 24th North Carolina Aug. 24, 1862
    VA25
McNish, S. - Co. I 6th South Carolina Aug. 30, 1862 VA25
McNurran, L.M. - Died Nov. 20, 1862 VA19
McPearson, __ - Colonel Feb. 8, 1865 VA25
McPearson, H. - May 3, 1862 VA25
McPeters, T. - May 20, 1862 VA25
McPeters, T. - Co. B 22nd North Carolina May 20, 1862
    VA25
McPhail, A. - Co. I 20th North Carolina Aug. 7, 1862 VA25
McPhail, C.H. - Norfolk Virginia July 1862 VA25
McPherson, R.J. - Co. G 9th Louisiana May 18, 1862 VA25
McPherson, William D. - Pvt. - Co. C 14th North Carolina
    MW May 12, 1864 Died May 18, 1864 VA28
McRae, J.J. Capt. - KIA Aug. 1, 1864 age 35 VA19
McRae, James - VA20
McRavy, J. - Co. F 2nd MC April 8, 1865 VA25
McRay, A. - Co. D 3rd North Carolina July 30, 1864 VA25
McRay, D. - Co. A 9th Georgia Jan. 16, 1863 VA25
McRay, D. - Co. H 26th North Carolina Oct. 13, 1863 VA25
McRee, J.R. - Co. A 49th Virginia June 7, 1863 VA25
McRidy, C. - Co. G 37th North Carolina April 8, 1865 VA25
McRorie, William F. - Capt. - Co. A 4th North Carolina KIA
    Spotsylvania Court House May 12, 1864 Headstone
    reads: 'W.L VA28
McRovie, W.L. - see McRorie, William F. VA28
McRunnel, Wm. - Died Apr. 16, 1862 VA19

McShane, William - VA15
McShell, __ - Lt.- Co. D 14th Louisiana April 22, 1862 VA25
McTuck, W.J. - Co. G 11th Alabama Aug. 19, 1862 VA25
McVay, J.D. - Co. B 13th South Carolina July 26, 1864 VA25
McWharton, H.J. - 15th Alabama VA18
McWilliams, S. - 3rd South Carolina VA18
McWithers, J.B. - Co. E 2nd South Carolina Oct. 7, 1864 VA25
Mead, Wm. Z. - KIA - buried Dec. 3, 1865 VA19
Meade, Andrew - Tennessee VA20
Meadow, A.L. - 4th Texas Oct. 4, 1862 VA25
Meadow, J. - Georgia 1862 VA25
Meadow, M.S. - Co. G 57th Virginia Aug. 6, 1862 VA25
Meadow, N. - Hampton's Legion Aug. 26, 1862 VA25
Meadow, W. M. - Co. B 24th Virginia June 25, 1862 VA25
Meadows, J. - Alabama June 23, 1862 VA25
Meadows, Peter C. - Pvt. - Co. G 48th Georgia DOD at Guinea station on March 7, 1863 VA28
Means, Geo. A. - Lt.- Co. K 6th Virginia VA10
Meares, Henry L. - Pvt. - Co. A 46th North Carolina Died May 10, 1864 VA28
Medham, W. - Aug. 1862 VA25
Medlin, J. - Co. H 46th North Carolina July 2, 1864 VA25
Medlin, John - Pvt. - Co. B 47th North Carolina Died May 18, 1864 VA28
Medlock, James - Co. K 15th Georgia VA28
Meek, V.P. - Georgia VA20
Meekings, A. - Co. G 38th Georgia Oct. 2, 1862 VA25
Meeks, __ Alabama Aug. 9, 1862 VA25
Meeks, B. - Co. B 1st North Carolina April 2, 1865 VA25
Meeks, Elisha - Pvt. - Co. C 38th Georgia Died May 10, 1864 VA28
Meeks, J.A. - Jeff. Davis Artillery Aug. 8, 1862 VA25
Meeks, J.C. - Co. A 24th Georgia March 25, 1865 VA25
Meeks, Jno. - Co. F 38th Georgia Sept. 7, 1862 VA25
Meeks, W. - Co. E 12th Georgia March 10, 1865 VA25

Meers, S.M. - Lt.- Co. F 16th North Carolina July 11, 1862 VA25
Mellen, B.C. - Co. D 24th Georgia July 28, 1863 VA25
Melton, C. - 16th North Carolina July 16, 1862 VA25
Melton, J.A. - Co. H 7th South Carolina Sept. 3, 1863 VA25
Melton, J.D. - Co. E 48th North Carolina July 5, 1862 VA25
Melton, J.J. - Co. B 16th Georgia July 22, 1864 VA25
Melton, J.W. - Sgt. - Co. B 16th Georgia July 22, 1864 VA25
Melton, T.H. - Co. F 8th North Carolina Aug. 29, 1862 VA25
Melvin, J.W. - Co. B 10th Alabama June 22, 1862 VA25
Menger, Bruce - Lt. Colonel - Co. I 5th Louisiana Died May 12, 1864 VA28
Menifer, J. - Co. B 7th Virginia June 7, 1862 VA25
Mercer, C.W. - Co. A 36th North Carolina March 29, 1865 VA25
Mercer, D. - VA06
Mercer, J.T. - Co. D 51st Georgia Feb. 7, 1863 VA25
Mercer, James - Pvt. - Co. A 18th Virginia Bat. Died April 27, 1865 VA26
Mercer, James M. - Corp. - Co. C 45th Georgia Died May 18, 1864 VA28
Mercer, Jasper - Pvt.- Co. K 26th Georgia Died May 15, 1863 VA28
Merchant, A.H. - 49th Virginia June 5, 1862 VA25
Merchant, Z. - Co. B 49th Georgia July 21, 1862 VA25
Meredith, J. - Co. K 24th Virginia Oct. 8, 1861 VA25
Merrell, E.A - Pvt.- Co. C 11th Virginia Died June 14, 1865 VA26
Merrill, A. - Co. K 1st Louisiana Jan. 3, 1862 VA25
Merrit, J.W. - VA12
Merritt, B.F. - Co. I 8th Georgia Dec. 21, 1862 VA25
Merritt, G.B. - Palmetto Sharp Shooters (South Carolina) July 8, 1864 VA25
Merritt, M.A. - Co. F Palmetto Sharp Shooters (South Carolina) July 8, 1864 VA25
Merritt, Robt. - Tennessee VA20

Merriwether, T.N. - Co. F 3rd Alabama VA18
Merryman, B. - Co. E 21st South Carolina Aug. 1, 1864 VA25
Merryman, T.J. - Co. I 13th North Carolina March 19, 1863 VA25
Merwith, W.N. - Co. A 49th Georgia July 23, 1862 VA25
Meryell, David - 9th Louisiana VA18
Messey, J.K. - Co. H 28th Georgia Sept. 18, 1862 VA25
Metzells, J.S. - Co. B 11th South Carolina June 17, 1864 VA25
Michael, J. - Co. G 1st North Carolina Bat. July 16, 1864 VA25
Mickleson, H.T. - June 30, 1862 VA25
Midgett, W.H. - Co. F 33rd North Carolina VA11
Midlong, W. - Co. E 5th North Carolina Oct. 29, 1862 VA25
Milam, Alfred Richardson - Corp. - Co. B 3rd South Carolina Battalion Died May 8, 1864 Headstone reads 3rd South Carolina Infantry VA28
Milan, J.A. - Co. B 55th North Carolina July 12, 1864 VA25
Milbourne, J. - Clark Cavalry VA06
Miles, J. - Co. G 27th North Carolina July 1, 1863 VA25
Miles, Putman E. - Pvt. - Co. B 50th Virginia KIA – Spotsylvania Court House - May 12, 1864 VA28
Miles, W.B. - Co. C 7th South Carolina June 26, 1864 VA25
Milford, Thos. J. - Pvt.- Co. A 26th Mississippi Died May 22, 1865 VA26
Millard, G.S. - 13th Alabama Oct. 19, 1861 VA25
Millard, W.H.C. - Co. H 11th South Carolina June 10, 1864 VA25
Mille, F. - Capt. - DOD Oct. 12, 1864 VA19
Miller, __ - 2nd Alabama April 29, 1862 VA25
Miller, A. - Co. I 2nd Mississippi May 13, 1862 VA25
Miller, A. - 16th Alabama Nov. 8, 1862 VA25
Miller, A. Shultz (MD) - medical doctor VA15
Miller, A.A. - Co. H 28th North Carolina May 3, 1864 VA25
Miller, A.A. - 23rd Georgia June 3, 1862 VA25
Miller, A.J. - Co. H 28th North Carolina May 3, 1864 VA25

Miller, C. - Died Dec. 1, 1862 VA19
Miller, C.C. - Co. A 18th South Carolina Aug. 10, 1862 VA25
Miller, C.J. - Georgia VA20
Miller, C.L. - Co. H 1st South Carolina Oct. 2, 1864 VA25
Miller, D. - Co. B 28th North Carolina Nov. 19, 1862 VA25
Miller, D. - Co. A 19th Alabama May 24, 1862 VA25
Miller, E.B. - Died April 6, 1864 VA17
Miller, Harry D. - Co. I 5th North Carolina VA11
Miller, I. - Co. A 15th Virginia VA08
Miller, J. - Navy Brigade Apr. 28, 1865 VA25
Miller, J. - Co. H 48th North Carolina Nov. 19, 1862 VA25
Miller, J. - Co. C 49th North Carolina June 25, 1864 VA25
Miller, J. - Co. K 6th Georgia Oct. 12, 1862 VA25
Miller, J.H. - Louisiana Artillery May 7, 1862 VA25
Miller, J.H. - Capt. - Co. F 23rd North Carolina June 3, 1862 VA25
Miller, J.L. - Colonel- 13th South Carolina May 7, 1862 VA25
Miller, J.M. - Colonel- 12th South Carolina May 7, 1862 VA25
Miller, J.M.A. - Co. A 6th Georgia Oct. 4, 1861 VA25
Miller, Jacob H. - Pvt. - Co. I 58th Virginia Died May 16, 1864 (MW - Spotsylvania Court House - May 12, 1864) VA28
Miller, L.A.J. - Pvt. - Georgia March 25, 1865 VA22
Miller, M. - Co. D 11th North Carolina Oct. 2, 1862 VA25
Miller, W. - 6th South Carolina VA18
Miller, W. - Co. D 5th North Carolina Nov. 24, 1863 VA25
Miller, W.D. - Co. E 13th Georgia Feb. 19, 1865 VA25
Miller, W.F. - June 15, 1862 VA25
Miller, W.H. - Co. A 42nd Mississippi Nov. 25, 1862 VA25
Miller, William H. - VA12
Millon, W.B. - Co. D 13th Georgia Feb. 20, 1865 VA25
Mills, B.J. - Co. C 49th Georgia Sept. 21, 1862 VA25
Mills, Benjamin F. - Pvt.- Co. B 59th Georgia Died May 10, 1864 VA28
Mills, H. - Co. C 18th Alabama Nov. 8, 1862 VA25

Mills, Isaac (Jr.) - Co. K 13th Virginia VA11
Mills, J. - Co. G 12th Virginia June 4, 1863 VA25
Mills, J.F. - Co. K 5th Georgia June 29, 1862 VA25
Mills, J.J. - 8th Alabama Nov. 8, 1862 VA25
Mills, J.M. - Co. E 11th Virginia June 27, 1863 VA25
Mills, Simeon - 7th South Carolina VA18
Mills, Simeon - Co. D 17th Virginia InfantryVA10
Mills, W.R. - 3rd Alabama May 2, 1863 VA25
Millsap, J. - Co C 20th North Carolina July 20, 1864 VA25
Milsler, M. - POW - Federal Soldier Died Dec. 23, 1861 VA19
Milton, __ - 24th Virginia July 3, 1862 VA25
Milton, J. - Co. G 2nd South Carolina June 3, 1862 VA25
Milton, T. - Co. D 3rd North Carolina Nov. 17, 1862 VA25
Milton, W.M. - Co. G 6th South Carolina June 5, 1862 VA25
Mimms, Martin M. - Pvt. - Co. C 16th Mississippi M W May 12, 1864 Died May 13, 1864 VA28
Mines, William - Co. F 12th Alabama VA11
Minion, J. - North Carolina VA28
Minnick, Dallas - Pvt. - Co. H 10th Virginia VA28
Minniss, H.J. - Co. H 42nd North Carolina Dec. 24, 1864 VA25
Minns, E.J. - Co. I 32nd North Carolina Jan. 9, 1865 VA25
Minor, A.L. - Texas VA20
Minor, W.D. - Co. F 35th Georgia July 2, 1862 VA25
Minsall, R.H. - Co. F 2nd South Carolina Dec. 12, 1863 VA25
Minter, A. - Pvt. - Co. A 1st Engineers. Died May 12, 1865 VA26
Mintz, __ - Oct. 17, 1862 VA25
Miss, H. - North Carolina Oct. 9, 1862 VA25
Missman, C.W. - Co. G 7th Tennessee June 5, 1863 VA25
Mital, G.L. - VA28
Mitcham, J.T. - Co. D 4th Georgia Aug. 8, 1862 VA25
Mitchel, G.R. - May 13, 1862 VA25
Mitchel, J.D. - Louisiana Dec. 9, 1862 VA25
Mitchel, J.H. - Co. H 24th Virginia April 20, 1862 VA25

Mitchel, R. - King William Artillery (Virginia) June 5, 1862 VA25
Mitchel, R.R. - Co. E 44th Alabama Feb. 3, 1863 VA25
Mitchell, J. - Clark Cavalry VA06
Mitchell, J.P. 40th Virginia July 2, 1862 VA25
Mitchell, John - Nurse - North Carolina VA08
Mitchell, M.D. - Co. H 12th Virginia June 18, 1864 VA25
Mitchell, P.G. - Clark Cavalry VA06
Mitchell, T.J. - Virginia VA20
Mitham, J.T. - Co. D 4th Georgia Aug. 7, 1862 VA25
Mittier, G. - Virginia VA07
Mixen, James - Co. A 7th South Carolina May 25, 1864 VA25
Mize, J.H. - Co. B 13th Mississippi July 8, 1862 VA25
Mizell, E. - Lt.- Co. D 26th Georgia April 27, 1863 VA25
Mizelle, Alexander - Pvt. - Co. I 41st Virginia KIA –
    Spotsylvania Court House - May 12, 1864 VA28
Mobley, Francis - Co. H 13th Georgia VA11
Mockla, D. - Co. C 11th Georgia July 5, 1862 VA25
Mocksley, H.W. - Co. h 13th Georgia May 28, 1863 VA25
Moffett, __ - Co. H 13th North Carolina May 28, 1863 VA25
Moffett, T.G. - Co. E 18th Mississippi July 1, 1862 VA25
Moffitt, J.R. - Tennessee VA20
Moise, John L. - Co. H 17th Artillery VA11
Molby, H.C. - 35th Georgia June 25, 1862 VA25
Molby, Jno. - Tennessee VA20
Molby, S. - Co. B 6th Georgia July 13, 1862 VA25
Molly, J.F. - 8th South Carolina VA18
Mon, A. - Co. E 23rd North Carolina June 15, 1862 VA25
Money, E.F. - Sgt. -8th Virginia Infantry VA10
Monoghon, Wm. - Pvt.- Co. H 57th North Carolina Died June
    19, 1865 VA26
Monroe, J. - Co. C 11th Virginia June 8, 1862 VA25
Monroe, J. Berkley - Co. E 6th Virginia VA10
Monroe, J.J. - Co. I 11th Alabama Aug. 11, 1862 VA25
Montague, W.H. - Co. B 1st North Carolina Aug. 18, 1864 VA25

Montgomery, B. - VA25
Montgomery, C. - Citizen - Alabama March 24, 1863 VA25
Montgomery, J. 5th - Virginia VA18
Montgomery, J. - Co. K 21st North Carolina Aug. 7, 1862 VA25
Montgomery, J.G. - Co. H 22nd Georgia May 25, 1864 VA25
Montgomery, J.H. - Co. E 11th North Carolina Sept. 7, 1864 VA25
Montgomery, Thos. W. - 25th South Carolina VA04
Moody, John W. - DOW July 23, 1862 age 19 VA19
Moody, Peter - Pvt. - Co. K 7th South Carolina Died May 8, 1864 VA28
Moon, L.N. - 8th Louisiana March 7, 1862 VA25
Moon, L.W. - Purcell Battery (Virginia) May 9, 1863 VA25
Moon, M.J. - 11th Alabama VA18
Mooney, J.G. - 5th Alabama Jan. 15, 1863 VA25
Mooney, P. - Co. I 56th Georgia June 12, 1864 VA25
Mooney, W.D. - 13th North Carolina Infantry - KIA - Battle of Williamsburg - May 5, 1862 VA02
Moons, T.B. - Co. G 8th Louisiana Dec. 8, 1862 VA25
Moor, Stafford William - Pvt. - Co. A 4th Cavalry Virginia KIA - Spotsylvania Court House Headstone reads: "William S. Moor" VA28
Moor, William S. see Moor, Stafford William VA28
Moore, A.J. - Co. B 57th Virginia June 8, 1862 VA25
Moore, A.R. - Co. E 23rd North Carolina July 12, 1864 VA25
Moore, B.L. - Co. A 18th Mississippi July 17, 1862 VA25
Moore, B.P. - 5th Alabama VA18
Moore, C.R. - South Carolina July 8, 1862 VA25
Moore, D. - Co. H 48th Georgia Sept. 9, 1862 VA25
Moore, D.T. - Washington Artillery (Louisiana) Aug. 16, 1864 VA25
Moore, E. - Lt.- Co. K 5th South Carolina June 13, 1864 VA25
Moore, E.W. - Co. B 22nd North Carolina May 11, 1862 VA25

Moore, Eli W. - Co. K 6th North Carolina VA11
Moore, F. - Clark Cavalry VA06
Moore, F. -June 3, 1862 VA25
Moore, Greenlee M. - Pvt. - Co. E 3rd South Carolina
    Battalion Died May 8, 1864 VA28
Moore, J. - Carter's Artillery VA18
Moore, J. - 3rd South Carolina Nov. 4, 1862 VA25
Moore, J. - North Carolina July 8, 1864 VA25
Moore, J. - Co. C 21st North Carolina April 15, 1865 VA25
Moore, J. - Co. C 45th North Carolina Feb. 1, 1864 VA25
Moore, J.A. - Co. F 18th Mississippi May 12, 1862 VA25
Moore, J.D. - Co. E 8th South Carolina June 1, 1862 VA25
Moore, J.G. - Co. D 8th Virginia July 15, 1862 VA25
Moore, J.R. - Co. C 28th North Carolina June 10, 1862 VA25
Moore, J.R. - Co. G 13th Mississippi April 29, 1862 VA25
Moore, James G. - Louisiana. - Died March 17, 1863 age 35
    VA19
Moore, John M. - Corp. - Co. K 26th Mississippi Died May 12,
    1864 VA28
Moore, Joseph C. - Co. H 17th Georgia VA11
Moore, M. - Co. B 5th Georgia June 29, 1862 VA25
Moore, M. - Co. G 24th Georgia June 16, 1862 VA25
Moore, M.J. - Co. H 5th Alabama Feb. 4, 1863 VA25
Moore, N. - Co. E 14th Louisiana June 15, 1862 VA25
Moore, R. - Camp Winder Oct. 30, 1862 VA25
Moore, R.H. - Co. B 5th Alabama June 27, 1862 VA25
Moore, R.M. - 4th__ VA18
Moore, R.W. - Co. H 9th Louisiana Jan. 16, 1863 VA25
Moore, S. - Colonel- 11th Alabama Aug. 22, 1862 VA25
Moore, Stephen - 7th Georgia VA18
Moore, T.H. - 10th Alabama Infantry - KIA - Battle of
    Williamsburg - May 5, 1862 VA02
Moore, T.W. - Co. A 1st Louisiana June 2, 1862 VA25
Moore, W. - Co. I 11th Virginia VA10
Moore, W. - Sgt. - Clark Cavalry VA06

Moore, W. - Co. D 18th North Carolina June 10, 1862 - age 21 VA25
Moore, W. - 26th Georgia Sept. 24, 1862 VA25
Moore, W. - Co. A 14th North Carolina July 3, 1862 VA25
Moore, W.A. - 13th North Carolina VA18
Moore, W.G. - Co. B 5th North Carolina VA11
Moore, W.L. - Co. E 27th North Carolina Dec. 30, 1864 VA25
Moorer, Duane W. - Pvt. - Co, M6th Alabama DOW VA28
Moorhead, S.D. - 11th Mississippi Infantry DOW - Berry's Ferry - Aug. 10, 1861 VA06
Moot, J.B. - Co. C 24th North Carolina Nov. 26, 1864 VA25
Moquest, E. - 12th Louisiana July 20, 1862 VA25
Moral, P. - Co. B 2nd Battalion March 14, 1862 VA25
Moran, F. - Maryland Nov. 12, 1862 VA25
Moran, G.W. - Co. D 8th Virginia July 2, 1862 VA25
Moran, H.H. - Co. D 15th North Carolina June 13, 1864 VA25
Morecock, J.N. - Lt.- Co. H 5th Virginia Cavalry Died Aug. 30, 1864 VA23
Morell, S.J. - 4th Louisiana Oct. 11, 1862 VA25
Morgan, A.M. - Co. G 47th Alabama Jan. 8, 1863 VA25
Morgan, B.R. - Co. A 10th Alabama VA11
Morgan, C.D. - Clark Cavalry VA06
Morgan, Charles W. - POW - Federal Soldier Died June 5, 1862 VA19
Morgan, F. - Co. M 30th Georgia June 2, 1864 VA25
Morgan, F.A. - Co. C 44th North Carolina June 14, 1864 VA25
Morgan, G. - 2nd Reserves March 25, 1865 VA25
Morgan, J. - 1st Mississippi Batt. VA18
Morgan, J. - Co. F 24th Georgia June 3, 1862 VA25
Morgan, J.B. - Co. E 4th North Carolina June 19, 1862 VA25
Morgan, J.L. - Co. C 42nd Mississippi Aug. 23, 1862 VA25
Morgan, J.W. - Co. H 5th Florida May 1, 1862 VA25 Morgan, John S. - Lt.- Co. B 32nd North Carolina Died May 10, 1864 VA28
Morgan, L. - Alabama July 30, 1863 VA25

Morgan, S.M. - 5th Alabama July 20, 1863 VA25
Morgan, T.M. - Co. E 6th Georgia July 27, 1864 VA25
Morgan, T.W. - Alabama Aug. 11, 1863 VA25
Morgan, W. - 2nd Alabama. Battalion June 10, 1862 VA25
Morgan, Wm. - Co. A 6th South Carolina Died May 7, 1863 VA03
Morgon, L.J. - 2nd "As." Battalion June 10, 1862 "As." was listed as the state in the burial roster. VA25
Morice, M.R. - Co. I 14th North Carolina Sept. 4, 1862 VA25
Moring, T. - June 5, 1862 VA25
Morris, Andrew J. - DOW Aug. 2, 1862 moved to Hollywood - 1863 (not listed in Hollywood) VA19
Morris, D. - Co. F 16th Mississippi VA28
Morris, Dempsey - see Morris, Demsey VA28
Morris, Demsey - Co. B 2nd North Carolina Headstone reads: ' Dempsey" VA28
Morris, J.H. - 12th Alabama Infantry VA08
Morris, O.W. - Pvt.- Co. H 34th Virginia Died June 26, 1865 VA26
Morris, Robert J. - 16th Mississippi VA04
Morris, W.J. - 20th Georgia VA18
Morrison, __ - Co. B 26th Alabama Sept. 16, 1862 VA25
Morrison, H. - Co. B 5th Louisiana June 7, 1862 VA25
Morrison, J.M. - Co. B 53rd North Carolina Dec. 21, 1863 VA25
Morriss, A.R. - Co. D 5th Alabama Jan. 2, 1863 VA25
Morriss, B.C. - Co. C 25th Virginia Bat. May 12, 1864 VA25
Morriss, H. - Co. F 6th South Carolina June 23, 1862 VA25
Morriss, H. - 6th North Carolina June 19, 1862 VA25
Morriss, J. - Co. I 13th South Carolina Feb. 27, 1865 VA25
Morriss, J.M. - Lt.- Co. G 26th South Carolina July 22, 1864 VA25
Morriss, J.R. - Co. K 26th North Carolina Dec. 25, 1864 VA25
Morriss, L.W. - Co. H 14th North Carolina Sept. 1, 1862 VA25

Morriss, M. - Co. H 2nd Georgia Aug. 20, 1862 VA25
Morriss, P.B. - 13th Alabama Sept. 30, 1861 VA25
Morriss, P.L.H. - Co. I 18th South Carolina March 12, 1865 VA25
Morriss, T.J. - Cobb's Legion (Georgia) May 9, 1863 VA25
Morriss, W.L. - Livingston Guards (Texas) July 21, 1861 VA25
Morrissey, Thos. - Artillery June 4, 1862 VA25
Morton, Isaacs - Died Nov. 11, 1862 VA19
Morton, J. - Co. B 35th Georgia June 22, 1862 VA25
Morton, M.E. - Co. F 25th Georgia Sept. 1862 VA25
Morton, W.S. - Co. I 1st South Carolina Sept. 3, 1864 VA25
Moseley, J.W. - Co. G 35th Mississippi July 17, 1863 VA25
Moseley, W. - Georgia VA18
Mosely, J. - Co. F 14th Alabama Sept. 11, 1862 VA25
Moses, A.J. - Co. A 46th North Carolina Nov. 1, 1863 VA25
Moses, W. - VA08
Mosley, J. - Co. D 10th Georgia Bat. June 11, 1864 VA25
Moss, A. - Co. E 8th Virginia March 29, 1862 VA25
Moss, Alfred - Major - General Ewell's Staff VA10
Moss, J. - Co. B 53rd Georgia June 6, 1864 VA25
Moss, J.W. - Co. B 13th Arkansas May 14, 1862 VA25
Moss, Jessee - Co. G 51st Virginia VA11
Moss, S. - Co. C 8th Louisiana Dec. 23, 1862 VA25
Moss, T. - Co. C 10th Georgia June 20, 1863 VA25
Moss, W.A. - July 2, 1862 VA25
Mosson, J.A. - Co. G 25th North Carolina July 24, 1864 VA25
Motes, J.B. - Co. K 1st South Carolina May 25, 1864 VA25
Motherly, M. - Co. E 21st North Carolina July 31, 1863 VA25
Motley, N.R. - Co. D 25th Virginia Bat. May 2, 1864 VA25
Moulden, Geo. - Co. K 19th Georgia Infantry VA10
Mount, J.M. - 11th Georgia May 24, 1862 VA25
Moy, J. - Co. K 24th North Carolina Sept. 2, 1864 VA25
Moyers, George W. - VA15
Muff, J.N. - Co. C 14th South Carolina June 6, 1864 VA25

Muley, Jacob - Capt. - Co. B 27th Virginia May 25, 1864 VA25
Mulford, G.W. - Co. G 16th Virginia July 4, 1862 VA25
Mulholand, B. - Co. C 56th Virginia Aug. 17, 1864 VA25
Mulholand, H.G. - Co. C 56th North Carolina July 24, 1864 VA25
Mull, James - Co. K 35th North Carolina Oct. 30, 1864 VA25
Mullas, F.M. - Co. E 48th North Carolina June 27, 1864 VA25
Mullen, H.L. - Aug. 17, 1862 VA25
Mullen, J.W. - Co. D 7th Virginia June 22, 1864 VA25
Mullen, M. - Co. A 10th Louisiana Aug. 26, 1862 VA25
Mullens, John - C.S. Navy Aug. 20, 1862 VA25
Mulley, A.A. - Lt.- Co. A 51st Georgia Jan. 12, 1863 VA25
Mullinuxes, A. - 19th Mississippi VA18
Mulroon, Jno. - see Mulrooney, John VA28
Mulrooney, John - Sgt. - Co. I 6th Louisiana Died May 12, 1864   Napier Bartlett's *Military Record of Louisiana* identifies this soldier as "Jno. Mulroon" VA28
Muncheson, J. - Sgt. - 27th Georgia June 25, 1864 VA25
Munn, J. - Co. G Palmetto Sharp Shooters (South Carolina) Aug. 21, 1862 VA25
Munsey, H. - Co. F 1st South Carolina Aug. 27, 1862 VA25
Murcheson, W. - Co. C 5th Texas Aug. 3, 1862 VA25
Murden, R. - Co. F 41st Virginia June 4, 1863 VA25
Murdin, M. - Co. B 6th Virginia May 21, 1863 VA25
Murdock, W.C. - VA25
Muren, L. - 13th Alabama Sept. 22, 1861 VA25
Murgrave, S.A. - Co. G 1st North Carolina July 14, 1864 VA25
Murmith, J.W. - Co. B 8th Alabama Nov. 27, 1862 VA25
Murphy, __ - July 30, 1862 VA25
Murphy, C. - 54th North Carolina Oct. 2, 1864 VA25
Murphy, Duncan - Lt.- Co. I 1st South Carolina Died May 12, 1864 VA28
Murphy, G.W. - VA12
Murphy, H. - 9th Alabama July 25, 1862 VA25

Murphy, J. - Co. C 11th Alabama Aug. 5, 1862 VA25
Murphy, J.B. - Co. B 1st Virginia VA08
Murphy, J.C. - Co. C 44th North Carolina Feb. 19, 1864 VA25
Murphy, J.E. - 9th South Carolina Oct. 7, 1861 VA25
Murphy, J.J. - 11th Mississippi VA18
Murphy, J.M. - Co. K 9th Virginia June 19, 1862 VA25
Murphy, J.W. - Virginia VA20
Murphy, J.W. - Co. G 40th North Carolina March 17, 1865 VA25
Murphy, John - Co. F 8th North Carolina 1862 VA25
Murphy, L. - Co. J 19th Virginia VA08
Murphy, T. - Co. E 48th Georgia Oct. 9, 1863 VA25
Murphy, W.F. - Co. K 5th North Carolina June 16, 1865 VA25
Murphy, W.H. - Co. F 50th Georgia Aug. 12, 1864 VA25
Murphy, W.K. - Co. I 19th Mississippi May 22, 1862 age 26 VA25
Murrall, D.J. - 12th Mississippi April 28, 1863 VA25
Murray, A. - May 7, 1862 VA25
Murray, G. Nov. 12, 1864 VA25
Murray, George W. - Lt.- Co. F 14th North Carolina VA28
Murray, H. - Co. E 2nd North Carolina Aug. 16, 1862 VA25
Murray, J.T. - Co. E 35th North Carolina June 6, 1864 VA25
Murray, Thos. - Mecklenburg Guards (Virginia) Sept 1861 VA25
Murray, W.B. - Corp. - Co. D 5th South Carolina Cavalry July 23, 1864 VA25
Murth, __ - July 30, 1862 VA25
Muse, Wm. T. - Commodore - C.S. Navy VA10
Myer, C.C. - Co. H 9th Alabama July 19, 1862 VA25
Myers, A. - Sgt. - Co. A 18th Mississippi Jan.30, 1863 VA25
Myers, D.J. - Co. F 7th South Carolina Cavalry June 7, 1864 VA25
Myers, F. - Co. E 7th Louisiana Oct. 1, 1863 VA25
Myers, J.A. - Co. B 17th North Carolina Oct. 13, 1864 VA25
Myers, S.G. - Co. H 14th North Carolina Oct. 7, 1863 VA25

Myers, W. - Co. F 1st South Carolina . June 5, 1862 VA25
Myers, W.A. - Arkansas June 23, 1861 VA25
N __, D.P. - Co. A 16th North Carolina July 1, 1862 VA25
Nabes, J.W. - Co. C 10th Alabama Aug. 17, 1862 VA25
Nahall, S.S. - Mississippi Artillery July 27, 1864 VA25
Nail, E.A. - Co. F 7th North Carolina June 27, 1863 VA25
Nail, H.C. - Co. H 24th North Carolina Aug. 8, 1864 VA25
Nail, N. - Co. F 42nd MC Jan. 12, 1865 VA25
Nailbin, W.J. - Co. E 28th Georgia June 4, 1863 VA25
Nailer, J.C. - South Carolina July 20, 1862 VA25
Nalle, J.L. - 4th Alabama VA18
Name, A. - Co. H 52nd North Carolina July 8, 1864 VA25
Nance, J.W. - 3rd Arkansas May 4, 1862 VA25
Nance, W. - Co. H 46th North Carolina April 28, 1865 VA25
Nash, B.S. - Co. G 40th Virginia Jan. 18, 1863 VA25
Nash, C.W. - 20th Georgia VA18
Nash, H.T. - Co. I 13th Mississippi July 26, 1862 VA25
Nash, T.H. - Co. K 49th Virginia July 8, 1862 VA25
Nash, W.M. - Co. E 7th Georgia July 17, 1862 VA25
Nation, Jas. - North Carolina VA20
Neal, G.W. - 7th South Carolina VA18
Neal, Gerry W. - Corp. - Co. H 53rd North Carolina Died May 12, 1864 Headstone reads: 'J.W. Neal" VA28
Neal, H.L.C. - Co. C 2nd Arkansas July 2, 1862 VA25
Neal, J. W. - see Neal, Gerry W. VA28
Neal, J.H. - Co. H 4th Texas Nov. 12, 1861 VA25
Neal, J.T. - 4th North Carolina Cavalry June 18, 1864 VA25
Neal, W. - Co. K 14th South Carolina June 16, 1864 VA25
Neale, J.J. - 17th Mississippi VA18
Nealey, T.E. - Lt.- Co. B 11th Mississippi June 1862 VA25
Neason, B.F. - Co. H 16th Louisiana May 24, 1865 VA25
Needham, C. - 11th Georgia VA18
Needham, Thomas - 1st Mississippi VA18
Neese, George M. - VA13
Neff, John Francis - VA14
Neighbor, B.J. - Co. B 3rd Georgia Jan. 1, 1863 VA25

Neighbors, H.R. - Co. I 17th Mississippi July 26, 1862 VA25
Neilson, John H. - Capt. - Co. E 44th Alabama Died May 8, 1864 VA28
Nelmes, F. - Co. D 45th Georgia May 30, 1862 VA25
Nelson, E. - Co. I 44th North Carolina Nov. 9, 1863 VA25
Nelson, G.W. - Co. K 15th Georgia July 29, 1864 VA25
Nelson, Hugh Mortimer - Aide-de-Camp to General Ewell Died of typhoid fever - Aug. 6, 1862 VA06
Nelson, J.F. - South Carolina VA20
Nelson, James - Co. I 11th Virginia VA10
Nelson, Jas. - Georgia VA20
Nelson, Joseph - Co. I 11th Virginia VA10
Nelson, L. - Co. C 1st North Carolina May 17, 1862 VA25
Nelson, R.P. - VA20
Nelson, T.S. - Lt.- Co. I 4th South Carolina Cavalry June 4, 1864 VA25
Nesbitt, P.L. - Co. D Palmetto Sharp Shooters (South Carolina) Oct. 22, 1864 VA25
Nestor, A. Virginia - VA20
Netherly, T.W. - Co. D 5th Texas April 1, 1862 VA25
Nevitt, Edward - Co. A 6th Virginia VA10
Newbill, Lewis E. - DOW June 14, 1864 age 21 VA19
Newcomb, Jno. - Co. D 17th Virginia InfantryVA10
Newell, A.H. - Co. E 11th North Carolina Aug. 27, 1864 VA25
Newell, G. - Co. F 2nd North Carolina June 17, 1864 VA25
Newell, J.M. - Lt.- Co. G 47th Alabama June 9, 1864 VA25
Newman, Garrett - Lulley's Virginia Art VA23
Newman, H.T. - Co. C 21st Georgia May 22, 1862 VA25
Newman, John W. - VA12
Newman, M.A. - Co. C 28th Georgia June 17, 1864 VA25
Newman, S. - Co. B 38th North Carolina March 29, 1865 VA25
Newman, T.F. - Carter's Artillery (Virginia) May 16, 863 VA25
Newman, Walter - VA12

Newson, A. - Co. A 48th Georgia Sept. 22,, 1862 VA25
Newson, J.H. - Co. F 34th Georgia Aug. 4, 1862 VA25
Newton, Andrew H. - Pvt.- Co. I 22nd Georgia Died at Gaines Mill station - March 1864 VA28
Newton, E. - Co. H 34th North Carolina July 27, 1864 VA25
Newton, J.D. - May 13, 1862 VA25
Newton, N. - Co. I 26th Alabama April 10, 1862 VA25
Newton, W.D. - Co. I 10th Alabama May 24, 1862 VA25
Nexas, Thos. - Co. I 3rd South Carolina Oct. 28, 1861 VA25
Nich, S.G. - Co. E 6th South Carolina Aug. 30, 1862 VA25
Nicham, W. - Co. G 24th North Carolina June 3, 1862 VA25
Nichols, G. - Co. B 22nd North Carolina July 4, 1862 VA25
Nichols, J. - Pvt. - North Carolina April 7, 1865 VA22
Nichols, J. - C.S.N. April 28, 1865 VA25
Nichols, J.A. - Co. B 12th South Carolina Aug. 25, 1864 VA25
Nichols, Jno. - Co. B 8th Alabama Dec. 24, 1862 VA25
Nichols, John J. - Wright's Heavy Artillery (Virginia)Died June 2, 1863 VA03
Nichols, Joshua L. - POW - Federal Soldier Died Dec. 23, 1861 VA19
Nichols, R. - Co. B 1st Louisiana July 13, 1862 VA25
Nichols, R.C. - Co. D 24th Georgia VA28
Nichols, Simpson - 7th Virginia VA18
Nichols, W. - Co. I 28th North Carolina July 7, 1862 VA25
Nickson, G.W. - Co. A 5th Georgia May 17, 1862 VA25
Nicots, I. - POW - Federal Soldier Died Dec. 23, 1861 VA19
Nifong, S. - Co. H 48th Georgia May 5, 1864 VA25
Night, J.J. - Co. K 6th Alabama June 12, 1862 VA25
Nipis, R. - POW - Federal Soldier Died Dec 14, 1861 VA19
Nitt, R.S. - Pvt. - Co. F 58th Virginia KIA - Spotsylvania Court House - May 12, 1864 VA28
Nix, C.C. - Co. C 24th Georgia July 4, 1864 VA25
Nix, W.M. - Co. G 44th North Carolina Sept. 2, 1864 VA25
Nixon, C.J. - Co. A 53rd Georgia March 15, 1863 VA25
Nixon, John - Co. E 27th North Carolina June 5, 1864 VA25

Nixon, Wm. - Pvt.3rd North Carolina Died June 19, 1865 VA26
Noah, A.H. - Co. K 34th North Carolina June 17, 1862 VA25
Nobbs, A. - Co. G 51st North Carolina Sept. 2, 1864 VA25
Nobles, A.B. - Co. E 14th South Carolina Aug. 1, 1864 VA25
Nobles, C.W. - 12th Alabama Nov. 7, 1861 VA25
Nobles, E. - Co. K 57th North Carolina April 22, 1865 VA25
Nobles, W.J. - Co. B 51st Georgia Nov. 12, 1862 VA25
Nolan, J. - Co. G - Orr's Rifles (South Carolina) June 5, 1864 VA25
Nolen, P. - VA08
Noll, W.A. - 18th Virginia VA18
Nored, T.W. - 26th Alabama June 2, 1862 VA25
Norfleet, William Henry - Pvt. - Co. B 16th Virginia DOW May 17, 1864 (MW Po River May 11, 1864)
 Headstone reads: ' William H. Norfult" VA28
Norflut, William H. - see Norfleet, William Henry VA28
Norman, C.H. - Co. K 44th North Carolina Aug. 27, 1864 VA25
Norman, H.H. - C.S. Navy April 1, 1865 VA25
Norman, J. - Co. F 24th North Carolina May 11, 1863 VA25
Norman, J.B. - Co. A 15th Georgia Sept. 16, 1861 VA25
Norman, R. - Co. K 64th Georgia Oct. 20, 1864 VA25
Norris, J.P. - Pvt.- Co. H 22nd Georgia Died May 14, 1864 VA28
Norris, T.J. - 2nd Mississippi June 17, 1862 VA25
Norris, W.B. - South Carolina VA20
Norriss, J.N. - Co. C 13th Alabama April 20, 1862 VA25
Norton, J. - 28th North Carolina Aug. 27, 1862 VA25
Norton, L. - 11th North Carolina VA18
Norton, N.H. - Co. B 24th North Carolina Sept. 14, 1864 VA25
Norton, P. - 21st Georgia VA18
Norton, P. - Co. A 28th North Carolina 1862 VA25
Norwood, J. - Co. A 1st South Carolina June 9, 1862 VA25
Norwood, J. - Co. I 18th North Carolina Nov. 10, 1862 VA25

Nowlan, L.S. - 5th South Carolina Cavalry Aug. 7, 1861 VA25
Nowlan, R.T. - Co. B 14th Tennessee July 7, 1862 VA25
Nowlan, W.C. - Sgt. - Co. H 27th Georgia VA25
Nuby, Thos. - North Carolina VA24
Nucum, J.A. - Sgt. - 17th Virginia June 6, 1864 VA25
Nugant, J. - Co. A 9th Louisiana April 4, 1863 VA25
Nun, J.A. - Co. E 34th Georgia April 4, 1863 VA25
Nun, T.C. - Cobb's Legion (Georgia) Oct. 1, 1862 VA25
Nun, T.P. - Co. F 12th Georgia June 21, 1864 VA25
Nun, V.S. - 49th Georgia June 27, 1863 VA25
Nunn, Andrew - Pvt. - Co. K 34th Virginia Died June 12, 1865 VA26
Nunn, Wm. - Co. D 15th Georgia Died Jan 1, 1862 VA23
Nuson, W.H. - Co. G 33rd North Carolina July 8, 1864 VA25
O'Bannon, __ - Lt. Colonel - 16th Georgia VA23
O'Brien, Michael - Co. B Tiger Rifles (Wheat 1st Special Louisiana Battalion) - Executed Dec 9, 1861 VA16
O'Neal, Andrew J. - Pvt.- Co. F 13th Georgia Accidentally killed at Guinea Station - Dec. 1, 1862 VA28
O'Neal, J.B. - 21st Georgia VA18
O'Neal, S.C. - 8th Louisiana VA18
O'Niel, Jo. - M. Died Dec. 18, 1862 VA19
O'Roark, Branson - VA12
Oakley, James - Pvt.- Co. I Hampton's Artillery Died May 31, 1865 VA26
Oats, H.S. - This soldier's unit is listed as "17th Georgia South Carolina" VA18
Ober, G. - Co. I 5th Texas Aug. 20, 1862 VA25
Obersey, A. - 1st North Carolina Aug. 11, 1861 VA25
Obrey, W.F. - Co. F 1st Georgia Nov. 19, 1861 VA25
Obrien, __ - Co. D 13th North Carolina July 8, 1862 VA25
Odemhofer, Albert - Pvt. - Co. B 8th Louisiana KIA Spotsylvania Court House May 12, 1864 Considerable confusion about the spelling of this soldier's name in the old cemetery records. VA28

Oden, B.J. - Co. A 8th South Carolina June 13, 1862 VA25
Oden, W. - Co. E 44th North Carolina Jan. 11, 1865 VA25
Odom, J. - Co. F 7th Mississippi March 15, 1865 VA25
Odom, J.B. - Co. C 6th Georgia Oct. 17, 1864 VA25
Odom, R. - Co. B 2nd North Carolina Jan. 14, 1864 VA25
Odom, S. - 8th South Carolina Aug. 28, 1861 VA25
Odonnel, J.W. - Co. G 1st Virginia May 24, 1862 VA25
Ogle, John - Virginia VA20
Oglesby, M.O. - Pvt.- Co. B 10th Florida Died June 20, 1865 VA26
Oglesby, R.L. - Co. G 19th Georgia Oct. 8, 1862 VA25
Oglesby, W.B. - Co. D 60th Georgia VA11
Oglethrope, J. - Co. B 6th Louisiana Nov. 19, 1861 VA25
Ogletree, J. - Co. A 11th Alabama June 24, 1862 VA25
Ogletree, J. Leonard - Pvt.- Co. I 13th Georgia Died May 12, 1864 VA28
Olinger, I. - VA12
Olinger, William - VA13
Oliphant, R. - Louisiana July 29, 1861 VA25
Oliver, J. - Co. K 35th North Carolina July 8, 1862 VA25
Oliver, J. - Co. H 2nd Louisiana May 11, 1863 VA25
Oliver, J.T. - Co. B 60th Georgia June 8, 1863 VA25
Oliver, W.G. - Co. E 23rd North Carolina VA11
Omans, A.M. - 6th Alabama Jan. 5, 1863 VA25
Omer, D. - South Carolina May 4, 1864 VA25
Oniel, C.P. - Co. H 6th Georgia May 24, 1862 VA25
Oniel, W.R. - Co. A 1st South Carolina April 28, 1864 VA25
Onino, J. - Co. C 2nd North Carolina March 5, 1865 VA25
Only, __ - 61st Virginia May 29, 1862 VA25
Only, J. - Co. D 61st Virginia Oct. 16, 1864 VA25
Oral, J.T. - Cooper's Rifles (South Carolina) Nov. 18, 1862 VA25
Ord, N. - 48th Georgia VA18
Organ, T. W. - Co. I 3rd Virginia Cavalry July 1, 1864 VA25
Organ, W.A. - Co. I 11th Virginia May 27, 1862 VA25
Osborne, B. - Co. A 37th North Carolina Nov. 7, 1861 VA25

Osborne, J.A. - Cobb's Legion (Georgia) Nov. 18, 1863 VA25
Osborne, J.P. - 14th South Carolina Nov. 20, 1862 VA25
Osborne, J.T. - Parker's Battery (Virginia) April 22, 1865 VA25
Osborne, L.Y. - Co. E 3rd North Carolina Sept. 14, 1862 VA25
Osborne, R. - Co. H 1st North Carolina Batt. Oct. 30, 1864 VA25
Osbrook, J. - Co. H 17th North Carolina Oct. 16, 1864 VA25
Osbrook, W. - Battery Number 9 (Virginia) June 13, 1862 VA25
Otley, P. - Co. C 28th Georgia June 12, 1864 VA25
Otts, J. - Co. C 13th South Carolina July 3, 1862 VA25
Otts, J.M. - Co. G 20th South Carolina July 12, 1864 VA25
Oury, S. - 16th Mississippi Died June 10, 1861 VA17
Outland, W.S. Letcher's Artillery (Virginia) April 4, 1862 VA25
Outlaw, H. - Moore's Co. May 1862 VA25
Ovabal, E.J. - Co. B 11th North Carolina Died Sept 21, 1861 VA23
Overby, Thomas - Mosby's Virginia Cavalry hung while POW - Sept 23, 1864 VA23
Overcash, D.W. - Co. B 57th North Carolina Jan. 5, 1863 VA25
Overcash, J.C. - Co. K 46th North Carolina May 3, 1864 VA25
Overcash, S. - 54th North Carolina VA18
Overlay, A. - Co. I 20th North Carolina Aug. 12, 1864 VA25
Overlay, O. - Co. I 44th North Carolina July 1, 1864 VA25
Overstreet, H. - Co. G 11th Arkansas April 7, 1865 VA25
Overstreet, Wm. - Capt. G.'s - Co. May 18, 1862 VA25
Owen, B. - Georgia VA20
Owen, G.W. - Georgia Sept. 21, 1861 VA25
Owen, G.W. - Co. A 6th Alabama Oct. 11, 1861 VA25
Owen, J.N. - Baughman's Artillery March 4, 1865 VA25
Owen, W.H. - Virginia VA20

Owens, __ - Aug. 20, 1862 VA25
Owens, A. - Co. B 37th North Carolina July 7, 1862 VA25
Owens, A.W. - Virginia Sept. 8, 1864 VA25
Owens, Archibald Young - see Owings, Archibald Young VA28
Owens, C. - Pvt. - 37th North Carolina Infantry DOW June 15, 1862 VA09
Owens, Daniel L. - Pvt. - 37th North Carolina Infantry DOW VA09
Owens, J. - Co. E 56th North Carolina Sept. 2, 1864 VA25
Owens, J. - Georgia - Nov. 1, 1861 VA25
Owens, J. - Co. D 49th North Carolina Feb. 6, 1865 VA25
Owens, J.C. - Co. A 44th South Carolina July 20, 1865 VA25
Owens, J.Q. - Co. A 1st South Carolina Aug. 20, 1864 VA25
Owens, J.S. - Nov. 12, 1863 VA25
Owens, J.W. - Co. G 21st Mississippi Aug. 1, 1862 VA25
Owens, James - 1st Georgia VA18
Owens, M. - Co. B 48th North Carolina Oct. 11, 1864 VA25
Owens, S.S. - Co. I 8th South Carolina June 8, 1864 VA25
Owens, T. - Co. E 1st South Carolina April 19, 1865 VA25
Owens, W. - Co. A 23rd South Carolina Aug. 24, 1863 VA25
Owens, W.H. - Co. E 14th South Carolina Aug. 9, 1864 VA25
Owens, W.T. - Sgt. - Co. G 9th Georgia Oct. 27, 1864 VA25
Owings, Archibald Young - Pvt. - Co. E 3rd South Carolina Battalion Died May 8, 1864 Headstone reads: 'Owens - 3rd South Carolina Infantry" VA28
Owley, J. - Co. F 1st Kentucky Cavalry June 27, 1865 VA25
Oxner, D. - Co. I 1st South Carolina 1864 VA25
P __, L. - June 4, 1862 VA25
Pacey, E. - 13th Alabama Sept. 16, 1861 VA25
Pack, J.J. - Co. D 22nd Georgia Oct. 2, 1864 VA25
Paders, H.C. - Co. H 47th North Carolina July 20, 1864 VA25
Padget, H.J. - April 6, 1862 VA25
Padget, John - Co. K 3rd North Carolina Sept. 12, 1862 VA25
Padgett, B.T. - 17th Virginia VA18
Padgett, E.M. - Co. C 26th South Carolina Nov. 8, 1864 VA25

Padgett, J.H. - Co. C 28th North Carolina July 20, 1862 VA25
Padgett, James - 13th Alabama Aug.28, 1861 VA25
Padgett, Joseph - Co. E 6th Virginia VA10
Padue, T. - Co. F 56th North Carolina Sept. 4, 1864 VA25
Pagaud, L.W. - Petersburg (Virginia) Oct. 17, 1864 VA25
Page, D.H. - Co. B 8th South Carolina April 26, 1863 VA25
Page, J.F. - Co. E 37th North Carolina VA11
Page, J.M. - VA20
Page, J.V. - Co. F 15th South Carolina June 24, 1862 VA25
Page, L.T. - Co. C 5th Alabama March 11, 1863 VA25
Page, Leonard H. - Lt.- Co. H 31st Georgia Died May 11, 1864 VA28
Page, Virginia E. - Civilian -Killed in explosion of C.S. Laboratory - March 16, 1863 age 13 VA19
Page, W. - Co. B 8th Louisiana Oct. 7, 1862 VA25
Page, W.S. - VA06
Paine, __ - Nov. 1862 VA25
Paine, __ - Co. I 2nd Mississippi June 28, 1862 VA25
Paine, __ - South Carolina July 5, 1862 VA25
Paine, G. - W. South Carolina July 3, 1862 VA25
Paine, H. - Co. A 13th Alabama May 27, 1862 VA25
Paine, H.S. - Nov. 18, 1862 VA25
Paine, J. - Co. I 19th Georgia May 27, 1862 VA25
Paine, J.T. - March 23, 1863 VA25
Paine, W. - 13th Alabama July 31, 1861 VA25
Paine, W.F. - Co. A 49th Virginia May 24, 1862 VA25
Painter, J.W. - Co. K 28th Virginia May 7, 1864 VA25
Palditn, S. - Co. D 13th South Carolina Sept. 22, 1864 VA25
Pall, B.T. - Co. E 3rd Georgia Dec. 24, 1862 VA25
Palmer's, Mrs. - "Box from, by Belvin" - This appears to be a box of bones that were disinterred from Mrs. Palmer's farm near Belvin, Virginia. VA25
Palmer, A. - Co. F 6th Georgia Aug. 3, 1864 VA25
Palmer, J.H. - Sgt. - Georgia Artillery July 24, 1864 VA25
Palmer, L.B. - Co. F 9th Louisiana Dec. 7, 1862 VA25
Palmer, S. - Co. F 6th Georgia Sept. 1, 1864 VA25

Palmer, V.A. - Pvt.- Co. E Cobb's Georgia Legion Died May 30, 1865 VA26
Palmer, W.L. - Co. I 22nd Georgia Aug. 3, 1862 VA25
Palson, __ - July 8, 1862 VA25
Palson, J.M. - Co. E 6th South Carolina June 28, 1862 VA25
Panley, M.B. - Co. H 21st Georgia June 10, 1863 VA25
Parater, M. - Palmetto Sharp shooters (South Carolina) Aug. 19, 1864 VA25
Parham, G.L. - Capt. Davis' Co.(Virginia) Aug. 23, 1861 VA25
Parham, W. - Co. D 26th South Carolina Dec. 1, 1865 VA25
Paris, M.R. - Co. H 2nd North Carolina Battery VA28
Paris, W.H. - Co. I 7th North Carolina Nov. 6, 1864 VA25
Parish, A. - Co. C 21st North Carolina June 29, 1864 VA25
Parish, J. - South Carolina Artillery June 1, 1862 VA25
Parish, J.M. - Co. A 3rd Alabama Aug. 24, 1862 VA25
Parish, J.R. - Co. C 11th North Carolina June 9, 1863 VA25
Parish, J.W. - Co. A 38th Georgia July 19, 1862 VA25
Parish, N.H. - Co. H 3rd North Carolina June 13, 1865 VA25
Parish, S. - Co. E 27th North Carolina Dec. 16, 1865 VA25
Parish, Thomas - Pvt.- Co. D 48th North Carolina Died May 29, 1865 VA26
Parist, C. - Co. B 22nd North Carolina March 28, 1862 VA25
Parker, __ - Co. K 5th Louisiana Nov. 18, 1862 VA25
Parker, __ - July 1862 VA25
Parker, A. - Co. B 31st North Carolina July 9, 1864 VA25
Parker, A. - Co. D 6th South Carolina June 8, 1862 VA25
Parker, A.E. - Co. D 10th Georgia July 6, 1864 VA25
Parker, Amos - POW - Federal Soldier Died Jan. 17, 1862 VA19
Parker, E.M. - Co. B 6th Virginia 1865 VA25
Parker, G.N. - Co. F 2nd Louisiana June 20, 1862 VA25
Parker, H. - Co. D 28th Virginia July 25, 1862 VA25
Parker, H.D. - 18th Virginia VA18
Parker, Hardy - DOW July 15, 1862 VA19
Parker, J. - Holcomb Legion VA18

Parker, J. - Co. H 18th North Carolina May 18, 1863 VA25
Parker, J. - Co. F 7th South Carolina July 21, 1864 VA25
Parker, J. - Co. B 56th Georgia April 2, 1865 VA25
Parker, J. - Co. B 24th Georgia March 8, 1865 VA25
Parker, J.A. - Co. D 10th Georgia Battalion July 24, 1864 VA25
Parker, J.D. - Lt.- 31st Virginia July 7, 1862 VA25
Parker, J.J. - Co. D 14th South Carolina June 19, 1862 VA25
Parker, J.W. - Co. C Palmetto Sharp Shooters (South Carolina) May 9, 1865 VA25
Parker, J.W. - Co. D 37th North Carolina June 1864 VA25
Parker, J.Y.- VA18
Parker, James E. - Pvt. - Co. D 37th North Carolina Died either May 12, 1864 or June 9, 1864 at North Anna VA28
Parker, John - Capt. - British Steamer *Modern Grace* Sept. 23, 1862 VA25
Parker, John - Co. C 56th North Carolina June 22, 1862 VA25
Parker, John S. - Sgt. - Co. A 4th Georgia MW May 10, 1864 VA28
Parker, L.L. - Co. I 47th Virginia Dec. 30, 1862 VA25
Parker, M. - Pvt. - South Carolina Aug. 21, 1864 VA22
Parker, M. - 1st Confederate Bat. (South Carolina) Aug. 21, 1864 VA24
Parker, R.H. - Co. H 47th Virginia July 1862 VA25
Parker, R.J. - Phillips' Legion 1864 VA25
Parker, S.M. - July 1862 VA25
Parker, W.T. - Co. B 18th Georgia VA11
Parker, W.T. - Co. D 27th North Carolina July 16, 1863 VA25
Parkhill, G. Washington - Capt. DOW June 28, 1862 VA19
Parkins, A. - 2nd Virginia Infantry VA06
Parks, J.A. - Co. A 28th North Carolina July 25, 1862 VA25
Parks, J.H. - 12th Georgia May 27, 1863 VA25
Parks, Marian - 11th Mississippi VA18
Parks, W.A. - Co. G 10th Georgia Dec. 21, 1864 VA25
Parmer, Joseph - Co. K 2nd North Carolina VA11

Parr, T.P. - 10th Alabama Infantry - KIA - Battle of
   Williamsburg - May 5, 1862 VA02
Parris, D. - Co. A 13th South Carolina Aug. 13, 1862 VA25
Parrish, W. - Dec. 7, 1862 VA25
Parsons, J. - Marine Corps Jan. 24, 1863 VA25
Parsons, M.L.D. - Co. K 36th North Carolina July 23, 1863
   VA25
Parsons, T.F. - Co. C 48th Georgia July 17, 1864 VA25
Parter, C.H. - Co. H 43rd North Carolina Oct. 3, 1863 VA25
Parton, J.W. - Co. C 14th Alabama Feb. 5, 1862 VA25
Partrick, A. - 30th Georgia July 10, 1862 VA25
Partridge, Amos - POW - Federal Soldier Died Jan. 17, 1862
   VA19
Paschell, S.M. - Co. F 42nd Mississippi VA25
Pascon, J. - Co. I 10th Louisiana May 20, 1862 VA25
Pasley, Agustus - Co. D 13th Virginia VA11
Pate, Alexander - Pvt. - Co. D 54th North Carolina Died Jan.
   11, 1863 VA28
Pate, T.A. - Co. K 13th Alabama May 21, 1862 VA25
Pate, T.J. - Co. B 27th Georgia June 25, 1862 VA25
Pathishall, G.G. - Co. E 8th North Carolina March 17, 1865
   VA25
Patrick, A.H. - Co. E 27th North Carolina Dec. 28, 1865
   VA25
Patrick, M. - Co. H 7th Georgia July 6, 1864 VA25
Patrick, W. - Co. C 3rd Louisiana Battalion Jan. 27, 1862
   VA25
Patterson, A. - Co. D 14th North Carolina March 12, 1863
   VA25
Patterson, D.M. - Co. I 18th Alabama Dec. 28, 1862 VA25
Patterson, G. - VA06
Patterson, G.B. - Co. B 30th North Carolina Sept. 3, 1863
   VA25
Patterson, J. - Maryland Nov. 23, 1862 VA25
Patterson, J.A. - Co. D 49th North Carolina Sept. 22, 1864
   VA25

Patterson, J.R. - Orr's Rifles (South Carolina) June 30, 1862 VA25
Patterson, Josiah B. - Lt.- Co. E 14th Georgia Died May 12, 1864 VA28
Patterson, L.G. - Co. G 35th North Carolina Aug. 25, 1862 VA25
Patterson, P. - Alabama Nov. 6, 1862 VA25
Patterson, S.S. - Co. A 4th North Carolina Feb. 26, 1864 VA25
Patterson, W.D. - Co. E 52nd North Carolina April 26, 1863 VA25
Patterson, William R. - Co. K 60th Georgia VA11
Patton, A.E. - 11th Alabama July 14, 1862 VA25
Patton, J. - Virginia VA20
Patton, W.H. - Co. H 14th South Carolina Dec. 7, 1863 VA25
Paul, James J. - Pvt. - Co. E 13th Georgia Died May 12, 1864 VA28
Pauley, L. - Virginia VA20
Paxton, R. - Capt. - Co. G 26th Georgia Feb. 24, 1863 VA25
Pay, J. - 7th North Carolina Feb. 5, 1865 VA25
Payman, Jas. - 38th Georgia July 22, 1862 VA25
Payne, Alex. - Virginia VA20
Payne, Daniel - Co. A 7th North Carolina VA11
Payne, E.B. - Died Nov. 22, 1862 VA19
Payne, Jo. D. - KIA near Fredericksburg, Virginia, Dec 15, 1862 age 19 VA19
Payton, L.S. - VA12
Peacock, J.L. - Co. A 30th Georgia Sept. 12, 1862 VA25
Peacock, John - Aug. 29, 1864 VA25
Peacock, M.J. - Co. E 49th Georgia Sept. 6, 1862 VA25
Peacock, R. - Co. D 27th Georgia April 28, 1862 VA25
Peacock, W.H. - Co. A 16th Georgia Oct. 7, 1862 VA25
Peak, J. - Co. H 33rd North Carolina June 15, 1864 VA25
Peal, C. - Co. K 17th North Carolina Sept. 16, 1864 VA25
Peal, D. - Co. H 18th North Carolina Feb. 6, 1865 VA25
Peal, E.E. - 1st North Carolina Aug. 26, 1861 VA25

Peal, T.J. - Co. I 14th South Carolina July 7, 1862 VA25
Pearce, G. - Co. C 18th South Carolina Nov. 6, 1862 VA25
Pearce, R.S. - Lt. - KIA May 26, 1864 age 26 VA19
Pearce, W. - 4th Texas Oct. 20, 1862 VA25
Pearson, A. - Letcher art. (Virginia) Aug. 7, 1862 VA25
Pearson, A. - Co. B 24th Georgia May 24, 1862 VA25
Pearson, A.M. - Co. G 8th Virginia Jan. 11, 1862 VA25
Pearson, Elthum - 8th Virginia Infantry VA10
Pearson, F.F. - Co. G 48th Georgia July 18, 1864 VA25
Pearson, J. - VA12
Pearson, J.E. - 1st South Carolina Jan. 2, 1863 VA25
Pearson, J.G. - Co. F 47th Alabama Feb. 13, 1863 VA25
Pearson, J.H. - South Carolina VA20
Pearson, J.J.M. - Co. G 9th Louisiana May 3, 1862 VA25
Pearson, J.S. - Co. F 9th Alabama June 25, 1862 VA25
Pearson, John - Pvt. - Co. E 14th South Carolina Died May 12, 1864 VA28
Pearson, M. - Co. F 20th North Carolina March 19, 1865 VA25
Peasley, G.A. - Co. H 4th Texas May 19, 1862 VA25
Peasley, W.M. - Sgt. - Co. B 27th North Carolina July 13, 1864 VA25
Peat, T. - 4th Virginia Artillery Jan. 27, 1862 VA25
Peck, Asa - 8th Virginia Infantry VA10
Peck, H. - Co. G 29th Virginia May 26, 1863 VA25
Pecor, C.A. - Co. A 47th North Carolina Jan. 4, 1865 VA25
Pedigo, John S. - Sgt. - Co. B 4th Virginia VA28
Peebles, A. - Co. A 2nd North Carolina Nov. 16, 1863 VA25
Peebles, J. - 2nd Florida Nov. 18, 1863 VA25
Peebles, R.F. - Co. A 7th South Carolina July 29, 1864 VA25
Peebles, R.H. - Co. G 60th Georgia July 7, 1862 VA25
Peebles, W.W. - Long's Regiment May 13, 1862 VA25
Peerless, P. - Co. C 51st Virginia VA08
Pegram, J.H. - 12th North Carolina July 4, 1862 VA25

Pegram, John – "General" - Infantry born 1832, KIA - Hatcher's Run - Feb. 6, 1865 D.S. Freeman lists Pegram as a "Colonel of Artillery. VA25
Pegues, C.C. - Colonel- 5th Alabama July 15, 1862 VA25
Pellam, E. - Co. G 1st South Carolina Oct. 24, 1864 VA25
Pelp, __ - Co. B 13th North Carolina Jan. 20, 1862 VA25
Pelt, Jacob - Pvt. - Co. B 23rd North Carolina Died May 10, 1864 VA28
Pemmington, J.W. - Co. B 3rd Virginia April 17, 1862 VA25
Pence, A. - Co. F 44th North Carolina June 27, 1864 VA25
Pence, G.B. - 5th Alabama VA18
Pendergrass, Alexander - Co. A 57th (37th)North Carolina VA28
Pendergrass, D. - Co. E 7th North Carolina VA11
Pendergrass, J.M. - Co. G 11th North Carolina Sept. 4, 1864 VA25
Pendly, Benjamin - Co. E 27th Georgia VA11
Penn, J.A. - Co. I 10th Alabama Feb. 13, 1863 VA25
Penn, J.B. - 17th Virginia Infantry - KIA - Battle of Williamsburg - May 5, 1862 VA02
Pennington, __ - Co. A 4th North Carolina June 15, 1862 VA25
Pennington, J.S. - Co. B 8th Alabama May 24, 1862 VA25
Penny, J.T. - Orr's Rifles (South Carolina) June 5, 1862 VA25
Pennybacker, Benjamine - VA12
Penyear, A.T. - 13th North Carolina VA18
Pepper, J.H. - South Carolina Aug. 19, 1862 VA25
Pepps, __ - May 30, 1862 VA25
Perdew, Augustus M. - Pvt. - Co. G 54th North Carolina Died May 20, 1863 at Fredericksburg VA28
Perdon, O.P. - Co. H 1st South Carolina 1865 VA25
Perdue, Hazzard - Pvt. - Co. I 13th North Carolina KIA - Fredericksburg - Dec. 13, 1862 VA28
Perdy, James - Co. H 24th Virginia July 8, 1862 VA25
Perkins, H. - Virginia VA20

Perkins, J.F. - Co. A 26th Alabama Nov. 22, 1862 VA25
Perkins, Thos. N. - Hanover Artillery (Virginia) May 26, 1862 VA25
Perkins, W. - Co. F 1st South Carolina June 4, 1862 VA25
Perkle, B.C.T. - Co. A 24th Georgia May 10, 1862 VA25
Perrin, W.B. - 15th Georgia Oct. 27, 1861 VA25
Perry, F. - Louisiana Artillery May 4, 1863 VA25
Perry, I.C. - Co. G 11th Virginia VA11
Perry, J. - Co. E 8th Georgia June 10, 1862 VA25
Perry, J. - Co. H 14th Georgia Jan. 25, 1863 VA25
Perry, J.E. - 49th Virginia July 14, 1862 VA25
Perry, W.H. - Co. A 38th Georgia March 14, 1865 VA25
Perry, W.H. - 6th South Carolina Jan. 29, 1862 VA25
Perry, William - Co. G 4th North Carolina VA28
Perryman, C.W. - 3rd Georgia July 17, 1862 VA25
Perryman, M.M. - Co. I 13th Alabama May 10, 1862 VA25
Perryman, W.H. - Co. G 47th Alabama VA11
Pervis, A. - Co. K 28th Georgia Sept. 9, 1862 VA25
Pervis, E.S. - Co. E 5th Louisiana This soldier's name is listed in Napier Bartlett's *Military Record of Louisiana*, however he is not listed in the cemetery's burial roster. VA28
Pestics, __ - 1st North Carolina July 1862 VA25
Pete, W.A. - Co. G 60th Georgia Nov. 19, 1863 VA25
Peters, J.T. - Co. A 11th Georgia May 21, 1862 VA25
Petitt, Robt. - Co. D 17th Virginia Infantry VA10
Pettington, Zion - Virginia VA20
Pettus, __ - KIA Grave not marked VA01
Petty, T. - 13th Alabama Oct. 6, 1861 VA25
Pettyjohn, T.J. - 18th Georgia Sept. 15, 1861 VA25
Peugh, W. - 13th Georgia 1862 VA25
Peyler, J.N. - Co. A 4th North Carolina VA28
Phaps, H. - Co. G 13th North Carolina June 15, 1864 VA25
Phelan, T. - Capt. - Co. A 8th Alabama 1862 VA25
Phelin, M. - 2nd Mississippi VA18
Phelps, F. - North Carolina April 20, 1862 VA25

Phelps, William Hampton - Sgt. - Co. E 13th Georgia Died at Hamilton's Crossing - March 25, 1863 VA28
Philips, A. - Co. G 37th North Carolina July 15, 1864 VA25
Philips, A. - Co. H 13th South Carolina Sept. 4, 1864 VA25
Philips, C. - Co. E 14th South Carolina Nov. 12, 1864 VA25
Philips, E. - Co. G 12th Alabama July 8, 1862 VA25
Philips, J. - Co. C 66th North Carolina July 17, 1864 VA25
Philips, J.H. - Co. I 14th Alabama Aug. 7, 1862 VA25
Philips, L.H. - Co. B 3rd Louisiana July 19, 1862 VA25
Phillips, __ - Co. E 32nd Virginia May 5, 1864 VA25
Phillips, __ - 2nd Mississippi Nov. 26, 1862 VA25
Phillips, A. - Co. H 56th North Carolina June 4, 1864 VA25
Phillips, Benj. - 3rd Virginia Cavalry Aug. 5, 1862 VA25
Phillips, Charles M. - VA12
Phillips, E.A. - 53rd Virginia VA18
Phillips, F. - Co. E 4th Texas June 1, 1862 VA25
Phillips, George W. - VA12
Phillips, H. - Co. H 14th Virginia Aug. 8, 1862 VA25
Phillips, Jas. M. -Died Dec. 10, 1862 VA19
Phillips, John - VA15
Phillips, R.L. - Co. H 22nd North Carolina May 9, 1863 VA25
Phillips, Robert L. - Pvt. - Co. G 12th Virginia KIA – Spotsylvania Court House - May 12, 1864 VA28
Phillips, T.A. - Moore's Battery April 10, 1862 VA25
Phillips, T.J. - Co. F 18th Georgia Sept. 12, 1861 VA25
Phillips, V.S. - Co. C 61st North Carolina July 1, 1864 VA25
Phillips, W.H. - Co. I 19th Mississippi July 18, 1862 VA25
Phillips, Z. - Co. D 12th Alabama June 18, 1862 VA25
Philson, W.F. - 1st South Carolina April 29, 1862 VA25
Phipps, Monroe - Pvt. - Co. K 45th North Carolina MW May 19, 1864 VA28
Pickering, H. - Pvt.- Co. H 6th Georgia Died May 23, 1865 VA26
Pickering, J. - Co. C 4th North Carolina June 20, 1862 VA25
Pickett, E. - South Carolina Nov. 8, 1862 VA25
Pickett, H. - Co. A 36th North Carolina July 25, 1864 VA25

Pickett, H. - 14th South Carolina July 8, 1862 VA25
Pilkinton, J.T. - Essex County (Virginia) July 24, 1864 VA25
Pillard, A. - Co. H 46th North Carolina Dec. 30, 1864 VA25
Pinder, Jno. - Co. G 1st South Carolina June 15, 1862 VA25
Pinder, W. - Co. D 20th Alabama April 26, 1863 VA25
Pine, C. - Co. B 26th Alabama June 2, 1862 VA25
Pine, C. - Co. C 46th Georgia May 30, 1862 VA25
Pinkard, T.C. - Sgt. - Co. I 40th Virginia July 25, 1862 VA25
Pinson, J.N. - Pvt. - Texas Oct. 29, 1864 VA22
Piper, F.D. - Co. I 1st South Carolina Sept. 2, 1862 VA25
Pipkin, __ - South Carolina May 18, 1862 VA25
Pipkin, W. - Co. B 20th Georgia July 28, 1862 VA25
Pippen, __ - 1862 VA25
Pippen, A.J. - Co. F 15th North Carolina May 4, 1862 VA25
Pippen, B.B. - Mississippi Nov. 16, 1862 VA25
Pippet, James - Aug. 2, 1861 VA25
Pitch, W. - Aug. 1, 1861 VA25
Pitt, William - Palmetto Regt. - South Carolina VA02
Pittman, J.D. - Co. H 4th South Carolina Jan. 29, 1865 VA25
Pittman, R. - 60th Georgia VA04
Pitts, David J. - Drum Major - Co. K 24th Georgia Died Dec. 13, 1862 VA28
Pitts, E.S. - Capt. - Co. F 25th Texas May 25, 1863 VA25
Pitts, F.M. - Co. I 14th Alabama June 20, 1862 VA25
Pitts, J. - Co. A 2nd South Carolina June 26, 1864 VA25
Pitts, W.S. - Co. F 18th Georgia Sept. 20, 1861 VA25
Plagmin, __ - July 8, 1862 VA25
Planter, Michael - Pvt. - Co. I 24th Virginia Died May 20, 1865 VA26
Plaskett, Mathew - Co. K 19th Georgia Infantry VA10
Plaster, J.S. - Co. I 34th Virginia April 26, 1862 VA25
Plaster, W. - Co. D 12th Virginia July 2, 1862 VA25
Platt, W.M. - Co. C 5th South Carolina Oct. 26, 1864 VA22
Player, T.F. - Co. K 2nd Florida Nov. 7, 1862 VA25
Pleant, P.G. - Died Nov. 22, 1862 VA19
Pleet, J. - Co. H 1st Mississippi July 1, 1863 VA25

Plies, J. - Co. I 57th North Carolina June 21, 1862 VA25
Plineton, A. - Co. F 37th North Carolina March 10, 1865 VA25
Plumer, H. - Co. B 4th North Carolina Nov. 1, 1862 VA25
Plumer, J.C. - Co. A 26th North Carolina Aug. 30, 1864 VA25
Plunkett, J.D. - Pvt.- Co. F 3rd Georgia Died June 24, 1865 VA26
Poag, P.W. - Co. F 16th South Carolina Oct. 18, 1864 VA25
Pod, R. - Aug. 22, 1861 VA25
Poe, L. - Co. A 2nd North Carolina March 11, 1863 VA25
Poe, N.H. - Co. G 28th North Carolina July 25, 1862 VA25
Poer, J.B. - Died Nov. 4, 1862 VA19
Pofe, J.C. - 37th Virginia VA18
Poindexter, G.H. - VA18
Polars, B.F. - Artillery June 9, 1864 VA25
Pollard, J.W. - Sept. 12, 1862 VA25
Pollock, Clarence J. - Pvt. - Co. C 1st South Carolina Died May 12, 1864 A memorial stone for this soldier is located in Hebrew Cemetery in Columbia, South Carolina VA28
Pollock, L.S. - 4th Georgia VA18
Pon, W.O. - Co. B 13th Mississippi Oct. 28, 1862 VA25
Pone, M. - Co. B 13th Mississippi Aug. 23, 1862 VA25
Ponidexter, J.G. - Co. I 33rd North Carolina June 1, 1862 VA25
Pool, D.P. - Co. D 5th North Carolina May 27, 1862 VA25
Pool, H. Franklin - Pvt. - Co. A 48th Georgia Died March 28, 1863 VA28
Pool, J. - Co. B 22nd Georgia Nov. 22, 1862 VA25
Pool, L. - Co. H 14th South Carolina June 28, 1862 VA25
Pool, S. - Co. E 38th Georgia May 30, 1864 VA25
Pool, W.F. - 6th Alabama May 30, 1864 VA25
Pooser, J.H. - Capt. - 2nd Florida May 31, 1862 VA25
Pope, A.A. - Co. H 38th North Carolina May 28, 1864 VA25
Pope, D. - Co. G 38th North Carolina June 13, 1863 VA25
Pope, J.R. - Co. B 52nd North Carolina Dec. 25, 1864 VA25

Pope, W.A. - Co. I 5th Alabama Jan. 25, 1863 VA25
Pope, W.C. - Co. C 51st Georgia July 27, 1864 VA25
Pope, W.F. - Co. K 22nd Georgia July 15, 1864 VA25
Pophand, G. - Co. I 28th Georgia May 24, 1864 VA25
Poplar, G. - Pvt. - Virginia April 19, 1865 VA22
Poplin, J. - Co. C 13th North Carolina May 10, 1862 VA25
Poppel, J.T. - Co. E 26th Georgia March 13, 1863 VA25
Poppy, A. - Pvt. - Virginia April 18, 1865 Cemetery roster lists this soldier as "E.A." Poppy VA22
Pops, J.A. - Co. E 25th Virginia Sept. 4, 1862 VA25
Poral, A. - Co. H 17th North Carolina Aug. 17, 1864 VA25
Pornis, L. - Co. A 1st Tennessee Sept. 2, 1862 VA25
Porter, Elisha - Pvt. - Troop Artillery (Georgia)KIA May 5, 1864 in the Wilderness VA28
Porter, Granville Penn - Pvt. - Co. D 1st Artillery KIA - Spotsylvania Court House - May 10, 1864 Headstone reads: " 3rd Virginia Howitzers (Richmond Howitzers) VA28
Porter, H.F. - Co. C 9th Virginia Cavalry June 24, 1864 VA25
Porter, I.M. - Co. K 61st Alabama VA11
Porter, J. - 5th North Carolina Nov. 12, 1862 VA25
Porter, J.E. - Co. A 62nd Georgia Died Jan. 19, 1863 VA03
Porter, John - 12th Alabama VA11
Porter, P.P. - Capt. - Co. H 4th Texas July 14, 1862 VA25
Porter, S.L. - 49th North Carolina Sept. 11, 1864 VA25
Porter, S.P. - Co. E 3rd Tennessee Cavalry Died Aug 1, 1864 (1861?) VA06
Porter, Thos. - Co. A 13th North Carolina June 10, 1862 VA25
Porter, W. - 15th Georgia Oct. 19, 1861 VA25
Porterfield, H.H. - Co. D 16th Georgia July 31, 1861 VA25
Porterfield, J.W. - Co. E 31st South Carolina July 1864 VA25
Portlock, Gustavus W. - 6th Virginia VA04
Posey, J.M. - Co. C 59th Georgia May 7, 1865 VA25
Posey, Robert - Kemper's Battery VA10

Poss, William R. - Pvt. - Co. G 61st Georgia KIA at Gaines Mill - June 27, 1862 VA28
Poston, Henry A. - Pvt. - Co. G 15th South Carolina Died May 12, 1864 VA28
Potter, H.W. - DOW Aug. 18, 1862 age 23 VA19
Potter, John - POW - Federal Soldier NY (NJ?) Regt. Died Oct. 5, 1861 VA19
Potts, H.N. - 11th Alabama VA18
Powe, E.W. - Miss VA20
Powell, A. - Alabama VA20
Powell, D.A. - 60th Louisiana March 2, 1864 VA25
Powell, H. - Co. A 27th North Carolina Jan. 8, 1863 VA25
Powell, J. - Edwards' Battalion March 10, 1865 VA25
Powell, J. - Co. F 56th North Carolina June 18, 1864 VA25
Powell, J.A. - Co. A 20th Georgia Sept. 20, 1864 VA25
Powell, J.M. - Co. E 9th Virginia Aug. 1, 1862 VA25
Powell, J.T. - Co. C 5th North Carolina Aug. 29, 1864 VA25
Powell, J.W. - Co. E 4th North Carolina June 16, 1864 VA25
Powell, W. - Sgt. - Co. D 10th North Carolina Nov. 10, 1864 VA25
Powell, W. - Co. G 49th Georgia July 5, 1862 VA25
Powell, W.P. - Co. F 40th North Carolina April 24, 1865 VA25
Powells, E.S. - Co. E 47th Virginia July 15, 1862 VA25
Powers, __ - Sept. 2, 1862 VA25
Powers, A. - Co. D 13th South Carolina July 1, 1864 VA25
Powers, G. - Co. A 50th Georgia June 5, 1863 VA25
Powers, J. - Co. I 9th Louisiana Jan. 7, 1862 VA25
Powers, J.J.A. - Co. C Phillips Legion (Georgia) VA28
Powers, Jno. - Co. E 15th Ala Died Feb 8, 1862 VA23
Powers, L. - Co. C 42nd Mississippi Sept. 2, 1862 VA25
Powers, N.F. - Maryland Dec. 3, 1861 VA25
Powers, W.M. - 6th Alabama June 3, 1862 VA25
Powers, W.T. - Co. G 5th Virginia July 5, 1862 VA25
Prasby, M.R. - Co. D 6th North Carolina July 18, 1864 VA25
Prater, B. - Co. D 47th Alabama May 11, 1865 VA25

Prathen, A. - Co. E 46th North Carolina Sept. 14, 1864 VA25
Pratler, W. - Co. F 28th Virginia May 18, 1862 VA25
Pratt, Wm. F. - "Killed by powder explosion" Aug. 6, 1862
 age 20 - This appears to have been a civilian working in a gunpowder "laboratory". VA19
Pratter, J.T. - Texas Aug. 5, 1863 VA25
Pray, J.W. - Co. E 44th North Carolina Sept. 3, 1864 VA25
Prescott, __ - 7th South Carolina VA18
Presler, J.L. - Co. I 48th North Carolina Aug. 27, 1864 VA25
Presson, __ - July 1, 1862 VA25
Presson, J.E. - July 5, 1862 VA25
Price, A.D. - Baltimore, Md. Oct. 20, 1862 VA25
Price, B.F. - Co. G 40th Virginia Nov. 11, 1862 VA25
Price, Berryman Z. - VA13
Price, C. - Co. I 1st North Carolina June 7, 1863 VA25
Price, E. - Co. B 23rd Mississippi Aug. 24, 1863 VA25
Price, F. - Co. H 49th Georgia July 1, 1862 VA25
Price, G.W. - Co. K 13th North Carolina July 8, 1862 VA25
Price, J. - Co. H 2nd North Carolina May 21, 1864 VA25
Price, J.B. - Co. A 42nd Mississippi Aug. 16, 1862 VA25
Price, J.D.U. - Co. H 23rd North Carolina June 2, 1863 VA25
Price, J.G. - Co. H 15th Alabama Aug. 11, 1862 VA25
Price, J.R. - Co. B 27th Georgia June 12, 1862 VA25
Price, J.T. - Lt.- Co. H 31st Georgia July 15, 1862 VA25
Price, R. - Co. G 5th Texas June 18, 1862 VA25
Price, S.H. - Co. D 27th North Carolina Jan. 11, 1865 VA25
Price, T. - Co. F 3rd North Carolina VA28
Price, T. - July 15, 1861 VA25
Price, W.L. - Co. B 22nd North Carolina May 21, 1862 VA25
Price, W.N. - 13th Alabama Sept. 7, 1861 VA25
Prichett, R.P. - Co. K 53rd Georgia VA11
Pridd, S. - Co. F 52nd North Carolina March 17, 1865 VA25
Pridemore, E.J. - Co. H 11th Alabama May 28, 1862 VA25
Priest, F. - 10th Georgia Battalion July 28, 1864 VA25
Prince, C. - Co. H 1st South Carolina July 12, 1864 VA25
Prince, Elias - Kentucky VA20

Prince, H. - Co. I 2nd Texas Aug. 21, 1862 VA25
Prince, J.F. - 4th South Carolina VA18
Print, __ 4th North Carolina Aug. 22, 1861 VA25
Prior, S.J. - South Carolina Nov. 10, 1864 VA25
Prisnall, A. - Co. F 46th North Carolina May 4, 1864 VA25
Pritchard, J.M. - Co. D 7th Georgia July 17, 1862 VA25
Pritchard, T.R. - Co. K 55th Virginia Dec. 8, 1863 VA25
Pritchee, __ - Died July 14, 1862 age 35 VA19
Privel, J. - 18th South Carolina Sept. 5, 1862 VA25
Proctor, A.P. - Co. C 66th North Carolina June 12, 1862 VA25
Proctor, Henry G. - 25th South Carolina VA04
Proctor, J.S. - Co. D 48th Georgia July 19, 1862 VA25
Proctor, W.W. - Co. I 45th Georgia July 21, 1864 VA25
Profit, W.C. - Co. G 18th North Carolina VA11
Propes, Thos. - Co. E 16th North Carolina June 1, 1862 VA25
Prophet, J.N. - Co. K 49th Virginia June 13, 1862 VA25
Propst, H.H. - Co. F 62nd Virginia VA11
Propter, H.J. - Co. G 24th Georgia June 16, 1862 VA25
Pross, W.H. - North Carolina June 1, 1862 VA25
Pruitt, H. - Co. B 19th Georgia June 10, 1862 VA25
Pruitt, L. - Co. B 38th Georgia April 26, 1863 VA25
Pruitt, R. - Alabama June 16, 1865 VA25
Publes, J. - 6th Louisiana VA18
Public, V.E. - Co. B 34th North Carolina June 7, 1862 VA25
Pucket, Floyd - Died March 29, 1863 age 26 VA19
Puckett, A. - Co. K 6th Mississippi Sept. 3, 1863 VA25
Puckett, A.W. - Co. H 35th Georgia June 19, 1862 VA25
Puckett, F. - Co. C 21st Georgia Jan. 25, 1863 VA25
Puckett, G.D. - Co. K 49th Virginia June 26, 1862 VA25
Puckett, W.H. - Co. K 49th Virginia June 9, 1862 VA25
Pucketts, G.W. - Co. H 3rd South Carolina July 30, 1862 VA25
Pugh, C.H. Patterson's - Co. May 29, 1862 VA25
Pugh, J.H. - 2nd Virginia June 26, 1864 VA25
Pugh, J.W. - Artillery May 31, 1862 VA25

Pugh, James M. - Sgt. - see Pugh, John M. VA28
Pugh, John M. - Corp. - Co. D 50th Virginia KIA - Spotsylvania Court House - May 12, 1864 Headstone reads: "Sgt. James M. Pugh" VA28
Pullen, W.B. - Capt. Gregory's - Co. June 1, 1862 VA25
Puller, A. - 2nd Virginia Infantry VA06
Pulliam, L.B.- see Pulliam, Lark D. VA28
Pulliam, Lark D. - Pvt. - Co. D 13th Georgia Died May 12, 1864 Headstone reads "L.B. Pulliam" VA28
Pumphery, I.- 26th Alabama April 29, 1862 VA25
Punks, J.G. - 45th Georgia May 26, 1864 VA25
Punley, S.M. - Co. G 38th North Carolina March 29, 1865 VA25
Purcell, Timothy - KIA July 13, 1862 age 19 VA19
Purdell, J.H. - Co. I 45th North Carolina Sept. 2, 1864 VA25
Purdon, A. - 30th Georgia Dec. 30, 1862 VA25
Purvis, Frank S. - Pvt. - Co. E 5th Louisiana Died May 12, 1864 VA28
Pusa, W.M. - Co. A 8th Mississippi Jan. 1, 1865 VA25
Pyfer, W.H. - Maryland Nov. 8, 1863 age 22 VA25
Pyson, R.W. - Co. I 5th Virginia 1862 VA25
Quayon, Lewis - POW - Federal Soldier Died June 10, 1862 VA19
Quesenbury, J. - Co. I 50th Virginia April13, 1865 VA25
Quick, B. - Co. C 8th South Carolina June 9, 1864 VA25
Quillin, Spencer - Virginia VA20
Quinn, D. - Co. B 22nd North Carolina July 1, 1862 VA25
R __, D.J. - Co. F 48th Georgia Jan. 3, 1863 VA25
R __, J.B. - 54th Georgia Jan. 8, 1863 VA25
Rackley, J.H. - Co B - Palmetto Sharpshooters (South Carolina) Died June 1, 1863 VA03
Raddin, J.F. - Co. G 35th North Carolina June 6, 1864 VA25
Ragen, T.C. - 4th Louisiana Battalion Oct. 15, 1864 VA25
Ragin, W. - Co. D 1st North Carolina May 19, 1864 VA25
Ragland, R.W. - Co. B 19th Georgia June 14, 1863 VA25
Raglon, W.R. - 11th Mississippi VA18

Railburn, __ - 12th South Carolina July 18, 1862 VA25
Raines, A.N. - Co. E 11th North Carolina April 27, 1863 VA25
Raines, R.N. - Co. G 60th Virginia Nov. 8, 1862 VA25
Rainey, T. - Orr's rifles (South Carolina) July 24, 1863 VA25
Rains, J.W. - 8th Georgia VA18
Rainwater, A. - Co. E 11th Alabama May 31, 1864 VA25
Rainwater, M.A. - Co. A 11th Alabama Aug. 14, 1862 VA25
Rainwater, W. - Co. E 11th Alabama Aug. 15, 1862 VA25
Raisedale, A.K. - Co. G 3rd South Carolina Nov. 19, 1862 VA25
Raivus, J.P. - Co. K 13th North Carolina June 22, 1864 VA25
Rakes, S.J. - Virginia VA20
Ralton, D.L. - Co. H 15th Alabama Died Nov 15, 1862 VA23
Ramble, W. - Co. A 44th Georgia Sept. 29, 1862 VA25
Ramel, J. - Co. D 4th Alabama Aug. 27, 1862 VA25
Ramsaur, W.G. - Co. I 11th North Carolina Oct. 28, 1863 VA25
Ramsey, D.R. - Pvt. (Corp.) - Virginia June 2, 1864 Cemetery roster lists both ranks. VA22
Ramsey, G. - 54th North Carolina VA11
Ramsey, J. - Co. F 2nd South Carolina July 24, 1864 VA25
Ramsey, James A. - Pvt. - Co. L 3rd Alabama Died May 12, 1864 VA28
Ramsey, T.A. - Pvt. - Virginia March 28, 1865 VA22
Randolph, A. - Co. A 14th South Carolina VA11
Randolph, Bev. - VA06
Randolph, Beverly - age 17 KIA - Greenwood Depot - March 2, 1865 VA06
Randolph, G.W. - Co. D 11th Virginia Aug. 21, 1864 VA25
Randolph, I.P. - Co. C 14th North Carolina April 24, 1863 VA25
Randolph, J. Tucker - Lt. -Died June 7, 1864 age 21 VA19
Randolph, John - 15th Georgia Feb. 20, 1862 VA25
Randolph, R. - Co. A 7th South Carolina Battalion June 5, 1863 VA25

Randolph, Robrt Carter - Capt. - Co. C 2nd Virginia KIA - Cedar Creek (Belle Grove), Virginia- Oct. 19, 1864 age 25 VA06

Randolph, T.H.B. - veteran Died 1900

Randolph, William Wellford - Colonel - 2nd Virginia - KIA - Wilderness - May 5, 1864 VA06

Ranel, R. - Co. H 34th North Carolina June 18, 1864 VA25

Rangden, J.T. - Co. C 10th Georgia May 10, 1863 VA25

Rankin, D.C. - Co. E 11th South Carolina July 21, 1862 VA25

Raper, John - Co. I 2nd North Carolina VA11

Rapidan, Daniel - Pvt. - Co. C 32nd North Carolina Died May 9, 1865 VA26

Rasbury, Newton - Alabama VA20

Rash, James - 15th Alabama VA18

Rasinger, D. - Co. D 15th South Carolina April 24, 1863 VA25

Rason, T. - Co. I 17th Georgia May 15, 1862 VA25

Ratcliff, Jno. R. - Co. D 17th Virginia InfantryVA10

Ratcliffe, W.T. - Co. H 14th North Carolina June 20, 1864 VA25

Ratman, W. - Carter's Artillery (Virginia) June 2, 1863 VA25

Ratteral, H. - Co. B 5th South Carolina Aug. 22, 1864 VA25

Ravel, J. - Co. C 59th Georgia Oct. 24, 1864 VA25

Ravil, E. - Co. C 15th South Carolina Sept. 12, 1862 VA25

Ravin, J.J. - Co. b 12th South Carolina July 10, 1862 VA25

Rawhn, D.O. - 8th Louisiana Artillery VA11

Rawkin, __ - 25th Georgia June 16, 1862 VA25

Rawle, J.A. - North Carolina March 3, 1865 VA25

Rawles, T.F. - Lt.- Co. G 23rd Georgia July 20, 1863 VA25

Rawling, D.H. - 14th Texas 1862 VA25

Rawlings, S.C. - 47th Louisiana Sept. 16, 1862 VA25

Rawner, L. - Co. K 14th Louisiana Aug. 10, 1862 VA25

Ray, A.G. - Co. H 60th Georgia June 28, 1863 VA25

Ray, D. - Pvt. - Co. E 57th Virginia Died June 11, 1865 VA26

Ray, J.B. - 15th Alabama VA18

Ray, J.C. - Co. B 5th Alabama Aug. 6, 1862 VA25

Ray, J.D. - Alabama VA20
Ray, J.H. - Pvt. - Georgia Aug. 21, 1864 VA22
Ray, Jno. H.- VA20
Ray, M. - Co. C 35th North Carolina July 20, 1862 VA25
Ray, M.J. - Co. H 25th South Carolina July 19, 1862 VA25
Ray, O.P. - Co. H 61st Georgia June 22, 1863 VA25
Ray, P.F. - "S.S." (Virginia) Sept. 30, 1861 VA25
Ray, R. - Co. G 19th Mississippi Jan. 29, 1863 VA25
Ray, S.B. - Georgia VA20
Rayburn, W. - 9th Georgia Oct. 19, 1861 VA25
Raylor, B.W. - Co. B 15th North Carolina July 28, 1864 VA25
Rayman, D. - Co. B 46th North Carolina May 18, 1864 VA25
Raysdale, E.W. - Co. E 38th Virginia Sept. 2, 1861 VA25
Raysdale, T. - Co. C 23rd North Carolina June 10, 1862 VA25
Rdcliffe, J. - 24th Virginia VA18
Read, J.F. - 30th Georgia VA18
Read, J.H. - VA12
Readfree, John - Co. C 14th North Carolina June 16, 1862 VA25
Reaney, H.B. - 2nd Virginia Artillery April 10, 1862 VA25
Reason, Jas. - Died July 28, 1862 age 21 VA19
Reason, R.H. - Co. G 13th North Carolina Jan. 24, 1865 VA25
Rebel, __ - June 15, 1865 VA25
Rector, W.L. - 11th Virginia Infantry - KIA - Battle of Williamsburg - May 5, 1862 VA02
Redden, J. - 42nd Virginia Vols. VA18
Redding, J.O. - Co. H 2nd Mississippi July 16, 1862 VA25
Redding, S.F. - Co. F 15th North Carolina June 10, 1863 VA25
Redding, S.F. - Co. F 15th North Carolina June 10, 1863 VA25
Redding, W. - Pvt. - Co. H 56th North Carolina Died June 14, 1865 VA26
Redman, E. - Co. D 20th South Carolina Sept. 9, 1864 VA25
Redman, J. - 2nd Virginia Battalion May 9, 1865 VA25
Redmon, Jacob W. - 25th South Carolina VA04

Redwood, John M. - DOW Sept. 26, 1862 age 21 VA19
Redwood, John Tyler - DOW July 9, 1862 age 21 VA19
Ree, Thomas - Co. E 13th Alabama May 28, 1864 VA25
Reed, A.J. - Corp. - Co. H 7th Georgia Aug. 12, 1864 VA25
Reed, C.E.B. - Virginia VA20
Reed, C.W. - Sgt. -8th Virginia Infantry VA10
Reed, E.M. - Co. C 7th Georgia May 13, 1862 VA25
Reed, G.H. - Co. G 48th Alabama July 25, 1862 VA25
Reed, G.W. - 1st South Carolina Rifles VA24
Reed, H.C. - Co. F 3rd Alabama Aug. 9, 1864 VA25
Reed, J. - Co. K 27th North Carolina Jan. 17, 1865 VA25
Reed, J.A. - Co. C 17th North Carolina July 27, 1864 VA25
Reed, J.W. - Pvt.- Co. G 13th Georgia . Died May 27, 1865 VA26
Reed, M.H. - Co. H 22nd North Carolina May 6, 1862 VA25
Reed, S.C. - Co. B 1st North Carolina May 13, 1865 VA25
Reed, W.N. - Co. F 49th North Carolina July 19, 1862 VA25
Reese, B.H. - Co. G 11th Alabama Aug. 5, 1862 VA25
Reese, B.R. - Co. C 22nd South Carolina July 17, 1863 VA25
Reese, D.L. - Co. K 56th North Carolina Oct. 13, 1864 VA25
Reese, H. - Co. H 3rd Alabama July 5, 1862 VA25
Reese, Jno. - (Rev.) Chaplin - Virginia VA23
Reese, T.A. - 21st North Carolina VA18
Reese, W.R. - 63rd North Carolina Cavalry Nov. 20, 1864 VA25
Reese, W.T. - Georgia Sept. 11, 1862 VA25
Reeves, __ - Co. F 16th North Carolina June 27, 1862 VA25
Reeves, __ - Lt.- 3rd Alabama July 20, 1862 VA25
Reeves, H.H. - Co. G 31st Georgia VA11
Reeves, J. - Co. B 20th Georgia Dec. 17, 1861 VA25
Reeves, S.- 7th Georgia VA18
Reeves, T.J.- South Carolina VA20
Register, Benjamin T. - Pvt. - 7th North Carolina Infantry DOW May 27, 1862 VA09
Register, William - Pvt. - Co. H 14th Georgia Died May 12, 1864 VA28

Reid, G.W. - Pvt. - South Carolina Oct, 27, 1864 VA22
Reid, O. - Co. K 19th Georgia July 8, 1862 VA25
Reid, R.J. - Lt. and Adjutant - 2nd Florida May 9, 1864 VA25
Reid, Thomas - 8th Virginia Infantry VA10
Reison, Wm. - 11th North Carolina VA23
Renfree, J.H. - 11th Alabama Aug. 31, 1861 VA25
Reordon, J. - 2nd Virginia Infantry VA06
Resby, W.O. - Co. I 30th North Carolina May 22, 1864 VA25
Resenver, __ - Co. D 6th Alabama June 20, 1862 VA25
Rets, W.T. - Georgia - Sept. 11, 1862 VA25
Revel, W.D. - Co. H 3rd Virginia March 6, 1863 VA25
Rever, __ - Co. H 55th Virginia Sept. 7, 1862 VA25
Revere, Elias Henry - Corp. - Woolfolk's Battery (Virginia) (Ashland Light Artillery) KIA - Spotsylvania Court House - May 12, 1864 VA28
Reynolds, D.S. - Co. K 15th Georgia April 23, 1862 VA25
Reynolds, D.T. - 2nd Florida June 2, 1862 VA25
Reynolds, F. - Artillery May 14, 1862 VA25
Reynolds, H. - Co. F 27th Georgia May 31, 1864 VA25
Reynolds, J. - Co. I 45th Georgia May 13, 1862 VA25
Reynolds, J. - Texas Aug. 27, 1861 VA25
Reynolds, J. - Co. F 31st Georgia April 24, 1863 VA25
Reynolds, J. W. - Hampton's Legion (Georgia) Aug. 20, 1862 VA25
Reynolds, J.D. - Pvt.- Co. B 38th Virginia Died June 15, 1865 VA26
Reynolds, J.H. - Co. C 22nd South Carolina July 19, 1863 VA25
Reynolds, J.M. - Asst. Surgeon. - South Carolina June 22, 1862 VA25
Reynolds, J.S. - Pvt. - Co. C 46th Virginia Died May 10, 1865 VA26
Reynolds, J.T. - Co. G 14th North Carolina Nov. 17, 1863 VA25
Reynolds, R. - Co. E 23rd South Carolina July 8, 1864 VA25
Reynolds, R.N. - Co. K 53rd Georgia Jan. 23, 1865 VA25

Reynolds, W.H. - 4th Alabama June 26, 1862 VA25
Reynolds, W.P. - 2nd Georgia Sept. 31, 1861 VA25
Reynolds, W.T. - Co. A 28th Georgia May 14, 1862 VA25
Rhew, J.H. - Co. H 56th North Carolina May 7, 1865 VA25
Rhodes, A. - Co. H 25th North Carolina June 28, 1863 VA25
Rhodes, A.J. - Co. G 66th North Carolina July 13, 1863 VA25
Rhodes, A.J. - Co. D 18th Georgia Oct. 12, 1864 VA25
Rhodes, G.J. - Co. D 7th Mississippi Aug. 10, 1862 VA25
Rhodes, G.T. - Co. H 17th Mississippi Aug. 10, 1862 VA25
Rhodes, Henry C. - Mosby's Virginia Cavalry shot while POW - Sept 23, 1864 VA23
Rhodes, J.J.- 7th South Carolina VA18
Rhodes, J.R. - Co. H 66th North Carolina July 16, 1864 VA25
Rhodes, R.S. - Pvt. - Co. D 45th North Carolina Died May 13, 1865 VA26
Rice, Benjamin - Co. I 40th Alabama VA11
Rice, J.D. - Pvt. - Co. C 6th North Carolina Died June 11, 1865 VA26
Rice, J.P. - Co. C 40th Virginia Sept. 29, 1862 VA25
Rice, Jacob - VA15
Rice, John - Co. E 1st Georgia Died Jan 2, 1862 VA23
Rice, M. - Hampton's Legion (Georgia) Nov. 2, 1864 VA25
Rice, R.E. (MD) - medical doctor VA12
Rice, S. - Assistant Surgeon 38th Georgia Infantry VA08
Rice, S.S. - Virginia VA07
Rich, J. - Co. B 54th North Carolina June 27, 1863 VA25
Richards, C.H. - 2nd Virginia Infantry VA06
Richards, Stephen - Virginia VA20
Richards, William H. - Corp. - Co. G 12th North Carolina VA28
Richardson, A. - Texas Aug. 10, 1861 VA25
Richardson, A.K. - Pvt.- Co. B 18th Georgia Died June 30, 1865 VA26
Richardson, A.N. - Co. E 44th North Carolina June 29, 1864 VA25
Richardson, C. - Co. D 58th Virginia June 6, 1863 VA25

Richardson, G. - Co. E 4th Virginia VA11
Richardson, H.C. - Co. H 7th Louisiana June 18, 1864 VA25
Richardson, J.D. - Co. D 45th North Carolina June 8, 1863 VA25
Richardson, J.J. - Co. A 3rd North Carolina June 1, 1863 VA25
Richardson, J.J. - Co. K 47th Virginia May 30, 1862 VA25
Richardson, J.W. - Co. D 17th Virginia Infantry VA10
Richardson, J.W. - Lt.- Co. B 26th North Carolina Oct. 5, 1864 VA25
Richardson, J.W. - Co. H 15th South Carolina July 6, 1864 VA25
Richardson, N. - Co. D 26th North Carolina 1864 VA25
Richardson, W.A. - Co. D 1st South Carolina Oct. 26, 1862 VA25
Richardson, W.R. - 8th Louisiana VA18
Richardson, W.R. - Co. F 34th North Carolina Nov. 25, 1864 VA25
Richburg, P.S. - 23rd South Carolina VA18
Richel, G. - 11th North Carolina Died 1861 VA23
Richie, James - Co. F 9th Virginia Headstone reads "Ritchie" VA28
Rick, G.W. - Co. F 1st South Carolina Aug. 1, 1862 VA25
Rickburg, J.W. - Co. I 25th South Carolina May 23, 1864 VA25
Rickman, M.L. - Co. I 16th North Carolina July 24, 1862 VA25
Ricks, Nero - Co. I 12th North Carolina June 15, 1862 VA25
Ricks, T.L. - Co. D 10th Georgia July 19, 1864 VA25
Ricks, W.R. - Co. G 66th North Carolina July 28, 1864 VA25
Ricks, William Edward - Pvt. - Co. K 45th North Carolina born March 14, 1830 Died May 11 (12), 1864 VA28
Ricks, William J. - Pvt. - Co. C 35th Georgia MW May 12, 1864 (Died May 20, 1864) VA28
Ridder, W.R. - Co. A 24th North Carolina July 3, 1863 VA25
Riddick, J.C. - Co. C 2nd North Carolina May 23, 1864 VA25

Riddick, T.F. - Co. D 20th Georgia Batt. June 19, 1864 VA25
Riddle, J.F. - Co. I 26th Mississippi Dec. 1, 1864 VA25
Riddle, Melmouth - Pvt. - Co. E 3rd South Carolina Battalion
    Died May 8, 1864 Headstone reads 14th South VA28
Riddlebury, F. - Co. A 60th Virginia Sept. 9, 1862 VA25
Rideway, J.B. - Co. H 13th Alabama June 11, 1862 VA25
Ridge, D. - Co. G 14th South Carolina July 11, 863 VA25
Ridley, John - Co. G 14th Georgia VA11
Rierson, J.W. - Major - North Carolina March 26, 1865 VA22
Rife, Joseph- VA15
Rigan, H.J. - Co. D 9th South Carolina Nov. 20, 1862 VA25
Rigell, A.L. - Co. A __th Georgia VA28
Rigell, Jason - Pvt. - Co. C 31st Georgia Died May 18, 1864
    VA28
Riggle, G. - VA06
Riggs, W. - Co. G 50th Georgia Sept. 9, 1863 VA25
Right, A. - Co. G 11th Alabama May 29, 1862 VA25
Right, H. - Co. H 12th Alabama July 18, 1862 VA25
Riley, C.W. - Co. A 5th South Carolina Feb. 27, 1863 VA25
Riley, Chas. - VA06
Riley, E.O. - Lt.- 6th Louisiana Infantry - Taylor's Brigade
    VA08
Riley, G. - Co. G 15th Alabama Jan. 2, 1863 VA25
Riley, John J. - Co. C 5th Alabama VA11
Riley, R. - Georgia Nov. 17, 1862 VA25
Rinker, __ - Virginia Infantry - "body removed" VA08
Rinker, W. - Co. D 49th Virginia April 24, 1865 VA25
Ripts, James - Louisiana Nov. 16, 1862 VA25
Rislett, J. - Co. D 10th Louisiana July 7, 1862 VA25
Ritchens, W.E. - 7th South Carolina Sept. 9, 1862 VA25
Ritcher, W.E. - South Carolina Sept. 9, 1862 VA25
Ritchie, James - see Richie, James VA28
Ritchie, T.B. - Co. E 4th Alabama Aug. 11, 1862 VA25
Ritter, J. - 2nd Virginia Infantry VA06
Ritter, J.Q. - Co. B 26th Alabama Sept. 1862 VA25
Rival, E. - Co. C 15th South Carolina Sept. 12, 1862 VA25

River, __ - Co. H 55th Virginia Sept. 7, 1862 VA25
Rivers, James J. - Corp. - Co. I 10th Georgia Accidentally killed May 17, 1864 VA28
Rives, __ - 1862 VA25
Rives, H. - Co. I 35th North Carolina Nov. 23, 1864 VA25
Rives, J. - Co. K 23rd Georgia Aug. 21, 1864 VA25
Rives, R.M. - Co. K 34th North Carolina Sept. 30, 1862 VA25
Rives, W. - Co. G 22nd Georgia Sept. 4, 1864 VA25
Rives, W. - Co. I 66th North Carolina Aug. 9, 1864 VA25
Rives, W.A. - Co. F 44th North Carolina Aug. 7, 1864 VA25
Roane, S.A. - Jan. 12, 1863 VA25
Roanes, S. - July 5, 1861 VA25
Robb, C.W. - Co. E 3rd South Carolina Aug. 9, 1864 VA25
Roberson, A.F. - Co. F 52nd North Carolina Dec. 4, 1864 VA25
Roberson, D. - Virginia Sept. 7, 1863 VA25
Roberson, E.H. - see Robinson, E.H. VA28
Roberson, G. North Carolina June 14, 1864 VA25
Roberson, J. - Co. A 5th South Carolina Aug. 1, 1862 VA25
Roberson, J.A. - Asst. Surgeon. - Virginia Cavalry Aug. 4, 1864 VA25
Roberson, J.A. - Co. H 6th North Carolina June 5, 1865 VA25
Roberson, J.W. - Co. G 18th South Carolina Nov. 27, 1864 VA25
Roberson, T.J. - Palmetto Sharp hooters (South Carolina) Aug. 19, 1864 VA25
Roberson, T.W. - Co. B 37th North Carolina June 16, 1862 VA25
Roberts, Absalom M. - Pvt. - Co. F 61st Georgia Died May 17, 1864 VA28
Roberts, Augustus - Co. F 22nd Georgia VA28
Roberts, B. - Co. B 49th Virginia May 31, 1864 VA25
Roberts, C.W. - Co. K 14th North Carolina June 23, 1862 VA25
Roberts, D. - Co. A 7th Georgia May 31, 1864 VA25
Roberts, G. - Co. B 6th North Carolina Infantry VA08

Roberts, H. - Co. D 26th North Carolina Sept. 17, 1864 VA25
Roberts, H.F. - Co. H 54th North Carolina VA11
Roberts, J. - 1st North Carolina Cavalry June 25, 1864 VA25
Roberts, J. - Co. I 14th Georgia June 2, 1862 VA25
Roberts, J. - Co. K 26th Georgia July 31, 1862 VA25
Roberts, J.C. - June 10, 1862 VA25
Roberts, J.T. - Co. F 23rd North Carolina Aug. 23, 1862 VA25
Roberts, James J. - Pvt. - Co. D 11th Alabama VA28
Roberts, P. - Co. G 15th North Carolina June 8, 1863 VA25
Roberts, R.J. - Co. E 13th Alabama Sept. 17, 1861 VA25
Roberts, S.B. - Co. G 38th North Carolina Feb. 19, 1862 VA25
Roberts, T.M. - Co. A 5th Alabama July 6, 1862 VA25
Roberts, Thomas J. - Co. I 12th Georgia headstone reads "3rd Georgia Artillery" . VA28
Roberts, W. - Co. B 14th North Carolina May 24, 1862 VA25
Roberts, W.D. - Co. D 58th Virginia March 25, 1865 VA25
Roberts, W.P. - Co. A 20th Georgia June 3, 1862 VA25
Roberts, W.P. - Co. A 40th North Carolina Nov. 19, 1862 VA25
Roberts, W.T. - Co. B 8th Louisiana June 1, 1862 VA25
Roberts, W.T. - Co. G 10th Alabama May 23, 1862 VA25
Robertson, __ - Co. F 16th Virginia July 19, 1862 VA25
Robertson, D.A. - Sgt. - Co. B 13th Virginia May 17, 1864 VA25
Robertson, F. - North Carolina Artillery July 14, 1864 VA25
Robertson, J. - Co. H 22nd South Carolina Nov. 20, 1864 VA25
Robertson, J.A. - Pvt. - North Carolina May 13, 1865 VA22
Robertson, J.C. - Co. H 23rd North Carolina June 4, 1862 VA25
Robertson, J.M. - Lt.- Co. C 27th Georgia VA11
Robertson, James - Corp. - Co. D 45th North Carolina Died May 19, 1864 VA28
Robertson, L.W. - Pvt.- Co. A 20th Virginia Bat. Died May 29, 1865 VA26

Robertson, P.M. - Co. K 48th Alabama VA11
Robertson, S.T. - June 5, 1862 VA25
Robertson, W. - Co. E 7th Georgia Died Feb 19, 1862 VA23
Robertson, W.H. - Co. F 7th Georgia July 3, 1864 VA25
Robertson, W.H.R. - Co. C 13th (North Carolina ?) Died Jan 22, 1862 VA23
Robertson, W.N. - Pvt. - Alabama March 29, 1865 VA22
Robertson, W.T. - Co. F 53rd Georgia May 11, 1863 VA25
Robertson, W.T. - Co. H 3rd Louisiana June 4, 1862 VA25
Robertson, William - Pvt. - Co. D 19th Mississippi M W May 12, 1864 Died May 13, 1864 VA28
Robey, James - Co. E 6th Virginia VA10
Robin, Jackson - Co. E 13th South Carolina VA11
Robinett, A. - Co. G 37th North Carolina June 25, 1862 VA25
Robinett, J.F. - Co. G 37th North Carolina Sept. 9, 1862 VA25
Robins, D.S. - Co. A 37th Virginia Aug. 29, 1862 VA25
Robins, H. - Co. B 37th North Carolina Aug. 23, 1862 VA25
Robins, J. - Co. B 34th North Carolina Dec. 7, 1863 VA25
Robins, M. - Co. B 14th North Carolina May 22, 1862 VA25
Robins, S.F. - Co. E 13th South Carolina July 8, 1862 VA25
Robins, W. - Co. K 5th South Carolina Aug. 24, 1862 VA25
Robinson, A. - 15th Georgia Died Jan 26, 1863 VA17
Robinson, A.J. - Jeff. Davis' Guards Oct. 1, 1861 VA25
Robinson, B. - Co. H 27th North Carolina May 1, 1864 VA25
Robinson, C.A. - Co. B 19th Mississippi Oct. 25, 1862 VA25
Robinson, C.L. - Co. H 16th North Carolina May 29, 1863 VA25
Robinson, E.H. - Pvt. - Co. G 2nd South Carolina Died May 26, 1864 MW Spotsylvania C. H. Last name also spelled "Roberson" VA28
Robinson, J.R. - 46th North Carolina Nov. 12, 1864 VA25
Robinson, J.T. - Co. D 26th Georgia July 24, 1862 VA25
Robinson, John - 5th Mississippi VA18
Robinson, John - May 9, 1862 VA25
Robinson, John - Co. G 28th Georgia Feb. 19, 1862 VA25

Robinson, L. - Co. A 13th North Carolina May 13, 1862 VA25
Robinson, R. - Co. G 44th Alabama Feb. 22, 1863 VA25
Robinson, W.H. - Co. C 14th South Carolina May 3, 1864 VA25
Robinson, W.J. - Co. I 17th South Carolina Aug. 6, 1864 VA25
Robinson, W.R. - Co. C 28th North Carolina Sept. 4, 1862 VA25
Robuck, S.L. - Co. H 17th North Carolina July 30, 1864 VA25
Robuck, W. - Co. K 42nd Mississippi Aug. 26, 1862 VA25
Robuck, William P. - Pvt. - Co. K 3rd South Carolina DOW May 17, 1864 (MW - May 9, 1864) VA28
Rochan, __ - April 1862 VA25
Roche, B.F. - 30th Virginia Oct. 11, 1863 VA25
Rochelle, J.C. - Co. B 15th Georgia June 4, 1862 VA25
Rockley, W. - Co. A 20th South Carolina June 18, 1864 VA25
Rodding, J.C. - Co. H 44th Georgia July 20, 1862 VA25
Rodes, R. - Co. G 2nd North Carolina Aug. 2, 1862 VA25
Rodgers, H. - Co. A 2nd North Carolina July 8, 1862 VA25
Rodgers, H.T. - Co. H 61st North Carolina Oct. 13, 1864 VA25
Rodgers, I.W. - Co. K 28th North Carolina June 28, 1863 VA25
Rodgers, J.J. - Co. F 53rd Georgia Jan. 22, 1863 VA25
Rodgers, J.L. - 57th Virginia Oct. 21, 1861 VA25
Rodgers, J.N. - 7th South Carolina VA18
Rodgers, James - Co. B 26th North Carolina Oct. 28, 1863 VA25
Rodgers, John - Co. B 61st Alabama VA11
Rodgers, Mike - 6th South Carolina VA18
Rodgers, T.P. - Co. I 18th Georgia June 2, 1862 VA25
Rodgers, W. - Virginia March 5, 1864 VA25
Rodgers, W.D. - Co. C 1st South Carolina July 4, 1862 VA25
Rodgers, W.H. - Co. F 5th Virginia Dec. 26, 1862 VA25
Rogan, R. - Capt. - Co. D 10th Alabama May 25, 1864 VA25

Rogers, C. - Gray's Batt. (North Carolina) Oct. 29, 1864 VA25
Rogers, David - 1st South Carolina VA04
Rogers, I.S. - Sgt. - Co. F 14th South Carolina Aug. 24, 1864 VA25
Rogers, J.A. - Co. F 1st South Carolina Aug. 10, 1862 VA25
Rogers, J.C. - Co. D 7th North Carolina VA11
Rogers, J.L. - Georgia July 17, 1863 VA25
Rogers, R.C. - Co. D 27th North Carolina Nov. 2, 1864 VA25
Rogerson, R.S. - Co. H 61st North Carolina Aug. 24, 1864 VA25
Rogerson, W.R. - Co. E 17th North Carolina Aug. 10, 1864 VA25
Rogue, A.J. - McIntosh Batt. (North Carolina) May 30, 1863 VA25
Rogus, J. - 28th North Carolina June 2, 1863 VA25
Roina, __ - Oct. 5, 1864 VA25
Roland, J.W. - 16th North Carolina July 6, 1862 VA25
Roland, R. - Co. B 50th Georgia June 20, 1863 VA25
Roland, W. - Co. D 23rd Georgia June 30, 1862 VA25
Roland, W.N. - Co. B 50th Georgia May 27, 1863 VA25
Roles, L.S. - Co. E 47th North Carolina April 26, 1864 VA25
Rolison, John - Co. K 22nd Virginia VA11
Rollin, J.D. - Co. B 28th North Carolina Oct. 27, 1865 VA25
Rolly, D.M. - Co. E 13th North Carolina June 16, 1862 VA25
Ronage, W.R. - Co. H 14th North Carolina July 19, 1863 VA25
Roods, T.G. - Died Oct. 22, 1862 VA19
Roof, Daniel - 10th Virginia VA18
Rooks, Zachariah - 2nd Lt.- Co. B 62nd Georgia Died Dec. 31, 1862 VA03
Roper, D. - "Rifles" (South Carolina) Oct. 16, 1864 VA25
Roquemore, Benj. W. - Lt.- Alabama March 29, 1865 VA22
Rose, D.A. - Corp. - Co. K 47th North Carolina June 27, 1863 VA25
Rose, Jesse -VA20

Rose, S. - 4th Virginia June 14, 1862 VA25
Rose, S.C. - Co. C 12th South Carolina June 10, 1862 VA25
Rosenberg, J. - Georgia VA17
Rosenberger, George W. - VA12
Rosenberger, Harvey - VA15
Rosenbrew, T.J. - Co. F 1st Tennessee Feb. 5, 1864 VA25
Ross, J.B. - 28th Virginia VA18
Ross, J.G. - Lt.- Co. I 9th Louisiana May 9, 1864 VA25
Ross, J.J. - Co. A Sumpter Artillery (South Carolina) May 6, 1862 VA25
Ross, W.D. - Co. H 61st Georgia Aug. 9, 1862 VA25
Rossell, Tolmond D. - 17th Mississippi VA18
Rosser, J. - Sgt. - Co. E 64th Georgia Sept. 5, 1864 VA25
Rossil, Euphrates - 17th Mississippi VA18
Rousey, W. - Pvt.- Co. H 38th Georgia Died June 18, 1865 VA26
Rousley, William - Pvt. - Co. E 4th North Carolina Died June 10, 1865 VA26
Routh, Alexander - Lt.- Co. K 46th North Carolina VA28
Row, D.M. - Co. A 11th Georgia Sept. 6, 1864 VA25
Rowan, S. C. - Co. D 25th North Carolina Aug. 19, 1864 VA25
Rowe, C. - Sgt. - Co. B 9th Virginia Cavalry Aug. 27, 1864 VA25
Rowe, I. - Co. I 37th North Carolina Aug. 31, 1864 VA25
Rowe, M. - Lloyd's Batt. July 3, 1863 VA25
Rowe, R. - Co. E 22nd Georgia Oct. 18, 1864 VA25
Rowe, R.A. - Oct. 21, 1861 VA25
Rowell, __ - Co. K 12th Alabama June 2, 1862 VA25
Rowell, H.D. - Co. H 48th Georgia June 18, 1864 VA25
Rowell, W. - Alabama Aug. 11, 1862 VA25
Rowers, J.R. - Co. C 2nd North Carolina March 5, 1864 VA25
Rowland, D.H. - 14th Tennessee June 30, 1862 VA25
Rowland, W.D. - Co. K 14th Georgia March 22, 1865 VA25
Rowler, J.M. - Louisiana Artillery Nov. 30, 1862 VA25
Roy, J.H. - Co. E 47th North Carolina Aug. 27, 1864 VA25

Roy, M. - Co. C 35th North Carolina July 20, 1862 VA25
Roy, T. - Co. A 5th Tennessee Sept. 30, 1864 VA25
Royal, Thos. T. - VA04
Royall, J.R. - Co. D 18th Georgia Sep. 20, 1861 VA25
Royalston, L.R. - Co. I 5th South Carolina June 18, 1864 VA25
Royster, J. - May 14, 1862 VA25
Royster, J.W. - Co. G 18th Mississippi May 13, 1863 VA25
Royster, W.G. - Co. E 36th North Carolina Dec. 1864 VA25
Royston, A.B. - Corp. - Co. H 47th North Carolina June 17, 1864 VA25
Ruck, W.J. - Co. A 48th Alabama Dec. 26, 1862 VA25
Rucket, H.M. - Co. A 23rd North Carolina May 23, 1863 VA25
Ruckman, J.W. - 19th Virginia Cavalry Oct. 17, 1864 VA25
Rudd, A. - Co. I 9th Virginia June 19, 1862 VA25
Rudd, L. - North Carolina March 1, 1862 VA25
Rudisell, R.D. - Co. G 57th North Carolina July 15, 1863 VA25
Rudisil, Jacob - Pvt. - Co. B 54th North Carolina Died May 17, 1865 VA26
Rudsell, J.J. - Co. E 37th Georgia June 6, 1862 VA25
Ruduck, J. - Co. I 6th Louisiana Nov. 20, 1862 VA25
Ruff, J.J. - Co. C 1st North Carolina June 15, 1864 VA25
Ruffin, E.T. - North Carolina May 28, 1864 VA25
Ruffner, H. - Co. C 7th Virginia Died Jan. 29, 1862 VA23
Rumpla, J.M. - Co. C 23rd North Carolina June 15, 1864 VA25
Rumsey, H.M. - Co. C 16th Georgia Feb. 25, 1865 VA25
Ruppe, J.W. - Hampton's Legion (Georgia) Nov. 26, 1864 VA25
Rush, W. - Tiger Rangers Dec. 18, 1861 VA25
Rushen, J.J. - Co. F 26th South Carolina Nov. 13, 1864 VA25
Rushing, J.C. - Co. I 48th North Carolina April 23, 1864 VA25
Rushing, W. - Co. F 26th South Carolina Sept. 22, 1864 VA25

Russel, J.A. - Sgt. - Co. A 60th North Carolina April 21, 1865 VA25
Russel, J.J. - Co. K 7th North Carolina Jan. 11, 1863 VA25
Russel, J.N. - Co. K 8th South Carolina Aug. 30, 1862 VA25
Russell, A.E. - VA20
Russell, B. - Clark Cavalry VA06
Russell, C. - Sgt. - South Carolina - 1864 VA22
Russell, James P. - Sgt. - Co. I 20th Georgia Died May 12, 1864 VA28
Rutherford, A. - Co. K 34th North Carolina April 24, 1863 VA25
Rutherford, B.H. - Co. E 23rd Georgia Sept. 11, 1864 VA25
Rutherford, William - Pvt. - Co. E 49th Virginia KIA Fredericksburg - Dec. 13, 1862 VA28
Rutledge, D.J. - Co. R 21st North Carolina Died Jan 19, 1862 VA23
Rutledge, I.H. - Co. C 60th Georgia June 18, 1864 VA25
Rutler, E.M. - VA06
Ryals, J.J. - Co. D 61st Georgia VA11
Ryan, C.W. - Co. B 14th Virginia Feb. 27, 1863 VA25
Ryan, John - Co. K 21st North Carolina March 24, 1863 VA25
Ryane, W.W. - DOW June 5, 1863 age 21 VA19
S __, F. - Georgia Feb. 3, 1863 VA25
S __, M. - July 7, 1862 VA25
Saal, Calvin - 3rd Georgia Bat. VA18
Sadberry, J. - Co. K 34th North Carolina June 12, 1864 VA25
Sadler, J.A. - Co. D 7th South Carolina Nov. 5, 1862 VA25
Sail, R.C. - Co. C 13th North Carolina May 25, 1863 VA25
Sailers, John - Co. D 16th Georgia Oct. 8, 1861 VA25
Saitor, __ - Co. C 33rd North Carolina Oct. 4, 1864 VA25
Salcott, T. - 4th Georgia June 16, 1862 VA25
Salf, H. - Co. F 48th Alabama July 4, 1862 VA25
Salman, James - Co. I 12th Virginia March 11, 1863 VA25
Saltskiver, William - 17th Mississippi VA18

Samford, I. - Co. C 16th Virginia July 12, 1862 VA25
Sammons, E.W. - 4th South Carolina VA18
Sammuels, John F. - KIA June 3, 1864 age 35 VA19
Sampson, E.J. - 4th Texas KIA - June 27, 1862 VA17
Sampson, H. W. - Co. K 47th North Carolina Sept. 18, 1864 VA25
Sampson, W.H. - Co. A 40th Virginia April 20, 1865 VA25
Samuel, Archer T. - Pvt. - Co. C 14th Tennessee VA28
Samuels, J.D. - Parker's Battery March 15, 1863 VA25
Sancy, J.L. - Co. A 48th North Carolina June 19, 1864 VA25
Sanderfer, S.T. 5th South Carolina Nov. 14, 1862 VA25
Sanders, E. - VA12
Sands, A. - Co. A 2nd North Carolina Battalion June 5, 1864 VA25
Sandy, __ - 40th Virginia May 31, 1862 VA25
Sandy, C.C. - Virginia July 18, 1863 VA25
Sanford, R. - Co. A 55th Virginia Sept. 4, 1862 VA25
Sanford, T. - Co. B 18th Louisiana Oct. 2, 1862 VA25
Sanford, T.S. - Co. C 18th Alabama July 16, 1862 VA25
Sanford, W.J. - July 30, 1861 VA25
Sanford, Wade B. - Pvt. - Co. C 15th South Carolina Died May 9, 1864 VA28
Sanzer, C.G. - Co. E 56th North Carolina Sept. 4, 1864 VA25
Sappe, A.F. - 22nd North Carolina June 16, 1862 VA25
Sappenfield, E. - Co. H 48th North Carolina Sept. 18, 1864 VA25
Sartin, C.J. - Co. G 45th North Carolina March 10, 1865 VA25
Sasser, Phillip E. - Pvt. - Co. F 4th North Carolina KIA - Fredericksburg - Dec. 13, 1862 VA28
Satchwell, T.M. - Co. I 3rd South Carolina Sept. 26, 1862 VA25
Saton, I.F. - Co. B 6th Alabama May 31, 1862 VA25
Satterfield, I.T. - Co. B 9th Georgia June 4, 1862 VA25
Satterfield, R.S. - Co. K 50th Georgia Nov. 8, 1862 VA25
Satterwhite, M.E. - Co. I 11th Georgia June 10, 1862 VA25

Saucer, C. - Co. H 21st Mississippi July 29, 1862 VA25
Saunders, A. - Adjutant- 23rd Georgia July 18, 1862 VA25
Saunders, A. - 23rd Georgia Aug. 22, 1862 VA25
Saunders, H.S. - Co. B 24th Georgia June 10, 1862 VA25
Saunders, I.H. - Co. D 1st Tennessee Sept. 12, 1862 VA25
Saunders, J. - Steamer *Pat. Henry* April 1, 1865 VA25
Saunders, J. M. - Capt. - 53rd Virginia Oct. 16, 1862 age 25 VA25
Saunders, J.H. - Co. I 11th Virginia VA10
Saunders, J.Z. - Co. H 14th Louisiana May 13, 1863 VA25
Saunders, L.D. - Co. C 15th North Carolina April 29, 1864 VA25
Saunders, Q. - 1st North Carolina Battalion May 28, 1862 VA25
Saunders, S.D. - Co. A 5th South Carolina June 22, 1862 VA25
Saunders, T. - 2nd Louisiana June 2, 1862 VA25
Saunders, W.H. - Co. C 42nd Virginia May 18, 1863 VA25
Saunders, W.T. - Co. B 5th North Carolina Nov. 17, 1862 VA25
Savage, B. - Co. A 7th North Carolina June 7, 1863 VA25
Savage, W. - Co. H 55th North Carolina Jan. 4, 1865 VA25
Sawley, C. - 19th Virginia July 4, 1862 VA25
Sawyer, S. - C.S. Navy June 1, 1865 VA25
Saxin, H.H. - Co. E 10th Alabama VA11
Saxon, J.F. - Co. K 53rd Georgia Dec. 2, 1862 VA25
Sayford, A. - Co. K 42nd North Carolina Sept. 2, 1864 VA25
Scabb, W. - Co. D 6th Virginia July 7, 1863 VA25
Scarbor, William - Co. K 28th Georgia VA11
Scarlett, G.W. - Co. G 14th North Carolina VA11
Scarvega, C.W. - Co. I 8th Louisiana Dec. 23, 1861 VA25
Scherzinger, Jos - Co. D 19th Mississippi July 7, 1862 VA25
Schupe, Charles - Civilian -Killed in explosion of C.S. Laboratory - Feb. 6, 1862 age 19 VA19
Schweinfurt, John - VA15
Scoff, M. - Co. K 21st South Carolina VA24

Scoffee, J.S. 14th Alabama July 20, 1862 VA25
Scoggins, S. - Co. E 56th North Carolina Aug. 13, 1864 VA25
Scoss, M. - Pvt. - South Carolina Aug. 25, 1864 VA22
Scott, A.A. - Co. H 57th North Carolina Dec. 30, 1862 VA25
Scott, Benjamin W. - Corp. - Co. G 57th Virginia DOD - Feb. 7, 1863 VA28
Scott, G.W. - Co. C 33rd North Carolina May 13, 1863 VA25
Scott, H. - North Carolina May 11, 1862 VA25
Scott, I.S. - Co. B 26th Alabama July 18, 1862 VA25
Scott, J. - July 4, 1862 VA25
Scott, J.C. - Co. D 2nd Louisiana 1862 VA25
Scott, J.W. - 2nd Mississippi VA18
Scott, Nichols Ewing - Pvt. - Co. G 12th Georgia Died May 10, 1864 VA28
Scott, Oliver P. - Pvt. - Co. K 9th Georgia Died May 10, 1864 VA28
Scott, Pat. - Fitzerald's Artillery May 9, 1862 VA25
Scott, T.J. - Alabama July 18, 1862 VA25
Scott, Thomas F. - Co. G 52nd Virginia VA11
Scott, Thos. - Co. H 11th North Carolina VA23
Scott, W.T. - Virginia VA20
Scotts, A.B. - Co. B 13th Georgia VA11
Scruggins, Samuel - Died Feb. 7, 1863 age 42 VA19
Scullas, R.A. - Co. C 2nd Mississippi Sept. 22, 1862 VA25
Sea, R.A. - Co. G 14th North Carolina May 28, 1863 VA25
Seabrooke, S.A. - Corp. - Co. B 27th South Carolina Aug. 5, 1864 VA25
Seaford, S. - 8th Georgia VA18
Seagars, M.L. - Co. D 42nd North Carolina Oct. 16, 1864 VA25
Seago, I.A. - Co. F 49th Georgia July 25, 1862 VA25
Seal, H. - Co. B 24th Georgia May 18, 1862 VA25
Seal, T.J. - Co. A 24th Georgia May 18, 1862 VA25
Sealey, J. - 2nd South Carolina Sept. 2, 1861 VA25
Seamans, T. - Heavy Artillery July 6, 1864 VA25
Seamour, H. - 1st South Carolina July 17, 1862 VA25

Seay, C. - Georgia May 14, 1862 VA25
Seay, D.H. - 2nd Georgia April 27, 1862 VA25
Seay, G.W. - 27th South Carolina July 15, 1864 VA25
Sedgworth, J. - Co. I 4th North Carolina June 20, 1862 VA25
Seine, A. - Co. G 2nd Mississippi Battalion June 19, 1862 VA25
Seit, J.T. - Co. G 21st Mississippi June 22, 1862 VA25
Seldner, Isaac 6 - th Virginia, Infantry Born Dec. 23, 1837 KIA - Chancellorsville - May 3, 1863 VA17
Selecman, Templeton - 4th Virginia VA10
Self, J. - Co. C 60th Georgia Jan. 5, 1863 VA25
Self, M. - Co. C 6th Georgia June 10, 1863 VA25
Sell, H. - Nov. 14, 1861 VA25
Sellars, G.B. - VA18
Sellers, __ - Co. B 28th South Carolina May 12, 1861 VA25
Sellers, A. - Co. E 37th North Carolina Sept. 29, 1864 VA25
Sellers, G.W. - Co. E 17th Georgia March 19, 1865 VA25
Sellers, John - Co. D 16th Georgia Sept. 1, 1861 VA25
Semn, A.D. - Co. C 20th South Carolina July 31, 1864 VA25
Semple, James A. - Veteran - Paymaster U.S. Navy - C.S. Navy Feb. 24, 1819 - 1886 VA02
Serge, David - Co. C 5th North Carolina VA11
Serrett, __ - June 16, 1862 VA25
Session, T.J. - Capt. - 4th Texas Nov. 9, 1861 VA25
Sett, W. - Co. K 47th Alabama Feb. 23, 1863 VA25
Setters, R. - Co. C 27th South Carolina July 25, 1864 VA25
Sexton, C.P. - Co. K 1st South Carolina Cavalry June 21, 1864 VA25
Sexton, W. - Aug. 21, 1861 VA25
Sexton, W.B. - 18th South Carolina Oct. 8, 1862 VA25
Shacklford, A.J. - F. Guards (Louisiana) Nov. 6, 1861 VA25
Shacklford, J.E. - Co. H 5th North Carolina Cavalry June 22, 1864 VA25
Shacklford, J.M. - Co. E 47th Virginia July 24, 1862 VA25
Shacklford, R.L. - Co. A 40th Virginia June 6, 1862 VA25
Shacklford, W. - Co. A 32nd Virginia April 22, 1862 VA25

Shaddock, J.M. - Co. E 47th Virginia July 24, 1862 VA25
Shaff, J.R. - Co. H 42nd North Carolina July 25, 1864 VA25
Shaffer, G. - Louisiana July 5, 1862 VA25
Shafin, J. - Co. C 9th Georgia July30, 1864 VA25
Shafnor, I.S. - Co. H 13th North Carolina May 15, 1863 VA25
Shalley, __ - July 1862 VA25
Shamble, W.M. - Co. K 42nd Mississippi Aug. 5, 1862 VA25
Shamble, W.N. - Co. E 7th Georgia July 27, 1862 VA25
Shanha, J.A. - Co. H 11th North Carolina May 15, 1863 VA25
Shannon, Hiram - Pvt. - Co. F 6th South Carolina Died May 14, 1864 VA28
Sharp, A. - Co. A 31st North Carolina May 27, 1864 VA25
Sharp, A.C. - Co. B 48th North Carolina Jan. 7, 1865 VA25
Sharp, L.D. - Co. A 49th North Carolina Aug. 17, 1864 VA25
Sharpley, J.O. - Co. G 1st Mississippi May 24, 1862 VA25
Sharpley, J.O. - Co. G 1st Mississippi May 24, 1862 VA25
Shaw, A. - Lt.- Co. K 38th North Carolina VA25
Shaw, C. - Co. A 61st Georgia March 6, 1865 VA25
Shaw, G. - Co. K 28th Georgia June 3, 1862 VA25
Shaw, J. - Co. B 2nd South Carolina June 14, 1863 VA25
Shaw, J.B. - Co. G 17th__Died March 186_ VA23
Shaw, James W. - Pvt. - Co. A 44th Georgia MW in 1864 VA28
Shaw, M. - 2nd Mississippi May 4, 1862 VA25
Shaw, R.S. - Pvt. - Co. K 45th North Carolina .Died May 14, 1865 VA26
Shaw, W.T. - Co. K 1st South Carolina July 21, 1862 VA25
Shawman, O.J. - Co. I 28th Virginia Oct. 17, 1861 VA25
Shealy, Wesley Walter - Pvt. - Co. I 15th South Carolina Died May 8, 1864 Headstone reads: "Sheely" VA28
Sheaning, E.C. - Co. B 30th North Carolina Nov. 3, 1862 VA25
Shed, A.J. - Co. E 51st Georgia May 29, 1863 VA25
Sheeley, A. - Co. A 7th South Carolina July 8, 1864 VA25
Sheeley, J.J. - Co. C 20th North Carolina July 26, 1864 VA25
Sheely, Wesley Walter - see Shealy, Wesley Walter

Sheffield, A.M. - Georgia VA07
Sheffner, J. - Co. K 57th North Carolina VA11
Shehorn, H. - Moody's Artillery (Virginia) Sept. 29, 1864 VA25
Sheilds, __ - May 20, 1862 VA25
Shelan, A.F. - Co. A 5th South Carolina July 7, 1862 VA25
Shelbern, C.W. - Goochland Artillery (Virginia) June 7, 1865 VA25
Shell, __ - Nov. 13, 1861 VA25
Shelton, J.L. - Co. C 4th South Carolina Cavalry July5, 1864 VA25
Shelton, J.M. - Feb. 8, 1865 VA25
Shelton, T. J. - Virginia Aug. 27, 1863 VA25
Shelton, T. S. - Arkansas Cavalry April 28, 1865 VA25
Shelton, W. - 7th North Carolina Sept. 2, 1863 VA25
Shelton, W.L. - Pvt.- Co. H 38th Virginia .Died May 25, 1865 VA26
Shempert, A. - Georgia Sept. 1, 1861 VA25
Shepard, __ - Co. B 27th Georgia June 5, 1864 VA25
Shepard, A. - Co. G 16th North Carolina Nov. 16, 1862 VA25
Shepard, Chas. - "supposed deserter" Dec. 31, 1864 VA24A
Shepard, J.T. - Stewart's Artillery (Virginia) Aug. 14, 1862 VA25
Shepard, J.W. - Co. F 52nd North Carolina Nov. 16, 1865 VA25
Shepard, R.F. - Co. A 4th Virginia May 15, 1863 VA25
Shepherd, __ - Virginia Infantry VA08
Shepherd, A. - Co. I 66th North Carolina July 10, 1864 VA25
Shepherd, A.J. - Co. B __th Georgia Battalion June 10, 1864 VA25
Shepherd, I.W. - Co. E 1st South Carolina July 7, 1864 VA25
Shepherd, J.P. - Co. B 27th North Carolina Sept. 23, 1864 VA25
Shepherd, J.W. - Co. G 19th Mississippi May 3, 1862 VA25
Shepherd, M. - Co. H 45th Georgia July 12, 1864 VA25
Shepherd, W.C. - VA06

Shepp, J.F. - Alabama VA20
Sheral, A. - Co. K 14th Virginia April 18, 1863 VA25
Sheral, A.S. - Co. G 37th North Carolina Aug. 24, 1862 VA25
Sherala, G.B. - Co. F 36th North Carolina Jan. 7, 1865 VA25
Sherard, W.J. - Co. I 61st Georgia Nov. 12, 1864 VA25
Sherard, W.Y. - Lt.- Co. E 2nd South Carolina Oct. 21, 1864 VA25
Sherer, W.H. - Capt. - Co. B 13th Virginia July 5, 1862 VA25
Sheridan, S.W. - Alabama Oct. 14, 1861 VA25
Sherley, J.D. - 15th Georgia May 27, 1862 VA25
Sherley, R.S. - May 22, 1862 VA25
Sherman, J. - 2nd Florida Infantry - KIA - Battle of Williamsburg - May 5, 1862 VA02
Sherman, W. - Co. I 14th Alabama May 20, 1862 VA25
Sheron, N. - Co. D 24th North Carolina Oct. 28, 1864 VA25
Sherrott, R.M. - 45th Georgia Sept. 23, 1862 VA25
Sheuer, Jonathan - Louisiana. VA17
Shewmake, H.C. - C.S. Navy March 24, 1865 VA25
Shey, __ - Co. A - 21st Mississippi May 13, 1862 VA25
Shields, A.H. - Co. A 18th Virginia May 20, 1862 VA25
Shields, J.A. - Co. K 48th Georgia Nov. 9, 1862 VA25
Shields, J.D. - Jeff Davis Legion VA18
Shields, Thomas - Pvt. - Co. E 5th Louisiana KIA 2nd Battle of Fredericksburg May 4, 1863 VA28
Shiffen, G.L. - Co. A 5th Louisiana March 26, 1865 VA25
Shiffery, M. - Co. C 2nd Mississippi Nov. 30, 1862 VA25
Shiflet, M.W. - Georgia May 23, 1862 VA25
Shine, J. - Cobb's Legion (Georgia) Aug. 30, 1861 VA25
Shiney, J.W. - Co. H 37th North Carolina May 31, 1864 VA25
Shinher, W.S. - April 20, 1863 VA25
Shinin, M.A. - 48th Alabama July 8, 1862 VA25
Shino, J.N. - Capt. - Florida 1865 VA25
Ship, J.H. - Hampton's Legion (Georgia) July 30, 1864 VA25
Shipp, John M. - Co. I 6th North Carolina Infantry VA08
Shipper, J.J. - Co. K 5th South Carolina Cavalry June 3, 1864 VA25

Shira, M. - Co. K 13th North Carolina Oct. 11, 1861 VA25
Shirley, Christian - VA12
Shirley, S.A. - Pvt. - Co. H 16th Mississippi Died May 12, 1864 Headstone reads: ' S.C. Shirley" VA28
Shirley, S.C. - see Shirley, S.A. VA28
Shirley, T.W. - Co. G 5th Texas May 26, 1862 VA25
Shirran, A.R. - Co. C 46th North Carolina Sept. 5, 1864 VA25
Shiver, Abner - Pvt. - Co. F 11th Florida Died May 9, 1865 VA26
Shivery, J. - 5th North Carolina Oct. 17, 1861 VA25
Shives, J.P. - Co. G 4th North Carolina VA28
Shoat, A.M. - Co. K 1st North Carolina April 21, 1864 VA25
Shoat, F. - Co. F 22nd North Carolina Sept. 12, 1862 VA25
Shoat, W.T. - 2nd Florida Oct. 21, 1861 VA25
Shoe, Levi - Co. B 7th North Carolina Died July 1, 1862 VA28
Shoemaker, H. - Co. D 47th North Carolina Sept. 2, 1864 VA25
Shoemaker, Wm. - Pvt.- Co. A 24th Virginia Cavalry Died June 23, 1865 VA26
Shoff, D.A. - Co. A 42nd North Carolina Oct. 4, 1864 VA25
Shomo, D.L. - VA12
Shoot, G.H. - Co. G 48th Georgia Oct. 29, 1862 VA25
Shoot, W.H. - Co. B 32nd North Carolina Sept. 20, 1862 VA25
Shooter, Washington Pickney - Lt. Colonel - Co. E 1st South Carolina Died May 12, 1864 VA28
Short, A.G. - Co. F 54th North Carolina June 29, 1864 VA25
Shory, A. - June 7, 1862 VA25
Shuler, S. McL. - 5th South Carolina Infantry - KIA - Battle of Williamsburg - May 5, 1862 VA02
Shuler, W.A. - Co. B 1st South Carolina Aug. 15, 1863 VA25
Shuley, O.A. - Co. K 13th Louisiana June 16, 1862 VA25
Shuley, Sam'l - Co. K 13th South Carolina June 15, 1862 VA25
Shull, H.M. - Co. H 28th South Carolina Sept. 9, 1864 VA25
Shultz, H. - 6th Louisiana VA18
Shumaker, J. - Co. G 6th Alabama Nov. 19, 1862 VA25

Shumaker, L.J. - 14th Virginia May 4, 1862 VA25
Shumate, G.H. - Clark Cavalry VA06
Shumate, Jno. -Clark Cavalry VA06
Shumpert, I.P. - Co. C 23rd South Carolina March 1, 1865 VA25
Shunston, W. - Co. F 1st Virginia Reserves April 1, 1865 VA25
Sibbet, John - Pvt. - 18th North Carolina Infantry DOW June 11, 1862 VA09
Sibert, G.W. - 10th Virginia VA18
Sibert, John M. - VA12
Sibert, Marion M. - VA12
Sider, R.S. - Co. B 15th North Carolina July 16, 1864 VA25
Sides, P.S. - Pvt. - North Carolina April 4, 1865 VA22
Sight, A.A. - Co. G 5th North Carolina May 18, 1863 VA25
Sigman, A. - Co. F 38th North Carolina June 25, 1864 VA25
Sigman, S. - Co. B 13th South Carolina Aug. 28, 1862 VA25
Signs, J.W. - Co. C 26th South Carolina April 27, 1862 VA25
Sikes, F. - Co. H 11th North Carolina Aug. 23, 1864 VA25
Siley, J.H. - Co. H 17th North Carolina Sept. 2, 1864 VA25
Sillcott, T. - Co. D 8th Virginia June 18, 1862 VA25
Sills, A.N. - Co. I 14th South Carolina May 27, 1864 VA25
Sills, W.M. - Co. F 10th Georgia March 26, 1865 VA25
Silman, B.T. - Co. I 1st Texas June 8, 1862 VA25
Simmonds, D. - Co. A 35th North Carolina Sept. 14, 1862 VA25
Simmons, C. - Pvt.- Co. K 30th North Carolina Died June 18, 1865 VA26
Simmons, James R. - Sgt. - Co. K 2nd South Carolina Died May 12, 1864 VA28
Simmons, W.J. - Co. D 4th Georgia Sept. 20, 1864 VA25
Simms, F. - Co. F 17th Virginia InfantryVA10
Simms, I.R. - Co. A 15th Georgia May 17, 1862 VA25
Simms, J.A. - 8th Virginia Infantry VA10

Simms, Josiah Calvin - Pvt. - Co. F 16th Georgia Died at Winchester (Virginia) - Dec. 1, 1862 Name also spelled Sims VA28

Simms, L.H. - Co. I 5th Georgia May 8, 1862 VA25

Simms, S. - Pvt. - Co. D 20th North Carolina Died May 6, 1865 VA26

Simms, T.A. - Co. B 20th North Carolina May 23, 1865 VA25

Simonds, J. - Cooper's Rifles (South Carolina) Oct. 14, 1861 VA25

Simons, A. - 53rd North Carolina Dec. 5, 1863 VA25

Simons, A.B. - Co. A 46th Georgia Sept. 20, 1864 VA25

Simons, I.M. - Price's Co. May 24, 1862 VA25

Simons, J. - Co. A 2nd South Carolina July 29, 1862 VA25

Simons, J.B. - Co. D 20th North Carolina Nov. 18, 1862 VA25

Simons, J.E. - Pvt.- Co. I 2nd Louisiana Died June 28, 1865 VA26

Simpson, J.C. - Engineer Corps Nov. 4, 1863 VA25

Simpson, S.J. - Co. K 28th North Carolina Jan. 7, 1863 VA25

Simpson, Thomas - Mosby's Cavalry VA10

Simpson, W. - Co. K 21st Mississippi June 6, 1863 VA25

Simpson, W.R. - 8th Fla. VA18

Sims, A.J. - 16th Mississippi May 26, 1864 VA25

Sims, E.R. - Co. C 42nd Mississippi Sept. 21, 1862 VA25

Sims, G.A. - Co. G 27th North Carolina June 17, 1864 VA25

Sims, G.S. - Co. I 12th South Carolina Sept. 7, 1864 VA25

Sims, Josiah, Calvin - see Simms, Josiah, Calvin VA28

Sims, M.G. - "H.L" (Hampton Legion ?) Georgia Nov. 5, 1864 VA25

Sims, M.J. - Sgt. - Co. D 1st South Carolina Oct. 12, 1864 VA25

Sims, W.R. - Dec. 23, 1861 VA25

Sinanthy, H.J. - Co. I 50th Georgia May 17, 1863 VA25

Sines, H. - Co. G 6th Georgia Sept. 22, 1862 VA25

Singfield, G. 14th Georgia April 29, 1862 VA25

Singfield, P. - Co. C 20th Georgia April 29, 1862 VA25

Singleton, I.H. - Sgt. - Co. F 19th Mississippi Oct. 2, 1864 VA25
Singleton, R. - Co. G 38th Virginia April 20, 1862 VA25
Singletree, W.W. - Co. B 18th North Carolina June 14, 1862 VA25
Sink, C.B. - Virginia April 22, 1862 VA25
Sink, G. - Co. I 14th North Carolina June 8, 1862 VA25
Sink, G.W. - Co. F 15th North Carolina Dec. 28, 1862 VA25
Sintmons, J.F. - 11th Alabama Vols. VA18
Sise, R.M. - South Carolina VA20
Sites, William H. - VA12
Sithers, Eliza - Killed by "Explosion (of) Magazine" April 17, 1865 VA19
Siviason, Geo. - Arsenal Battalion (Virginia) Aug. 11, 1863 VA25
Sizeman, J. - Co. I 26th North Carolina June 9, 1864 VA25
Sizeman, L. - June 16, 1863 VA25
Sizemore, __ - Co. A 22nd South Carolina Jan. 12, 1865 VA25
Skilman, B.W. - Co. I 8th Virginia June 27, 1862 VA25
Skilman, W. - Co. A 9th Louisiana July 3, 1862 VA25
Skinner, W.N. - Co. C 20th Georgia March 17, 1863 VA25
Skipper, J.S. - Co. E 59th Alabama June 10, 1865 VA25
Skipper, Wesley W. - 30th North Carolina VA04
Slater, C. - Pvt. - Co. H 11th Florida Died June 9, 1865 VA26
Slaughter, J. - Co. C 5th Georgia Aug. 20, 1862 VA25
Slaughter, J.H. - Co. G 30th North Carolina Nov. 15, 1863 VA25
Slaughter, Wm. - Pvt.- Co. F 9th Virginia Died July 2, 1865 VA26
Slaver, J.W. - Winder's Cavalry Jan. 30, 1863 VA25
Slawter, W. - Co. G 49th Georgia 1865 VA25
Sligh, John T. - see Sly, John T. VA28
Sloane, J.J. - Co. D 34th North Carolina June 15, 1862 VA25
Sloane, R.E. - Co. C 10th North Carolina Oct. 27, 1863 VA25
Slone, Wm. - Co. E 10th North Carolina July 22, 1864 VA25
Slower, I.H. - Corp. - Winder's Cavalry Jan. 29, 1863 VA25

Slupton, W.D. - Co. G 5th North Carolina Nov. 14, 1862 VA25
Sly, John T. - Pvt. - Co. C 48th Alabama Died May 8, 1864 name on headstone - "Sligh" VA28
Small, R.S. - Lt.- Co. G 47th North Carolina July 27, 1862 age 23 VA25
Smallwood, __ - Co. H 2nd Georgia Aug. 11, 1861 VA25
Smallwood, W. - Co. E 6th Georgia Sept. 4, 1862 VA25
Smecher, Pascal - VA20
Smery, Joshua - VA18
Smiley, A.E. - Co. F 5th Alabama Jan. 1, 1863 VA25
Smith, __ - Palmetto Sharp Shooters (South Carolina) July 18, 1862 VA25
Smith, __ - July 5, 1862 VA25
Smith, __ - Colonel 1st South Carolina July 5, 1862 VA25
Smith, __ - Co. E 4th North Carolina Oct. 7, 1864 VA25
Smith, __ - Georgia July 2, 1862 VA25
Smith, __ - Co. F 1st Louisiana July 8, 1862 VA25
Smith, __ - 11th Mississippi June 6, 1862 VA25
Smith, A. - Co. H 9th Georgia July 18, 1864 VA25
Smith, A. - Co. A 66th North Carolina Sept. 2, 1864 VA25
Smith, A.B. - Pvt. - Co. C 46th North Carolina Died May 18, 1865 VA26
Smith, A.D. - Co. K 26th Georgia Jan. 24, 1863 VA25
Smith, A.J. - Co. E 10th Georgia March 28, 1863 VA25
Smith, A.N. - Co. F 66th North Carolina July 11, 1864 VA25
Smith, A.S. - Co. G 57th Alabama March 25, 1865 VA25
Smith, Abraham - Capt. - Co. I 13th Virginia DOW May 27, 1864 (MW Spotsylvania Court House - May 19, 1864) VA28
Smith, Amelia - Died Feb. 23, 1863 age 55 VA19
Smith, Asa R. - DOW July 14, 1862 age 52 VA19
Smith, B. - Co. A 47th North Carolina Jan. 3, 1865 VA25
Smith, B.F. - 45th North Carolina Infantry VA08
Smith, Berrien - Pvt. - Co. C 50th Georgia DOD May 1, 1862 VA28

Smith, Booker - Sgt. - Co. C 46th Virginia Died May 3, 1865 VA26
Smith, D. - Co. C 3rd North Carolina May 24, 1863 VA25
Smith, D. - Virginia Aug. 9, 1862 VA25
Smith, D. - Co. D 42nd Mississippi Nov. 16, 1862 VA25
Smith, D.J. - Lt.- Co. G 4th North Carolina May 21, 1864 VA25
Smith, D.N. - Lt.- Co. H 5th Alabama Died May 10, 1864 VA28
Smith, D.N. - Co. F 1st South Carolina May 17, 1863 VA25
Smith, D.P. - 13th South Carolina June 5, 1862 VA25
Smith, David - Lt. KIA July 12, 1864 VA19
Smith, E. - Co. C 46th North Carolina Nov. 21, 1862 VA25
Smith, E.A. - Co. I 11th South Carolina June 15, 1864 VA25
Smith, E.M. - Co. I 4th Georgia VA11
Smith, E.P. - Co. D 47th Virginia June 24, 1862 VA25
Smith, F. - Co. K 8th Georgia May 14, 1862 VA25
Smith, F.A. - Co. H 22nd Georgia Aug. 29, 1864 VA25
Smith, F.B. - Co. E 11th Alabama July 8, 1862 VA25
Smith, F.M. - 17th __ VA18
Smith, F.O. - Co. C 7th Georgia Cavalry Jan. 25, 1865 VA25
Smith, G. - Pvt. - Georgia June 27, 1865 VA22
Smith, G. - 3rd Alabama Feb. 8, 1963 VA25
Smith, G.B. - Died Nov. 22, 1862 VA19
Smith, G.B. - 5th Louisiana VA18
Smith, G.C. - Co. I 15th Georgia April 19, 1864 VA25
Smith, G.W. - Co. E 15th Georgia Aug. 6, 1864 VA25
Smith, G.W. - Co. A 14th North Carolina Nov. 12, 1864 VA25
Smith, George - Corp. - Co. C 49th Virginia KIA 1864 VA28
Smith, George - May 12, 1862 VA25
Smith, H. - Co. I 27th North Carolina April 24, 1864 VA25
Smith, H. - Co. B 2nd Georgia Jan. 13, 1865 VA25
Smith, H. - 61st Georgia June 10, 1863 VA25
Smith, H. - Co. I 17th Mississippi Jan. 2, 1863 VA25
Smith, H. - Co. C 12th Louisiana Aug. 9, 1862 VA25

Smith, H.C. - 5th North Carolina Nov. 26, 1862 VA25
Smith, H.M. - Co. E 4th Virginia VA25
Smith, I.A. - Co. D 37th North Carolina June 17, 1862 VA25
Smith, I.B.E. - Co. E 4th South Carolina July 17, 1862 VA25
Smith, I.F. - Co. H 1st Virginia July 8, 1862 VA25
Smith, I.H. - Hampton's Legion (Georgia) May 4, 1862 VA25
Smith, I.S. - 7th North Carolina Dec. 29, 1862 VA25
Smith, I.S. - Co. F 14th Georgia Aug. 2, 1862 VA25
Smith, I.W. - Alabama Feb. 11, 1863 VA25
Smith, J. - Maryland VA11
Smith, J. - Pvt. - Alabama April 1, 1865 VA22
Smith, J. - Co. C 38th Virginia May 16, 1862 VA25
Smith, J. - July 30, 1862 VA25
Smith, J. Wesley - DOW April 27, 1865 age 25 VA19
Smith, J.A. - Co. H 30th Georgia VA11
Smith, J.D. - Co. I 35th North Carolina VA11
Smith, J.D. - Co. I 8th Louisiana Dec. 17, 1862 VA25
Smith, J.G. - Co. G 13th Alabama Nov. 19, 1862 VA25
Smith, J.H. - Co. C 61st Georgia Oct. 27, 1862 VA25
Smith, J.H. - Co. C 42nd Alabama March 29, 1865 VA25
Smith, J.J. - 3rd Virginia Artillery June 11, 1862 VA25
Smith, J.M. - VA20
Smith, J.M. - Co. I 19th Georgia May 27, 1862 VA25
Smith, J.M. - Co. I 52nd North Carolina Oct. 14, 1864 VA25
Smith, J.N. - Co. B 7th South Carolina June 24, 1864 VA25
Smith, J.P. - 12th Mississippi Aug. 9, 1862 VA25
Smith, J.R. - Co. A 52nd North Carolina Nov. 15, 1864 VA25
Smith, J.T. - 24th Georgia July 2, 1862 VA25
Smith, J.W. - Co. E 11th South Carolina July 28, 1864 VA25
Smith, J.W. - Co. B 1st South Carolina Sept. 12, 1862 VA25
Smith, John - Co. F 7th Georgia May 14, 1861 VA25
Smith, John F. - Pvt. - Co. I 47th Alabama Died May 10 (12?), 1864 VA28
Smith, John Tyler - Sgt. - Co. B 49th Georgia Died May 12, 1864 VA28

Smith, John Wesley - Pvt. - Co. D 2nd Georgia Died May 17, 1864 VA28
Smith, Joseph A. - Lt.- Co. C 45th Georgia Died May 12, 1864 VA28
Smith, K.G. - Lt.- Co. K 39th Georgia Died in Mississippi - Jan. 23, 1863 VA28
Smith, L. - Co. C 2nd North Carolina VA11
Smith, L.A. - Co. E 53rd Georgia Oct. 16, 1864 VA25
Smith, L.B. - Co. B 24th Georgia June 17, 1862 VA25
Smith, L.H. - Co. D 3rd Alabama Aug. 12, 1862 VA25
Smith, L.J. - 2nd Louisiana Aug. 14, 1861 VA25
Smith, L.M. - 24th Virginia VA18
Smith, Lew L. - Pvt. - Co. G 13th Georgia Died May 12, 1864 VA28
Smith, M. - Co. G 12th North Carolina July 5, 1862 VA25
Smith, N. - Cobb's Legion (Georgia) July 10, 1862 VA25
Smith, N.W. - Lt.- Co. A 18th Mississippi June 14, 1862 VA25
Smith, Newton A. - Pvt. - Co. H 16th Georgia DOD April 20, 1863 VA28
Smith, P.W. - Co. F 7th North Carolina July 15, 1863 VA25
Smith, R. - South Carolina Oct. 21, 1861 VA25
Smith, R.B. - Virginia April 14, 1863 VA25
Smith, R.C. - Co. F 2nd South Carolina June 25, 1864 VA25
Smith, R.F. - Corp. - Co. E 33rd North Carolina May 28, 1864 VA25
Smith, R.P. - Co. D 47th Virginia June 22, 1862 VA25
Smith, R.T. - Co. D 16th Alabama May 28, 1865 VA25
Smith, S.A. - Co. C 37th North Carolina Aug. 5, 1862 VA25
Smith, S.B. - Co. C 17th Virginia July 20, 1862 VA25
Smith, S.G. - Co. B 61st Alabama July 21, 1864 VA25
Smith, S.H. - Alabama VA25
Smith, S.M. - Co. A 56th North Carolina July 20, 1864 VA25
Smith, S.T. Courtney Artillery (Virginia) Dec. 27, 1862 VA25
Smith, S.T. - 21st Mississippi June 6, 1862 VA25
Smith, S.T. - Co. D 61st Alabama July 4, 1865 VA25

Smith, S.T. - Aug. 2, 1862 VA25
Smith, T.G. - Palmetto Sharp Shooters (South Carolina) July 18, 1862 VA25
Smith, T.H. - Co. A Hampton's Legion (South Carolina) May 4, 1862 VA25
Smith, T.I. - Co. B 6th Alabama Sept. 19, 1862 VA25
Smith, T.W. - 5th Georgia May 24, 1862 VA25
Smith, Thos. - Co. D 4th Texas Sept. 17, 1862 VA25
Smith, Virginia S. - "Killed in an engagement with the Federal Army." March 15, 1865 age 24 VA19
Smith, W. - 13th North Carolina VA18
Smith, W. - 7th Georgia June 5, 1862 VA25
Smith, W. - Co. B 42nd Mississippi Aug. 27, 1862 VA25
Smith, W. - Co. B 42nd Mississippi Sept. 26, 1862 VA25
Smith, W. - 27th Georgia June 5, 1862 VA25
Smith, W.A. - Sharp Shooters (South Carolina)July 15, 1862 VA25
Smith, W.A. - Virginia Oct. 26, 1862 VA25
Smith, W.A. - Co. A 4th North Carolina April 29, 1864 VA25
Smith, W.H. - Co. A 13th Mississippi June 17, 1862 VA25
Smith, W.H. - Co. E 3rd Virginia July 27, 1862 VA25
Smith, W.H. - Co. A 13th North Carolina June 13, 1862 VA25
Smith, W.J. - DOD May 21, 1863 VA19
Smith, W.M.A. - KIA May 2, 1862 - VA19
Smith, W.P. - Co. A 1st Georgia July 28, 1864 VA25
Smith, W.R. - Co. C 23rd North Carolina May 16, 1863 VA25
Smith, W.S. - Lt.- Co. C 6th Alabama June 3, 1862 VA25
Smith, W.T. - Co. G 12th Alabama April 2, 1862 VA25
Smith, W.T. - Co. G 4th Georgia July 17, 1864 VA25
Smith, W.T. - Co. G 27th North Carolina July 3, 1864 VA25
Smith, William A. - Died June 2, 1862 age 21 VA19
Smith, William T. - Pvt. - Co. H 59th Georgia Died May 10, 1864 VA28
Smith, Z. - Co. B 35th North Carolina Aug. 2, 1862 VA25
Smith, Z. - Co. B 6th Georgia Oct. 27, 1862 VA25

Smithdale, J.D. - Co. C 48th North Carolina Aug. 13, 1864 VA25

Smither, H. - Louisiana Zouaves June 14, 1862 VA25

Smithers, J.W. - Co. C 25th North Carolina Aug. 1, 1864 VA25

Smithgan, A. - 1st South Carolina June 16, 1862 VA25

Smithson, __ - Co. H 5th Alabama July 1, 1862 VA25

Smithson, E.L. - Pvt. - Co. A 56th Virginia Died June 13, 1865 VA26

Smithtrick, W.J. - Co. A 17th North Carolina Oct. 28, 1864 VA25

Smittenberg, A.M. - see Swittenberg, A.M. VA28

Smoke, J. - Co. K 11th South Carolina June 5, 1864 VA25

Smoot, A. - 3rd Alabama July 29, 1862 VA25

Smoot, W. - Cooper's Rifles (South Carolina) Sept. 17, 186 VA25

Smothus, S. - Co. C 21st South Carolina March 12, 1865 VA25

Smyle, J.R. - Co. E 2nd South Carolina Nov. 19, 1862 VA25

Snatchmell, __ - Co. I 3rd North Carolina Sept. 29, 1862 VA25

Snead, __ - 1862 VA25

Snead, D.V. - 11th Alabama VA18

Snead, Rich - Co. I 11th North Carolina Died Sept 27, 1861 VA23

Snead, Thos. - Aug. 2, 1861 VA25

Snelgrove, A.L. - Co. C 1st South Carolina April 28, 1864 VA25

Snells, J. - Tennessee VA20

Snider, E.W. - Texas VA11

Snider, H.M. - Pvt. - North Carolina April 7, 1865 VA22

Snipes, Alfred G. - Co. E 5th North Carolina VA11

Snipes, J. - Co. F 13th Georgia July 26, 1862 VA25

Snipes, R.P. - Co. E 23rd South Carolina Aug. 28, 1864 VA25

Snipes, T.E. - Co. H 5th North Carolina Cavalry June 23, 1864 VA25

Snipes, W.B. - Co. D 14th North Carolina July 28, 1864 VA25

Snodgrass, H. - Pvt. - Virginia April 20, 1865 VA22
Snodgrass, W. - VA12
Snow, F. - Co. K 1st South Carolina July 23, 1862 VA25
Snow, J.R. - Co. C 21st North Carolina March 26, 1865 VA25
Snow, James - Co. I 18th North Carolina VA11
Snow, T. - Lt.- Co. C 21st North Carolina May 6, 1863 VA25
Snow, Winston - Co. G 2nd North Carolina VA28
Snyder, Eli - Co. B 11th North Carolina Died Oct 4, 1861 VA23
Snyder, H.J. - Co. A 9th Louisiana Jan. 19, 1862 VA25
Snyder, M.D. - Co. F 56th North Carolina July 24, 1864 VA25
Snyder, R.D.B. - Lt.- 40th Virginia VA25
Snyder, T. - Co. K 27th North Carolina Aug. 8, 1864 VA25
Snyder, W. - 18th South Carolina Aug. 5, 1862 VA25
Snyder, W.F. - Co. G 27th Virginia Dec. 26, 1862 VA25
Soel, Setes - POW - Federal Soldier Died Nov. 16, 1861 VA19
Sogill, J. - Co. K 37th North Carolina Oct. 18, 1864 VA25
Sopps, W. - Co. D 48th Georgia Sept. 20, 1862 VA25
Sorrow, S.P. - 15th Georgia VA18
Souratt, A. - Co. H 59th Georgia March 2, 1865 VA25
Southall, D. - Co. E 2nd North Carolina Nov. 25, 1862 VA25
Southall, R.G. - 6th Alabama June 2, 1862 VA25
Southerland, John - 16th Mississippi Nov. 21, 1863 VA25
Southern, L.W. - 11th Georgia VA18
Southgal, R. - Surry County (Virginia) March 25, 1864 VA25
Sowers, G.A. - Co. B 26th Virginia June 11, 1865 VA25
Sowers, James Kerfoot - Pvt. - Co. H 4th Virginia Cavalry KIA - Spotsylvania Court House - May 12, 1864 VA28
Sowers, Wm. - VA06
Spafford, G.E. - Pvt. - Virginia July 17, 1864 VA22
Spail, W.T. - Co. G 52nd North Carolina Nov. 13, 1864 VA25
Spalding, Jas. W. - Colonel VA19
Sparker, M.R. - Co. E 5th Florida Aug. 23, 1862 VA25
Sparkman, S. - Co. D 8th Florida July 11, 1863 VA25

Sparks, __ - Co. D 14th North Carolina July 8, 1862 VA25
Sparks, J.T. - 18th South Carolina Nov. 23, 1862 VA25
Sparrow, W. - Co. G 56th Georgia July 5, 1864 VA25
Spear, S. - 11th North Carolina VA18
Speargla, A. - Co. I 11th North Carolina Oct. 8, 1864 VA25
Spears, D. - 12th Alabama Sept. 5, 1862 VA25
Spears, J. - Co. D 12th Mississippi May 19, 1864 VA25
Spears, J.W. - Co. K 8th North Carolina March 12, 1865 VA25
Spears, S.C. - 8th South Carolina May 19, 1864 VA25
Spears, T. - Co. B 13th South Carolina Oct. 29, 1862 VA25
Spears, W.C. - Co. B 44th Georgia April 26, 1864 VA25
Spears, W.N. - Co. F 28th North Carolina Jan. 7, 1863 VA25
Speck, I.M. - Co. C 11th Mississippi Feb. 8, 1863 VA25
Spemwill, H.L. - Co. G 2nd North Carolina Sept. 7, 1864 VA25
Spence, J.H. - Virginia VA20
Spence, J.L. - Co. I 32nd North Carolina Aug. 28, 1864 VA25
Spencer, Charles - Co. E 15th Virginia VA11
Spencer, J. - Co. E 25th North Carolina Sept. 7, 1864 VA25
Spencer, J.L. - 1st Texas Aug. 24, 1861 VA25
Spencer, James - Co. A 5th Alabama VA11
Spennard, J.T. - Co. G 17th North Carolina June 22, 1864 VA25
Spennel, R. - Co. A 38th North Carolina April 11, 1865 VA25
Sperger, T.H. - Co. B 4th Virginia July 21, 1862 VA25
Sperrin, L.P. - 18th Mississippi Jan. 30, 1863 VA25
Sperry, S. - Co. I 11th North Carolina(?) - Died Oct 28, 1861 VA23
Spicemer, S. - Pvt. - Alabama April 1, 1864 VA22
Spickard, Sam'l. - Sgt. - Co. H 24th Virginia Died June 4, 1865 VA26
Spidds, Geo. - May 18, 1862 VA25
Spikes, W. - 12th Mississippi Jan. 8, 1863 VA25
Spikes, W.T. - Co. K 27th Georgia May 2, 1862 VA25
Spiller, A. - Co. B 17th Mississippi May 30, 1862 VA25

Spina, M.A. - Co. B 46th Alabama June 15, 1863 VA25
Spiney, E.W. - Co. D 13th Alabama June 22, 1862 VA25
Spinkle, R. - 4th North Carolina June 4, 1862 VA25
Spirlin, G.W. - Co. I 56th North Carolina June 5, 1864 VA25
Spiva, James N. - Pvt. - Co. A 11th Alabama VA28
Spradlin, W. - Co. A 26th Alabama June 6, 1863 VA25
Spray, H.R. - Co. F 48th North Carolina June 2, 1864 VA25
Sprigne, R.W. - Co. A 42nd North Carolina Dec. 27, 1864 VA25
Sprinkle, F.R. - Co. H 4th North Carolina May 30, 1862 VA25
Sprout, F. - Co. F 19th Virginia May 13, 1862 VA25
Spurgess, A. - Co. A 26th South Carolina April 27, 1862 VA25
Spurley, B. - Co. K 9th Georgia May 20, 1862 VA25
Spurlock, J.M. - Co. C 36th Virginia Battalion Apr. 10, 1865 VA25
Spyrer, P.H. - Co. H 20th South Carolina Infantry VA08
Stader, B.G. - Co. E 13th North Carolina Nov. 22, 1863 VA25
Staidon, J.M. - Co. I 37th North Carolina June 29, 1863 VA25
Stanard, Jacqueline Beverly - VMI Cadet -KIA - Battle of New Market - May 15, 1864 - Buried in Orange, Virginia VA21
Stanberry, __ - July 1, 1862 VA25
Standard, __ - Co. A 23rd South Carolina July 1862 VA25
Standent, J.H. - Co. H 43rd North Carolina Jan. 21, 1865 VA25
Stanfell, J.W. - Co. A 20th Georgia Battalion June 29, 1864 VA25
Stanfell, J.W. - Co. A 20th Georgia Battalion June 29, 1864 VA25
Stanfield, H.A.P. - KIA May 18, 1864 age 22 VA19
Stanford, D.D. - Co. K 42nd Mississippi July 20, 1862 VA25
Stanford, J.B. - Co. H 15th North Carolina Feb. 20, 1865 VA25
Stank, A. - Co. A 37th North Carolina June 5, 1863 VA25
Stanley, C.C. - Co. H 27th North Carolina June 7, 1862 VA25

Stanley, G.W. - 5th North Carolina Dec. 29, 1862 VA25
Stanley, H.J. - Co. F 25th South Carolina Jan. 13, 1865 VA25
Stanley, Hardy B. - Capt. - Co. G 49th Georgia Died May 12, 1864 VA28
Stanley, J.A. - 5th Alabama VA18
Stanley, J.P.D. - Co. D 20th Georgia June 14, 1864 VA25
Stanley, P.R. - Sgt. - Co. D 20th Georgia June 5, 1864 VA25
Stanley, S. - Co. A 28th Louisiana Sept. 9, 1862 VA25
Stanley, W. - Co. G 7th North Carolina July 10, 1864 VA25
Stansbury, E. - 4th Maryland Battalion April 16, 1863 VA25
Stant, C.H. - C.S. Navy 1865 VA25
Stapler, W.H. - Georgia Artillery July 6, 1864 VA25
Staples, E.E. - 3rd Tennessee VA18
Stapleton, Jos. - 18th Mississippi VA18
Star, A.J. - Co. G 28th North Carolina July 5, 1864 VA25
Star, W.A. - 6th Georgia May 20, 1862 VA25
Starburn, I.F. - Co. H 33rd North Carolina Aug. 15, 1862 VA25
Starch, J. - Co. D 37th North Carolina June 10, 1862 VA25
Stark, F. - POW - Federal Soldier Died Oct. 23, 1861 VA19
Starke, T.H. - Co. B 8th Florida April 3, 1863 VA25
Starling, R. - Co. A 2nd South Carolina May 7, 1861 VA25
State, S. - Co. H 3rd South Carolina Dec. 23, 1862 VA25
Staten, T. - Co. I 13th Alabama June 2, 1863 VA25
Staten, Uriah G. - Pvt. - Co. I 49th Virginia KIA -Spotsylvania Court House - May 12, 1864 VA28
Statin, Samuel E. - POW - Federal Soldier Died June 19, 1862 VA19
Staton, Uriah G. - see Staten, Uriah G. VA28
Steading, G.F. - South Carolina VA22
Steadman, J. - Co. G 18th North Carolina June 27, 1863 VA25
Steadwell, H.C. - Co. K 35th North Carolina Nov. 8, 1864 VA25
Steame, J. - Co. B 6th South Carolina July 3, 1864 VA25
Stears, G. - Lt.- Co. H 15th South Carolina May 25, 1864 VA25

Stedman, T.E. - Co. E 8th North Carolina Jan. 8, 1863 VA25
Steel, J.L. - Co. A 22nd North Carolina June 9, 1864 VA25
Steel, Jno. R. - Sgt. - Co. D 17th Virginia Infantry VA10
Steele, A.J. - Co. I 4th Alabama Sept. 7, 1862 VA25
Steele, Dan'l. - Co. D 23rd Georgia Sept. 7, 1862 VA25
Steele, Frank - 8th Virginia Infantry VA10
Steele, R. - Co. G 60th Virginia VA11
Stegall, L. - Co. A 7th North Carolina Nov. 27, 1864 VA25
Stephens, __ - 13th North Carolina July 16, 1862 VA25
Stephens, A. - Co. G 7th South Carolina Battalion July 10, 1864 VA25
Stephens, A.J. - Co. C 13th North Carolina July 21, 1862 VA25
Stephens, E.P. - Texas VA20
Stephens, E.W. - Co. I 17th Mississippi May 12, 1861 VA25
Stephens, G.W. - Co. B 6th Georgia July 3, 1864 VA25
Stephens, I.P. - VA08
Stephens, J. - Co. H 53rd North Carolina April 28, 1864 VA25
Stephens, J.B. - Co. A 7th South Carolina June 2, 1863 VA25
Stephens, R.C. - Co. I 19th Georgia May 20, 1862 VA25
Stephens, R.M. - Co. G 35th Georgia July 19, 1862 VA25
Stephens, S.F. - Co. G 14th Alabama June 26, 1862 VA25
Stephens, T.W. - Co. C 18th North Carolina Jan. 9, 1863 VA25
Stephenson, __ - Co. H 9th Louisiana July 16, 1862 VA25
Stephenson, A. - VA12
Stephenson, A.J. - 5th Alabama May 25, 1862 VA25
Stephenson, J.D. - Co. G 1st North Carolina VA11
Stepp, Tisdale - Pvt. - Co. F 14th North Carolina Died May 12, 1864 VA28
Stepps, __ - Texas Aug. 14, 1861 VA25
Steptoe, J. - Co. D 59th Georgia Sept. 1, 1864 VA25
Sterens, J.H. - Co. F 11th North Carolina Died Sept 28, 1861 VA23
Sterling, J.C. - Co. B 4th South Carolina Cavalry July 1, 1864 VA25

Sterling, J.T. - Co. G 50th Georgia Jan. 1, 1864 VA25
Steuart, Charles C. - Pvt. - Co. B 31st Virginia DOW June 6, 1864 (MW Spotsylvania Court House) VA28
Stevens, A. - Co. I 19th Mississippi May 24, 1862 VA25
Stevens, F.W. - 1st South Carolina Sept. 9, 1862 VA25
Stevens, J.D. - South Carolina Artillery July 17, 1864 VA25
Stevens, J.F. - Co. D 26th North Carolina Dec.18, 1864 VA25
Stevens, W. - Co. C 3rd Georgia July 14, 1864 VA25
Stevenson, J.H. - Artillery June 18, 1864 VA25
Stevenson, L.J. - Co. A 13th North Carolina July 5, 1864 VA25
Steward, __ - Co. I 49th Georgia July 1, 1862 VA25
Steward, B. - July 25, 1861 VA25
Steward, C.L. - Co. A 25th Georgia May 24, 1864 VA25
Steward, I. - Co. A 20th South Carolina July 27, 1864 VA25
Steward, J.W. - Georgia VA20
Stewart, B.F. - Co. H 64th Georgia Aug. 31, 1864 VA25
Stewart, Benjamin Franklin - Lt.- Co. K 40th Virginia DOW May 20, 1864 (MW Spotsylvania Court House - May 12, 1864) VA28
Stewart, J.F. - Co. A 13th South Carolina June 17, 1862 VA25
Stewart, J.J. - Co. I 21st Mississippi July 23, 1862 VA25
Stewart, J.S. - Co. G 1st South Carolina Sept. 16, 1864 VA25
Stewart, T.J. - Co. G 38th Georgia VA11
Stewart, W.S. - Co. F 20th South Carolina May 5, 1865 VA25
Still, D.C. - 1st South Carolina July 26, 1862 VA25
Stillard, G.C. - Co. G 3rd South Carolina VA11
Stillman, Charles E. - KIA June 9, 1862 VA19
Stills, W.A. - Co. A 18th North Carolina Nov. 7, 1862 VA25
Stoater, William R. - KIA May 20, 1864 VA19
Stock, E.B. - Co. F 25th South Carolina March 17, 1865 VA25
Stokes, A.W. - Co. H 27th North Carolina Dec. 30, 1863 VA25
Stokes, David E. - DOW Aug. 25, 1862 age 23 VA19
Stokes, J.A. - Co. H 27th North Carolina Oct. 12, 1864 VA25
Stol, George - POW - Federal Soldier Died June 8, 1862 VA19

Stone, F.M. - Pvt. - Co. D Hampton's Legion Died June 12, 1865 VA26
Stone, H. - Co. B 3rd Virginia Aug. 30, 1861 VA25
Stone, J. - Co. E 1st South Carolina VA22
Stone, M.W. - Co. A 4th North Carolina Dec. 29, 1862 VA25
Stone, P.T. - Co. G 15th South Carolina May 24, 1863 VA25
Stone, T. - Co. D 16th Georgia Sept. 29, 1864 VA25
Stone, W.J. - 18th Virginia VA18
Stoner, H.D. - Co. D Maryland Artillery Aug. 16, 1862 VA25
Stoner, I.D. - Maryland Artillery Aug. 17, 1862 VA25
Stonescope, S.C. - North Carolina VA20
Stoop, J. - Capt. - Co. C 18th Virginia Heavy Art. Aug. 4, 1864 VA25
Storm, Henry A. - 14th South Carolina VA04
Story, I.W. - Co. A 22nd North Carolina May 9, 1862 VA25
Story, John - 9th Alabama July 17, 1861 VA25
Stoulman, __ - Co. A 16th North Carolina Jan. 17, 1863 VA25
Stoup, J.S. - 5th North Carolina VA18
Stoutman, A.M. - Co. I 7th North Carolina Sept. 14, 1864 VA25
Stovall, Alfred B. - Pvt. - Co. K 19th Mississippi MW May 12, 1864 Died May 22, 1864 VA28
Stovall, F.M. - 42nd Virginia VA18
Stowe, __ - June 9, 1862 VA25
Stowe, J.C. - Co. A 11th North Carolina Jan. 3, 1864 VA25
Stowe, R.H. - Co. B 13th North Carolina Nov. 7, 1863 VA25
Stower, W. - Co. A 4th Alabama Oct. 19, 1864 VA25
Strahan, R.G. - Co. G 27th North Carolina July 3, 1864 VA25
Strain, John - Sgt. - Co. C 53rd North Carolina Died May 15, 1864 VA28
Stranch, __ - Aug. 13, 1862 VA25
Strand, A.J. - Co. C 41st North Carolina July 20, 1863 VA25
Strand, T.J. - Co. A 31st Georgia Aug. 12, 1862 VA25
Strand, W.T. - Capt. - Co. G 2nd South Carolina July 10, 1864 VA25
Stratton, W.H. - 18th Mississippi May 22, 1862 VA25

Straws, A.J. - Co. C 41st Georgia June 18, 1863 VA25
Street, H. - POW - Federal Soldier Died June 25, 1862 VA19
Street, P. - Co. F 2nd North Carolina June 3, 1863 VA25
Street, R.G. - 6th Alabama VA18
Strell, H. - POW - Federal Soldier Died June 25, 1862 VA19
Stribley, J.M. - Co. C 15th Georgia Dec. 21, 1864 VA25
Strickland, __ - Died Nov. 22, 1862 VA19
Strickland, __ - Alabama Aug. 20, 1862 VA25
Strickland, C. - 2nd Florida Sept. 2, 1861 VA25
Strickland, H. - Co. K 50th Georgia Nov. 5, 1862 VA25
Strickland, H. - Co. A 64th Georgia Oct. 20, 1864 VA25
Strickland, I.P. - 4th Georgia July 5, 1862 VA25
Strickland, J. - Co. G 45th Georgia Sept. 4, 1862 VA25
Strickland, J.P. - Capt. - Georgia Nov. 5, 1864 VA25
Strickland, M. - Aug. 8, 1862 VA25
Strickland, M.R. - 8th South Carolina Oct. 25, 1862 VA25
Strickland, P. - 7th North Carolina VA22
Strickland, R.S. - Co. K 50th Georgia Nov. 8, 1862 VA25
Strickland, S.J. - Co. E 61st Georgia VA11
Strickland, W.A. - Co. I 57th Virginia June 15, 1864 VA25
Strickland, W.R. - 50th Georgia March 22, 1863 VA25
Strickland, W.W. - Co B 8th South Carolina Died Dec 18, 1861 VA23
Strickland, Wm. - Co. I 31st North Carolina June 21, 1864 VA25
Strickler, John W. - VA15
Stricklin, John - DOW Oct. 3, 1862 age 20 VA19
Stricklin, W.G. - Co. K 56th Georgia March 31, 1865 VA25
Strickling, E.C. - Co. C 7th North Carolina Aug. 8, 1862 VA25
Stringfellow, __ - 15th Alabama Nov. 30, 1861 VA25
Stringfellow, A.W. - Corp. - Co. I 3rd Virginia June 24, 1862 VA25
Stringfellow, E. - Co. G 42nd Mississippi July 23, 1862 VA25
Stringfellow, L. - Co. A 1st South Carolina March 1, 1865 VA25
Stringfield, J.W. - Co. G 6th Georgia Sept. 22, 1862 VA25

Stromoar, William - Virginia VA22
Strond, B.T. - Co. B 5th Texas Aug. 31, 1861 VA25
Strong, C. - Co. F 2nd Mississippi June 10, 1862 VA25
Stroop, C. - Co. H 52nd North Carolina June 18, 1864 VA25
Strother, A. - Stribling's Artillery Sept. 1, 1862 VA25
Strower, W. - Co. A 4th Alabama Oct. 19, 1864 VA25
Struna, __ - July 1, 1862 VA25
Stuart, Charles C. - Pvt. - Co. B 31st Virginia DOW June 6, 1864 (MW Spotsylvania Court House) VA28
Stuart, J.E.B. (James Ewell Brown) - Major General - Cavalry 1833 - May 12, 1864 - MW at Yellow Tavern on May 11, 1864 VA25
Stuart, James M. - Corp. - 48th Virginia VA04
Stuart, N.B. - Co. G 21st Mississippi July 1, 1862 VA25
Stuart, R. - Co. A 1st South Carolina June 20, 1862 VA25
Stuart, Washington - Kemper's Battery VA10
Stuckey, R.D. - 13th Mississippi VA18
Studemuir, A.J. - 13th South Carolina VA18
Stump, John H. - VA20
Stunson, G.W. - Co. K 47th North Carolina June 22, 1864 VA25
Sturnes, M.B. - Co. I 28th Georgia Oct. 1, 1862 VA25
Styles, John - Co. G 5th Texas June 11, 1862 VA25
Sugal, M. - May 21, 1864 VA25
Suggs, J.S. - Tennessee VA20
Suggs, Wiley - Co. F 14th North Carolina VA11
Sulivan, A.J. - 12th South Carolina June 19, 1864 VA25
Sulivan, D.C. - Co. H 7th Louisiana April 28, 1865 VA25
Sulivan, J.S. - Co. G 27th Georgia Sept. 28, 1864 VA25
Sulivan, P.M. - Virginia Cavalry June 24, 1862 VA25
Sullen, A. - 24th North Carolina March 11, 1865 VA25
Sullivan, John D. - Pvt. - Co. D 52nd Virginia DOW June 20, 1864 (MW May 18, 1864) Other sources place this soldier in Fredericksburg Cemetery VA28
Sullivan, M. - North Carolina VA22
Sullivan, T. - Co. B 2nd South Carolina June 13, 1864 VA25

Sullivan, W.H. - Co. A 49th Virginia June 12, 1864 VA25
Sumerit, J.L. - Co. K 46th North Carolina Sept. 9, 1864 VA25
Sumery, R.H. - South Carolina July 26, 1861 VA25
Summens, __ - Georgia Oct. 8, 1864 VA25
Summer, J.B. - Sgt. - Co. H 16th Mississippi Died May 12, 1864 VA28
Summerlin, M.P. - 15th Louisiana VA18
Summerline, H.J. - 14th Alabama Infantry - KIA - Battle of Williamsburg - May 5, 1862 VA02
Summers, __ - Aug. 16, 1862 VA25
Summers, D. - Co. F 4th North Carolina July 11, 1862 VA25
Summers, E.T.W. - Portsmouth Artillery (Virginia) July 15, 1862 VA25
Summers, J. - Co. G 22nd North Carolina June 10, 1862 VA25
Summers, J.D. - Co. E 13th South Carolina June 20, 1862 VA25
Summers, J.R. - Co. F 22nd North Carolina July 5, 1862 VA25
Summers, John - Co. H 48th Georgia Aug. 25, 1864 VA25
Summers, P.H. - South Carolina July 26, 1861 VA25
Summers, W.B. - Alabama VA20
Summerty, G. - Co. A 18th North Carolina Dec. 25, 1862 VA25
Summett, J.W. - Co. F 18th North Carolina Dec. 23, 1862 VA25
Summonds, A. - Co. I 46th North Carolina Nov. 27, 1863 VA25
Sumner, H.J. - Co. C 47th Alabama Feb. 3, 1863 VA25
Sumner, M.M. - Co. B 15th South Carolina June 12, 1864 VA25
Sunnett, D. - 1st North Carolina July 30, 1862 VA25
Surenger, J.E. - Florida VA20
Surley, H. - Co. C 34th North Carolina Aug. 4, 1864 VA25
Surratt, R. - Co. F 34th North Carolina May 14, 1864 VA25
Sutler, C.S. - Co. K 38th Georgia May 30, 1864 VA25
Suttlefield, J. - Co. H 5th Florida Aug. 24, 1862 VA25

Sutton, C.G. - Co. D 45th Georgia May 30, 1864 VA25
Sutton, D.B. - Co. D 12th Alabama July 1, 1862 VA25
Sutton, J. - Co. C 13th North Carolina June 19, 1862 VA25
Suwell, L.W. - "P.L." - Co. H Georgia Nov. 6, 1864 VA25
Swan, I.M. - Co. G 3rd Georgia July 17, 1862 VA25
Swann, J. - Co. B 35th Georgia June 20, 1862 VA25
Swann, J.K. - Co. G 38th Georgia Feb. 8, 1865 VA25
Swapard, W.J. - Co. I 4th Alabama April 17, 1865 VA25
Swarford, H. - May 20, 1862 VA25
Swartzwelder, Z. - Clark Cavalry VA06
Sweat, A.S. - Co. F 13th Georgia June 5, 1864 VA25
Sweeney, Jonathan - Lt. -KIA March 2, 1864 moved to Hollywood - Nov. 25, 1899 (not listed in Hollywood) VA19
Sweet, David - Pvt. - Co. E 7th Tennessee Died June 10, 1865 VA26
Sweet, I.F. - Co. F 14th Alabama May 27, 1864 VA25
Sweetland, James - POW - Federal Soldier Died May 7, 1862 VA19
Swindle, I.W. - Co. C 3td North Carolina April 21, 1862 VA25
Swingdolph, W.E. - Co. D 14th Alabama June 22, 1862 VA25
Swink, G.W. - Lt.-8th Virginia InfantryVA10
Swink, J. - Co. F 7th Virginia July 1, 1863 VA25
Swinson, Z.B. - Co. B__th Virginia Aug. 23, 1864 VA25
Swittenberg, A.M. - Corp. - Co. H 16th Mississippi Died May 12, 1864 Headstone reads:" Smittenberg" Soldier's name is also spelled:" Smittenburg" VA28
Switzer, __ - Co. F 52nd Virginia July 30, 1862 VA25
Sykes, __ - Co. K 44th North Carolina Jan. 3, 1865 VA25
Sykes, I.N. - Co. B 16th North Carolina April 7, 1864 VA25
Sykes, John - Co. I 26th Alabama Aug. 18, 1862 VA25
Sykes, L. - Co. I 36th North Carolina April 9, 1865 VA25
Sykes, L.W. - Lt.- Aid de Camp - Mississippi Sept. 1, 1864 VA25
Sykes, R. - Georgia Artillery July 25, 1862 VA25

Sykes, W.T. - Co. B 16th Georgia May 13, 1863 VA25
Sykes, William - 11th North Carolina VA18
Syle, J. - 16th Virginia May 18, 1862 VA25
Sylmen, D. - Co. D 37th North Carolina June 6, 1864 VA25
Syman, J.H. - Co. C 6th Virginia June 24, 1864 VA25
Symk, __ - 21st Mississippi July 10, 1862 VA25
Symmonds, John - 7th Georgia VA18
Synk, J. - Co. F 15th North Carolina Oct. 29, 1863 VA25
T __, G. W. - Co C__ Died Dec 1861 VA23
T __, J. - Co. C 61st Georgia Dec. 23, 1862 VA25
T __, W.J. - Aug. 20, 1861 VA25
T __, W.P. - Sgt. - Co. I 21st Arkansas July 5, 186_ VA25
Tabb, James - DOW Sept. 17, 1862 VA19
Tabb, Jas. - Died Sept 17, 1862 age 53 VA19
Tabb, Robert - KIA May 2, 1862 VA19
Taff, G.W. - Co. I 28th Georgia March 1863 VA25
Taff, T.W. - Co. D 31st Georgia July 16, 1862 VA25
Taffwel, L. - Co. H 5th Louisiana June 3, 1863 VA25
Taggard, J.B. - North Carolina VA22
Tailor, S.C. - Co. G 12th Alabama Sept. 16, 1862 VA25
Talbert, A.G. - Co. D 21st South Carolina Jan. 1, 1865 VA25
Talbot, J.H. - Co. I 5th Alabama June 17, 1862 VA25
Talley, __ - Co. I 37th North Carolina Aug. 30, 1864 VA25
Talley, J.S. - Co. K 14th North Carolina May 29, 1862 VA25
Talliaferro, J.C. - Aug. 8, 1862 VA25
Tanner, John - Pvt. - Co. F 11th Virginia Died May 4, 1865 VA26
Tansell, B. - Co. B 49th Virginia June 15, 1862 VA25
Tanton, R.W. - Co. E 25th North Carolina July 22, 1864 VA25
Tarn, John - Co. K 49th North Carolina July 21, 1864 VA25
Tarpley, Ashburg - 12th Mississippi VA04
Tarpley, J.S. - Co. K 47th North Carolina June 28, 1864 V25
Tarr, W. - Buckingham County (Virginia) Dec. 4, 1862 VA25
Tarrance, T.O. - Co. F 34th North Carolina Aug. 26, 1862 VA25

Tarrance, W.B. - Co. B 13th North Carolina July 23, 1863 VA25
Tarrans, S. - North Carolina VA07
Tash, S. - Co. H 15th North Carolina Dec. 19, 1864 VA25
Tasnew, J. - Co. I 9th North Carolina Nov. 9, 1864 VA25
Tate, R.J. - Co. H 27th Georgia Aug. 5, 1864 VA25
Tate, T.F. - 9th Louisiana Oct. 23, 1861 VA25
Tate, W.P. - Co. K 6th North Carolina May 16, 1862 VA25
Tatum, H.S. - Co. G 3rd North Carolina March 25, 1862 VA25
Taulbert, W.N. - Co. A 47th North Carolina July 16, 1864 VA25
Tavon, Jasper - 48th Georgia VA11
Taylor, __ - 49th Virginia July 3, 1862 VA25
Taylor, A. - North Carolina Aug. 30, 1864 VA25
Taylor, A.J. - Co. B 46th North Carolina July 19, 1864 VA25
Taylor, Christopher C. - DOW Aug. 15, 1862 VA19
Taylor, D. - Co. H 5th North Carolina July 1, 1862 VA25
Taylor, D.T. - Co. B 13th South Carolina July 22, 1862 VA25
Taylor, F.L. - Lt. Colonel- 12th Virginia Oct. 3, 1862 VA25
Taylor, F.W. - Co. F 28th North Carolina July 25, 1864 VA25
Taylor, G. - Co. H 14th South Carolina June 10, 1862 VA25
Taylor, G. - 9th Louisiana May 18, 1862 VA25
Taylor, G.P. - Co. E 34th North Carolina Aug. 1, 1864 VA25
Taylor, G.T.A. - Arkansas July 5, 1861 age 24 VA25
Taylor, G.W. - Co. B 9th Alabama Sept. 2, 1864 VA25
Taylor, Geo. - Died Dec. 16, 1862 VA19
Taylor, H. - C.S. Navy Nov. 18, 1864 VA25
Taylor, H. - Co. H 2nd North Carolina Aug. 24, 1862 VA25
Taylor, J. - Pvt. - Co. K 54th North Carolina Died May 2, 1865 VA26
Taylor, J. - Co. K 45th Georgia June 21, 1862 VA25
Taylor, J. - Co. K 13th South Carolina July 10, 1862 VA25
Taylor, J. F. - Co. F 44th Virginia Aug. 24, 1862 VA25
Taylor, J.R. - Co. G 30th North Carolina July 12, 1862 VA25

Taylor, J. Stratton - Resident of Confederate Soldiers Home Died July 19, 1918 age 74 VA19
Taylor, J.C. - Co. A 2nd Arkansas June 29, 1862 VA25
Taylor, J.H. - Pvt. - Co. A 3rd Alabama Died May 08, 1864 VA28
Taylor, J.P. - Co. D 12th Georgia Aug. 12, 1862 VA25
Taylor, J.P. - Co. H 9th Louisiana Dec. 29, 1862 VA25
Taylor, J.S. - 13th South Carolina June 15, 1862 VA25
Taylor, J.W. - Virginia VA20
Taylor, James - Co. K 61st North Carolina Aug. 19, 1864 VA25
Taylor, Jas. - Co. F 1st Virginia Cavalry VA23
Taylor, Jas. T. - Co. E 7th Virginia Infantry VA10
Taylor, John - Co. C 4th Virginia July 23, 1863 VA25
Taylor, M. - Co. F 25th South Carolina March 5, 1865 VA25
Taylor, M.M. - Co. I 22nd North Carolina March 5, 1865 VA25
Taylor, Ma __ - VA06
Taylor, Milton - VA12
Taylor, R. - 13th South Carolina June 10, 1862 VA25
Taylor, R. - Co. F 17th North Carolina Sept. 28, 1864 VA25
Taylor, S. - Co. C 26th Alabama Sept. 14, 1862 VA25
Taylor, T. - Co. K 13th South Carolina July 8, 1862 VA25
Taylor, W. - Sgt. - Co. E 56th North Carolina Dec. 2, 1864 VA25
Taylor, W.B. - Co. A 46th North Carolina July 22, 1864 VA25
Taylor, W.I. - Co. H 53rd Georgia May 24, 1864 VA25
Taylor, W.J. - 5th Alabama VA18
Taylor, W.J. - Co. G 17th Georgia June 5, 1862 VA25
Taylor, W.L. - Co. E 27th North Carolina May 22, 1864 VA25
Taylor, W.L. - Alabama May 10, 1862 VA25
Taylor, W.S. - Co. A 47th North Carolina April 27, 1864 VA25
Taylor, Wm. W. - 25th South Carolina VA04
Teal, J. - May 5, 1863 VA25

Tebbitts, Charles F. - POW - Federal Soldier Died Nov. 14, 1861 VA19
Tedder, B.W. - Co. B 28th Georgia June 20, 1862 VA25
Tedder, W. - Co. D 17th Mississippi May 18, 1864 VA25
Tednal, W.T. - Co. E 53rd Georgia May 16, 1863 VA25
Teel, James - POW - Federal Soldier Died June 9, 1862 VA19
Teever, W.H. - 13th Georgia Aug. 11, 1862 VA25
Telison, __ - Co. F 18th Mississippi Oct. 4, 1864 VA25
Templeton, J.M. - Co. I 7th North Carolina Oct. 18, 1864 VA25
Templeton, W.A. - Co. F 28th Georgia May 17, 1862 VA25
Tenant, J.S. - Co. K "H.L." (Hampton Legion?) Georgia June 17, 1864 VA25
Tending, J.W. - Co. H 7th South Carolina Sept. 29, 1862 VA25
Tensell, B. - Co. B 18th North Carolina June 15, 1862 VA25
Tensell, T.M. - Prince William County (Virginia) May 26, 1862 VA25
Terrel, I. - POW - Federal Soldier Died Dec. 25, 1861 VA19
Terrell, Andrew J. - Pvt. - Co. B 52nd Virginia DOW May 17, 1864 (MW Spotsylvania Court House) VA28
Terrell, S. - Alabama Jan. 24, 1863 VA25
Terrett, A.H. - 1st Brigade (South Carolina) April 12, 1862 VA25
Terrett, John - Co. I 11th Virginia VA10
Terrill, E.H. - 19th Mississippi VA18
Terry, C. - Co. H 42nd Mississippi Aug. 16, 1862 VA25
Terry, C.H. - Co. K 15th Alabama June 6, 1862 VA25
Terry, C.W. - Co. C 13th Mississippi July 26, 1862 VA25
Terry, G.W. - 49th Virginia July 14, 1862 VA25
Terry, H. - Co. E 1st South Carolina Artillery June 27, 1864 VA25
Terry, H. - Co. A 1st Alabama June 30, 1864 VA25
Terry, H. - Co. B 49th Virginia Aug. 16, 1862 VA25
Terry, I. - Co. K 12th Alabama Dec. 16, 1861 VA25
Terry, J. - Co. F 60th Georgia Oct. 14, 1861 VA25

Terry, J.P. - Co. A 22nd South Carolina Nov. 10, 1864 VA25
Terry, W.G. - Co. C 27th North Carolina Jan. 3, 1863 VA25
Terry, William - Co. B 15th Georgia VA11
Tessell, N. - Alabama Aug. 30, 1862 VA25
Thacher, J. - Co. B 38th North Carolina Nov. 5, 1864 VA25
Thacker, B. - 10th Louisiana Aug. 12, 1861 VA25
Thacker, E. - Co. D 24th Georgia May 28, 1862 VA25
Thaws, S.F. - Co. C 59th Georgia May 27, 1864 VA25
Thaxton, J.M. - Sgt. - Co. C 25th Virginia Battalion May 12, 1864 VA25
Thayer, M.B.- POW - Federal Soldier Died June 21, 1862 VA19
Theis, Christian - VA12
Theis, Henry W. - VA12
Therrell, Lewis - Co. D 8th South Carolina Died May 12, 1864 VA28
Thevis, __ - Co. C 13th North Carolina July 21, 1862 VA25
Thigfar, W.H. - Co. C 18th Mississippi April 29, 1861 VA25
Thigher, H.G. - Co. I 26th South Carolina Aug. 13, 1864 VA25
Thigher, J. - Co. H 26th South Carolina Aug. 15, 1864 VA25
Thigher, R. - Co. H 66th North Carolina Aug. 23, 1864 VA25
Thipling, J. - Co. K 38th Georgia July 3, 1862 VA25
Thiser, I.A. - Co. I 11th North Carolina Nov. 14, 1863 VA25
Thomas, B.F. - Co. K 12th North Carolina VA25
July 16, 1862
Thomas, C. - Sgt. - Co. A 28th North Carolina June 3, 1864 VA25
Thomas, E.A. - Co. I 53rd Virginia July 22, 1862 VA25
Thomas, E.J. - 15th Alabama VA18
Thomas, Edgar - Co. D 17th Virginia Infantry VA10
Thomas, G.W. - Co. E 60th Georgia June 25, 1864 VA25
Thomas, H. - Co. F 20th South Carolina Cavalry June 21, 1864 VA25
Thomas, H. - Co. E 12th North Carolina July 16, 1862 VA25
Thomas, H. - Co. D 49th North Carolina Aug. 5, 1864 VA25

Thomas, I.M. - 38th North Carolina Dec. 30, 1862 VA25
Thomas, J. - Co. H Cooper's Rifles (South Carolina) June 12, 1864 VA25
Thomas, J. - Co. F 21st South Carolina July 21, 1864 VA25
Thomas, J.E. - Co. E 27th Alabama May 24, 1862 VA25
Thomas, J.H. - Hawe's Battery (Virginia) May 7, 1865 VA25
Thomas, J.R. - Co. I 33rd North Carolina May 24, 1864 VA25
Thomas, J.R. - Co. B 52nd North Carolina June 13, 1864 VA25
Thomas, J.W. - Co. H 30th North Carolina Aug. 8, 1862 VA25
Thomas, John - VA15
Thomas, L. - Colter's Battery (Virginia) Oct. 17, 1864 VA25
Thomas, L.J. - Co. H 5th Florida Aug. 27, 1862 VA25
Thomas, M.H. - Co. G 49th Georgia Aug. 2, 1862 VA25
Thomas, Michael - VA15
Thomas, P. - Co. K 14th Louisiana July 24, 1862 VA25
Thomas, P.A. - Co. G 14th Alabama June 8, 1862 VA25
Thomas, Paul - 16th Mississippi VA18
Thomas, R. - Co. H 26th South Carolina March 9, 1865 VA25
Thomas, R.G. - Pvt.- Co. H 3rd North Carolina Died June 24, 1865 VA26
Thomas, S.P. - Co. G 6th North Carolina Infantry VA08
Thomas, W. - Co. B 2nd Florida Oct. 2, 1864 VA25
Thomas, W.F. - Co. D 49th North Carolina Aug. 12, 1864 VA25
Thomas, W.G. - Co. G 23rd Georgia Oct. 8, 1864 VA25
Thomas, W.H. - Co. H 24th Virginia July 1, 1864 VA25
Thomas, W.J. - Co. G 9th Virginia June 15, 1862 VA25
Thomas, W.L. - Co. D 66th North Carolina July 28, 1864 VA25
Thomason, J.S. - Co. K 64th Georgia Oct. 18, 1864 VA25
Thompson, __ - Alabama Infantry VA08
Thompson, __ - Co. G 15th South Carolina July 8, 1862 VA25
Thompson, A. - Co. G 53rd Georgia May 18, 1863 VA25
Thompson, A. - Co. G 15th Louisiana June 9, 1863 VA25

Thompson, A.H. - Co. B 14th Georgia Dec. 13, 1861 VA25
Thompson, A.M. - Co. H 50th Georgia July 4, 1864 VA25
Thompson, A.V.Y. - Co. G 8th Louisiana June 8, 1863 VA25
Thompson, Armis'd - 8th Virginia Infantry VA10
Thompson, B.L. - 26th Alabama Sept. 6, 1862 VA25
Thompson, Charles - Co. I 19th Virginia VA11
Thompson, H. - Co. D 11th Alabama Nov. 10, 1861 VA25
Thompson, H.A. - Co. E 14th South Carolina May 21, 1864 VA25
Thompson, H.M. - Co. F 53rd Georgia VA11
Thompson, J. - Co. F 25th North Carolina June 29, 1862 VA25
Thompson, J.H. - 38th Georgia Nov. 4, 1864 VA25
Thompson, J.J. - Co. I 11th Georgia March 17, 1863 VA25
Thompson, J.J. - Oct. 11, 1861 VA25
Thompson, J.P. - Co. K 1st North Carolina July 14, 1862 VA25
Thompson, J.S. - Alabama VA20
Thompson, J.W. - Co. D 14th South Carolina June 28, 1862 VA25
Thompson, J.W. - 1st South Carolina Oct. 8, 1864 VA25
Thompson, L.B. - 3rd Alabama March 12, 1862 VA25
Thompson, N.N. - Mississippi Jan. 30, 1863 VA25
Thompson, R.E. - Co. C 45th Georgia June 12, 1862 VA25
Thompson, R.R. - Co. E 21st North Carolina Dec. 27, 1862 VA25
Thompson, R.S. - 26th Alabama Sept. 6, 1862 VA25
Thompson, R.W. - Co. A 6th Alabama June 17, 1863 VA25
Thompson, S.H. - Co. G 60th Virginia June 30, 1862 VA25
Thompson, T. - Co. G 23rd North Carolina June 1, 1864 VA25
Thompson, T.J. - 13th Mississippi Aug. 1, 1861 VA25
Thompson, T.W. - Co. G 6th North Carolina June 7, 1862 VA25
Thompson, V. - Lt.- Co. I 14th Louisiana July 23, 1862 VA25
Thompson, W. - Mississippi VA18

Thompson, W. - 2nd Georgia July 16, 1862 VA25
Thompson, W. - Co. A 55th North Carolina Dec. 7, 1863 VA25
Thompson, W.A. - Co. C 13th South Carolina Oct. 18, 1864 VA25
Thompson, W.A. - Co. C 49th North Carolina Oct. 18, 1864 VA25
Thompson, W.G. - Co. G 6th Georgia Oct. 10, 1864 VA25
Thompson, W.L. - 4th Alabama VA18
Thompson, W.L. - Co. K 4th Alabama May 3, 1865 VA25
Thompson, W.P. - Virginia VA20
Thompson, William L. - Lt.- Co. G 5th Virginia Died May 10, 1864 VA28
Thompson, William R. - Sgt. - Co. A 4th North Carolina VA28
Thorn, Y.P. - Co. I 1st North Carolina Cavalry Nov. 13, 1864 VA25
Thornton, J.A. - Co. G 5th Texas Jan. 6, 1862 VA25
Thornton, John W. - Pvt. - Co. A 47th Alabama Died May 08, 1864 VA28
Thornton, M.F. - Co. F 38th Georgia Aug. 7, 1862 VA25
Thornton, N. - Co. A 13th Alabama April 14, 1861 VA25
Thornton, N.H. - Co. A 9th Louisiana Feb. 5, 1862 VA25
Thornton, R.T. - Co. K 24th North Carolina June 14, 1864 VA25
Thoyman, B.J. - Co. H 58th Georgia May 15, 1863 VA25
Thrankett, G. - Co. F 43rd Mississippi June 25, 1864 VA25
Thrash, J.B. - Co. E 28th Georgia Aug. 11, 1862 VA25
Thrasher, L. - Sept. 24, 1861 VA25
Thrift, C.B. - 3rd South Carolina VA18
Thrift, James - Major - Co. G 8th Virginia Infantry VA10
Throgmorten, T. - Co. C 10th Mississippi Jan. 19, 1862 VA25
Throwbridge, Charles E. - POW - Federal Soldier Died Oct. 9, 1861 VA19
Thurman, Wm. - Died Dec. 11, 1862 VA19
Thurston, J.R. - 45th Georgia June 1864 VA25

Thuseat, S.W. - Co. A 2nd Georgia March 29, 1865 VA25
Tichell, J. - Co. K 49th North Carolina April 24, 1865 VA25
Tidler, George M. - VA12
Tidler, J.P.M. - VA12
Tidler, S.L. - VA12
Tidler, William J. - VA12
Tidwell, W.A. - Co. K 13th Georgia June 23, 1864 VA25
Tigue, G.W. - Co. A 37th North Carolina June 8, 1862 VA25
Tigue, J.B. - Co. I 13th Mississippi Jan. 28, 1863 VA25
Tigue, W. - Co. I 14th South Carolina Sept. 14, 1862 VA25
Tilley, W.D. - Co. K 2nd North Carolina June 22, 1864 VA25
Tillient, R.S. - Co. C 9th Virginia July 5, 1862 VA25
Tillis, J.L.- 20th Georgia VA18
Tillman, D. - Co. A 13th North Carolina June 4, 1863 VA25
Tillman, George W. - Pvt. - Co. G 4th Georgia Died May 10, 1864 VA28
Tillman, R. - 5th Texas May 26, 1862 VA25
Tillman, R. M. - 1st Texas May 26, 1862 VA25
Tilly, P.J. - 22nd North Carolina VA18
Timberlake, F.J. - Co. G 47th North Carolina July 18, 1864 VA25
Timberlake, J.F. - Co. E 53rd Virginia July 30, 1862 VA25
Tindal, J. - Co. A 26th North Carolina Aug. 18, 1864 VA25
Tindall, W.A. - Co. A 13th Georgia June 23, 1865 VA25
Tininson, W.A. - 69th Georgia Nov. 13, 1864 VA25
Tink, C. - Co. F 5th Tennessee Dec. 29, 1861 VA25
Tinkler, R.H. - Co. G 6th South Carolina June 26, 1864 VA25
Tinsley, J. - Co. D 42nd Mississippi M arch 22, 1862 VA25
Tiston, M. - Co. I 8th Virginia March 13, 1865 VA25
Tittle, L.P. - Corp. - Co. G 18th Georgia VA28
Titus, F. - Co. D 5th Alabama Feb 22, 1863 VA25
Todd, G.W. - 46th Virginia July 15, 1863 VA25
Todd, J.A. - 1st Texas July 4, 1862 VA25
Todd, J.F. - Capt. - 4th Georgia July 15, 1862 VA25
Todd, J.J. - Co. A 26th South Carolina March 8, 1865 VA25

Todd, James M. - Pvt. - Co. B 45th Georgia Died May 19, 1864 also listed as John M. Todd VA28
Todd, John M. - see Todd, James M. VA28
Todd, N.J. - 11th North Carolina April 21, 1865 VA25
Todd, O.G. - Co. F 45th Georgia Oct. 3, 1863 VA25
Todd, S.H. - 2nd North Carolina June 2, 1862 VA25
Todd, W.D. - Cobb's Legion (Georgia) Sept. 9, 1864 VA25
Toland, W. - Corp. - "H.L." (Hampton's Legion ?) Georgia Nov. 5, 1864 VA25
Toler, __ - 1st South Carolina Oct. 23, 1862 VA25
Toler, H. - Pvt. - North Carolina March 26, 1865 VA22
Tollison, W. - Co. I 13th South Carolina July 2, 1862 VA25
Tomberlin, M. - 27th Georgia VA18
Tomberlin, W. - VA12
Tomlin, John - Co. I 3rd Virginia March 25, 1862 VA25
Tomlin, W.A. - Camp Winder (Virginia) May 10, 1862 VA25
Tomodle, S.J. - Co. I 8th Louisiana May 27, 1863 VA25
Tompkin, R.D. - Co. E 9th Georgia VA11
Tompkins, __ - Aug. 18, 1864 VA25
Tompkins, S. - 2nd Florida Sept. 8, 1861 VA25
Tompkins, S.H. - Capt. - 60th Virginia June 27, 1862 VA25
Tompkins, T.H. - 2nd Florida Aug. 1, 1861 VA25
Tompson, James A. - DOW July 19, 1862 age 9 (sic) VA19
Toner, A. - Co. C 16th Mississippi VA28
Topans, N.B. - Sgt. - Co. H 32nd North Carolina VA28
Topper, F.R. - Clark Cavalry VA06
Towers, D.R. - Lt.- 8th Georgia VA25
Townsend, Charles C. - see Townsends, Charles C. VA28
Townsend, H.E. - Sgt. - Co. G 8th South Carolina Dec. 4, 1862 VA25
Townsends, Charles C. - Co. A 20th North Carolina Headstone reads: 'Townsend" VA28
Towson, J.S. - Co. B 9th Virginia Cavalry Aug. 16, 1864 VA25
Tracket, R.A. - 18th Virginia Sept. 10, 1861 VA25
Trakell, W.M. - June 8, 1862 VA25

Trammell, B.P. - Co. H 22nd South Carolina Aug. 6, 1864 VA25
Trammell, T. - Co. F 42nd Mississippi Oct. 5, 1862 VA25
Tramwill, A.C. - Co. D 53rd Georgia Aug. 6, 1862 VA25
Trapp, B.W. - Co. F 12th South Carolina May 4, 1864 VA25
Treadway, I.E. - Co. K 22nd South Carolina Cavalry Sept. 5, 1864 VA25
Treadway, J.A. - Co. H 43rdNorth Carolina Oct. 1863 VA25
Treadway, James - 12th Alabama Aug. 1, 1861 VA25
Tredaway, L.R. - 17th Georgia VA18
Tredden, W. - Co. I 26th North Carolina Sept. 15, 1862 VA25
Trent, J.H. - Co. B 3rd Virginia June 4, 1862 VA25
Trent, T.D. - Pvt.- Co. C 18th Virginia Bat. Died July 3, 1865 VA26
Trevell, T.C. - Sgt. - Co. B 35th North Carolina Oct. 30, 1864 VA25
Trexell, J. - POW - Federal Soldier Died Oct. 24, 1861 VA19
Tribbe, J. - Co. H 64th Georgia Aug. 14, 1864 VA25
Trice, J.H. - Co. B 37th North Carolina July 3, 1864 VA25
Trickle, S.C. - Co. F 55th Virginia June 25, 1862 VA25
Trimble, E. - Georgia VA20
Triplett, J.M. - Co. B 8th Virginia Aug. 1, 1862 VA25
Tripp, M.B. - Co. H 1st Texas July 5, 1862 VA25
Troth, B.Z. - Sgt. - Co. E 7th Virginia Infantry VA10
Trotter, J. - Co. A 42nd Mississippi Aug. 30, 1862 VA25
Trotter, J.B. - Co. B 2nd South Carolina Rifles Headstone reads: "2nd South Carolina Infantry" VA28
Troywick, J.F. - 15th Alabama June 12, 1862 VA25
Troywick, M.S. - Co. H 13th Alabama July 29, 1862 VA25
Truce, W. - Co. B 11th Alabama Aug. 31, 1862 VA25
Trucklin, W. - Co. E 36th North Carolina March 31, 1865 VA25
Trueheart, John H. - DOW Aug. 18, 1865 age 20 VA19
Truman, J.W. - Co. F 28th North Carolina Sept. 4, 1862 VA25
Trusdale, J.C. - Co. I 12th South Carolina June 19, 1864 VA25

Trutt, __ - Co. G 28th Georgia July 7, 1863 VA25
Tubb, M. - Co. I 12th Mississippi July 11, 1862 VA25
Tucker, A.J. - Lt.- Co. I 12th Georgia May 18, 1864 VA25
Tucker, B.F. - Co. F 1st South Carolina June 27, 1864 VA25
Tucker, R.A. - 11th Alabama July 14, 1862 VA25
Tucker, T. - Co. B 63rd North Carolina Aug. 9, 1863 VA25
Tucker, W. - Co. K 4th Georgia Jan. 7, 1863 VA25
Tucker, W.H. - Co. A 10th Georgia Battalion July 2, 1864 VA25
Tucker, W.T. - 8th Virginia Infantry VA10
Tuckley, R.W. - Co. F 22nd Mississippi Nov. 10, 1864 VA25
Tulbyfield, E.A. - Co. C 28th North Carolina June 5, 1862 VA25
Tuler, T. - Virginia Reserves Feb. 20, 1865 VA25
Tulson, A. - Co. I 14th North Carolina Oct. 16, 1864 VA25
Tune, N.B. - Co. G 6th Georgia July 25, 1864 VA25
Tunkerly, C. - Cobb's Legion, Georgia Sept. 14, 1861 VA25
Tunstill, A.H. - Pvt.- Co. E 44th Virginia Bat. Died May 23, 1865 VA26
Turboler, R.E. - Co. C 28th North Carolina June 12, 1862 VA25
Turk, I.G. - Co. D 45th Georgia May 22, 1864 VA25
Turke, Daniel A. - DOW July 3, 1863 age 19 VA19
Turkies, P. - Co. F 10th Louisiana Aug. 15, 1863 VA25
Turner, __ - 4th North Carolina Infantry VA08
Turner, __ - Co. I - "H.L" (Hampton's Legion?) Georgia March 3, 1865 VA25
Turner, A. - Co. G 11th North Carolina May 26, 1863 VA25
Turner, A. - Co. G 4th South Carolina June 19, 1862 VA25
Turner, A.R. - Co. G 64th Georgia Oct. 19, 1864 VA25
Turner, A.W. - Co. I 59th Georgia Aug. 28, 1864 VA25
Turner, Bruce - Died of measles in 1861 VA05
Turner, C. - 1st South Carolina Cavalry Oct. 15, 1864 VA25
Turner, C.C. - Co. K 20th North Carolina Sept. 1, 1862 VA25
Turner, C.P. - Co. D 17th North Carolina July 24, 1864 VA25
Turner, H. - Pvt. - Virginia April 19, 1865 VA22

Turner, J. - Co. G 64th Georgia Aug. 1, 1864 VA25
Turner, J. - Co. B 63rd Tennessee July 25, 1864 VA25
Turner, J. - Cobb's Legion (Georgia) June 25, 1863 VA25
Turner, J. A. - Virginia Artillery May 29, 1862 VA25
Turner, J. L. - Co. E 21st Mississippi June 2, 1862 VA25
Turner, J.B. - Co. H 4th North Carolina May 23, 1862 VA25
Turner, J.W. - Co. E 28th North Carolina Oct. 28, 1864 VA25
Turner, John - Pvt. - Co. A 20th North Carolina KIA -
  Spotsylvania Court House - May 19, 1864 VA28
Turner, John - Pvt. - Co. E 32nd North Carolina MW -
  Spotsylvania Court House - May 10, 1864 (Died May
  11, 1864 VA28
Turner, John - Co. B 1st Louisiana Aug. 22, 1862 VA25
Turner, L.B. - Co. A 2nd Florida June 25, 1862 VA25
Turner, R. - Co. D 2nd Mississippi VA25
Turner, R.K. - Co. K 22ndNorth Carolina Aug. 20, 1862
  VA25
Turner, S.E. - Co. E 49thGeorgia July 24, 1862 VA25
Turner, T. - Co. A 2nd North Carolina Aug. 8, 1862 VA25
Turner, T.W. - Co. K 47th Alabama Jan. 24, 1863 VA25
Turner, W. - Co. F 32nd North Carolina May 27, 1864 VA25
Turner, W.A. - Lt.- Co. C 7th Georgia Oct. 4, 1864 VA25
Turner, W.B. - Co. I 10th Alabama July 1, 1862 VA25
Turner, W.H. - Pvt. - Georgia March 30, 1864 VA22
Turner, W.S. - Co. R 17th Georgia Died Jan. 5, 1862 VA23
Turner, William L. - Co. G 57th Virginia Died at Quincy
  Station Jan. 17, 1863 VA28
Turnley, W. - Co. D 9th Alabama June 14, 1862 VA25
Turrentine, W.A.T. - 10th Alabama Sept. 26, 1862 VA25
Tusing, Ted - VA30
Tuttle, J.C. - 21st North Carolina May 29, 1863 VA25
Twyner, J.B. - __th Virginia Infantry - KIA - Battle of
  Williamsburg - May 5, 1862 VA02
Tyler, D.J. - Co. K 2nd Louisiana May 27, 1862 VA25
Tyler, George C. - KIA July 2, 1864 VA19
Tyler, R. - Hanover Artillery (Virginia) May 4, 1862 VA25

Tyler, W. - Co. F 18th Mississippi Jan. 20, 1863 VA25
Tyler, W. J. - Co. I 18th Mississippi Aug. 26, 1862 VA25
Tyson, D.P. - Co. H 26th North Carolina Oct. 27, 1864 VA25
Tyson, J.M. - Co. B 14th Texas June 8, 1864 VA25
Ulm, R.M. - Co. E 27thSouth Carolina Dec. 11, 1864 VA25
Ulsory, S. - Co. I 21st Mississippi June 5, 1862 VA25
Underwood, J.G. - Co. C 57th Virginia Oct. 9, 1861 VA25
Underwood, J.H. - Co. I 16th Georgia Sept. 14, 1861 VA25
Underwood, J.M. - Co. G 45th North Carolina June 9, 1864 VA25
Underwood, John - Mosby's Cavalry VA10
Upshaw, J.C. - Pvt. - Co. B 13th Georgia Died May 12, 1864 VA28
Ustick, J.L. - Co. G 5th Alabama June 2, 1863 VA25
Usury, J.B. - Co. F 14th Alabama June 30, 1862 VA25
Usury, J.T. - Co. D 55th Virginia July 10, 1862 VA25
Usury, W.P. - Co. D 10th Alabama Aug. 1, 1862 VA25
Utley, J.B. - Corp. - Co. D 48th Georgia Sept. 6, 1864 VA25
Utterbach, S.C. - Co. G 13th Virginia VA11
Vacas, C.J. - Virginia VA11
Vackers, B.A. - VA20
Vacking, J.S. - Co. K 24th Georgia March 11, 1863 VA25
Valentine, T.D. - Co. H 13th South Carolina June 22, 1862 VA25
Vallendingham, J.W. - Co. F 3rd Georgia May 27, 1864 VA25
Vance, Calvin - Georgia VA20
Vance, George - Virginia VA20
Vance, J.K. - Co. F 7th North Carolina March 9, 1865 VA25
Vance, T. - Co. F 45th North Carolina June 2, 1864 VA25
Vance, W. - 15th Alabama Oct. 13, 1861 VA25
Vancen, J.A. - North Carolina Cavalry Sept. 4, 1861 VA25
Vandaver, J.R. - 5th South Carolina VA18
Vangant, J. - 3rd Alabama Jan. 8, 1862 VA25
Vangant, T. - 4th Texas July 8, 1862 VA25
Vanley, J. - Co. K 48th Alabama June 9, 1864 VA25
Vans, W.H. - Co. E 27th South Carolina July 22, 1864 VA25

Vansickler, E. - Co. E 8th Virginia June 16, 1862 VA25
Vanter, J.E. - Capt. - July 4, 1862 VA25
Vardaman, Thomas W.R. - see Vardeman, Thomas W.R
 VA28
Vardeman, Thomas W.R. - Pvt. - Co. K 10th Alabama Died
 May 2, 1864 name on headstone - "Vardaman" VA28
Varings, __ - Nov. 5, 1862 VA25
Varuer, J.H. - Co. A 11th Alabama July 6, 1862 VA25
Vasseur, __ - "Doctor" Jan. 1862 VA25
Vaston, A.B. - Co. E 28th North Carolina Oct. 4, 1864 VA25
Vaughan, A. - Co. D 12th North Carolina June 18, 1862 VA25
Vaughan, C. - Co. E 38th Georgia July 28, 1862 VA25
Vaughan, F.O. - Sumpter Vol. (South Carolina) VA18
Vaughan, G.P. - Co. A 27th South Carolina Aug. 10, 1864
 VA25
Vaughan, J. - Co. G 56th North Carolina June 17, 1863 VA25
Vaughan, J.W. - Co. G 56th Georgia July 27, 1863 VA25
Vaughan, James D. - Adjutant / Lt.- 1st Virginia Cavalry Died
 May 7 (13?), 1864 Also listed as "James P.
 Vaughan" VA28
Vaughan, James P. - see Vaughan, James D. VA28
Vaughan, R.B. - Co. B 27th South Carolina July 21, 1864
 VA25
Vaughan, S. - June 2, 1862 VA25
Vaughan, W.A. - Co. F 53rd North Carolina VA11
Vaughan, W.A. - Co. B 13th South Carolina June 26, 1864
 VA25
Vaughan, W.S. - Co. D 3rd Virginia July 7, 1862 VA25
Vaughan, Z. - Co. C 13th Mississippi June 3, 1862 VA25
Vaughn, F.J. - Virginia VA20
Vaughn, Jesse - Co. H 20th Georgia VA11
Vaughn, John - Co. D 14th Virginia VA11
Vaughter, M.G. - Virginia VA20
Veal, W. - Co. E 45th Georgia March 11, 1863 VA25
Venable, R. - Co. F 23rd North Carolina VA11
Veringe, __ - Co. H 29th Virginia Nov. 5, 1862 VA25

Vern, V. - Sgt. - Co. C 6th Georgia Nov. 17, 1864 VA25
Vernon, J. - Co. D 20th North Carolina May 20, 1862 VA25
Verrell, R. - Co. I 17th North Carolina Nov. 4, 1864 VA25
Vest, Joseph L. - Died April 7, 1863 age 21 VA19
Vestall, J. - Nov. 25, 1862 VA25
Via, Josiah - Virginia VA20
Via, T.L. - Sgt. - Co. H 57th Virginia Died May 5, 1865 VA26
Vial, J.B. - Co. E 5th Alabama VA11
Vick, A.T. - Co. G 19th Mississippi Jan. 19, 1863 VA25
Vicker, William - Baltimore, Maryland VA11
Vickery, Robert - Sgt. - Co. G 26th Georgia MW May 12, 1864 (Died May 13, 1864) VA28
Vier, Jno. - Co. B 55th Georgia May 3, 1862 VA25
Vigues, J.J. - 19th Virginia VA18
Viles, Chas. - Georgia VA20
Villiness, __ - Co. I 12th Virginia Nov. 7, 1862 VA25
Vincent, C.C. - Co. C 1st Texas June 24, 1862 VA25
Vincent, P. - Co. I 18th Mississippi June 9, 1863 VA25
Vincent, T.J. - Corp. - Co. K 1st South Carolina June 14, 1864 VA25
Vinson, Jethro - Pvt. - Co. F 51st Georgia Died in Fredericksburg - Jan. 1, 1862 VA28
Vinyard, J.H. - Pvt.- Co. B 10th Florida Died June 21, 1865 VA26
Vinyard, R. - VA12
Vocal, A.L. - Co. E 25th South Carolina June 2, 1864 VA25
Von Kannon, William - see Cannon, William VA28
Von, John - Co. B 17th North Carolina July 21, 1862 VA25
Vonhandlier, T. - 1st South Carolina Dec. 27, 1862 VA25
Vorous, John - VA06
Voss, J.E. - Co. D 7th Virginia Aug. 5, 1862 VA25
Voulant, C. - Maryland Sept. 1, 1863 VA25
Vuncannon, William - see Cannon, William VA28
W __, G.H. - Louisiana 1864 VA25
W __, L. - June 10, 1862 VA25
Waddel, J. - Clark's Artillery June 10, 1862 VA25

Waddel, W.A. - Co. G 1st Tennessee Aug. 7, 1862 VA25
Waddell, Richard - 5th South Carolina VA18
Wade, H. - Co. D 3rd Georgia Sept. 7, 1864 VA25
Wade, M. - Jan. 17, 1863 VA25
Wade, S. - Virginia Jan. 27, 1863 VA25
Wade, W. - Co. E 38th Alabama July 30, 1865 VA25
Wade, W.G. - 7th Alabama July 30, 1864 VA25
Wade, Wm. - Co. C 57th Virginia July 30, 1863 VA25
Wade, Wm. H. - Died Aug 24, 1862 VA19
Wadsworth, J.D. - Co. K 26th North Carolina Nov. 2, 1864 VA25
Wagner, D.B. - Co. D 1st Virginia June 17, 1863 VA25
Wagner, M.P. - 28th North Carolina July 22, 1864 VA25
Wagnon, G. - 13th Louisiana Oct. 18, 1861 age 22 VA25
Wailsh, A. - Lt.- Co. C 24th North Carolina Nov. 25, 1864 VA25
Waiter, L. - Co. E 20th Georgia June 24, 1864 VA25
Wakeham, Samuel A. - Pvt. - Co. D 1st Artillery Died May 10, 1864 Headstone reads: "3rd Virginia (Richmond) Howitzers" VA28
Walbern, D.B. - Co. B 22nd North Carolina May 24, 1864 VA25
Walche, J.C. - Co. D 1st South Carolina June 30, 1862 VA25
Walden, J.G. - Co. F 26th Mississippi May 3, 1864 VA25
Walden, Thomas H. - Co. H 15th Alabama VA11
Walden, Wm. - Co. H 44th Georgia Nov. 19, 1862 VA25
Waldro(p), J.D. - Co. C 1st Texas May 27, 1862 VA25
Waldrop, __ - Lt.- 23rd Georgia July 18, 1862 VA25
Waldrop, C.P. - Co. F 20th South Carolina Jan. 26, 1865 VA25
Waldrop, J.R. - Co. K 16th Alabama June 18, 1862 VA25
Walford, J. - VA20
Walker, A.S. - Co. F 6th South Carolina June 24, 1864 VA25
Walker, B.F. - Co. B 46th North Carolina Sept. 29, 1863 VA25
Walker, D. - Co. F 49th Virginia June 30, 1862 VA25

Walker, F. - Palmetto Sharp Shooters (South Carolina) July 11, 1862 VA25
Walker, H.J. - Co. G 27th North Carolina Sept. 4, 1864 VA25
Walker, J.A. - Co. A 66th North Carolina Sept. 27, 1864 VA25
Walker, J.H. - Co. I 42nd Mississippi Oct. 2, 1862 VA25
Walker, J.J. - Toomb's Artillery(Georgia)May 13, 1862 VA25
Walker, J.R. - Co. A 14th North Carolina June 4, 1862 VA25
Walker, J.S. - Co. A 7th Georgia May 31, 1862 VA25
Walker, J.T. - Cobb's Legion (Georgia) May 29, 1862 VA25
Walker, J.T. - Co. A 14th South Carolina Feb. 25, 1865 VA25
Walker, J.W. - 1st Kentucky VA18
Walker, J.W. - Co. F 14th Georgia May 28, 1863 VA25
Walker, J.W. - Co. C 1st North Carolina July 27, 1862 VA25
Walker, J.W. - Co. F 48th North Carolina May 1, 1863 VA25
Walker, James H. - Co. D 11th Georgia Died Feb 25, 1862 VA23
Walker, L.W. - 33rd North Carolina June 14, 1862 VA25
Walker, M. - June 4, 1862 VA25
Walker, Milton F. - Sgt. - Co. H 4th North Carolina Headstone reads: "Corp." VA28
Walker, Reuben Lindsay - *Our Confederate Dead* published by the Ladies' Hollywood Memorial Association in 1916 lists this soldier as "General of Infantry", however Boatner's *The Civil War Dictionary* lists him as "Brigadier General of Artillery". 1827 - 1890 VA25
Walker, S.B. - Co. I 42nd Mississippi Aug. 5, 1862 VA25
Walker, Samuel T. - VA12
Walker, W.D. - Co. E 12th Georgia July 25, 1864 VA25
Walker, W.E. - South Carolina1862 VA25
Walker, W.J.R. - Co. D 5th Florida May 20, 1863 VA25
Walker, W.W. - Co. A 13th South Carolina July 3, 1862 VA25
Wall, __ - June 5, 1862 VA25
Wall, D. - Co. C 17th North Carolina Sept. 9, 1864 VA25
Wall, E. - Marine Corps - C.S.N. Oct. 22, 1863 VA25

Wall, G.W. - Jeff Davis Legion VA18
Wall, J.F. (?) - Co. J 11th Georgia Died March 1862 VA23
Wall, J.W. - Co. I 1st South Carolina Dec. 7, 1863 VA25
Wall, John - Co. H 8th Louisiana Sept. 1864 VA25
Wall, Martin N. - Pvt. - Co. E 3rd Georgia S.S. Died May 10, 1864 VA28
Wall, Richard - Died March 9, 1863 age 40 VA19
Wall, T.G. - Co. C 5th Louisiana Sept. 14, 1862 VA25
Wallace, C.S. - Co. C 37th North Carolina June 25, 1865 VA25
Wallace, J.B. - Sgt. - Co. E 7th South Carolina July 3, 1864 VA25
Wallace, J.F. - Co. B 5th South Carolina Nov. 23, 1862 VA25
Wallace, J.M. - 18th Mississippi VA18
Wallace, J.M. - Co. B 35th Georgia Jan. 12, 1862 VA25
Wallace, J.R. - Co. I 17th Virginia May 25, 1864 VA25
Wallace, M. - 49th North Carolina VA18
Wallace, May Ellan - Civilian -Killed in explosion of C.S. Laboratory - March 16, 1863 age 12 VA19
Wallace, T. - Co. B 5th Texas June 5, 1862 VA25
Wallace, W.C. - Dec. 18, 1862 VA25
Wallace, W.C. - Co. E 48th North Carolina May 29, 1864 VA25
Wallace, W.W. - 21st Georgia VA18
Wallen, H. - Co. E 27th Georgia July 27, 1862 VA25
Waller, David - KIA May 2, 1862 age 32 VA19
Waller, H. - Co. E 27th Georgia Aug. 9, 1862 VA25
Waller, I.W. - Co. E 13th Alabama June 16, 1862 VA25
Waller, J.D. - Co. H 59th Georgia Oct. 3, 1864 VA25
Waller, John H. - Co. D 10th Georgia VA28
Waller, T. - Co. C 17th Virginia May 1865 VA25
Walls, J.W. - March 10, 1865 VA25
Walraven, S. - Co. F 46th Alabama March 24, 1865 VA25
Walraven, S. - Co. F 46th Alabama March 24, 1865 VA25
Walsh, R.K. - Sgt. - Co. C 4th Virginia VA28
Walson, T.A. - Co. G 44th Georgia June 28, 1863 VA25

Walston, L. - 8th South Carolina VA18
Walters, W.D. - Co. C 10th Georgia June 14, 1864 VA25
Walton, A.P. - Co. G 46th Virginia July 9, 1865 VA25
Walton, J. - Co. E 3rd North Carolina July 29, 1862 VA25
Walton, J.F. - Corp. - Co. F 53rd Georgia (Headstone reads Co. D) VA28
Walton, J.W. - Fry's battery (Virginia) VA11
Walton, M.J. - Virginia VA20
Walton, R. - Co. B 46th North Carolina Aug. 17, 1864 VA25
Wamble, B.F. - Co. I 17th North Carolina July 10, 1864 VA25
Ward, F. - April 3, 1862 VA25
Ward, G.W. - VA20
Ward, G.W. - Colonel-2nd Florida Infantry - KIA - Battle of Williamsburg - May 5, 1862 VA02
Ward, G.W. - Co. K 34th Mississippi April 30, 1865 VA25
Ward, George T. - Colonel - 2nd Florida Infantry - KIA - Battle of Williamsburg - May 5, 1862 VA02
Ward, J. - 14th Alabama Oct. 13, 1862 VA25
Ward, J. - 13th Alabama Oct. 15, 1861 VA25
Ward, J. - May 25, 1864 VA25
Ward, J.B. - 44th GeorgiaDec.7, 1862 VA25
Ward, J.D. - 18th Mississippi May 6, 1862 VA25
Ward, Jno. - Virginia VA20
Ward, L. - Alabama Sept. 14, 1861 VA25
Ward, M. - Co. G 13th South Carolina Jan. 16, 1865 VA25
Ward, N. - Virginia Jan. 22, 1863 VA25
Ward, T.B. - Co. K 20th North Carolina Aug. 24, 1862 VA25
Ward, T.F. - Co. I 42nd North Carolina Jan. 23, 1865 VA25
Ward, W. - 13th Georgia Dec. 2, 1861 VA25
Ward, W. - Co. G 14th Alabama June 10, 1862 VA25
Ward, W.W. - Sgt. - Co. I 1st Maryland Died Nov 12, 1861 VA23
Wardian, J.M. - 4th South Carolina VA18
Wardlaw, F.H. - Sgt. - Orr's Rifles (South Carolina) June 30, 1862 VA25
Ware, W.J. - 1st South Carolina VA18

Warlick, W.T. - Pvt. - Co. F 23rd North Carolina Died May 10, 1864 VA28
Warmack, __ - Co. A 38th Georgia Feb. 7, 1865 VA25
Warner, J.J. - Co. A 61st Georgia July 8, 1862 VA25
Warns, B. - Co. H 10th Alabama Sept. 29, 1862 VA25
Warren, D.B. - Co. F 52nd North Carolina April 29, 1865 VA25
Warren, Henry - Mississippi VA20
Warren, J. - Co. C 44th North Carolina Sept. 5, 1864 VA25
Warren, J.J. - Co. C 44th North Carolina Aug. 19, 1864 VA25
Warren, J.O. - Co. E 2nd North Carolina Died July 15, 1862 VA23
Warren, T.A. - Co. G 12th North Carolina July 13, 1864 VA25
Warren, Thomas J. - Pvt. - Co. H 14th Georgia Died May 12, 1864 VA28
Warren, W.C. - Co. H 5th North Carolina July 23, 1864 VA25
Warren, W.L. - Co. B 18th Georgia April 27, 1862 VA25
Warrew, W. - DeKalb County (Alabama) VA18
Warrick, J. - Co. D 15th Ala Died Jan. 20, 1862 VA23
Warrick, R. - Co. A 46th North Carolina Dec. 23, 1862 VA25
Warsham, A.B. - Co. K 56th North Carolina June 8, 1864 VA25
Warwack, A.T. - Co. B 11th North Carolina June 29, 1864 VA25
Warwack, T.J. - Co. A 30th North Carolina July8, 1864 VA25
Warwick, Clarence - DOW June 28, 1862 age 19 VA19
Washington, __ - Co. K 14th Georgia Jan. 3, 1863 VA25
Washington, A.A. - Co. E 46th North Carolina Jan. 3, 1865 VA25
Washington, J.H. - Co. B 11th Georgia May 9, 1862 VA25
Washington, T.J. - Co. A 13th Mississippi May 18, 1864 VA25
Washpon, J.E. - 1st Virginia Artillery Headstone reads "J.E. Washpow" VA28
Washpow, J.E. - see Washpon, J.E. VA28

Waters, A.G. - Capt. - Co. F 34th North Carolina June 29, 1862 VA25
Waters, Hosea M. - Pvt. - Co. H Palmetto Sharpshooters (South Carolina) Died May 8, 1864 VA28
Waters, W.J. - Pvt. - Co. K 66th Georgia Died June 13, 1865 VA26
Watkins, A.C. - Capt. - Co. A 24th Georgia May 24, 1863 VA25
Watkins, H.W. - Co. D 16th Virginia Aug. 18, 1862 VA25
Watkins, J. - 30th - North Carolina Aug. 1, 1862 VA25
Watkins, J. - 1st Mississippi Nov. 15, 1861 VA25
Watkins, J.T. - Co. H 6th Georgia Sept. 12, 1862 VA25
Watkins, L. - Co. K 8th Georgia May 7, 1862 VA25
Watkins, W. - North Carolina Artillery Aug. 8, 1864 VA25
Watkins, W.C. - Died May 26, 1864 age 23 VA19
Watley, W.D. - 21st Georgia VA11
Watson, __ - 15th South Carolina Oct. 28, 1862 VA25
Watson, A.J. - 10th Alabama June 5, 1862 VA25
Watson, A.J. - Co. B 10th South Carolina Nov. 8, 1864 VA25
Watson, F. - 11th Georgia VA18
Watson, J.C. - 19th Georgia VA18
Watson, J.D. - Co. D 27th South Carolina July 12, 1864 VA25
Watson, J.J. - North Carolina April 5, 1861 VA25
Watson, J.J. - Co. E 17th South Carolina June 23, 1864 VA25
Watson, J.S. - Co. G 11th Alabama Dec. 8, 1861 VA25
Watson, James K.P. - Pvt. - Co. D 45th North Carolina Died May 12, 1864 VA28
Watson, L. - Louisiana VA20
Watson, M. - Co. H 22nd South Carolina Aug. 6, 1864 VA25
Watson, R. - Co. I 51st Georgia April 10, 1863 VA25
Watson, R. - Co. C 14th North Carolina June 7, 1862 VA25
Watson, S.F. - Co. D 9th Louisiana Dec. 18, 1861 VA25
Watson, T.J. - Co. B 17th Georgia Dec. 30, 1861 VA25
Watson, W. - July 16, 1862 VA25
Watson, W.D. - Co. B 5th South Carolina June 4, 1862 VA25
Watson, W.F. - Co. D 10th Georgia July 2, 1864 VA25

Watson, W.H. - Co. F 10th Alabama June 16, 1862 VA25
Watt, Henry L. - MW - Battle of Big Bethel, Virginia, - June 10, 1861. This soldier's name does not appear in the cemetery's roster. VA25
Watts, D.E. - 4th Texas Nov. 9, 1861 VA25
Watts, J.F. - Co. G 37th North Carolina June 14, 1863 VA25
Watts, P.B. - Co. A 27th Georgia May 18, 1864 VA25
Watts, R.W. - Aug. 25, 1864 VA25
Watts, W. - Co. K 17th Georgia April 20, 1862 VA25
Waugh, W.R. - 3rd Alabama Sept. 16, 1862 VA25
Waugh, W.S. - Co. C 4th North Carolina July 13, 1863 VA25
Waver, J. - Co. H 39th North Carolina June 25, 1864 VA25
Wayde, W.G. - Georgia VA20
Wayland, B.B. - Co. F 13th Virginia May 24, 1863 VA25
Waymack, H. - Co. F 13th Alabama July 19, 1862 VA25
Wayne, H. - Co. B 8th Virginia June 23, 1862 VA25
Wayne, Joseph E. - Sgt. - Co. E 5th Virginia Cavalry KIA May 7, 1864 - Todd's Tavern VA28
Wayne, R.C. - 1st Georgia April 23, 1864 VA25
Weatherad, C.W. - Georgia Jan 15, 1863 VA25
Weatherford, W.J. - Co. G 25th North Carolina July 24, 1864 VA25
Weatherman, R.W. - Co. I 28th North Carolina July 7, 1863 VA25
Weaver, J.J. - Co. C 26th Alabama July 30, 1863 VA25
Weaver, S. - Co. C 27th Georgia July 15, 1862 VA25
Weaver, S.H. - Virginia Nov. 1861 VA25
Weaver, Samuel - VA15
Weaver, Virgil - Capt. - Co. H 6th Virginia Cavalry KIA May 7, 1864 - Todd's Tavern Headstone reads "Co. B 6th Virginia Cavalry VA28
Weaver, W.F. - Co. B 41st Georgia March 6, 1865 VA25
Weaver, W.H. - Co. F 15th Alabama VA11
Web, Isham - Kentucky - VA20
Webb, C. - Wardmaster (of hospital) VA08
Webb, D. - July 15, 1861 VA25

Webb, F.W. - Co. F 50th North Carolina June 6, 1864 VA25
Webb, J.R. - Co. I 17th North Carolina July 22, 1864 VA25
Webb, J.S. - Lt.- Tennessee VA20
Webb, Josiah - Co. F 3rd Tennessee Died Feb 4, 1862 VA23
Webb, T.W. - Co. H 26th Alabama June 17, 1862 VA25
Webb, Wm. - Co. K 28th North Carolina March 11, 1863 VA25
Webster, __ - Hung as "Yankee Spy" VA19
Webster, W. - 42nd Virginia VA18
Webster, W.E. - KIA June 29, 1862"disinterred and taken to Annapolis, Md. - Nov. 19, 1919" VA19
Weeks, __ - 49th Virginia June 18, 1862 VA25
Weeks, __ - Co. F 5th South Carolina July 15, 1861 VA25
Weeks, F.B. - Co. F 27th North Carolina May 12, 1864 VA25
Weeks, J.A. - Co. A 30th North Carolina May 11, 1863 VA25
Weeks, S.E. - Co. H 11th South Carolina June 22, 1864 VA25
Weiss, S. - Georgia - VA17
Welch, A.S. - Co. F 60th Georgia Feb. 28, 1865 VA25
Welch, G.W. - 18th Mississippi VA18
Welch, J. - 2nd Virginia Infantry VA06
Welch, J. - Alabama VA20
Welch, R. - Co. A 26th North Carolina July 26, 1864 VA25
Welcup, William - POW - Federal Soldier Died Nov. 14, 1861 VA19
Wells, A.B. - Co. C 9th Louisiana June 29, 1863 VA25
Wells, Andrews - Pvt. - Co. B 9th _la(Fla.?) Died June 12, 1865 VA26
Wells, C. - Georgia Nov. 27, 1862 VA25
Wells, G.W. - Co. B 38th Georgia June 6, 1862 VA25
Wells, George B. - Pvt. - Co. G 14th North Carolina Died May 12, 1864 VA28
Wells, H. - Co. A 10th Louisiana Sept. 4, 1861 VA25
Wells, H.B. - Georgia Aug. 20, 1863 VA25
Wells, J. - Fry's Battery Aug. 18, 1864 VA25
Wells, J. M. - Co. G 46th North Carolina March 4, 1865 VA25

Wells, James G. - Sgt. - Co. K 31st Virginia Died May 20, 1864 Headstone reads: "James G. Willis" also listed in Carrington's and Shoemaker's Battery VA28

Wells, James W. - Co. E 30th __ VA28

Wells, John - Kemper's Battery VA10

Wells, M.F. - Pvt.- Co. B 10th Virginia Died June 14, 1865 VA26

Wells, R. - Co. G 8th Virginia July 6, 1862 VA25

Wells, Robt. - 8th Virginia Infantry VA10

Wells, S.J. - 30th North Carolina May 12, 1863 VA25

Welsh, __ - Oct. 29, 1862 VA25

Werne, W.T. - Co. D 38th North Carolina June 27, 1863 VA25

Werson, D.D. - Co. F 56th North Carolina Aug. 12, 1864 VA25

Wert, S.B. - Co. K 26th Alabama June 2, 1862 VA25

Wesh, A. - Texas Rangers Sept. 4, 1861 VA25

Wesley, J. - Louisiana Jan. 1862 VA25

West, E.S. - 1st Maryland VA18

West, J.P. - Corp. - Co. B 11th North Carolina Aug. 28, 1865 VA25

West, K.- VA22

West, William - Co. H 13th North Carolina May 20, 1863 VA25

Westbrook, C.H. - Co. B 38th Georgia Dec. 23, 1862 VA25

Westbrook, William H. - Co. G 2nd North Carolina Headstone reads: 'William H.H. Westbrook" VA28

Westbrook, William H. H. - see Westbrook, William H. VA28

Westbrooks, J. - April 19, 1862 VA25

Wetcher, Daniel - POW - Federal Soldier Died Feb. 5, 1862 VA19

Wetzel, John M. - Appier's Corps (South Carolina) VA28

Weymouth, John - KIA - July 18, 1862 VA19

Whaley, J. - Co. F 13th Georgia VA11

Whaley, J.J. - Co. A 17th__ VA23

Whalley, A. - July 14, 1861 VA25

Wham, Ro. - Died Nov. 13, 1862 VA19
Wharton, T.R.M. - 15th Louisiana Sept. 23, 1861 VA25
Whatley, A.J. - Co. D 4th Georgia Dec. 24, 1862 VA25
Wheeler, Chas. - Virginia VA20
Wheeler, G. - VA06
Wheeler, J.H. - Co. E 18th North Carolina Aug. 30, 1864 VA25
Wheeler, P. - POW - Federal Soldier Died June 11, 1862 VA19
Wheeler, W.W. - Co. G 23rd Georgia Aug. 12, 1864 VA25
Wheelwright, Joseph Christopher - VMI Cadet -KIA - Battle of New Market - May 15, 1864 DOW June 2, 1864 - Buried at VMI VA21
Wheely, Ed. - POW - Federal Soldier Died June 11, 1862 VA19
Wheman, D.C. - Co. C 20th North Carolina June 19, 1863 VA25
Wherless, W. - Co. K 8th Georgia June 14, 1862 VA25
Whicker, Cy - Co. E 11th North Carolina Died Dec 9, 1861 VA23
Whidden, R. Lott - Co. F 59th Georgia VA18
Whisnatt, B.C. - Co. A 1st South Carolina July 3, 1862 VA25
Whitaker, D. - Lt.- Co. F 7th South Carolina Cavalry July 1, 1864 VA25
Whitaker, E.J. - Co. H 2nd Mississippi July 14, 1862 VA25
Whitaker, H.A. - Co. G 20th Georgia June 9, 1864 VA25
Whitaker, J.F. - 5th Virginia May 20, 1864 VA25
Whitaker, J.J. - Co. A 5th Alabama June 29, 1862 VA25
Whitaker, T.J. - Co. G 42nd North Carolina Oct. 10, 1864 VA25
Whitden, __ - Co. G 13th Mississippi Jan. 12, 1863 VA25
Whitden, __ - Co. I 27th Georgia Oct. 20, 1862 VA25
White, A. - see White, A.J. VA28
White, A. - Sgt. - Co. C 47th North Carolina June 10, 1864 VA25
White, A.B. - Co. E 6th Alabama July 25, 1862 VA25

White, A.F. - Alabama July 21, 1861 VA25
White, A.J. - Co. F__ th North Carolina Headstone Reads: "A.White" VA28
White, A.J. - Co. I 22nd North Carolina Nov. 10, 1864 VA25
White, A.P. - North Carolina June 5, 1862 VA25
White, Christian A. - VA12
White, D. - Co. I 24th Georgia July 15, 1862 VA25
White, D. - Co. F 20th Georgia May 20, 1862 VA25
White, E. - Co. K 27th North Carolina Jan. 19, 1864 VA25
White, F.O. - Co. A 20th North Carolina VA11
White, G. - Capt. Mal's Company July 22, 1862 VA25
White, G.W. - Co. I 2nd Louisiana June 21, 1862 VA25
White, G.W. - Co. B 7th Georgia July 6, 1864 VA25
White, H. - Co. F 33rd North Carolina April 16, 1865 VA25
White, H.J. - Co. I 1st Texas Nov. 18, 1862 VA25
White, J. - Co. H 21st Alabama May 9, 1863 VA25
White, J. - Co. D 12th North Carolina Jan. 19, 1864 VA25
White, J.H. - VA12
White, J.M. - Pvt.- Co. A 18th Virginia Bat. Died June 4, 1865 VA26
White, J.M. - Co. G 49th Georgia June 27, 1864 VA25
White, James - Co. E 2nd North Carolina VA28
White, John - Co. D 61st Virginia May 16, 1863 VA25
White, Jonathan J. - Sgt. - Co. I 15th Alabama Died May 11, 1864 VA28
White, Joseph C. - Lt.- Co. C 4th North Carolina VA28
White, Joseph H. - Co. F 24th Virginia VA11
White, M. - North Carolina Aug. 24, 1862 VA25
White, M.A. - Co. F 5th North Carolina Jan. 20, 1862 VA25
White, P.J. - South Carolina Oct. 16, 1862 VA25
White, R. - Pvt. - Arkansas Nov. 7, 1864 VA22
White, R.C. - Co. C 48th North Carolina July 17, 1863 VA25
White, R.J. - Co. D 7th South Carolina Aug. 29, 1864 VA25
White, R.Q. - Co. D 2nd South Carolina July 28, 1864 VA25
White, R.S. - Co. D 7th South Carolina Battalion Aug. 1, 1864 VA25

White, R.S. - Co. C 18th Georgia June 2, 1864 VA25
White, T. - Georgia Oct. 16, 1862 VA25
White, T.J. - Co. A 9th Alabama March 17, 1865 VA25
White, T.O. - Co. G 7th South Carolina June 28, 1864 VA25
White, Thomas - Pvt. - Co. D 16th Mississippi Died May 12, 1864 VA28
White, Thomas J. - Charlottesville Artillery (Virginia) Died May 18, 1864 VA28
White, W. - Co. K 1st South Carolina June 24, 1862 VA25
White, W.H. - Co. D 12th Mississippi July 9, 1863 VA25
White, W.H. - Co. K 17th North Carolina July 27, 1864 VA25
White, W.M. - Co. H 10th South Carolina Oct. 4, 1864 VA25
White, Wm. T - Sgt. - 3rd South Carolina VA04
Whitefield, B.F. - Co. I 14th Alabama June 10, 1864 VA25
Whitefield, J.M. - Co. D 20th Georgia Aug. 29, 1863 VA25
Whiteford, W.T. - Lt.- Co. B 50th Georgia May 11, 1863 VA25
Whitehead, __ - Capt. -16th Georgia VA23
Whitehead, B.T. - Co. C 27th South Carolina Sept. 1864 VA25
Whitehead, J. - Co. I 2nd Louisiana June 16, 1862 VA25
Whitehead, J.H. - 3rd Georgia Battalion VA18
Whitehead, J.W. - Co. K 15th North Carolina July 14, 1864 VA25
Whitehead, J.W. - Co. B 15th South Carolina July 16, 1864 VA25
Whitehead, L.T. - Co. A 47th Georgia June 10, 1862 VA25
Whitehead, S.M. - Co. B 15th South Carolina Jan. 5, 1865 VA25
Whitehead, W.D. - Co. D 2nd Georgia July 1, 1862 VA25
Whiteheart, C. - Corp. - Co. C 56th North Carolina Aug. 24, 1864 VA22
Whiteley, W. - Co. D 35th Georgia July 21, 1862 VA25
Whitely, D. - Co. G 5th North Carolina May 18, 1862 VA25
Whitely, S.J. - Co. F 1st North Carolina Dec. 26, 1862 VA25

Whitely, Wm. - Co. H 42nd North Carolina Sept. 22, 1864 VA25
Whitemore, J.B. - Co. G 2nd South Carolina Sept. 26, 1864 VA25
Whitemore, J.W. - Co. K 12th South Carolina July 15, 1864 VA25
Whitesel, Addison - Co. H 7th Virginia Cavalry VA11
Whitfield, J.A. Capt. - Co. C 2nd Mississippi May 3, 1863 VA25
Whitfield, R.B. - Co. D 17th North Carolina Aug. 12, 1864 VA25
Whiting, Carlyle - Clark Cavalry VA06
Whiting, Carlyle F. - Clarke Cavalry KIA - Nov. 3, 1864 VA06
Whiting, H. - Co. C 25th North Carolina July 25, 1864 VA25
Whitley, J.W. - Died of smallpox - Nov. 20, 1862 VA19
Whitley, W.P. - Sept. 3, 1862 VA25
Whitlock, __ - July 27, 1862 VA25
Whitlock, A.S. - Co. I 24th Georgia May 16, 1862 VA25
Whitlock, J.W. - Co. I 5th North Carolina June 26, 1864 VA25
Whitman, John A. - Pvt. - Co. K 57th North Carolina .Died May 6, 1865 VA26
Whitmer, M.S. - Co. A 1st South Carolina June 2, 1862 VA25
Whitmore, John - Co. B 9th Alabama Feb. 3, 1863 VA25
Whitnell, J.O. - Nov. 16, 1862 VA25
Whitsal, J.M. - Co. D 1st South Carolina Cavalry July 15, 1864 VA25
Whitten, __ - Co. G 49th North Carolina March 5, 1865 VA25
Whitten, J.P. - 31st North Carolina Oct. 19, 1864 VA25
Whitten, M. - Co. F 2nd Alabama March 5, 1865 VA25
Whitter, G. - 2nd Virginia Infantry VA06
Whittingdon, J. - Petersburg (Virginia) Jan. 2, 1865 VA25
Whitworth, R.H. - Co. A 4th South Carolina Jan. 9, 1861 VA25
Whorley, J.D. - 2nd Virginia Reserves Aug. 15, 1864 VA25

Whurley, S. - Co. C 57th Virginia Nov. 20, 1861 VA25
Wickes, Gustavus - VA12
Wickes, William W. - VA12
Wicklin, __ - June 27, 1862 VA25
Wicks, L.R. - 5th Texas VA18
Widdle, W.C. - Virginia VA20
Wiggan, C.H. - Co. H 23rd South Carolina July 1862 VA25
Wiggins, A.T. - Co. D 5th Alabama May 3, 1862 VA25
Wiggins, Henry E. - Pvt. - Co. F (I?) 61st Georgia KIA at
    Fredericksburg - Dec. 13, 1862 VA28
Wiggins, J.V. - Aug. 25, 1862 VA25
Wiggins, John - Co. K 23rd South Carolina Aug. 14, 1862
    VA25
Wiggins, S.M. - Co. H 15th Alabama VA11
Wiggs, N. - Sgt. - Co. K 6th North Carolina Aug. 2, 1864
    VA25
Wilas, C.A. - Co. F 22nd North Carolina Oct. 16, 1864 VA25
Wilbern, G.C. - Wright's Artillery May 31, 1862 VA25
Wilbern, J.L. - Co. K 7th Alabama Oct. 24, 1864 VA25
Wilbern, P. - North Carolina Artillery June 30, 1862 VA25
Wilberson, S. - Co. K 55th North Carolina July 6, 1864 VA25
Wilbons, __ - 11th Georgia Sept. 4, 1861 VA25
Wilbons, G. - 11th Georgia Sept. 4, 1861 VA25
Wilbran, W. - Co. H 2nd Georgia July 1, 1864 VA25
Wilburn, __ - VA18
Wilburn, D.W. - 11th Alabama VA18
Wilburn, J. - Co. D 5th Florida Nov. 1, 1862 VA25
Wilburne, T. - 1st Virginia Artillery May 13, 1862 VA25
Wilcox, B.R. - 12th Alabama VA18
Wilcox, George - Co H, 20th Georgia Died Dec 27, 1861
    VA23
Wild, Thos. - Co. C 10th North Carolina Jan. 10, 1864 VA25
Wilder, A.J. - Co. F 4th South Carolina July 13, 1864 VA25
Wilder, C.B. - Co. F 6th South Carolina March 20, 1863
    VA25
Wilder, J.E. - Co. E 3rd Georgia Aug. 13, 1861 VA25

Wilder, W.A. - Co. G 5th Alabama May 26, 1862 VA25
Wildman, A.G. - North Carolina July 6, 1864 VA25
Wiley, P. - Co. I 24th Georgia May 21, 1864 VA25
Wiley, R.P. - 4th Georgia July 6, 1863 VA25
Wiley, T. - Co. E 4th Virginia Battalion April 8, 1865 VA25
Wilfong, E. - VA12
Wilford, W.W. - 10th Georgia Sept. 10, 1861 VA25
Wilkerson, __ - Virginia June 8, 1862 VA25
Wilkerson, __ - Co. I 14th Virginia June 9, 1862 VA25
Wilkerson, J.C. - Co. G 13th North Carolina Feb. 3, 1863 VA25
Wilkerson, James W. - Pvt. - Co. I 7th Tennessee KIA at Fredericksburg - Dec. 13, 1862 VA28
Wilkerson, N.R. - Co. C 11th Mississippi June 20, 1863 VA25
Wilkerson, W.A. - 22nd North Carolina June 20, 1863 VA25
Wilkerson, W.R. - Co. G 11th Mississippi Aug. 16, 1863 VA25
Wilkerson, W.W. - Co. D 25th Virginia April 6, 1865 VA25
Wilkes, John - South Carolina March 9, 1864 VA25
Wilkes, M.F. - Feb. 5, 1862 VA25
Wilkins, E. - Co. E 59th Georgia Feb. 7, 1865 VA25
Wilkins, Edmund D. - Pvt. - Co. F 13th Virginia Cavalry KIA Spotsylvania Court House VA28
Wilkins, G.A. - Co. F 6th Virginia July 8, 1862 VA25
Wilkins, J. - Co. B 6th South Carolina July 30, 1864 VA25
Wilkins, J.A. - Co. A 6th South Carolina Oct. 22, 1864 VA25
Wilkins, T.B. - Co. B 11th North Carolina Sept. 18, 1864 VA25
Wilkinson, B. - Pvt. - Co. G 18th Virginia Died May 20, 1865 VA26
Wilkinson, M. - Tennessee VA20
Wilkinson, S. - Co. F 13th Georgia March 15, 1863 VA25
Wilkinson, W. - Georgia Nov. 7, 1862 VA25
Wilks, M. - Co. C 51st Georgia June 11, 1864 VA25
Wilks, R. - Co. H 1st South Carolina June 8, 1864 VA25
Wilks, W. - Co. H 53rd Georgia Nov. 18, 1862 VA25

Wilkwright, J.F. - Co. D 8th Georgia July 1, 1864 VA25
Will, __ - Co. C 13th South Carolina Oct. 30, 1862 VA25
Will, Reuben B. - VA15
Willard, J.W. - Co. I 3rd South Carolina May 12, 1862 VA25
Willcox, C.T. - Price's Artillery (Virginia) May 6, 1862 VA25
Willcox, J.A. - "M.C." - Texas 1864 VA25
Willey, J. - Georgia Feb. 15, 1863 VA25
Williams, __ - Lt. - 1862 VA25
Williams, A. - Co. G 38th North Carolina Aug. 1, 1863 VA25
Williams, A. F. - Co. E 1st North Carolina Nov. 24, 1863 VA25
Williams, A.E. - Pvt.- Co. A 18th Virginia Bat. Died June 3, 1865 VA26
Williams, A.M. - Pvt. - Co. H 2nd South Carolina Died May 10, 1864 Headstone reads: " W.A.M. Williams" VA28
Williams, A.T. - Co. B 9th Louisiana July 30, 1863 VA25
Williams, Augustus G. - Co. I 11th Virginia VA10
Williams, B. - Oct. 28, 1861 VA25
Williams, B. - Co. E 43rd North Carolina April 29, 1865 VA25
Williams, B. - Co. A 14th Georgia Nov. 19, 1862 VA25
Williams, B. - Co. D 11th North Carolina Dec. 24, 1864 VA25
Williams, B.L. - Sgt. - Died Jan. 4, 1865 age 34 VA19
Williams, Burwell - Died Aug 21, 1862 VA19
Williams, C. - Seaman - C.S. Navy Nov. 1, 1862 VA25
Williams, C.M. - Co. K 49th Virginia June 7, 1862 VA25
Williams, D.C. - Co. C 2nd Mississippi Battalion June 4, 1862 VA25
Williams, E. - Co. B 6th Alabama May 21, 1862 VA25
Williams, G. - 5th Alabama VA18
Williams, G. - Co. E 49th Virginia May 9, 1862 VA25
Williams, G.L. - 8th Virginia Infantry VA10
Williams, G.W. - Pvt. - Co. B 2nd South Carolina Died May 15, 1864 (MW May 8, 1864) VA28
Williams, H. - 18th South Carolina VA18
Williams, H. - Co. A 2nd South Carolina March 7, 1865 VA25

Williams, H. - Co. G 17th South Carolina Sept. 27, 1864 VA25
Williams, H. - Co. C 43rd Georgia May 30, 1864 VA25
Williams, H.J. - Co. E 6th North Carolina July 13, 1864 VA25
Williams, H.L. - Co. B 38th North Carolina July 16, 1862 VA25
Williams, I.H. 16th Georgia Sept. 12, 1861 VA25
Williams, J. - Corp. - Co. H 66th North Carolina Sept. 27, 1864 VA25
Williams, J. - June 7, 1865 VA25
Williams, J. - 10th Alabama Cavalry Nov. 2, 1864 VA25
Williams, J. - Co. I 7th Louisiana Jan. 1, 1865 VA25
Williams, J. - Co. F 60th Georgia July 29, 1862 VA25
Williams, J.B. - 14th South Carolina June 2, 1862 VA25
Williams, J.E. - Co. G 47th North Carolina March 7, 1864 VA25
Williams, J.H. - Co. I 1st North Carolina June 19, 1864 VA25
Williams, J.H. - Co. E 16th North Carolina July 3, 1864 VA25
Williams, J.H. - Co. A 8th Louisiana May 3, 1862 VA25
Williams, J.L. - 2nd South Carolina VA18
Williams, J.N. - Co. H 42nd Mississippi Sept. 9, 1862 VA25
Williams, J.R. - Co. G 29th Georgia July 7, 1864 VA25
Williams, J.T. - Mississippi Aug. 24, 1863 VA25
Williams, J.T. - Co. G 8th Virginia Aug. 1, 1862 VA25
Williams, J.W. - 8th Virginia Infantry VA10
Williams, J.W. - Co. E 40th North Carolina March 17, 1865 VA25
Williams, Jasper - Mississippi VA20
Williams, John B. - Co. L 2nd South Carolina Rifles Died May 26, 1863 VA03
Williams, John L. - Co. F 12th Mississippi VA28
Williams, John W. - Pvt. - Co. C 4th Georgia Died 1864 VA28
Williams, L.H. - Co. G 2nd North Carolina Sept. 29, 1862 VA25
Williams, L.P. - Co. K 35th Alabama July 27, 1862 VA25

Williams, M.J. - Co. F 45th North Carolina July 31, 1864 VA25
Williams, M.J. - Co. E 12th South Carolina July 15, 1862 VA25
Williams, M.W. - 61st Virginia June 10, 1863 VA25
Williams, Owen - Died Nov. 18, 1862 VA19
Williams, R. - Co. G 13th Alabama Nov. 7, 1862 VA25
Williams, R.G. - Co. G 10th Alabama Nov. 16, 1862 VA25
Williams, Robert L. - Capt. - Co. C 12th North Carolina Died June 6, 1864 (MW Spotsylvania Court House) VA28
Williams, Roger - Co. I 11th Virginia VA10
Williams, S. - Co. I 22nd South Carolina Jan. 26, 1865 VA25
Williams, S.B. - Lt.- Co. C 44th North Carolina Dec. 2, 1864 VA25
Williams, T. - Co. G 12th North Carolina Oct. 28, 1862 VA25
Williams, T. - Co. K 5th Alabama May 17, 1864 VA25
Williams, T.W. - 2nd Louisiana Oct. 4, 1862 VA25
Williams, W. - Co. E 14th North Carolina Sept. 15, 1864 VA25
Williams, W.A.M. - see Williams, A.M. VA28
Williams, W.G. - Co. A 14th North Carolina June 2, 1862 VA25
Williams, W.H. - Co. H 28th Georgia July 12, 1864 VA25
Williams, William - Virginia VA20
Williams, William M. - Pvt. - Co. K 26th Georgia Died May 12, 1864 VA28
Williamson, Gilbert - VA12
Williamson, J. - Co. H 46th North Carolina Oct. 4, 1864 VA25
Williamson, J.D. - VA12
Williamson, Matthew W. - VA12
Williamson, R. - 12th Georgia Oct. 1, 1862 VA25
Willingford, J. - Co. B 51st Georgia May 24, 1863 VA25
Willingham, J.R. - VA06
Willingham, W.J. - 4th Texas Aug. 4, 1861 VA25
Willis, __ - July 7, 1862 VA25

Willis, __ - Co. I 13th South Carolina Aug. 6, 1862 VA25
Willis, A.C. - Mosby's Virginia Cavalry hung while POW - October 1864 VA23
Willis, D. - Co. E 18th Georgia May 19, 1862 VA25
Willis, George W. - 50th Georgia VA18
Willis, J. - Co. K 12th Georgia Battalion Oct. 1, 1864 VA25
Willis, J.J. - 6th Alabama Oct. 17, 1861 VA25
Willis, J.M.(Jr.) - KIA May 17, 1864 age 27 VA19
Willis, James G. - see Wells, James G. VA28
Willis, John J. - Pvt. - Co. I 53rd Georgia VA28
Willis, T.W. - 1st Virginia Reserves July 6, 1865 VA25
Willoughby, J.P. - Pvt. - Co. C Hampton's Legion Died May 7, 1865 VA26
Wills, Jno. - Kentucky VA20
Wilmouth, J. - Lt.- Co. A 1st Tennessee May 22, 1864 VA25
Wilmouth, J. - Co. K 3rd Virginia July 5, 1862 VA25
Wilson, __ - Nurse - "West Virginia" VA08
Wilson, A.N. - Cobb's Legion (Georgia) Oct. 9, 1863 VA25
Wilson, C.L. - Co. D 31st Georgia July 14, 1862 VA25
Wilson, Edward - 4th South Carolina VA18
Wilson, F.B. - 2nd Virginia Infantry VA06
Wilson, G. - Co. E 49th Georgia Sept. 1, 1862 VA25
Wilson, G.R. - Co. G 9th South Carolina Oct. 15, 1862 VA25
Wilson, H. - Co. H 5th Texas June 13, 1862 VA25
Wilson, H. - Co. I 20th Georgia Aug. 10, 1864 VA25
Wilson, I. - Georgia - April 14, 1863 VA25
Wilson, J. - Pvt.- Co. H 2nd North Carolina Died June 24, 1865 VA26
Wilson, J. - Gregory's Company May 18, 1864 VA25
Wilson, J.C. - Co. I 4th Alabama Aug. 13, 1864 VA25
Wilson, J.T. - Co. C 4th North Carolina Aug. 10, 1864 VA25
Wilson, John - 14th Alabama VA18
Wilson, Joseph Harvey - Pvt. - Co. B 53rd North Carolina DOW VA28
Wilson, L.E. - Co. G 11th Georgia July 1861 VA25
Wilson, M. - Co. H 15th North Carolina Sept. 22, 1862 VA25

Wilson, Mark A. - Pvt. - Co. E 23rd Virginia Died May 24, 1864 VA28
Wilson, R.. - Lt.- Virginia April 20, 1865 VA22
Wilson, R.C. - Co. D 18th Mississippi Jan. 19, 1863 VA25
Wilson, S. - Sgt. - Co. C 64th Georgia Aug. 23, 1864 VA25
Wilson, T. Burr - Co. D 13th South Carolina May 30, 1862 VA25
Wilson, T.B. - Co. D 13th North Carolina May 30, 1862 VA25
Wilson, T.H. - Co. H 8th North Carolina May 20, 1862 VA25
Wilson, Thomas W. - Lt.- Co. F 23rd North Carolina VA28
Wilson, W. - June 1, 1862 VA25
Wilson, W. - Co. H 96th North Carolina April 1, 1865 VA25
Wilson, W. B. - Co. K 49th North Carolina June 25, 1864 VA25
Wilson, W.A. - Pvt. - Co. A 38th Georgia DOD May 5, 1863 at Hamilton's Crossing VA28
Wilson, W.J. - Co. K 1st Texas Sept. 1, 1862 VA25
Wilson, W.L. - Co. K 1st Tennessee Sept. 2, 1862 VA25
Wilten, M.T. - Co. F 5th Virginia Aug. 18, 1862 VA25
Wimberly, C. - 17th Georgia VA18
Wimbish, William M. - Pvt. - Co. I 5th Alabama Died May 10, 1864 VA28
Wimmer, J.F. - Virginia VA20
Wimsett, Riley - Co. H 55th North Carolina Died April 3, 1863 VA03
Wincey, Ephraim W. - Sgt. - Co. C 61st Georgia Died May 18, 1864 VA28
Winder, A. - Co. C 9th North Carolina May 24, 1864 VA25
Winder, C. - North Carolina May 28, 1864 VA25
Winder, J.H. - July 11, 1864 VA25
Winder, L.A. - July 11, 1864 VA25
Windle, Hugh - VA12
Windle, Peter - VA12
Windley, H.A. - Co. I 13th North Carolina Sept. 6, 1862 VA25

Wingate, M.F. - 23rd South Carolina Dec. 4, 1861 VA25
Wingate, O.J. - Co. F 8th Florida Nov. 10, 1862 VA25
Wingfield, J.W. - Co. B 18th Georgia May 25, 1864 VA25
Winham, E. - 6th Alabama May 27, 1862 VA25
Winhart, C. - 10th Louisiana Aug. 22, 1861 VA25
Winley, W.J. - Co. I 15th Louisiana Dec. 2, 1861 VA25
Winston, Harry C. - age 22 DOW Oct.7, 1864 VA19
Winston, S.F. - Co. D 9th Louisiana Nov. 14, 1861 VA25
Winstread, G.W. - Nurse - North Carolina VA08
Winter, B. - VA18
Winting, G.A. - 1st South Carolina Rifles April 23, 1864 VA25
Wirt, S. - Co. A 11th South Carolina July 3, 1862 VA25
Wisdom, J.T. - Co. A 14th Georgia April 24, 1862 VA25
Wise, C.M. - Co. H 45th Georgia Aug. 22, 1862 VA25
Wise, H. - Co. B 14th South Carolina Oct. 9, 1864 VA25
Wise, J. - Co. B 3rd North Carolina Dec. 22, 1863 VA25
Wise, T.H. - Co. D 20th South Carolina Oct. 12, 1864 VA25
Wise, W. - Co. K 4th North Carolina May 17, 1864 VA25
Wise, W.H. - Co. A 14th Alabama July 21, 1862 VA25
Wise, W.S. - Co. G 17th North Carolina Nov. 29, 1864 VA25
Wissinger, J.W. - Co. I 15th South Carolina Nov. 14, 1863 VA25
Witer, S.B. - Co. G 26th Georgia July 28, 1864 VA25
Withers, R.P. - Co. H 22nd North Carolina Aug. 24, 1864 VA25
Withers, S.W. - Co. D 13th Alabama May 7, 1862 VA25
Wofford, William Thomas - Pvt. - Co. K 3rd South Carolina Died May 10, 1864 VA28
Wolf, W.M. - Lt. - Hagood's South Carolina Brigade Died May 9, 1864 VA17
Wolfe, G.- North Carolina VA17
Wolfe, J.A. - 13th South Carolina Nov. 3, 1861 VA25
Wolfe, J.D. - Co. G 14th Alabama May 25, 1862 VA25
Womble, F.M. - Died Nov. 14, 1862 VA19
Womble, S.C. - Co. D 2nd Alabama July 7, 1862 VA25

Wood, A.C. - Co. C 23rd Georgia Sept. 21, 1862 VA25
Wood, Alonzo - Kentucky VA20
Wood, Chas. - Co E 1st Maryland Died Nov 11, 1861 VA23
Wood, D.F. - Co. B 28th Georgia Aug. 5, 1864 VA25
Wood, David - Co. D 10th Georgia VA28
Wood, E. - Exchanged Prisoner Aug. 9, 1862 VA25
Wood, F.W. - Co. F 22nd Georgia March 9, 1865 VA25
Wood, G.W. - Co. A 13th Mississippi May 21, 1862 VA25
Wood, J. - Co. F 49th North Carolina May 24, 1864 VA25
Wood, J.H. - Co. A 7th Georgia Aug. 13, 1861 VA25
Wood, J.W. - Co. G 37th North Carolina VA28
Wood, J.W. - March 18, 1863 VA25
Wood, Kilen - 61st Virginia VA18
Wood, P.C. - Corp. - Co. A 28th Georgia Sept. 25, 1864 VA25
Wood, Samuel - Pvt. - Co. B 11th Virginia Died May 12, 1865 VA26
Wood, Thomas A. - Adjutant /- Pvt. - Co. C 42nd Virginia KIA Spotsylvania Court House - May 12, 1864 VA28
Wood, W.H. - Virginia Artillery Sept. 16, 1861 VA25
Wood, W.J. - Corp. - Co. K 11th Georgia Aug. 1, 1864 VA25
Woodall, __ - Sept. 12, 1862 VA25
Woodall, B. - Co. D 52nd Virginia April 21, 1865 VA25
Woodall, J.A. - Lt.- Co. F 45th Georgia Aug. 1, 1862 VA25
Woodall, J.W. - Co. A 53rd Virginia July 30, 1862 VA25
Woodall, James - Co. F 42nd Mississippi Sept. 9, 1862 VA25
Woodall, L. - Co. F 45th Georgia July 29, 1864 VA25
Woodall, Thos. - Capt. Clay's Company May 7, 1862 VA25
Woodar, A. - Co. A 21st Virginia June 29, 1863 VA25
Woodard, F.S. - 4th Texas Nov. 1, 1861 VA25
Woodard, G.W. - Co. E 11th Alabama Aug. 22, 1862 VA25
Woodard, H. - VA20
Woodard, J.B. - Co. C 17th North Carolina July 19, 1864 VA25
Woodard, S. - Co. H 56th North Carolina Aug. 3, 1864 VA25
Woodard, W. - Co. K 66th North Carolina July 25, 1864 VA25

Wooden, J.W. - Pvt.- Co. E 5th North Carolina Died June 4, 1865 VA26
Woodes, J. - Co. I 20th North Carolina June 14, 1863 VA25
Woodhouse, E.S. - Sgt. - Co. B 8th North Carolina Sept. 7, 1864 VA25
Woodiff, Thomas J. - Co. B 38th Georgia KIA at Fredericksburg - Dec. 13, 1862 VA28
Wooding, Jno. W. - Co. G 57th Virginia Aug. 12, 1863 VA25
Woodly, __ - VA18
Woodmyre, Thomas H. - POW - Federal Soldier Died Dec. 7, 1861 VA19
Woodrow, J. - Co. I 6th South Carolina Feb. 7, 1865 VA25
Woodruff, George W. - Pvt. - Co. B 53rd Georgia DOD April 1, 1863 (1864?) at Fredericksburg VA28
Woods, __ - Sept. 3, 1861 VA25
Woods, C. - Virginia VA20
Woods, J. - Co. D 66th North Carolina Aug. 18, 1864 VA25
Woods, J. - Co. A 66th North Carolina June 4, 1864 VA25
Woods, J.W. - Co. E 37th Virginia Battalion VA11
Woods, Jackson - VA14
Woods, Jacob Harvey - VA14
Woods, James A. - Co. A 8th Virginia VA11
Woods, L. T. - Co. C 15th North Carolina Aug. 22, 1864 VA25
Woods, S. - Co. H 38th North Carolina June 16, 1863 VA25
Woods, Thomas G. - Pvt. - Co. E 48th Georgia DOD March 26, 1863, at Guinea Station VA28
Woodward, J.R. - Major - Co. E 1st Tennessee Died Sept 18, 1862 VA23
Woodworth, H. - Frazier's Battery July 6, 1864 VA25
Woody, David - Corp. - Co. I 45th North Carolina MW May 19, 1864 VA28
Woody, J.N. - Co. B 27th North Carolina Jan. 17, 1865 VA25
Woody, S. - Co. A 34th North Carolina Nov. 18, 1863 VA25
Wooldridge, James M. - Pvt.- Co. B 46th Virginia Died June 29, 1865 VA26

Woolley, D.H. - 10th Alabama Infantry - KIA - Battle of Williamsburg - May 5, 1862 VA02
Wooter, Geo. J. - Co. A 56th Georgia 1863 VA25
Wootten, A.J. - Co. A 6th Alabama June 21, 1862 VA25
Wootten, J.W. - Co. B 24th Georgia May 29, 1862 VA25
Wootten, Z. - 65th Virginia May 20, 1862 VA25
Wordal, R. - Sgt. - Co. B 12th Georgia May 25, 1864 VA25
Wordsworth, B. - 15th Alabama Nov. 18, 1861 VA25
Workman, A.T. - Co. B 19th South Carolina July 24, 1864 VA25
Workman, W. - Co. F 38th North Carolina June 14, 1864 VA25
Workman, W.A. - Corp. - Co. H 12th South Carolina Died May 12, 1864 VA28
Worley, D.E. - 23rd Georgia July 18, 1864 VA25
Wormes, James - POW - Federal Soldier Died June 9, 1862 VA19
Worsham, George A. - Lt. - Co. F 17th Georgia Died May 12, 1864 VA28
Worsham, W. - Co. C 37th North Carolina June 7, 1862 VA25
Worsham, Wm. - Co. A 22nd Georgia Aug. 18, 1862 VA25
Worthington, H. - Kentucky VA20
Worthlington, T. - Co. H 27th North Carolina Oct. 4, 1864 VA25
Worthy, Leonard C. - Pvt. - Co. D 13th Georgia Died May 12, 1864 VA28
Wrenn, Henry - Co. D 17th Virginia Infantry VA10
Wrenn, J. - Co. B 48th North Carolina July 2, 1864 VA25
Wrenn, James - Co. E 6th Virginia VA10
Wright, __ - Nov. 10, 1862 VA25
Wright, A. - Co. K 2nd Florida July 13, 1862 VA25
Wright, A. F. - Co. A 44th South Carolina Oct. 6, 1863 VA25
Wright, A.M. - Co. C 10th Georgia June 27, 1864 VA25
Wright, B.W. - Alabama April 15, 1863 VA25
Wright, Columbus G. - Sgt. - Co. B 60th Georgia Died May 14, 1864 VA28

Wright, D. - Capt. - KIA - Dec. 17, 1864 VA19
Wright, D. - C.S. Navy April 2, 1865 VA25
Wright, F. - Surgeon - Maryland Nov. 20, 1862 VA25
Wright, Fletcher - Virginia VA20
Wright, G.W. - Pvt.- Co. B 34th North Carolina Died May 23, 1865 VA26
Wright, J. - 12th - Virginia Battalion June 19, 1862 VA25
Wright, J. - 22nd North Carolina July 29, 1862 VA25
Wright, J.B. - Co. E 46th Georgia July 14, 1864 VA25
Wright, J.H. - Lt.- Virginia May 27, 1865 Cemetery roster lists this soldier as "J.A. Wright". VA22
Wright, J.J. - Co. F 35th North Carolina June 13, 1862 VA25
Wright, L.F. - Sept. 18, 1863 VA25
Wright, M. - Co. A 1st Georgia March 14, 1865 VA25
Wright, P.R. - 13th North Carolina Infantry - KIA - Battle of Williamsburg - May 5, 1862 VA02
Wright, Richard (Richmond) - DOW - July 22, 1862 age 39 VA19
Wright, S. - 17th North Carolina Sept. 17, 1864 VA25
Wright, T.C. - Co. A 20th North Carolina Sept. 3, 1862 VA25
Wright, W.A. - Co. D 11th North Carolina Oct. 7, 1864 VA25
Wright, W.D. - Pvt. - Co. K 11th Virginia Died June 4, 1865 VA26
Wroten, Thomas J. - Co. K 21st Georgia VA11
Wyatt, G.B. - Co. C 5th South Carolina June 19, 1862 VA25
Wyatt, J. - Co. E 20th North Carolina July 8, 1864 VA25
Wyatt, J.J. - 24th Virginia May 14, 1862 VA25
Wyatt, O. - 16th North Carolina Sept. 29, 1862 VA25
Wyatt, T.O. - Co. K 8th North Carolina March 27, 1865 VA25
Wyatt, W. - Co. I 6th South Carolina Oct. 11, 1861 VA25
Wyatt, Young - 1st North Carolina "First Martyr" 1861 VA25
Wynn, A. - Co. E 25th Virginia June 20, 1863 VA25
Wynn, J.P. - Co. C 17th North Carolina Sept. 9, 1864 VA25
Wynn, R.J. - 5th South Carolina Oct. 12, 1861 VA25
Wynne, J. - Sumpter Artillery (South Carolina) Oct. 1, 1861 VA25

Wynne, T. - Sumpter Artillery (South Carolina) May 3, 1862 VA25
Wynne, W.C. - South Carolina May 26, 1864 VA25
Wythers, J.L. - Co. A 44th North Carolina June 2, 1863 VA25
Wytherston, J.W. - Co. B 11th Georgia June 14, 1863 VA25
Wywatt, J.W. - Co. F 37th North Carolina July 18, 1864 VA25
Yancey, A. - Co. F 19th Georgia Jan. 14, 1862 VA25
Yancey, A. T. - Co. D 19th Georgia Dec. 13, 1862 VA25
Yans, C.A. - Co. B 44th Georgia Jan. 31, 1864 VA25
Yarbrough, A. - Co. E 35th North Carolina July 17, 1864 VA25
Yarbrough, D.P. - Co. A Cobb's Legion (Georgia) Aug. 12, 1864 VA25
Yarbrough, S.H. - Co. E 14th Georgia April 28, 1864 VA25
Yarbrough, W.J. - Co. D 35th North Carolina July 8, 1862 VA25
Yates, John - VA12
Yearwood, B.J. - Co. I 2nd Georgia Dec. 23, 1862 VA25
Yeates, G.W. - Co. D 13th Mississippi May 10, 1862 VA25
Yeatman, __ - Co. D 40th Virginia April 2, 1862 VA25
Yeatts, __ - Co. G 14th Alabama June 5, 1862 VA25
Yeatts, __ - June 10, 1862 VA25
Yeatts, C. - C.S. Navy Jan. 1, 1865 VA25
Yeatts, F. - Co. F 46th North Carolina Oct. 26, 1863 VA25
Yeatts, J. - Co. E 18th Virginia July 5, 1862 VA25
Yeatts, J. T. - Co. A 37th North Carolina July 26, 1862 VA25
Yeatts, John - Co. G 3rd North Carolina July 22, 1862 VA25
Yeolton, J.H. - Co. A 49th North Carolina Oct. 25, 1864 VA25
Yerby, J.M. - Co. D 26th Alabama June 26, 1862 VA25
Yesner, W. - Co. H 31st Virginia June 22, 1864 VA25
Yoder, John A. - Co. F 23rd North Carolina VA28
Yon, R.A. - Sgt. - Co. I 27th South Carolina Feb. 12, 1865 VA25
York, J.C. - T. Artillery (Georgia) July 30, 1862 VA25
York, John - Co. I 48th North Carolina Sept. 22, 1864 VA25

York, V. - Co. C 30th South Carolina 1865 VA25
Yost, M.A. - Lt.- 24th Mississippi Infantry VA08
Youn, J.C. - Pvt. - Co. I 2_th South Carolina (This may be North Carolina) Died May 12, 1865 VA26
Young, A. - Co. C 31st Virginia July 12, 1864 VA25
Young, A. - 1st South Carolina Oct.9, 1861 VA25
Young, A. - Co. G 6th Louisiana May 11, 1863 VA25
Young, C.B. - Co. C 16th North Carolina June 24, 1862 age 27 VA25
Young, Cyrus - 4th South Carolina VA18
Young, D. - Co. D 10th Alabama Nov. 26, 1862 VA25
Young, D. W. - Lt.- Co. C 38th Georgia Dec. 12, 1862 VA25
Young, F.M. - Co. F 13th South Carolina July 8, 1862 VA25
Young, George B. - KIA - May 30, 1864 age 28 VA19
Young, H.S. - Co. D 48th North Carolina Nov. 30, 1863 VA25
Young, I.W. - 24th Virginia May 27, 1862 VA25
Young, J. - Co. H 37th North Carolina June 23, 1863 VA25
Young, J.F. - Co. B 13th South Carolina July 3, 1862 VA25
Young, J.H. - Co. H 11th Mississippi July 9, 1863 VA25
Young, J.H. - Co. B 26th North Carolina April 12, 1865 VA25
Young, J.J. - Co. G 38th Georgia July 22, 1862 VA25
Young, J.W. - 18th Virginia April 6, 1862 VA25
Young, John - Wheat's Batt. (Louisiana) April 21, 1862 VA25
Young, L. - May 29, 1862 VA25
Young, M.P. - Co. D 41st Georgia Feb. 19, 1865 VA25
Young, P. - Co. G 7th Tennessee Dec. 24, 1862 VA25
Young, P. - Co. G 6th North Carolina Nov. 27, 1864 VA25
Young, W. - Cutt's Battery May 24, 1862 VA25
Young, W.M. - Co. I 14th North Carolina June 24, 1862 VA25
Youngblood, A.J. - Lt.- Co. K 8th Florida Aug. 1, 1862 VA25
Youngblood, Augustus K. - Pvt. - Co. G 13th Georgia Died at Hamilton's Crossing - May 9, 1863 VA28
Youngblood, C.S. - Co. H 2nd Louisiana May 16, 1863 VA25
Younger, A.J. - Pvt.- Co. E 45th Virginia Died June 29, 1865 VA26

Yount, A. - 13th North Carolina Oct. 10, 1861 VA25
Yount, Luther - Pvt.- Co. C Pogue's Artillery Died June 2, 1865 VA26
Zabra, Jno. A. - May 13, 1863 VA25
Zackary, T. - Sept. 24, 1862 VA25
Zadford, Joe - Co. I 48th North Carolina Aug. 12, 1864 VA25
Zark, Julius - 7th Louisiana. VA17
Zeigle, D.C. - VA23
Zeigler, H.H. - Co. B 20th South Carolina Infantry VA08
Zeihum, Mary - Civilian -Killed in explosion of C.S. Laboratory - March 16, 1863 age 12 VA19
Zelaff, W.N. - 2nd Texas VA18
Zimmerman, J. - Co. I 26th North Carolina Aug. 6, 1862 VA25
Zirkle, Abraham - VA13
Zirkle, Moses - VA12
Zirkle, Noah - VA13

Appendix

Monument to 63 Confederate Dead in Massanutten Cemetery—Woodstock, Virginia
All photographs by the author unless noted

The Pyramid Monument to the 17,000 Confederate Dead Buried in Hollywood Cemetery, Richmond, VA

A new marker alongside an old marker.
Hollywood Cemetery, Richmond, VA

Wooden Headboards in Hollywood Cemetery—1865
Library of Congress, Prints and Photographs
Division [LC-B8171-0931]

Hollywood Cemetery in 2001

Unknown Section in Hollywood Cemetery

Grave of Gen. J.E.B. Stuart in Hollywood Cemetery
ca. 1865 (with temporary marker)
Library of Congress, Prints and Photographs
Division [LC-B811-3618]

Marker to Confederate Dead—Fairview Cemetery
Culpeper, VA

Some of the Names on the Marker to Confederate Dead
Fairview Cemetery—Culpeper, VA

VMI Cadet Samuel Francis Atwell
Mortally Wounded in the Battle of New Market
Virginia Military Institute Archives

Culpeper National Cemetery

Body of a Confederate soldier in the Trenches at
Spotsylvania Court House, VA
Photographed by Timothy H. O'Sullivan in
May 1865
Library of Congress, Prints and Photographs
Division [LC-B811-0723]

Spotsylvania Confederate Cemetery

Body of a Confederate soldier near
Mrs. Alsop's house
Spotsylvania Court House
Photographed by Timothy H. O'Sullivan in
May 1864
Library of Congress, Prints and Photographs
Division [LC-B811-0725]

Spotsylvania Confederate Cemetery

Spotsylvania Confederate Cemetery

Spotsylvania Confederate Cemetery

Mount Jackson, Virginia

Mount Jackson, Virginia

Front Royal, Virginia

Front Royal, Virginia

**Monument to Mosby's Men
Front Royal, Virginia**

Monument to Mosby's Men
Front Royal, Virginia

City Point National Cemetery
Graves of Confederate POW's

Yorktown National Cemetery

Bibliography

Books

Barnes, Joseph K. [Surgeon General of the United States Army]. *The Medical and Surgical History of the War of the Rebellion.* Washington, DC: 1870.

Bartlett, Napier. *Military Record of Louisiana.* New Orleans: 1875.

Bible, Donahue. *Vaughn's Brigade at Piedmont.* Mohawk, Tennessee: Dobson Creek Publishers, 1995.

Boatner, Mark M. (III). *The Civil War Dictionary.* New York: Vintage Books, 1988.

Bowie, Oden. *A Descriptive List of the Burial Places of the Remains of Confederate Soldiers, who fell in the Battles of Antietam, South Mountain, Monocay, and other Points in Washington and Frederick Counties in the State of Maryland.* Hagerstown, Maryland: Free Press, n.d.

Charles Broadway Rouss Camp of United Confederate Veterans. *Report on the Re-Burial of the Confederate Dead in Arlington Cemetery.* Washington, DC: Judd and Detweiler, 1901.

Confederated Southern Memorial Association. *History of the Confederated Southern Memorial Associations of the South.* n.d.

Courtland Baptist Church. *Courtland Baptist Church's Ancestral History 1845 – 1982.* n.d.

Davidson, James West, et al. *Nation of Nations* Vol. 2. New York: McGraw-Hill, 1990. 2 vols.

Freeman, Douglas Southall. *Lee's Lieutenants.* New York: Charles Scribner's Sons, 1944.

Handy, Isaac K. *United States Bonds.* Baltimore, Maryland: Turnbull Brothers, 1874.

Hughes, Mark. *Bivouac of the Dead.* Bowie, Maryland: Heritage Books, Inc., 1995.

Joslyn, Mauriel Phillips (ed). *Valor and Lace.* Mufreesboro, Tennessee: Southern Heritage Press, n.d.

Ladies' Hollywood Memorial Association. *Our Confederate Dead.* Richmond, Virginia, 1916.

Ladies' Hollywood Memorial Association. *Register of the Confederate Dead, Interred in Hollywood Cemetery, Richmond, Virginia.* Richmond, Virginia, 1869.

Ladies Memorial Association [Charleston, South Carolina]. *A Brief History of the Ladies Memorial Association of Charleston, SC.* Charleston, South Carolina: H.P. Cooke and Co., 1880.

National Library of Medicine. *Medicine of the Civil War.* n.d.

Emerson, Bettie Alder Calhoun. *Historic Southern Monuments.* New York and Washington: Neale Publishing Company, 1911.

Norris, L. David. *The Autobiography of Wilburn Hill King.* Hillsboro, Texas: Hill College Press, 1996.

Quartermaster General [of the United States Army]. *Roll of Honor: Names of Soldiers Who Died in Defense of the American Union, Interred in the National Cemeteries.* Washington, DC, 27 vols. (1865-1871).

Quartermaster General [of the United States Army]. *Statement of the Disposition of Some of the Bodies of Deceased Union Soldiers and Prisoners of War Whose Remains Have Been Moved to National Cemeteries.* Washington, DC, 4 vols., 1868.

Racine, J. Polk. *Recollections of a Veteran: or Four Years in Dixie.* Elkton, Maryland: Appeal Printing Office, 1894

Robertson, James I. *Civil War Sites in Virginia: A Tour Guide.* Charlottesville, Virginia: University of Virginia Press, 1982.

Smith, [Mrs.] S.L. *North Carolina's Monuments and Memorials.* Raleigh, North Carolina: Edwards and Broughton, Co., 1941.

Stotelmyer, Steven R. *The Bivouacs of the Dead.* Baltimore, Maryland: Toomey Press, 1992.

United States Christian Commission. *Record of the Federal Dead.* Philadelphia, 1865.

Whitehorne, Joseph A. *The Battle of New Market.* Center of Military History, Washington, DC, 1988.

Manuscripts

National Archives Record Groups

RG92-576. "General Correspondence and Reports Relating to National and Post Cemeteries." 1865-1890.

RG92-587. "Correspondence Relating to the Administration of National Cemeteries." 1907-1919.

RG92-695. " Correspondence - Office of the Commissioner for Marking Graves of the Confederate Dead." n.d.

The Library of Virginia (Richmond, Va.) - Archives Research Services

Kavanagh, F.E. " Confederate Cemetery Records: Hopewell, Virginia" Typescript (accession # 21107). Cemetery Records Collection.

Transcript of Confederate Cemetery Records: Newport News, Virginia (accession # 20717). Cemetery Records Collection.

Smith, Julia D., Comp. Confederate Cemetery Records: Warren County, Virginia: Prospect Hill Cemetery (accession # 26253). Cemetery Records Collection.

Shockoe Cemetery, Richmond, Virginia, Miscellaneous Reels 926-931 (accession 31702d). Local Records Collection.

University of Virginia
(Albert H. Small Special Collections Library)

Richard Heath Dabney Papers (accession # 2533).

Roster of Buried Confederate Soldiers Collection (accession # 1235).

Other Manuscripts

Avent, Joseph C. (III) "Information Regarding North Carolina's Confederate Soldiers Buried in Yorktown's National Cemetery." 1995.

Avery, Carrie White. "Cemetery Records." Library of Congress. 1923.

Mack, Oscar. *Report of the Inspector of National Cemeteries for the Years 1870 and 1871.* 1871.

Mack, Oscar. *Report of the Inspector of National Cemeteries for the 1874.* 1874.

Berry, James H. *Report of the Commissioner for Marking Confederate Graves.* 1912.

McMillen, Greg. "Confederate Soldiers Buried at Emory, Va." 2001.

Mumma, Calvin. *Washington Cemetery.* Pamphlet in the files of Antietam National Battlefield.

National Park Service. "A Brief History of Spotsylvania Confederate Cemetery." n.d.

National Park Service. "Spotsylvania Confederate Cemetery." n.d.

National Park Service. "Roster of Burials in Spotsylvania Confederate Cemetery." n.d.

Sellers, Jesse and Barbara Blakey. "List of Confederate Soldiers Buried in and near New Market, Va." 1987.

Story, Hatcher P. "List of Confederate Soldiers Buried at Courtland Baptist Church." 1986.

Veterans' Administration. "Station Data Sheet - Jefferson Barracks National Cemetery." n.d.

Weaver, R.B. "Weaver File." Gettysburg National Military Park

Wright, M. "List of Confederate Soldiers Buried in the Bruton Parish Churchyard." 1986.

Other Sources

Newspapers

Boonsboro Oddfellow. 1866.

Culpeper Observer. 1921. Article located in Culpeper County Library's vertical file.

Washington Post. 1879.

Magazines

Confederate Veteran

Southern Historical Society Papers

Burton, David L. "Friday the 13th." *Civil War Times.* October 1982. pp 36-41

About The Author

Mark Hughes is an electronic technologist who relaxes by writing books about Civil War cemeteries. *Confederate Cemeteries, Volume 1*, is his third book. His first two books, *Bivouac of the Dead* and *The Unpublished Roll of Honor*, are about Union Civil War cemeteries. He has also written numerous articles about teaching, electronics, amateur radio, and Civil War cemeteries. Mark's amateur radio callsign is WB4UHI.

He is a graduate of Gaston College (AAS - 1971), and Southeastern Oklahoma State University (BS - 1985, Master of Technology - 1986). He grew up on his parents' turkey farms in the Carolinas. Currently an Electronic Instructor at Cleveland Community College in Shelby, North Carolina, he has also worked as an electronic technician and broadcast engineer.

He married Patricia McDaniel in 1970. They have one daughter: Anna Grace Hughes (born 1987).

www.ingramcontent.com/pod-product-compliance
Lightning Source LLC
Chambersburg PA
CBHW072022240426
43667CB00044B/1943